GLOBAL STRATEGIC MANAGEMENT

RONALD SERIES ON MARKETING MANAGEMENT

Series Editor: **FREDERICK E. WEBSTER, Jr.**
The Amos Tuck School
of Business Administration
Dartmouth College

Global Strategic Management

WILLIAM H. DAVIDSON

1807 1982

A RONALD PRESS PUBLICATION

JOHN WILEY AND SONS

New York · Chichester · Brisbane · Toronto · Singapore

Library of Congress Cataloging in Publication Data:

Davidson, William Harley, 1951–
   Global strategic management.

   (Ronald series on marketing management)
   "A Ronald Press publication."
   Includes index.
   1. International business enterprises—Management.
I. Title.   II. Title: Strategic management.   III. Series.

HD62.4.D38   1982   658'.049   82-8480
ISBN 0-471-09314-9   AACR2

Printed in the United States of America

10 9 8 7 6 5 4 3 2 1

To My Grandparents

Series Editor's Foreword

Marketing management is among the most dynamic of the business functions. On the one hand it reflects the everchanging marketplace and the constant evolution of customer preferences and buying habits, and of competition. On the other hand, it grows continually in sophistication and complexity as developments in management science are applied to the work of the marketing manager. If he or she is to be a true management professional, the marketing person must stay informed about these developments.

The Ronald Series on Marketing Management has been developed to serve this need. The books in the series have been written for managers. They combine a concern for management application with an appreciation for the relevance of developments in such areas of management science as behavioral science, financial analysis, and mathematical modeling, as well as the insights gained from analyzing successful experience in the marketplace. The Ronald Series on Marketing Management is thus intended to communicate the state-of-the-art in marketing to managers.

Virtually all areas of marketing management will be explored in the series. Books now available or being planned cover advertising management, industrial marketing research, brand loyalty, sales management, product policy and planning, public relations, overall marketing strategy, and financial aspects of marketing management. It is hoped that the series will have some effect in raising the standards of applied marketing management.

FREDERICK E. WEBSTER, JR.

Hanover, New Hampshire
June 1977

vii

Preface

This book attempts to define and analyze many of the issues and functions involved in managing a global business. The objective is to provide a set of frameworks for the development and analysis of global strategies and for the administration of multinational firms. The book seeks to structure the key dimensions of global strategy and to define the process of managing a global business. It addresses problems and issues commonly encountered in international business. Above all, it aims to structure and systematize management functions required in the development and administration of a global business.

Despite its management orientation, the book is intended to be useful and relevant to those who think about global management as well as to those who practice it. A considerable amount of new data, material, and research is presented here. Most of the background material used in this book derives from the research activities of the Harvard Multinational Enterprise Project. As research administrator for the project from 1975 to 1978, I was able to benefit greatly from opportunities to interview representatives of a wide range of U.S. and European multinational firms, to analyze the extensive data gathered by the project, and, most of all, to discuss international management issues with the Harvard faculty involved in the project. I am particularly indebted to Professor Raymond Vernon for his guidance and support. Professor Michael Yoshino, whose extensive case studies provide a rich foundation for analysis of global strategies, provided a second major source of ideas for this book.

I am indebted also to the National Science Foundation and The Amos Tuck School for support in the research and writing of this book. Typing was performed capably by Tammy Stebbins and Audrey Brown, who never complained about the many revisions. A set of excellent research assistants, including Laura Prescott, Bruce McKenzie, Kevin Davidson and Chris Gebhard, all made significant contributions to the completion of this book; and Marc Teatum created the artwork in an efficient and elegant fashion. My gratitude is great for all these sources of support.

WILLIAM H. DAVIDSON

Hanover, N.H.
July 1982

Contents

ONE

Global Strategic Management

Global strategic management is the process of defining, developing and administering a strategy and structure for a worldwide business. The words *global* and *strategic* define two important areas of emphasis. Global, as opposed to international management, suggests a comprehensive approach to both domestic and international operations. Strategic, as opposed to operating management, emphasizes analysis of environmental and internal factors in making those decisions that determine the position and profile of the organization in a dynamic environment.[1] These perspectives dominate the approach presented in this book.

The familiar concept of the strategic business unit serves as the starting point for global strategic management activities.[2] A strategic business unit consists of a set of products that share manufacturing, marketing and technical bases and common customers and competitors. The effective development and management of a global strategy for such a business unit is the focus and objective of global strategic management. In pursuing this objective, the elements of an integrated, comprehensive strategy for a global business must first be addressed individually in a static setting for single business units. Although many variables must be considered in developing a global strategy, the same key strategic issues and choices will apply to all global businesses. These universal issues will be developed within a framework that emphasizes the relationship between strategic choices and corporate performance.[3] That relationship is extremely hard to measure because of difficulties in defining and measuring variances in corporate objectives, resources, environmental conditions and time frame. Neverthe-

1

less, the relative competitive position of individual firms can and will be related to fundamental strategic choices.

In addition to common strategic choices, all global businesses share a critical set of management processes and needs. Effective management of a global business requires a means of gathering and internally distributing information about the world business environment. The success of a global business also depends on management's ability to share resources within the business unit and with the larger parent organization. Coordination of marketing, manufacturing and other activities is another critical issue. Mechanisms for internally transferring resources quickly and cheaply are essential. Successful global businesses also require a global perspective on customers and competitors while each operating affiliate remains responsive to its local environment. Effective management of a global business requires attentiveness to these processes and needs in addition to continuous concern for the strategic profile of the organization in its environment.

At the most basic level, the fundamental attribute of effective global management is an integrated strategy and structure. The simplicity of this statement is deceptive, but its importance can be seen by examining the principal alternative approach to management of international operations. The main alternative—decentralized, autonomous foreign operations—reflects an entirely different philosophy about global management. This alternative entails a holding company approach to management, an approach that is best documented in conglomerate companies such as Textron and Litton Industries. In such firms, the primary ties between central headquarters and individual operating units are financial ties. Such systems have performed effectively in the United States. However, it has yet to be shown that such an approach is effective as a global management system.

In order for a foreign affiliate to succeed, it must have strengths and resources superior to those of local and foreign competitors in its market. In almost every case, those strengths and resources must come from the parent firm. The conglomerate form consciously de-emphasizes the transmission of nonfinancial resources from parent to affiliate. Decentralization of decision making permits responsiveness to local markets, but does not encourage coordination with other units to share costs and resources, nor does it foster a global perspective on the objectives and problems of the business. In short, without a coordinated global management system, foreign affiliates are on their own abroad.

There are very few conglomerates among the list of major U.S. multinational enterprises. Conglomerates are broadly defined as firms active in a wide range of unrelated industries whose expansion has occurred primarily through acquisition. Regardless of how multinational enterprises are defined, very few conglomerates appear among the leaders in international activity. The primary exception, ITT, exhibits one of the most centralized management systems of any major corporation. Extensive efforts are made within ITT to encourage communication among managers, and intensive planning and staff activities are designed to coordinate and direct business units along global lines.[4] Despite these efforts, ITT has been forced to withdraw from a large number of foreign operations in recent years.[5]

An examination of the larger U.S. conglomerates reveals that foreign sales and profits generally account for very small percentages of their total revenues. Many of the 27 firms in Table 1-1 derive less than 10% of their revenues from foreign operations. The two firms with the largest percentage of sales abroad, ITT and W.R. Grace, are unique in that both were founded outside the United States. Grace was founded in Peru; ITT's origins were in Puerto Rico. Both entered the U.S. market only after years of activity abroad, and both have explicitly attempted to increase U.S. revenues in recent years while de-emphasizing foreign operations.

When conglomerates are active in foreign markets, they frequently use exports to serve those markets. Export sales account for a significant share of foreign revenues in many cases (Table 1-2). Few conglomerates operate significant networks of foreign subsidiaries. When they do, these networks have frequently been acquired. Such is the case with United Technologies (Otis), City Investing (Federal Pacific) and IC Industries (Pet), for example. The conglomerate system of management does not appear to be effective in developing international operations. There are several possible explanations for this observation, but one fundamental issue remains. The success of a foreign affiliate is largely a function of the support it receives from its parent corporation. A conglomerate parent transmits financial resources to its affiliates, but often cannot assist in other ways. In contrast, the affiliates of a company like IBM receive technology, marketing skills, a powerful brand name, information, management, components, complementary products and access to other foreign markets in addition to financial resources. If there are two affiliates in a foreign market and one has a parent like IBM, while the other has a conglomerate parent, there should be little question as to which company's performance will be superior in the long run.

The conglomerate firm does not prosper abroad for one fundamental

TABLE 1-1.   Overseas Operating Revenues for Major U.S. Conglomerates in 1979 (in thousands of dollars)

Company	Total Sales	Sales of Foreign Affiliates*	Percentages
Allied Products	332,549	9,900	3.0
Alco Standard	1,917,128	47,900	2.5
AMFAC	1,689,496	n.s.†	n.s.
AVCO	1,932,155	170,300	8.8
Bangor Punta	785,900	48,800	6.2
Brunswick	1,257,333	216,261	17.2
Chromalloy	1,536,489	n.s.	n.s.
City Investing	5,040,700	788,000	15.6
Dart−Kraft	2,403,266	648,835	27.0
Dayco	739,889	97,915	13.2
Fuqua	2,056,824	86,740	4.2
W.R. Grace	5,266,629	1,677,000	31.8
Gulf and Western	5,288,247	990,000	18.7
IC Industries	3,734,600	312,800	8.4
ITT	17,197,423	10,594,000	61.6
Walter Kidde	2,284,146	275,408	12.0
Lear Siegler	1,327,271	242,368	18.2
Litton	4,087,809	989,886	24.2
LTV	7,996,809	n.s.	n.s.
Northwest Industries	2,579,900	n.s.	n.s.
Ogden	2,241,408	68,611	3.0
Rockwell International	6,176,400	767,000	12.4
Textron	3,392,974	504,000	14.8
TransAmerica	4,044,167	n.s.	n.s.
United Technologies	9,053,358	2,092,128	23.1
White Consolidated	2,010,114	102,300	5.1
Zapata	524,935	103,694	19.7

Source: Corporate annual reports and 10-K's.
*Does not include exports from the United States.
†n.s. Signifies that the company reported sales of foreign affilitates to be insignificant.

reason. The success of a global business rests on integrated operations and coordinated strategy. The firm must transmit and share information, resources and experience throughout the enterprise. Without these system resources and supports, a foreign affiliate cannot compete with local firms or other foreign affiliates. The conglomerate firm cannot actively support its foreign affiliates without radically altering its management systems and basic business philosophy.

TABLE 1-2.   Exports as a Percentage of Total Foreign Sales (1980)

Company	Percentage
United Technologies	42
A-T-O (Figgie)	60
Brunswick	33
Textron	19
Allied Products	100
Alco Standard	32
W.R. Grace	13

Source: Company response to author's questionnaire.

Conglomerates are not the only firms to employ what could be called a loose or passive approach to managing foreign operations. It is quite common in the early stages of a firm's international expansion for foreign affiliates to operate autonomously.[6] Among well-established multinational companies, larger and more diverse companies can be expected to exhibit some of the approaches that are common among conglomerates. Such firms can be expected to exhibit relatively loose, passive approaches to global management because the problems of coordination, communication, and control are so great in large diversified firms. Size and diversity are important, but they do not dictate a particular approach to international management. Large and highly diverse firms such as ITT and General Electric have developed strong central management systems that ensure coordination, integrated planning, and a global orientation throughout their extensive foreign operations.

The management systems developed by ITT and GE reveal a common feature: Both are extremely costly. ITT line managers spend over 100 days per year in the areas of planning, budgeting, reporting, and meetings with central management.[7] General Electric's planning and reporting system also requires a major investment in management time. These are extreme cases, but the basic fact is that such systems require tremendous initial investments and absorb a significant share of management energy. Are such systems necessary for managing foreign operations?

The strategic business unit concept plays a useful role in addressing this issue. The process of evaluating an SBU to determine objectives and operating strategies, typically within a portfolio planning framework can also be employed to define the geographic dimensions of the unit's activities. Business units facing significant international opportunities and threats can be identified and managed accordingly. Assessment of the prospects for international activity in any given business area is an important aspect of global strategic planning.

PROSPECTS FOR INTERNATIONAL ACTIVITY

A global orientation is almost universally valuable in the present business environment, but its importance varies substantially in different industries. In some sectors, international factors do not play a major role in the environment facing a company. In assessing the importance of international considerations in any business, however, it is important to address not only their present role but their potential role. If an industry does not exhibit significant international activity, the prospects for increased activity must be explored. These prospects depend on the fundamental characteristics of the business in question. The importance of these characteristics can be seen by examining the degree of internationalization in other industries.

The degree of internationalization of an industry can be measured by examining the role of global competitors. In industries such as steel, cement and brewing, "local" enterprises control 90% or more of all world markets. Local enterprises are defined as firms deriving less than one-third of their revenues from foreign markets. In other industries, including computers, automobiles and civilian aerospace, global firms account for well over half of total market volume. Global firms are those companies with a third or more of their sales in foreign markets.

Analysis of the present role of global competitors serves a primary purpose in assessing prospects for international activity in an industry. However, the absence of global competitors should not be interpreted to mean that a global strategy would not be effective in the industry. The potential role of global competitors can be examined by analyzing a number of characteristics that correlate with the degree of internationalization of different industries.

Industries with high degrees of internationalization typically exhibit several characteristics. Industries dominated by global competitors tend to be technologically advanced.[9] Many of the industries dominated by global competitors are capital-intensive and offer significant economies of scale in manufacturing. The role of marketing skills also appears to be important. Many industries requiring intensive advertising and marketing efforts are highly internationalized. These characteristics are not conclusive signs that

TABLE 1-3.   Percentage of World Sales by Global Companies

Industry	1970	1975	1980
Automobiles	62.6%	67.3%	81.4%
Cement	8.0	9.1	8.2
Computers	89.7	84.7	69.5
Construction Machinery	24.8	39.6	42.1
Steel	7.0	14.3	11.8
Television	11.6	22.7	29.8
Tires	28.0	70.9	75.7
Plastics and resins	49.1	72.7	59.2
Soft drinks	25.1	41.2	65.2
Brewing	0.01	0.06	0.09
Aerospace	19.7	30.0	49.4

Source: Compiled from a wide range of sources on individual companies and industries by the author.

an industry can or will be internationalized, but most industries with successful global firms exhibit more than one of these characteristics. The aerospace industry, for example, exhibits a high level of technology and is subject to significant economies of scale in manufacturing. Break-even volumes are high: The cost of designing a new aircraft has been estimated to exceed $1 billion. These factors provide a powerful stimulus for global strategies. Global firms receive the benefit of unit cost reduction from additional sales realized in foreign markets.

A more basic issue lies behind these generalizations. Hymer concluded that the underlying determinant of the degree of internationalization in any industry involves the ability of globally oriented enterprises to dominate local firms.[10] This is the fundamental issue in deciding whether a global strategy is likely to succeed in a given business. The decision to pursue a global strategy should be based on a conviction that the business will or can be dominated by global competitors.

GLOBAL OR LOCAL MANAGEMENT STRATEGIES

An examination of actual market share trends provides a useful first step in approaching this decision. Two simple measures serve this purpose. The first measure, shown in Table 1-3, accounts for the overall market share held by firms considered to be global competitors. The second calculates the total world market share held by firms outside their home markets. In this case, the home market sales of all firms are compared to sales outside their home market in a given industry. The automobile industry provides an example of the use of this measure. The percentage of world sales accounted for by all firms outside their home markets stood at 47.7% in 1979. The equivalent percentages for 1970 were 62.6 and was 34.3% in 1970. Although the dominance of global competitors has been clear for some time in the automobile industry, such firms have only recently begun to play a major role in other industries. In the color television industry, for example, sales by global firms represented only 11.6% of world sales in 1970, but 29.8% in 1979. The color television industry provides a useful example of the internationalization of an industry by aggressive global competitors.

The Color Television Industry

The color television industry originated in the United States in 1952 with the introduction of the first commercial set by RCA. The industry grew very slowly in the United States, and it was not until 1960 that a significant annual sales volume was reached. Other large producers of black-and-white sets

TABLE 1-4.   Percentage of Sales Outside Firms' Home Markets

Industry	1970	1975	1979
Automobiles	34.3%	39.8%	47.7%
Cement	6.7	9.2	10.7
Computers	34.2	43.1	51.2
Construction machinery	12.4	23.7	27.4
Steel	12.1	14.8	13.6
Television	16.4	21.7	24.6
Tires	19.5	37.0	41.8
Plastic and resins	n.a.*	n.a.	n.a.
Soft drinks	17.0	25.3	41.5
Beer	0.4	0.7	0.9
Aerospace	14.4	40.3	35.6

Source: Compiled from a wide range of sources on individual companies and industries.
*n.a.:not available.

first entered the industry in the early 1960s, and the U.S. market began a period of rapid growth. Foreign markets for color television developed more slowly, partly because of political delays in approval of transmission standards. The debate over transmission standards prolonged the introduction of color television in foreign markets until the late 1960s.

Several factors discouraged the leading U.S. firms from pursuing a global strategy in the color television industry. Many nations adopted alternative transmission systems that were not compatible with U.S. standards. Disposable income in many countries was not sufficiently high to warrant the mass marketing techniques employed in the United States. Even in Great Britain, consumer purchases of color sets were rare; most sets were purchased by leasing companies and rented to the end user. In addition, strong local competition had developed in all major foreign markets by 1970. Over 20 local firms produced or assembled color sets in West Germany in 1970, for example. In the United Kingdom, Thorn Industries Ltd. controlled 40% of the market, while Thomson-Brandt dominated the French market.

The initial trend toward market dominance by local enterprises reversed itself in the 1970s as global competitors began to penetrate foreign markets through exports and direct investment. The first Japanese color sets were imported into the United States in 1967. By 1977, Japanese producers accounted for over 30% of the U.S. market. The Japanese producers generally followed a strategy highly similar to that already proven successful in the motorcycle and black-and-white television industries. Large-scale, capital-intensive manufacturing processes were employed to generate significant economies of scale, reduce unit costs and deliver a product of consistent quality. To achieve the unit volumes necessary to realize cost reduction, marketing efforts were focused on maximizing market penetration. With the exception of Sony, the product was positioned at the low end of the market to attract the largest possible consumer base. Prices were lowered and extensive distribution networks were developed. Successful marketing efforts generated the sales volume necessary to realize the cost leadership objectives implicit in their global strategy. As competitive position in the industry became increasingly reflective of sales volume, local competitors began to disappear. In the United States, the number of color television manufacturers declined from over 50 in 1970 to 14 in 1980. Ten of these 14 U.S. firms are now owned by foreign competitors.[11]

In Europe, the penetration of Japanese imports has not yet reached significant proportions outside of the United Kingdom, but fear of Japanese competition permeates the European industry. It is estimated that it takes 1.9 man-hours to produce a color set in Japan, as compared with 3.9 man-hours in Germany.[12] The importance of manufacturing scale and efficiency has already resulted in significant changes in the European industry. Levels of concentration have increased significantly. Philips, the volume leader in Europe, is active throughout Europe and has acquired an interest in Grundig, the largest German producer. In the United States, Philips has acquired Magnavox and the third largest U.S. producer, Sylvania.[13] Thomson-Brandt, the largest French producer, recently acquired three German color set manufacturers. The industry is becoming highly concentrated, and the leading firms are expanding into foreign markets, primarily through acquisition.

Success in the color television industry will continue to be based on a global strategy that emphasizes volume and market share on a worldwide basis. The importance of a global perspective appears to have been de-emphasized by many American manufacturers, however. The American firms that initiated the color television industry have yielded their positions as leading competitors in this industry.

Why did these U.S. firms fail to capture the dominant global position now held by foreign competitors? Preoccupation with the domestic market limited the international activity of many of the U.S. firms. A failure to monitor their competition on a global basis was particularly harmful, but more important was a failure to perceive and explore opportunities in foreign markets. The color television industry provided the opportunity for a successful global strategy, but none of the U.S. companies fully perceived its potential. The Japanese strategy was firmly based on the fundamental characteristics of the industry.

Managers must assess their industry's potential for international competition and act vigorously to anticipate potential threats from foreign firms. More importantly, a global strategic perspective will lead to aggressive pursuit of international opportunities. However, the pursuit of a global strategy requires careful analysis of the industry in question. Not all industries can be dominated by global competitors. In color television, the nature of the manufacturing process provided a basis for successful global strategies. Other factors also provide effective foundations for global strategies.

TABLE 1-5.   Leading Color Television Producers, 1979

	Annual Unit Volume (in thousands)
Matsushita	3,500
Philips	3,300
Sony	2,000
RCA	2,000
Toshiba	2,000
Sanyo	1,950
Zenith	1,900
Thomson-Brandt	1,600
Grundig	1,400
Hitachi	1,300
General Electric	1,200
Sylvania[a]	1,200
Sharp	900
AEG Telefunken	800
ITT	700
Thorn	500

Source: The Economist, company reports, author estimates. For a comparable set of estimates, see Financial Times, November 18, 1980.
[a] Acquired by Philips in 1981.

Foundations of a Global Strategy

If a business already exhibits a high degree of internationalization, the
mandate to the firm is clear. It must be prepared to deal with foreign
competition, and it should investigate foreign market opportunities. The
industry clearly supports, if not requires, global strategies. If global firms do
not presently dominate the business in question, further analysis of the
probability of success for a global strategy in the industry is warranted. This
assessment should focus on identifying the potential advantages a global
competitor can hold over locally oriented firms.

It is widely held that domestic companies will conquer foreign entrants in
their home market if everything else is equal. The domestic companies have
extensive knowledge of the market, better relations with the government,
and what might be called the benefit of primary position. Existing domestic
firms have had the benefits of first choice in establishing market positions,

distribution systems and promotion strategies. These benefits include not only any initial positional superiority they hold, but also in many cases a financial advantage if the cost of market entry has risen. To overcome these disadvantages, the foreign-owned firm must possess other resources or abilities that compensate for its implicitly inferior position.

There are several sources of such strengths for successful global firms. Some are economic, and some are strategic. Economic strengths permit a firm to do something more efficiently than others; strategic strengths allow the firm to do something that other firms cannot do at all, at least not in the short run. The economic sources are those that result in an immediate cost advantage. The foreign firm can derive such cost advantages from access to cheaper capital, for example. This advantage can result because its home capital markets are more efficient than local financial institutions, because of home or host government subsidies and investment incentives or because of the respective positions of home and host currencies in the international monetary system. All firms can raise capital, but some can do so much more cheaply than others.

The importance of this factor should not be underestimated. A large amount of U.S. foreign investment activity appears to have been stimulated by the lower cost of U.S. capital. Lower capital costs, provided by high price−earnings ratios in U.S. equity markets and the availability of low-cost, long-term financing in debt markets, encouraged U.S. firms to pursue projects in foreign markets whose returns were unsatisfactory to local competitors with higher discount rates. It also gave U.S. firms a significant advantage in existing businesses, especially those with high capital requirements.

Chinese Money and International Business

The conglomerate firm emerged in the United States in the 1960s. The concept of generating growth through acquisition fit with the growth orientation of the time. U.S. equity markets responded enthusiastically to this new phenomenon. The resulting price−earnings (P−E) ratios provided the conglomerates with the very means necessary to fuel further growth. In the well-known fashion, a company with a high multiple could generate the growth that supported its P−E ratio by acquiring other firms through an exchange of stock. In the following example, United Industries offers to acquire Acme by exchanging one half share of its own stock for each share of Acme. Since one half share of United is worth $15 and each share of Acme only $10, it is an attractive offer. The resulting combination leads to a 20%

increase in earnings for United. Most importantly, if the P−E ratio remains constant, the two firms combined are now valued at $450 million, an increase of $100 million over what they were worth spearately. That of course is the magic of Chinese money, a phrase used to describe acquisitions funded through such exchanges of shares.

	Before Acquisition				After Acquisition			
	Earn-ings	E.P.S.	P.E.	Market Value	Earn-ings	E.P.S.	P.E.	Market Value
United Industries	$10m	$1.00	30	$300m				
Acme Lock Company	$ 5m	$1.00	10	$ 50m	($15m	$1.20	30	$450m)

The conglomerate era is now presumed to be ended. However, perhaps another version of the game is still possible. The basic concept behind the conglomerate strategy is to acquire "cheap" earnings, repackage them and sell them to financial markets at a substantial premium over cost. Foreign operations provide one of the best sources of "cheap" earnings.

U.S. equity markets have consistently valued corporate earnings higher than equity markets in other countries. Average price−earnings ratios in the United States have exceeded those in foreign equity markets by substantial margins. The opportunity for arbitrage has been perceived by many U.S.-based corporations. By acquiring earnings abroad at lower P−E's and repackaging them for valuation in the U.S. market, surplus market value can be created. Between 1965−1975, the largest 180 U.S.-based multinational enterprises acquired 3,654 foreign companies, a 278% increase over the number of acquisitions in the previous decade.[14]

The capital-cost advantage enjoyed by American firms has diminished sharply in recent years, however. Price−earnings ratios in U.S. equity markets have declined relative to those in foreign bourses. The advantage of borrowing dollars in debt markets may also have diminished. At one time, international creditors preferred to loan in dollars because of the dollar's liquidity and stability. Aliber argues that this preference for holding dollar debt led to a "currency premium" that reduced dollar borrowing costs.[15] These benefits were available to all U.S.-based companies. However, creditors' preferences for holding dollar-denominated assets declined sharply in the 1970s, suggesting that the relative cost of borrowing in dollars has risen. It now appears American firms will be less able to utilize capital-cost advantages as a basis for global expansion. Foreign acquisition activity by U.S.-based firms can be expected to diminish.[16]

If capital markets no longer favor U.S. firms, there is very little basis for international activity by firms whose global strategy was based on advantages in the financial area. The only financial motive left to support international investment for such companies is diversification. The benefit of diversification is a theoretical reduction in the variance of aggregate cash flows for the parent. Since host country business cycles do vary significantly, foreign investment can serve to reduce variance in sales and profits.[17] This reduction in variance, however, may not offset the additional operating risks associated with international investments. Moreover, the same diversification benefits can be realized by investing in liquid foreign securities. In short, global operating strategies built primarily on financial strengths and the benefits of diversification rest on questionable foundations.

One result of the availability of cheap capital continues to contribute to the competitiveness of U.S. companies abroad. Lower capital costs encouraged U.S. firms to build capital-intensive manufacturing facilities. The effects of capital-cost advantages thus continue to be reflected in the existing international operations of U.S. companies. These facilities provide cost advantages as scale economies are realized on rising volume in growing markets. Other economies of scale provide important advantages to the global firm and represent an important support for global strategies. The global firm can spread a variety of fixed costs across a larger volume of business. This effect, however, will be significant only if resources such as management systems, technology, market research, components, products and personnel can be readily transferred to foreign markets. If such resources are inapplicable in foreign markets, these benefits cannot be

TABLE 1-6.   Average Price–Earnings Ratios on World Stock Exchanges

	1970	1980
United Kingdom	14.4	5.5
West Germany	10.4	7.9
Switzerland	9.3	12.3
Japan	8.6	18.1
Canada	15.9	9.1
Norway	14.0	12.5
Singapore	—	19.2
United States	17.2	8.3

Source: Capital International Perspectives, Geneva, Switzerland.

achieved. The transferability of such resources is a critical issue in determining whether a business can be developed on a global basis.

Another source of economic advantage lies in material and component sourcing. Global firms may gain advantages here because of larger purchasing volumes and production runs. The global firm can also achieve strategic superiority in this area if it controls sources of materials or components. Examples of this occur in many industries: chemical companies control upstream feedstock supplies; aluminum smelters control bauxite refining facilities; television manufacturers produce tubes; and computer and telecommunication companies manufacture their own integrated circuits and semiconductors. Control of supply markets permits the global firm to dominate local companies. The same effect will occur if the global firm controls captive user markets for a product. Vertical integration is a key motive for international expansion in a number of industries.[18]

Even when firms do not directly control sources of supply, they can gain advantages in sourcing through superior global information networks. Logistics, trading and sourcing skills and networks are principal reasons for the success of global trading companies, and they represent important resources for all global firms. Such networks provide the global firm with a significant strategic advantage not only in the area of sourcing but in other areas as well. Market intelligence systems can identify and evaluate the implications of competitors' and users' activities. Monitoring of broad environmental trends and events also yields information of commercial significance. Firms with such information are able to position themselves in anticipation of events and to predict the impact of global events on local markets.

Two additional sources of strategic strength provide primary advantages for successful global firms. Superior technology represents perhaps the principal strength of U.S. multinational enterprises. While superior process technology provides cost advantages, product innovations represent sound strategic strengths on which to base a global strategy. The high levels of export and foreign investment by high-technology companies indicate the important role of technology in the success of global strategies.[19] The second major strategic strength associated with multinational firms derives from marketing expertise. Firms with the ability to conduct market research and to effectively package, promote and distribute products possess skills that cannot be duplicated by many local competitors. These skills, which contribute to perceived product differentiation, are an important source of strategic strength in international markets.[20]

Examination of this set of criteria will give the firm an indication of the likelihood of success for a global strategy. Does the firm possess economic advantages or strategic strengths that will support a global strategy? Do other firms possess such strengths? Will they in the future?

Foundations of a Global Strategy

Economic Advantages	Strategic Strengths
Capital costs	Marketing
Material and component costs	Technology
Economies of scale	Information
Government subsidies	Quality control
	Management systems
	Market control
	Human resources

If the characteristics of the business are such that firms can achieve significant advantages in many of these areas, a global strategy can be successful. If the industry in question appears to offer promise for a global strategy, the firm has three options. It can adopt a defensive posture, monitoring for competitive threats in its home market and preparing contingency plans for that prospect. Second, it can adopt a follower strategy, waiting until other firms begin to carry out global strategies and then imitating their actions. Third, it can initiate its own actions to internationalize the business in question. The approach to be pursued depends on management's assessment of the prospects for success of global competitors in the industry, as well as assessment of the firm's own ability to pursue a global strategy.

Global strategic management includes all three approaches. The alternative of a purely domestic orientation rests on the explicit or de facto assumption that foreign opportunities and threats will not play a significant role in a business for the foreseeable future. This assumption is entirely appropriate in a wide, but shrinking, number of businesses. Such a management approach may be appropriate in businesses such as cement, brewing, service businesses and most public sector procurement areas. Even in these industries, however, examples of successful global strategies can be cited. Although the firm should always be sensitive to global trends, there are cases where the investment in management systems, information networks and planning is not justified. Global management is suitable only when the firm perceives the necessity of anticipating foreign competition or the potential benefit of developing global markets. That is the fundamental objective in determining whether a business should be managed as a global business unit or a local business.

Developing a Global Strategy

Firms pursuing domestic or defensive strategies in a global business are vulnerable in several respects. They cannot use cash flows from foreign operations to support their domestic operations in the event of recession or intense competition. Established global competitors, on the other hand, can increase market shares selectively by cutting prices, offering favorable terms and providing better services in individual markets. They can support such activities with cash flows from other stable markets. After acquiring a dominant share in a market through such tactics, the global competitor can raise prices and use resulting cash flows to support similar operations in other markets. Competition between global and local competitors is particularly one-sided if the product in question does not vary significantly from market to market. In such cases, the global firm can sequentially concentrate its resources on a single market, achieve a dominant position and then transfer its resources to the next target. The fragmented nature of its local competition permits the global firm to concentrate its resources selectively on individual markets at the most opportune moment without fear of retaliation in other markets.

An excellent example of the successful use of this type of strategy can be found in the writing instrument industry. Originally the industry was organized along national lines, with relatively little international activity. International activity emerged in the 1950s following the introduction of the ball-point pen. This new technology provided the basis for several global strategies. U.S. companies, notably Papermate and Scripto, established or acquired foreign affiliates to produce and sell ball-point pens. These affiliates were granted considerable autonomy by the parent firm. Another global competitor emerged in France in the late 1950s. Bic's low-priced, disposable product had created a broad new market for ball-point writing instruments in France. Bic's first ventures abroad occurred only after it had achieved an 80% market share in its home market. Using cash flows generated in the stable French market, Bic invested heavily in manufacturing, distribution and promotion when it entered the British market in 1957. The full resources of the parent company were used to support a carefully coordinated strategy in Great Britain. The local orientation of the British pen manufacturers gave Bic the advantage of surprise in introducing its standardized, low-priced, disposable pens in the United Kingdom.

Another global competitor had entered the British market at virtually the same time as Bic. Scripto Ltd. was a subsidiary of a leading U.S. producer of medium-priced ball-point pens. Operating under considerable autonomy, the manager of Scripto Ltd. decided that he could not risk a full commitment of the subsidiary's resources in an aggressive response to Bic's moves. His tentative response permitted Bic to achieve a dominant market position in the United Kingdom.

By failing to view the developments in Great Britain as a confrontation between two global competitors, Scripto was beaten before it started. Not only could Scripto have anticipated Bic's entry, it could have committed all its resources to achieving at least a stalemate in the United Kingdom. Scripto could then have been in a position to successfully preempt Bic's strategy in the low-priced segment of the pen market in its home market and elsewhere before Bic could enter those countries. Instead, Scripto and other pen manufacturers continued to operate in the United States almost as if nothing had happened. After capturing the British market, Bic used the same strategy to conquer the U.S. market and then other markets around the world. Effective monitoring of global developments would have permitted domestic pen manufacturers to anticipate the advent of low-priced, disposable pens and react accordingly. Instead, the local orientation of its competitors permitted Bic to dominate virtually all the world's pen markets without ever facing a serious competitive challenge. Faced with global competitors capable of executing such a strategy, local strategies, whether consciously defensive or simply myopic, appear to be inferior. A defensive global strategy, however, could be appropriate under some conditions.

Defensive strategies are suited to several conditions. They are clearly relevant if the firm does not believe it has the resources to compete internationally. There are also situations where a defensive approach holds merit in businesses that have already been internationalized. If foreign firms possess greater strengths in terms of technology or other resources, the home firm is justified in not pursuing foreign markets. Although the firm may not be able to compete against other global rivals in neutral ground, it may be able to do so in its home territory.

If the business in question is a product with significant and enduring variations in style and low economies of scale, the defensive approach again appears justified. The relative strength of local firms in such industries also can be expected to increase as a product matures. Market and capacity shares controlled by multinational firms have declined over time in many markets.[21] Foreign expansion will not be justified in such industries unless the firm can enhance the existing state of the art in the industry. The foreign expansion of a business also should be limited when the firm perceives greater returns on scarce resources in other businesses. Businesses outside a firm's principal area of expertise exhibiting promising global prospects often are restricted. Such product lines will not be within the charted direction of growth for the company.[22] The defensive approach can be justified under such conditions. In general, however, if the firm desires to do anything more than survive in a global business, it must adopt a strategy that emphasizes expansion into foreign markets as well. In many cases survival itself will be dependent on successful foreign expansion.

Strategic Choices

Once the decision has been made to enter foreign markets, management immediately faces a set of critical strategic choices. A number of issues must be faced in building and running a global business. How management approaches and resolves these issues determines the company's competitive position in world markets and, ultimately, its performance.

The challenge facing management in any industry lies in comparing performance with other competitors. For firms pursuing a global strategy, the relevant comparison is with other global competitors. Performance depends on many variables, some beyond the control of management, but each global competitor in any industry must make a set of common strategic choices. Six areas in particular are important to firms pursuing a global strategy.

Elements of Global Strategy

Participation policy

Market selection

Marketing mix management

Sourcing strategy

Financial policies

Organizational structure

Decisions in these six areas determine key dimensions of a global strategy. The resulting effects on performance are not always immediately visible, but the record of various firms in foreign markets suggests that management choices in these areas play a critical role in determining relative performance.

NOTES

1. This familiar framework serves as the foundation for virtually all business policy and strategic planning models. See, for example, Christensen, C.R., *Policy Formulation and Administration* (Homewood, Illinois: Irwin, 1976); King, W.R. and D.I. Cleland, *Strategic Planning and Policy* (New York: Van Nostrand Reinhold, 1978).
2. The concept of the strategic business unit was developed within the General Electric Company. The GE management system is described in: Springer, C.H., "Strategic Management in General Electric" *Operations Research*, November−December 1973. See also King, W.R. and D.I. Cleland, *Strategic Planning and Policy*, (New York: Van Nostrand Reinhold, 1978), pp. 56−57, 77−79, 299−300; Hall, W.K., "SBU's—Hot, New Topic in the Management of Diversification," *Business Horizons*, February 1978, pp. 17−25.
3. Many of the best studies of this relationship are drawn from the resources of the Profit Impact of Marketing Strategies (PIMS) project. See, for example, Schoeffler, Sidney, R.D. Buzzell and D.F. Heany, "Impact of Strategic Planning on Profit Performance," *Harvard Business Review*, March−April 1974.
4. ITT's management systems are described in: "ITT—Can Profits be Programmed?" *Dun's Review*, November 1965; "ITT—The view from the Inside," *Business Week*, November 3, 1973.
5. ITT sold over 40 business units between 1978 and 1980. The majority of these units were located outside the United States. These divestitures are summarized below.
6. This process is described by: Stopford, J.M. and L.T. Wells, Jr., *Managing the Multinational Enterprise* (New York: Basic Books, 1972), pp. 18−29. A similar pattern for European enterprises is described by Franko as the *tochtergesellshaft* relationship found to prevail in early stages of foreign expansion. Franko, L.G., *The European Multinationals* (New York: Harper and Row, 1976), pp. 187−211. For a case description of this type of relationship, see *Sigma Corporation in Italy* (A & B), ICCH Numbers 4-377-085, 086.

ITT Divestitures

Year	Units Sold	Annual Sales	Proceeds of Diverstiture
1978	8	$ 75m	$ 27m
1979	17	$221m	$ 74m
1980	17	$677m	$564m

Source: *Wall Street Journal*, April 1, 1981, p. 31. For details of specific divestitures, see the following.

Unit Divested	Country	Reference
Telephonique (68%)	France	*Wall Street Journal* June 16, 1976
Standard Telephones and Cables	South Africa	*Wall Street Journal* June 23, 1977, p. 8
Electro-Optical Division	France	*Electronics Week* January 12, 1977, p.1
Four Food Processing Affiliate	Western Europe	*Milling*, February 27, 1979 p. 48
Standard Electrica (51%)	Brazil	*Electronics Week* February 14, 1979
Standard Electric (25%)	Argentina	*New York Times* May 28, 1979, p. D2
Standard Telephone and Cable (15%)	United Kingdom	*Journal of Commerce* June 4, 1979, p. 4
Rimmel International	United Kingdom	*Wall Street Journal* January 3, 1980, p. 6
Ashe Laboratories	United Kingdom	*Chimie Art* June 27, 1980, p. 17
Steiner, S.A.	Switzerland	*Les Echos* March 23, 1980, p. 8
French TV Operations	France	*Wall Street Journal* July 25, 1980, p. 18
Rayonier	Canada	*Les Echos* August 20, 1980, p. 5
Indosat	Indonesia	*Wall Street Journal* January 2, 1981, p. 12.

7. From personal remarks to the author by Mr. Lyman Hamilton, former president of ITT.
8. This process is described in: Channon, D.F., *Multinational Strategic Planning* (New York: AMACOM, 1978), pp. 89–119; Prahalad, C.K., "Strategic Choices in Diversified MNC's," *Harvard Business Review*, September–October 1976.
9. The relationship between innovation and international investment at the micro level is presented in the well-known product life cycle model. See Vernon, Raymond, "International Investment and International Trade in the Product Cycle," *Quarterly Journal of Economics*, May 1966, pp. 190–207. At the macro level, the relationship between R & D intensity and international investment activity is developed by: Severn, A.K. and M.N. Lawrence, "Direct Investment, Research Intensity and Profitability," *Journal of Financial and Quantitative Analysis*, March 1974, pp. 181–190.
10. Hymer, S., *The International Operations of National Firms* (Cambridge: MIT Press, 1976).
11. Foreign producers of color televisions in the United States are Philips (Magnavox and Sylvania), Matsushita (Motorola and Panasonic), Sony, Sanyo, Sharp, Mitsubishi, Hitachi and Toshiba.

12. *The Economist*, June 28, 1980, pp. 80−81.

13. *Business Week*, February 23, 1981, p. 89.

14. Curhan, J.P., W.H. Davidson and Rajan Suri, *Tracing the Multinationals* (Cambridge: Ballinger, 1978), p. 21.

15. Aliber, R.Z., "A Theory of Foreign Direct Investment," in Kindleberger, C.P. (ed.), *The International Corporation* (Cambridge, MIT Press, 1970).

16. Daniels, J.D. and S. Patil, "U.S. Foreign Acquisitions: An Endangered Species?," *Management International Review*, Spring 1980, pp. 25−33.

17. The original theory of diversification was formalized by Moskowitz. Extensions of this theory to international investment have been made by a number of authors. Moskowitz, H., *Portfolio Selection: Efficient Diversification of Investment* (New York: Wiley, 1959); Solnik, B. "The International Pricing of Risk," *Journal of Finance*, May 1974, pp. 365−780; Grubel, H.G., "Internationally Diversified Portfolios," *American Economic Review*, December 1968, pp. 1299−1314; Lessard, D.E., "International Portfolio Diversification", *Journal of Finance*, June 1973; Rugman, A.M., "Risk Reduction by International Diversification", *Journal of International Business Studies*, Fall 1976.

18. The internalization of supply and user markets as a motive for international investment is described by Buckley, P.J., and M.C. Casson, *The Future of the Multinational Enterprise* (New York: Holmes and Meier, 1976).

19. Keesing, D.B., "The Impact of Research and Development on United States Trade," *Journal of Political Economy*, February 1967, pp. 38−49; Gruber, W.H., D. Mehta and Raymond Vernon, "The R & D Factor in International Trade and International Investment of U.S. Industries," *Journal of Political Economy*, February 1967, pp. 20−38.

20. The value of product differentiation is described by Hall, W.K., "Survival Strategies in a Hostile World," *Harvard Business Review*, September−October 1980, pp. 75−85. The importance of product differentiation per se as a source of strategic strength for global companies is developed in Caves, R.E., "International Corporations: The Industrial Economics of Foreign Investment," *Economica*, February 1971, pp. 1−27.

21. There are many examples of this phenomenon. The most obvious cases have occurred in extractive industries, but a similar pattern has occurred in manufacturing sectors as well. Deglobalization is apparent in the computer industry today. Indigenous firms in France and Japan, notably, have increased their share of market relative to global competitors. In the case of France, see *Business Week*, March 21, 1977, p. 48. For Japan, see "Japan's Big Push in Computers" *Fortune*, September 25, 1978, pp. 64−72.

    A similar pattern is occurring in the drug industry in many countries. See James, B.J., *The Future of the Multinational Pharmaceutical Industry to 1990* [New York: Halsted Press (Wiley), 1977], pp. 24−54.

    For a cross sectional view of different industries within specific countries, see: Connor, J.M., *The Market Power of Multinationals* (New York: Praeger, 1977), pp. 100−101.

22. The importance of this relationship can be seen in Biggadike, E.R., *Corporate Diversification: Entry, Strategy and Performance* (Boston: Harvard University Press, 1976); Rumelt, Richard, *Strategy, Structure and Performance* (Boston: Harvard Business School, Division of Research, 1974).

TWO

Participation Policies

The transition from a domestic orientation to a global perspective often occurs over a lengthy period of time. Commitment to international expansion builds gradually and generally is reflected in conservative, incremental patterns of expansion abroad. This process is often reflected in the firm's participation policy, most notably in initial preferences for licensing and joint venture agreements. One example of the importance of participation policy can be cited in the metal container industry. Continental Can, the leading U.S. producer, opted to pursue foreign markets primarily through licensing agreements with independent foreign firms. The president of the company described their participation policy at the 1953 annual meeting of shareholders:

> We limit participation in companies in foreign countries to a minority interest. We do not participate directly in management. We do provide them with any know-how and technical knowledge to the extent that they call on us. The only exceptions to that policy are in Canada and Cuba where we have wholly-owned subsidiaries. Our Canada company, however, is an autonomous, independent company.

While limiting investment abroad, Continental aggressively pursued licensing agreements in foreign markets, signing agreements with 36 foreign firms by 1960 and an additional 17 firms by 1965. One of these licenses was the principal British can company, Metal Box Ltd. Metal Box utilized Continental's technology in over 20 markets around the world through its network of

23

wholly owned affiliates. At the same time, a smaller U.S. competitor was expanding abroad at a rapid rate. Crown Cork and Seal established majority or wholly owned subsidiaries in 16 countries by 1960. Foreign sales accounted for 44% of Crown Cork and Seal revenues in 1960 and 48% of net profits.

When Continental Can found growth rates in its domestic market slowing in the early 1970s, the company decided to increase its commitment to faster-growing foreign markets. It was faced with several constraints in pursuing such a strategy, however. Its existing licensing agreements prohibited the company from entering many of the most desirable foreign markets. In other cases, aggressive global competitors such as Metal Box and Crown Cork and Seal had established a strong local presence. The results of Continental's early participation policy proved to be a severe deterrent to international expansion. Negotiation of release from licensing agreements with Metal Box required considerable time and expense. A shift in emphasis toward greater participation in foreign markets under such conditions proved difficult to implement. As this example suggests, participation policy plays an important role in determining relative competitive positions in an industry undergoing internationalization.

This discussion of participation decisions focuses primarily on strategic choices regarding the use of licensing, joint ventures and wholly owned subsidiaries in foreign markets. These alternative modes of activity represent only one dimension of participation policy, however. Choice of entry method—acquisition or subsidiary formation—is an important element in participation policy. In addition, participation covers not only a global firm's level of ownership in a foreign affiliate, but the extent of managerial, marketing and manufacturing activity in the host country. The legal form and the operating reality of participation can differ substantially. Choices about the nature and level of marketing and manufacturing activities in the host country are addressed in other chapters. The focus here is on choice of entry methods, managerial roles and ownership levels.

FACTORS AFFECTING PARTICIPATION DECISIONS

Several considerations influence the choice between wholly owned subsidiaries, joint ventures, licensees or agents in developing individual foreign markets. These choices often must be made under serious constraints imposed by host governments, but even in the absence of such constraints, a range of other factors affect participation decisions. Characteristics of the industry, product, and the firm, as well as host country conditions, are the principal determinants of participation decisions.

The importance of these factors can be seen by examining them in relation to actual participation patterns.[1] Different industries, for example, exhibit distinct patterns of participation in foreign markets. Table 2-1 provides an indication of participation patterns in a number of broadly defined industries. Wholly owned subsidiaries account for over 80% of all·foreign investments in the cosmetic, drug and computer industries. A far lower use of wholly owned subsidiaries appears in the paper, chemical, tire and motor vehicle industries. These differences reflect the underlying characteristics of these individual industries. Wells found that several types of global strategies result in a strong preference for wholly owned subsidiaries.[2] Such preferences are exhibited especially by firms that emphasize marketing

TABLE 2-1. Participation Patterns for Individual Industries, 1976

Industry	Percentage of Foreign Investment by Level of Ownership			
	Wholly Owned	Majority JV	Minority JV*	Total Number
Beverages	78.3%	12.8%	9.0%	78
Food	69.6	14.2	16.2	625
Textiles & apparel	60.6	10.6	28.8	94
Paper	51.9	17.5	30.6	206
Chemicals	53.8	11.5	34.7	741
Cosmetics & personal care	86.5	8.4	5.1	275
Drugs	80.2	12.3	7.5	536
Tires	48.3	34.8	16.9	89
Nonferrous metals	50.0	15.3	34.7	176
Computer & office machinery	84.2	6.6	9.2	76
Appliances & TV	74.3	15.0	10.7	113
Communication equipment	73.8	14.8	11.4	61
Motor vehicles	54.1	16.3	29.6	283
Scientific instruments	76.9	11.9	11.2	160

Source: Compiled from Curhan, J.P., W.H. Davidson and Rajan Suri, *Tracing the Multinationals* (Cambridge: Ballinger, 1977), pp. 318–319.
*Owned 50% or less by the multinational parent firm.

techniques to differentiate their product, and by firms that emphasize research and development to generate superior technologies.

The importance of complete ownership to firms in industries dominated by marketing activity is apparent in the high use of wholly owned subsidiaries in the beverage and cosmetics industries. The drug industry also represents a sector in which marketing efforts are pursued intensely. The drug industry actually spends a larger percentage of its sales on advertising than the beverage industry. At the same time, there is also a major emphasis on research and development in this industry. The computer and scientific instrument industries typify the emphasis on internal ownership present in most high-technology industries. Industries with lower levels of research and development and product differentiation tend to exhibit lower reliance on wholly owned subsidiaries.

This pattern reflects several important factors. Firms without superior technology or strong brand identification do not have the bargaining power to insist on complete control of a foreign venture in host countries that demand local ownership. In addition, these same firms may not possess sufficient strength to succeed in foreign markets without the assistance of a local partner. Participation patterns largely reflect these two primary issues. Host government restrictions on foreign equity ownership levels are largely applied as a function of the bargaining power of the foreign firm. Such bargaining power is determined by the degree to which its product is proprietary in nature. Firms without strong proprietary products can be required to accept local partners by governments intent on maximizing national participation in new business ventures. In the absence of official pressure, such firms frequently seek out local partners to aid in marketing, distribution, sourcing, government relations, personnel development and financing.

PRODUCT CHARACTERISTICS

One of the most important characteristics of a product with respect to participation policy is its technology content. High technology content is generally associated with policies that emphasize complete control and ownership of foreign affiliates. These policies reflect several basic concerns. High-technology firms possess strategic strengths that ensure them both market power and bargaining power. Consequently, they generally do not need local partners, and they are able to negotiate effectively in host countries that insist on national equity involvement. The most vivid example of such a policy is perhaps evident in the international activities of IBM. Its participation policy clearly states that it will not accept foreign ownership in any of its operations.[3] Even in Japan, IBM was able to negotiate full ownership of its local subsidiary because of its strong market position. When corporate policy was put to the test in India, the company opted to withdraw from the market rather than accept local ownership.

Such strength of commitment to a participation policy stems from several key concerns. On the most basic level, outside ownership in an affiliate reduces managerial flexibility. If the affiliate is engaged in extensive activity within a larger multinational system, local ownership can reduce the affiliate's responsiveness to the system's global objectives and opportunities. Conflicts between the local perspective of an outside owner and the global perspective of the multinational firm commonly appear in a number of areas. Local partners may wish to maximize dividend payments and minimize royalty payments, for example. If the local partner is closely tied to the host government, it may exert pressures to maximize local sourcing and to increase exports. The global firm, on the other hand, is often intent on sourcing from its affiliates in other countries for quality control, cost and financial reasons. At the same time, incentives to export from a joint venture are low because higher returns can be achieved by exporting from a wholly owned subsidiary. If a parent firm has a choice between a joint venture and a wholly owned affiliate to serve a third country market, a preference for the latter can be expected. Conflicts of this sort are common to all joint ventures, but they are more significant for high-technology companies. In other sectors, outside partners contribute significant resources to the affiliate that can be critical to its success. These contributions often outweigh the costs of dealing with an outside partner. The success of a high-technology venture rarely depends on such contributions. Consequently, outside ownership is considered strictly a cost in such ventures, because of the constraints and conflicts associated with such arrangements.

From another perspective, permitting outside ownership in such ventures can also be viewed as an uneven exchange. The outside owner shares in the rents associated with the affiliate's technology resources, but those resources are often capitalized at less than full value. This issue is a critical factor in participation decisions. Dunning found that foreign affiliates in the United Kingdom were substantially more profitable than local companies.[4]

This difference in profitability was greatest in high-technology industries. Such differences can be attributed largely to the fact that the foreign affiliates did not incur the overhead costs associated with research and other aspects of product line development.

These findings suggest that the resources transferred by the parent are substantially more valuable than the local partner's capital contribution. Valuation of these resources is the single most important issue in determining participation decisions. There is a great deal of evidence to suggest that these resources are systematically undervalued. If they were not undervalued, there would not be the rigid insistence on complete control and ownership by global firms. More fundamentally, if they were not systematically undervalued, *there would be no multinational firms.*

A Theory of Foreign Investment

International exploitation of business resources such as technology or a brand name need not be pursued through foreign affiliates. These resources can be sold to foreign firms for exploitation in their own home markets. Such local firms possess superior market-specific expertise and could effectively exploit a technology or brand name in their home market. This rationale is the basis for all licensing activity. Rather than developing a foreign affiliate at great cost, the proprietary resources essential to any business venture can be sold to an established firm in the foreign market.

Licensing occurs when the parent firm determines that it can realize a satisfactory return from selling its proprietary business resources to an independent foreign firm. In many cases, however, licensing does not offer returns comparable to those available through direct investment. This is particularly true in high-technology industries. International markets for technology appear to be highly inefficient.

Markets for technology are subject to the economics of information described by Arrow.[5] The value of technology is largely embodied in information. The seller of information or technology cannot adequately reveal the nature of the resource without effectively giving it away. The seller's reluctance to reveal information results in uncertainty about the good's value on the part of the potential buyers. Such buyer uncertainty leads to undervaluation of the technology. Since potential buyers will not offer the full value of the resource, returns from licensing will be unsatisfactory to the seller. Buckley and Casson argue that when external markets for technology or other proprietary business resources are inefficient, the result is "internalization" of foreign markets through direct investment.[6] In order to realize the full return from its resources, the parent firm must exploit them itself in foreign markets through direct investment. This rationale appears to be consistent with actual patterns of corporate activity in foreign markets.

Analysis of actual investment and licensing patterns confirm the importance of technology in participation decisions. Two of the most meaningful measures of technology content were found to correlate highly with the relative usage of foreign investment vis-á-vis licensing in exploiting a product in foreign markets. One recent study found that as the age of a product increases, the reliance on licensing in exploiting foreign markets also increased.[7] Product age represents one measure of the proprietary technology content associated with any product. As Table 2-2 reveals, an increase in age results in a significantly lower use of direct investment. The model developed in that study also shows that direct investment increases as the firm's research expenditure rate rises. With everything else equal, an increase in R&D expenditures from 2 to 5% of sales increases the incidence of direct investment from .74 to .82 of all foreign activity. Both measures suggest that the usage of direct investment is positively correlated with a product's technology content. Levels of research and development expenditure do not measure the technology of a particular product, but they do indicate the likelihood of continued technological advances. The expectation of future generations of technology permits the firm to amortize the fixed

TABLE 2-2.   Direct Investment and Measures of Technology Content

Product Age in Years	R&D as a Percent of Sales	Frequency of Direct Investment
1	.02	.74
5	.02	.68
10	.02	.65
15	.02	.63
1	.05	.82
5	.05	.78
10	.05	.76
15	.05	.74

Source: Davidson, W.H. and McFetridge, D.G., "International Technology Transactions and the Theory of the Firm," unpublished manuscript.

costs of direct investment over a larger product base and longer time frame. Research-intensive firms can also anticipate continued market and bargaining power to support a policy of complete ownership. For these reasons, high technology content is closely associated with participation policies that maximize the use of direct investment and minimize outside ownership.

Product-to-Parent Relationship

The impact of product characteristics on participation decisions must be evaluated within the context of the firm itself. An important issue is the relationship of an individual product line to the parent's industrial focus, resources and objectives. Products outside a firm's major lines of business exhibit significantly higher rates of licensing and outside ownership than those within. The firm's strategic commitment to such products often does not match that for its principal lines. In such cases, the company will not wish to invest heavily in building an international network of affiliates. If the product line is viewed as a secondary, short-term business, there is little justification for such long-term investments. Returns from licensing are highly attractive in such cases. In addition, the contribution of outside owners will be welcomed, and higher levels of joint venture activity can be expected.

Wells found that joint ventures occurred far more frequently for products outside the primary line of the parent. Joint ventures accounted for 42.3% of all foreign investment activity for such products, as compared to 33.6% for

TABLE 2-3.   Participation Patterns and Products Relationship to Parent's Principal Industry

Parent Participation Level	Within Principal Industry	Other
License	9.2%	19.7%
Minority	10.7	10.8
CO	7.2	5.8
Majority	8.6	7.4
Wholly owned	64.3	56.3

Source: Compiled from Davidson, W.H., *Experience Effects in International Investment and Technology Transfer* (Ann Arbor: UMI Research Press, 1980).

products within parents' principal line of business.[8] The occurrence of licensing is also significantly higher for products outside of a firm's principal industry. My own detailed study of participation patterns for 57 multinational enterprises reveals that licensing is used to exploit products within a parent's principal industry far less frequently than for other products. Licensing accounted for only 9.2% of all foreign ventures for products within firms' principal industries, while 19.7% of all foreign ventures for other products were conducted through independent licensees. Products within the parent's principal industry exhibit a significantly higher usage of wholly owned subsidiaries to exploit foreign markets. Secondary product lines are less likely to be introduced abroad through direct investment.

These patterns suggest the importance of the firm's strategic commitment to a product line in determining participation policy. In addition to strategic issues, economic factors also contribute to such participation patterns. Products outside the firm's principal industry will receive less benefit from the firm's existing operating infrastructure. The compatibility of a product with existing facilities plays an important role in determining participation patterns.

ECONOMIC EFFECTS

The economics of participation decisions are determined largely by the fixed costs associated with foreign investment decisions. Fixed costs include those expenses and investments incurred in establishing managerial, marketing and manufacturing activities in a foreign market. When these costs are substantial, preference for licensing or joint ventures will be relatively high. When they can be reduced, preferences for wholly owned subsidiaries will rise.

These costs are determined to a large extent by the level of existing infrastructure already in place in any market. The presence of a foreign subsidiary in a foreign market dramatically reduces the fixed costs of foreign investment. Managerial, marketing and manufacturing facilities will have largely been established, and the cost of market entry will be much lower than in markets without an existing subsidiary. These economic factors have several important effects on global management strategies. In the area of market selection, they result in a natural preference for countries with established subsidiaries. In participation decisions, the presence of an existing subsidiary leads to a strong preference for the use of that entity in introducing new products.

This effect can be seen quite clearly in Table 2-4, which describes participation patterns for the sample of 57 multinational corporations mentioned earlier. For markets in which the parent firm had no prior activity, licensees accounted for 31.8% of all market entries. If the firm had already made a direct investment in the market, however, only 17.2% of all subsequent product introduction were effected through licensees. The fact that licensing activity continues in the presence of a subsidiary reflects the importance of the product's relationship to the parent's principal industry. The economic benefits associated with an existing subsidiary will not be fully transferable to an unrelated product line. If existing manufacturing, distribution and managerial resources cannot be applied to a new product line, the economics of foreign investment for such lines will not be enhanced by the existence of an established subsidiary. Most licensing activity by firms in countries with an existing affiliate occurs under such conditions.

The realization of economic benefits in participation decisions is thus a function of the diversity of the firm. Highly diverse firms will be unable to apply existing resources to all products. Firms with narrow and closely related product lines will be able to utilize existing resources extensively in entering foreign markets. This factor contributes to an observed tendency for highly diverse firms to make greater use of joint ventures and licensing arrangements.[9]

The presence of an existing affiliate in a foreign market lends important economic effects to participation decisions. In general, the presence of an

TABLE 2-4. Participation Patterns and Parent's Status in Host Country, Ventures Entered Between 1945 and 1978 by 57 U.S. Multinational Firms

Parent Status in Host Country	Percentage of Entries Via:				
	Licensee	Minority Joint Venture	Majority Joint Venture	Wholly Owned	Total Number
No prior activity	31.8%	17.5%	7.2%	44.5%	236
Prior licensing only	59.5	7.4	5.4	27.6	257
Prior direct investment	17.2	18.4	4.8	59.6	1,350
TOTAL	25.9%	17.1%	5.2%	51.6%	1,843

Source: Compiled from Davidson, *Experience Effects in International Investment and Technology Transfer.*

affiliate eliminates the need to consider other market entry options. Other options should be considered, however, when the product in question is unrelated to the affiliate's activities.

EXPERIENCE EFFECTS

The ability to utilize existing subsidiary resources significantly enhances the use of wholly owned subsidiaries. A second, similar effect occurs at corporate headquarters. The development of central administrative systems, information banks, human resources and mechanisms for transferring resources to foreign markets all enhance the economics of foreign investment. These central resources can be applied to a range of foreign ventures to reduce the overhead costs associated with foreign investment. Measurement of the level of such central resources is extremely difficult. One measure does provide an indication, however. The number of market entries or product transfers already executed provides a measure of the firm's cumulative experience in introducing products into foreign markets.

This measure correlates highly with participation patterns. Products in industries where the parent firm has no prior transfer experience exhibit extremely high rates of licensing. The first foreign market entry for products in such instances occurred through independent licensees in 32.0% of all cases for the same sample of 57 firms. For products in industries where the parent had entered more than 10 markets, licensing accounted for only 10.9% of all market introductions.

These patterns reflect several basic effects. First, experience reflects scale economies in the use of fixed overhead resources at headquarters. Second, experience includes benefits associated with the learning curve phenomenon. Teece found that the variable cost of executing the transfer of a product to a foreign market declined as a function of the number of times the transfer had been executed.[10] Both these factors reduce the cost of market entry and stimulate foreign investment. A third factor also plays an important part in the tendency toward greater participation as experience rises. One of the principal benefits of experience is uncertainty reduction, and uncertainty appears to play a very important role in participation decisions.

One of the most widely observed phenomena in international business is the prevalence of conservative behavior in the early stages of global expansion. There is a strong tendency for firms to rely initially on licensees

TABLE 2-5.   Industry Experience Levels and Participation Patterns

Parent's Prior Transfers in Product's Industry	Licensees	Minority- Owned Joint Venture*	Majority- Owned Joint Venture	Wholly Owned Subsidiaries	Total
		Percentage of Transfers Via:			
0 prior transfers	32.0%	17.1%	3.7%	47.2%	870
1–4 prior transfers	24.3	15.6	6.9	53.2	518
5–10 prior transfers	22.4	18.9	4.6	54.1	216
11 or more prior transfers	10.9	13.0	7.1	69.0	239
TOTAL	25.9%	17.1%	5.3%	51.6%	1,843

Source: Compiled from Davidson, W.H., Experiences Effects International Investment and Technology Transfer (Ann Arbor: UMI Research Press, 1980).
*Includes affiliates owned 50% or less by the U.S. parent.

and joint ventures in entering foreign markets.[11] This tendency is illustrated by the data in Tables 2-4 and 2-5. The accumulation of experience results in a reduction of uncertainty about foreign operations. As perceived risk levels decline, the firm's willingness to increase its participation levels rises. The result is increasing participation in subsequent ventures.

Two distinct types of uncertainty can be identified. The first is associated with a particular product's potential in foreign markets. Uncertainty of this type sharply diminishes as successful market entries are completed. The second form of uncertainty relates to individual foreign markets. In entering a foreign market for the first time, a firm faces extremely high levels of uncertainty about a wide range of country characteristics. The presence of an existing affiliate largely eliminates this factor from participation decisions, but it appears to be an important factor in initial entries in any new market. Licensing and joint venture arrangements are popular means of entering new markets; wholly owned subsidiaries are used more frequently after a firm has gained experience in the country through export or licensing activities.

COUNTRY CHARACTERISTICS

The effects of country uncertainty on participation decisions are partially visible in the entry patterns found in a range of host countries for the 57 parent companies mentioned earlier. Markets highly similar to the United States, such as Canada, Australia and the United Kingdom, exhibit relatively low rates of licensing and joint venture formation. Lower uncertainty about the operating environment in these countries contributes to a preference for greater participation. It is notable in Table 2-6 that the group of markets labeled "other" exhibits an extremely high rate of licensing. Licensing accounts for half of all activity in this collection of secondary markets. In many of these cases, host country limitations on direct investment are not the principal reason for low levels of participation by multinational firms.

TABLE 2-6. Foreign Transfers of 580 Products by 57 U.S.-Based Firms, Classified by Type of Recipient and Host Country, 1945–1978

Host Country	Percentage of Transfers Via:				
	Independent Licensees	Minority-Owned Affiliates	Majority-Owned Affiliates	Wholly Owned Affiliates	Total Number
Canada	5.0%	6.2%	1.1%	87.8%	180
Colombia	7.7	11.5	26.9	53.8	26
Netherlands	10.0	30.0	8.3	51.7	60
Argentina	15.6	17.2	6.3	60.9	64
United Kingdom	17.0	12.9	6.7	63.4	194
Brazil	17.1	6.7	5.7	70.5	105
Australia	17.5	12.6	4.9	65.0	143
Mexico	17.6	30.6	13.9	38.0	108
Italy	23.3	14.4	4.4	57.8	90
France	26.2	5.4	10.0	58.5	130
Spain	26.3	14.1	3.5	56.1	57
Belgium	27.1	5.1	8.5	59.3	59
Germany	30.5	17.9	2.1	49.5	95
Turkey	30.8	38.5	15.4	15.4	13
Sweden	36.8	31.6	0.0	50.0	12
South Africa	37.5	20.0	0.0	42.5	40
India	41.7	8.3	0.0	50.0	12
Switzerland	41.7	8.3	0.0	50.0	12
Taiwan	44.4	0.0	5.6	50.0	18
Japan	45.9	53.4	0.7	0.0	146
Venezuela	58.3	20.9	0.0	20.8	24
Peru	62.5	25.0	0.0	12.5	8
Other	49.6	10.8	3.3	36.3	240
TOTAL	25.9%	17.1%	5.3%	51.6%	1,843

Uncertainty about operating in such countries as New Zealand, Kenya, Rhodesia, Finland, Portugal, Nigeria and the Ivory Coast leads to licensing rates in excess of 60% for each of these countries.

Uncertainty levels about such secondary markets contribute to low levels of participation. In most cases, firms will have relatively little knowledge and experience relevant to such markets. This uncertainty leads firms to discount investment opportunities in secondary markets. Several patterns result from this process. When investment opportunities are discounted, returns from licensing become more attractive. The result is a higher rate of licensing in secondary markets. In addition, total levels of activity in such markets may be reduced if suitable licensing arrangements can not be negotiated. When investment does occur in such markets, joint ventures are relied on more extensively than in primary foreign markets.

The larger sample of 180 firms studied by the Harvard Multinational Enterprise Project exhibit similar country participation patterns. In Canada, for example, minority joint ventures accounted for only 7.9% of all manufacturing subsidiaries formed or acquired before 1976. The United Kingdom and Australia also exhibit extremely low levels of minority joint venture formation. Levels of joint venture activity generally correlate with market size and similarity. Larger, similar markets tend to attract greater participation.

The highest levels of participation occur in English-speaking, Western-oriented markets. Even within the culturally distinct regions of South America and Asia, the highest participation rates occur in nations with the greatest similarities to Western society. Argentina is widely recognized as the most European-oriented culture in Latin America, and the Philippines is the only country in Asia where the predominant religion is Western. These two nations exhibit the greatest reliance on wholly owned affiliates of all countries in their respective regions. Even in continental Europe, the highest participation rate occurs in the Netherlands, a nation renowned for its ability to assimilate and accommodate foreign languages and cultures. France, with perhaps the most distinct culture in Western Europe, exhibits a relatively low usage of wholly owned subsidiaries. Market similarity appears to have an important impact on participation policy.

One other broad consideration plays a critical role in determining participation patterns. National policies with respect to foreign investment are primarily responsible for the high levels of joint venture formation in countries such as Japan, South Korea, India and Mexico. Restrictions on

TABLE 2-7. Participation Patterns for Foreign Subsidiaries Formed or Acquired by 180 U.S.-Based Multinational Enterprises, 1900–1976

Country	Percentage of Subsidiaries			
	Minority Joint Venture	Majority Joint Venture	Wholly Owned Subsidiary	Total Number
Canada	7.9%	5.4%	86.7%	576
Mexico	30.7	11.9	54.7	352
Central America & Caribbean	27.9	20.2	51.9	168
Chile	23.3	26.7	50.0	30
Colombia	36.7	11.2	52.1	98
Ecuador	27.3	13.6	59.1	22
Peru	24.3	21.6	54.1	37
Argentina	17.4	10.7	71.9	121
Brazil	24.2	18.0	57.8	244
Venezuela	24.7	23.5	51.8	170
United Kingdom	15.8	5.2	79.0	538
Belgium	20.4	10.5	69.1	152
France	23.9	27.4	48.7	343
Netherlands	15.5	10.6	73.9	123
Germany	20.3	12.9	66.9	380
Greece	29.6	11.1	59.3	27
Spain	40.8	21.7	37.5	184
Sweden	22.2	9.7	68.1	72
Turkey	28.6	28.6	42.8	21
North Africa & Middle East	44.5	22.9	32.6	96
South Africa & Rhodesia	20.8	10.1	69.1	178
Other Africa	26.2	16.7	57.1	84
Pakistan	21.7	52.2	26.1	23
India	54.4	15.2	30.4	79
Thailand	20.6	29.4	50.0	34
Indonesia	15.4	38.5	46.1	26
Philippines	18.5	20.0	61.5	65
South Korea	71.4	10.7	17.6	28
Taiwan	33.3	17.9	48.8	39
Japan	77.6	3.9	18.5	259
Australia & New Zealand	18.6	16.7	64.7	365

Source: Compiled from Curhan, J.P., W.H. Davidson and Rajan Suri, *Tracing the Multinationals* (Cambridge: Ballinger, 1977), pp. 316–317.

foreign investment in these and other countries limit participation options and result in a higher level of joint venture activity.

Host Country Investment Restrictions

Restrictions on foreign investment are an important national policy in a growing number of host countries.[12] The Japanese model has been widely cited as an example of the benefits of such restrictions. By limiting foreign participation in its domestic industry, Japan has been able to pursue a national industrial policy without concern for potential conflict with the interests of global firms. The protection, support and direction of infant industries by the government has led to the development of highly successful export-oriented sectors. These results would have been inconsistent with the interest of foreign investors, so that domestic control of industry was an essential element in Japan's development plans. Similar constraints on foreign investment have become highly common in the Far East and elsewhere. Rigid restrictions on foreign participation are enforced in India and South Korea. Indonesia and Malaysia have adopted foreign investment controls as well. Mexico has recently strengthened a policy limiting foreign participation in domestic companies. In the early 1970s, the Andean Pact countries adopted draconian measures designed to limit participation by foreign firms in industrial ventures within their borders. Such restrictions are also common in the Middle East and Africa. In many of these countries, restrictions on foreign ownership are supplemented by laws regulating licensing agreements as well. Article 20 of the Andean Pact, for example, cites that member countries are not to authorize licensing agreements that contain stipulations as to territorial limits on licensee exports; equipment, component or material purchases; or pricing or volume guidelines. Royalty rates are also strictly regulated in a large number of host countries.[13]

Constraints on foreign participation are differentiated by industry in most of these countries. In India, industrial sectors are divided into three broad categories. Foreign investment is permitted in the first category, which includes industries such as selected industrial machinery, office equipment, and precision instruments. In the second category, including such industries as appliance controls, mining machinery, chemicals and fertilizer, transformers and pulp and paper, foreign participation is limited to licensing agreements. No foreign participation of any form is permitted in the third category of industries, which includes the radio, battery, cable, railcar, and electrode sectors. The categories and composition of these national participation policies can vary significantly across countries and over time. In India and Indonesia, an increasing number of sectors have been added to categories in which foreign participation is prohibited as domestic industries become self-sufficient. In Japan, the number of sectors open to foreign direct investment has increased from 55 in 1967 to 228 in 1973 and to all but 5 sectors in 1980.[14] Understanding of host country sector ownership standards is of principal importance in making participation decisions for any product. Once these host government policies are understood, negotiations with host governments become critical in implementing many participation decisions.

Negotiating with Host Governments

Administration of national foreign investment policies is typically conducted by an agency such as MITI in Japan or the Foreign Investment Board in India.[15] Formal application for foreign investment licenses must be submitted to these agencies for approval. In many cases, a number of other official agencies must also approve foreign investment applications. In India, aproval of the Ministry of Industry and the Ministry of Finance are also required for market entry. The presence and power of these agencies is of course greatest in the state-run economies of the Eastern Bloc, China and the less developed world. Negotiations with such agencies are a critical management task in the area of participation policy.

Participation is only one of many issues arising in negotiations with host countries, but it often appears to be the principal area of contention in discussions between multinational firms and host governments. Much of the literature on this process is drawn from extractive industries, since host governments have been most active in this sector. The issue of ownership and control of existing companies has led to painful confrontations between host governments and foreign firms in many countries. The oil industry has a long history of incidents related to control and participation. Mexico nationalized the local affiliates of foreign petroleum companies in 1939. Peru assumed control of International Petroleum Corporation, an affiliate of Exxon, in 1967. Host governments have assumed control of oil company affiliates in over 20 countries since 1970, including key production companies in Venezuela, Iran, Libya, Iraq and Saudi Arabia. A similar pattern of increasing participation has occurred in other extractive industries. Copper mines in Zaire, Zambia and Chile have been nationalized.[16] Bauxite producers in Jamaica and Guyana have come under the control of the host government.[17] Management of iron ore mines in Venezuela and Brazil has been assumed by government-controlled enterprises.

New ventures in these industries are subject to intense negotiations over tax rates, infrastructure grants, depreciation schedules and of course, ownership patterns. Negotiating skills play a major role in the success of global firms in foreign markets under such conditions. A wide body of literature on the negotiation process details issues and approaches for negotiating with host governments.[18] Several general themes appear throughout this literature.

The negotiating process brings together two parties capable of viewing the outcome of their discussions as a zero-sum game confrontation. Every effort to reduce this perception and establish an expectation of mutual benefit will aid the negotiating process. Initial emphasis on issues that do not present major conflicts serves this purpose. A wide range of issues will be discussed in any negotiation, and certain issues can be conceded with little cost. Such tactics can help to establish a positive negotiating relationship. Ultimately, however, issues involving significant conflict of interest must be addressed. Resolution of such conflicts involves a wide range of tactics designed to maximize the benefits and minimize the costs of the agreement to each party. Approaches to this stage of negotiations vary considerably. In renegotiation proceedings, or those designed to alter the terms of an original extractive concession agreement, for example, the foreign investor is invariably recalcitrant and defensive in seeking to drag out and delay resolution of the negotiations. This approach is inappropriate in market entry negotiations. The firm will have to carry the initiative in such cases, while the host country will often use stalling, outside approval requirements and rival offer tactics to improve the terms of any agreement in its favor. The effectiveness of these tactics depends both on the negotiating skill and bargaining power of each party. Some of the key variables in host government negotiations are:

Ownership levels

Tax schedules

Depreciation schedules

Infrastructure support

Arbitrator mechanisms

Repatriation levels

Indiginous employment levels

Duties and quotas on imports

Export levels

Length of agreement

Capital structure

Debt sources

Import protection

Host countries' bargaining skills and power have increased rapidly over time. Consulting firms, United Nations agencies and advisors from third countries have all contributed to the impovement in host country bargaining skills. In many cases, the faces across the table from management either are outside professionals or are acting under their direction. In most other cases, government officials with extensive negotiating experience will represent the host country's interests. The general improvement in bargaining skills coincides with a sharp increase in host country bargaining ower.

Host country bargaining power has risen rapidly as a result of an increase in the number of firms vying for foreign markets. Competition for foreign markets has risen steadily in the post war period. Each year, additional firms from the United States and elsewhere have entered global markets. For example, the Harvard Multinational Enterprise Project identified 81 U.S.-based firms that operated manufacturing facilities in six or more nations in 1950. By 1975, there were 254 U.S. firms operating in six or more countries. This statistic does not adequately reflect the rate of increase in competition for foreign markets, however, because of a parallel trend towards increasing diversity. Not only has the number of firms active in global markets increased, but the range of activity for the average firm has expanded significantly. The 81 firms mentioned previously manufactured abroad in an average of four 3-digit Standard Industrial Classification (SIC) industries in 1950. In 1975, those same firms manufactured abroad in an average of 11 industries. In addition, the number of firms from Europe, Japan and elsewhere active in international markets has risen rapidly.

The explosive overseas expansion of U.S., British, European and Japanese firms has contributed greatly to the bargaining power of host

TABLE 2-8.   Number of Foreign Manufacturing Subsidiaries Established by
European and Japanese Companies*

	Nationality of Parent Firm		
	United Kingdom	Continental Europe	Japan
pre-1920	87	218	0
1920–1945	251	405	44
1946–1959	351	377	21
1960–1970	1,840	2,023	1,020

Source: Harvard Multinational Enterprise Project Data Base.
*These data represent activity by the largest 49 U.K.-based firms, 94 continental companies and
66 Japanese firms in the manufacturing sector as of 1970.

countries. These new entrants often undercut prevailing agreements in an
industry in order to establish a presence in foreign markets. In the oil
industry, new companies such as Ente Nazionale Idrocarburi (ENI) and
Occidental offered highly favorable terms to win concessions away from
established oil companies. The growing presence of such companies permitted host countries to shift the terms of concession agreements completely in
their favor. These new entrants disrupted the once united front the industry
had presented in negotiating concession arguments. Host governments soon
found that they could play firms off against each other and, by focusing on
companies with the most to gain or lose in any situation, extract vastly
improved terms on both new and existing agreements. Libyan pressure on
Occidental Petroleum, which derived over 90% of its crude supply from that
country, was the wedge that broke the oil industry ranks and led to the
emergence of the OPEC.

This process occurs in virtually all industries. The number of firms
competing for foreign markets has risen in virtually every sector of the global
economy.[19] The mere presence of additional competitors significantly
strengthens the bargaining position of host governments. As a result,
negotiations regarding market entry and participation levels present a
growing challenge to global firms. Incidents such as the departure of IBM
from India are indicative of the magnitude of this issue.

The growth in bargaining skill and power by host countries has several
implications. In extreme cases, severe participation restrictions appear to
result in a dramatic reduction in activity by multinational firms. For the 180
firms cited earlier, investment activity declined sharply in India and the

Andean Pact countries following adoption of investment restrictions. The relevant legislation was adopted in both cases in 1969, although the intent had been clear for several years. In each of the countries involved, foreign investment activity in manufacturing falls off significantly after 1965. Foreign investment activity in these countries during the 1965–1975 period was down 35% from the previous decade. Total foreign investment activity in all other countries by this sample of firms actually increased by 37% over this same period. The result of the imposition of restrictions on foreign investment can be seen clearly in Table 2-9.

One of the most important questions about the effect of such policies is their impact on licensing activity. The Japanese have been signally successful in encouraging licensing activity while restricting investment. Although no firm evidence is available, there are indications that the policies adopted in India and the Andean Pact may actually have resulted in reduced licensing activity. Licensing activity for my sample of 57 U.S. firms in these countries declined between 1955–1965 and 1965–1975. These firms entered 21 licensing agreements in these countries between 1955 and 1965 and 14 in the following decade. The number of products entering these markets through minority joint ventures also declined from 24 to 12 over the two decades. These reductions again coincide with an aggregate increase in both types of activity for other markets. It is important to note, however, that these firms represent only major U.S. multinational firms. Activity by secondary U.S. firms and foreign companies may have more than compensated for this decline.

TABLE 2-9. **Number of Manufacturing Subsidiary Entries for 180 U.S. Multinational Firms in Countries with Investment Restrictions**

Country	Period of Entry				
	pre-1950	1950–60	1961–65	1966–70	1971–75
India	7	22	32	14	11
Peru	13	18	17	13	5
Colombia	23	37	49	20	20
Ecuador	1	3	9	6	6
Venezuela	18	62	47	48	39
TOTAL	62	142	154	101	81

Source: Curhan, Davidson and Suri, *Tracing the Multinationals,* pp. 318–319.

These data suggest one form of corporate resonse to the rising power of host governments. The decision not to participate is a popular option under unfavorable conditions. In other cases where participation levels are negotiated, increasing emphasis on the use of joint ventures and licensing agreements can be expected. The most important implication of rising host country negotiating strength for participation decisions concerns the use of joint ventures and licensing agreements. As long as domestic ownership remains a principal ideological and strategic objective of host governments, global enterprises will be forced to accept lower levels of participation in many foreign ventures. Development and management of joint ventues and licensing agreements pose a rising challenge to global firms.

JOINT VENTURE FORMATION AND MANAGEMENT

The focus in this chapter, as well as in others in this section of the book, is on key strategic choices that determine the profile of a firm's global activities. There is less emphasis on management of ongoing operations. Nonetheless, it is imortant to recognize the issues and constraints associated with managing joint ventures. These factors are key inputs in decisions to form joint ventures, and in choices regarding the internal structure of any partnership.

Local partners offer a number of benefits to global firms. Franko found that U.S. managers perceived their most significant contributions, in order of importance, as general local knowledge, managerial personnel, marketing personnel, and access to distribution systems. Capital, sourcing and manufacturing contributions were considered less important.[20] These benefits are offset by a number of constraints. Potential conflicts in joint venture management typically occur in a number of areas. Pricing, dividends, export, sourcing, royalty, and product design policies often emerge as areas of conflict between global and local partners. Some of these conflicts relate to the financial returns received by each party from the joint venture. Dividend and royalty payments in particular are purely financial issues. Other conflicts derive from differences of opinion over operating procedures. Global firms often wish to standardize elements of marketing or manufacturing activity, while local partners have their own preferences. Where quality control and product consistency are critical, and where the credibility of an international brand name is at stake, a global firm should be reluctant to alter its production policies. If a local partner is unwilling to accept such policies, serious problems can result. On the other hand, local partners often have a better understanding of local marketing and distribution requirements. A global firm's failure to appreciate this ability can often lead to difficulties. Differences in administrative procedures also present universal and significant problems for joint ventures. Global firms wish to receive standardized financial and managerial information from their affiliates. The installation of a standard management information system generally is accompanied by standard capital budgeting, planning and evaluation procedures. These management systems are alien and undesirable to many local partners. Installation of such management systems is particularly problematic if the issue of management control has not been clearly resolved prior to formation of the joint venture.

An additional area of potential conflict is the definition of the venture's sourcing and marketing linkages. Numerous charges of transfer pricing manipulation have been alleged against both global and local partners. Prices for components, capital goods and materials purchased from the global parent will be scrutinized by local partners. On the other hand, it is not uncommon for local partners to form wholly owned marketing companies to purchase the output of a manufacturing joint venture for resale to consumers. In several cases, global firms with minority ownership positions in such a venture have alleged that the local partner shifted profits to the marketing subsidiary through transfer pricing manipulations.[21]

Another concern in joint ventures is the definition of the scope of the company's activities. As noted earlier, global partners generally are reluctant to use joint ventures to serve export markets if a wholly owned subsidiary can also supply the product. Local partners will naturally seek to maximize such activity. Local partners also may hold expectations about product line extensions that are not part of a global firm's plan for the joint venture.

All these issues and more must be considered and discussed in structuring a joint venture agreement. Not all of them can be resolved prior to the initial commitment to a partnership. It is important, however, to ascertain at least the respective contributions, responsibilities and policy jurisdiction of each party. It is also important to openly discuss each party's expectations of the other prior to engaging in a formal contract. Such precontractual discussion and negotiations can dramatically increase the chances of success for a joint venture. At the same time, however, it must be recognized that not all conflicts and contingencies can be anticipated. Arbitration mechanisms and procedures for such eventualities should be established prior to their occurrence. Even more important than formal arbitration procedures, perhaps, is the nature of the relationship with the partner. A positive relationship that extends beyond legal contractual commitments is the principal goal of any joint venture agreement.

Relationships with Local Partners

Selection of a local partner is a critical decision in joint venture formation. In the most general terms, the global firm requires a partner whose strengths meet the primary needs of the venture. If marketing and distribution are the principal requirements, the ideal local partner will be an experienced and established distributor of related products. If relations with the host government is critical, a local partner with close ties to the government is needed. The importance of these general principles can be seen in histories of many joint ventures.

Such considerations were critical in Raytheon's choice of partners for its initial joint venture in Italy in 1960. Raytheon's Hawk Missile System had been selected by the NATO command for installation in Europe in 1959. Because of the extensive role of government in this industry, Raytheon elected to manufacture Hawk components in a joint venture with a subsidiary of IRI, the state-owned Italian industrial holding company. The partnership flourished as the IRI lobbied for and assigned additional military contracts to the joint venture. In the first five years after its formation, the subsidiary contributed more than $15 million in earnings and royalties to the parent company. Its contribution in 1965 exceeded total earnings from the rest of the company in that year.

Shortly after the formation of this joint venture, Raytheon became an active partner in a second Italian company. This company's objectives were to enter the television components market in Europe. Raytheon's partners in this venture were an electrical utility company and several private individuals. These partners possessed some local political strength, but Raytheon already had an extremely positive relationship with the Italian government because of its other activities in the country. The venture's greatest needs were in the area of marketing, as Raytheon had no relevant experience in the television industry or, for that matter, in any area outside its defense activities. Its partners were unable to make an effective contribution, and the company lost more than $15 million in the first five years of its existence.

Choice of partners was not the only reason for the success and failure of these two ventures, but partner selection was an important factor in these results.

Partner selection requires extensive consideration of the fit between the joint venture's needs and the partner's strengths. Other characteristics of potential local partners are also important. The size and stability of the company are key factors. In most cases, the global firm will be larger than the local partner. When the reverse is true, it can prove difficult to keep the local partner focused on the activities of the joint venture, especially if the partner is diversified, and the joint venture falls outside its principal line of business. In addition, entry into an agreement with a larger local firm often eliminates the popular option of acquiring the joint venture or the partner itself at a future date.

The stability of local partners is another important issue. Involvement with a company suffering from financial problems is highly undesirable. Mitsubishi's recent experience with Chrysler, its Japanese joint venture partner and American distributor, shows that an otherwise healthy partnership can be undermined by the problems of a parent. The implications can be even more serious if the local partner in a joint venture goes bankrupt. Ataka's bankruptcy in 1976 posed severe problems for several U.S. firms that had formed Japanese marketing agreements with the parent company.[22]

Partner selection patterns for the 180 firms in the Harvard Multinational Enterprise Project sample provide some insight into the types of local partners chosen by U.S. multinational firms. Joint ventures are generally thought of in terms of partnerships between one foreign and one local company. This type of managment arrangement is the predominant form of joint venture, but other forms are also significant. For the 1,023 manufacturing joint ventures in which these firms participated in 1975, the principal partner in two thirds of the cases was a local private firm from the host country. The local partner in 81 of those joint ventures was a state-owned enterprise. Other multinational firms from outside the host country were the principal partner in 143 ventures, and in an additional 115 cases the outside equity ownership was widely dispersed among more than six equity holders. Each of these broad categories reflects a very different approach to partner selection.

Joint ventures with state-owned enterprises occur in virtually every industrial sector, but they are particularly common in the refining and chemical industries. These two sectors accounted for 40% of all joint ventures with state enterprises. The tire industry also makes conspicuous

TABLE 2-10.　Outside Owners in Manufacturing Joint Ventures for 180
U.S.-Based Multinational Firms, 1975

Type of Outside Partner	Percentage Ownership by Outside Partner				
	5–49%	50%	51–94%	Unknown	Total
Local private	230	243	166	45	684
Local state	35	18	22	6	81
Foreign private	72	42	19	10	143
Widely dispersed	52	9	41	13	115
TOTAL	389	312	248	74	1,023

Source:　Compiled from Curhan, Davidson and Suri, Tracing the Multinationals, p. 374.

use of state enterprises as local partners. The geographic distribution of such ventures is also extensive, although very little joint venture activity with state enterprises occurs in the principal industrial countries. Only two cases were reported in the combined markets of Canada, Australia, the United Kingdom and Germany, for example. A group of 10 secondary host countries accounted for almost exactly half of all joint ventures with state enterprises. Ventures with state agencies appear to be used primarily in highly restrictive, risky, secondary markets.

On the other hand, ventures with wide dispersion of ownership tend to occur in principal industrial markets. The existence of well-developed securities markets appear to be crucial in implementing this strategy. Canada, the United Kingdom, and Australia account for 20% of all ventures in which outside ownership is widely dispersed. Dispersion of ownership can also be viewed as a means of satisfying host equity participation requirements without relinquishing control. This approach is used extensively in Mexico and India, which together account for over 20% of such ventures.

Joint ventures with other global firms are most common in extractive industries, where such arrangements have long been used to share risks in exploration projects and to maintain industry stability. The classic partnerships involving global competitors were Aramco and the Iran consortium, which shared control of Middle Eastern oil supplies among the major U.S. and European oil companies. Joint ventures still dominate oil exploration activity. Similar partnerships are common in mining industries, but joint ventures between global competitors occur extensively in manufacturing sectors as well. The occurrence of such ventures is greatest in the refining and chemical industries and in the iron, steel, and nonferrous metal sectors.

TABLE 2-11.   Principal Sites of State-Owned Joint Ventures in 1975

	Number of Manufacturing Ventures in 1975 (all types)	Number of Joint Ventures in 1975	Number with State-Owned Partners
Nicaragua	13	11	3
Peru	40	28	3
Turkey	18	12	3
Iran	33	27	8
Kenya	16	7	3
India	72	58	5
Saudi Arabia	8	8	3
Morocco	18	14	3
South Korea	28	23	5
Taiwan	37	19	3
TOTAL	283	207	39

Source: Compiled from Curhan, Davidson and Suri, *Tracing the Multinationals*, pp. 34, 316, 378–79.

In addition, the paper, glass, electrical machinery and motor vehicle industries also exhibit extensive use of such ventures.[23] Oligopoly considerations appear to be the principal motives behind the formation of such partnerships. Each of these industries is highly concentrated and, with the exception of the paper industry, contains a number of large foreign competitors. Confrontations with such familiar foreign rivals can be best avoided by entering into joint ventures in contested markets. In such cases, the joint venture represents an ideal market-sharing arrangement.

Changes in Joint Venture Status

One of the most important decisions facing a participant in a joint venture is the issue of changing participation levels over time. Despite considerable pressure on firms in a number of countries to reduce ownership levels in existing affiliates, the overall trend continues to be toward rising participation by U.S. firms in foreign ventures. Overall, shifts in ownership have resulted in a larger number of wholly owned affiliates for U.S. firms. The number of minority-owned affiliates has declined. The trend can be seen in Table 2-12 by comparing the final column with the bottom row. While 7,741 of the subsidiaries of 180 U.S. firms active in 1975 entered as wholly owned affiliates, 8,059 were wholly owned in 1975. The number of majority-, co-owner and minority-owned affiliates each declined slightly. Underlying the relative stability in the aggregate numbers, however, were some significant shifts in partnership participation levels. Of the 1,050 affiliates active in 1975 that entered as majority-owned joint ventures, 314 had become wholly owned by the U.S. parent prior to 1975. Shifts of smaller but significant magnitude occurred for minority- and co-owned affiliates. A large number of affiliates entering in these categories become wholly owned subsidiaries before 1975.

Significant exceptions to this general trend appear in a number of countries. In Mexico, Peru, Norway, Turkey, Algeria, and India, the trend has been toward a reduction in the participation of U.S. companies in existing affiliates. With these exceptions, there is a general tendency for U.S. firms to ·gradually increase their participation levels in ongoing affiliates.

This observation neglects a second important trend in participation patterns, however. A very important indicator of participation trends is the incidence of complete withdrawals from joint venture agreements. Such activity has been increasing dramatically among the firms in this sample. These 180 firms withdrew from a total of 103 joint ventures between 1955 and 1965. The number of withdrawals in the following decade rose to 831 cases of sale or liquidation of foreign affiliates. This trend is a powerful indicator of the problems associated with joint venture management in an increasingly competitive and restrictive environment. Notably, the majority of these withdrawals do not appear to have been caused by business failure. Joint ventures were liquidated in less than one third of the cases involving the withdrawal of a U.S. parent. The majority of the cases involve a sale of

TABLE 2-12.   Changes in Ownership Levels for Subsidiaries Active in 1975

Ownership at Entry	Ownership in 1975					
	95−100	51−94	50	45−49	Unknown	Total
94−100%	7,216	182	58	62	223	7,741
51−94%	314	697	19	40	20	1,090
50%	148	34	595	49	20	846
5−49%	119	73	33	831	23	1,079
Unknown	262	39	20	54	67	442
TOTAL	8,059	1,025	725	1,036	353	11,198

Source: Harvard Multinational Enterprise Project Data Base.

TABLE 2-13. Means of Withdrawal from Joint Ventures, 1951−1976

Initial Ownership Level of U.S. Parent	Means of Withdrawal				
	Sold	Liquidated	Expropriated	United Kingdom	Total
51−94%	200	106	17	8	331
50%	176	91	8	3	278
5−49%	246	65	21	3	335
TOTAL	622	262	46	14	944

Source: Compiled from Curhan, Davidson and Suri, *Tracing the Multinationals*, p. 183.

the firm's interest in the joint venture; the purchaser in these instances is almost always the other partner in the company.

The decision to withdraw from a joint venture often results from unresolved conflicts about management of the venture. In other cases, conflicts resulting from a change in relative bargaining power can lead to pressure from the local partner or host govenment to reduce participation levels. The "obsolescing bargain" phenomenon cited by Vernon describes how the position of a local partner is strengthened over time by a number of natural processes.[24] As the partner gains experience and expertise in the business, and marketing and financial risks decline, the relative importance of the global partner's role diminishes. This process is stimulated if the business achieves a steady state, and the global firm is making no significant ongoing contribution to the business. Under such conditions, the local partner can easily manage the company without a foreign partner. Pressure to reduce the participation by global firms in such situations can lead to expropriations. A more frequent and less dramatic response is the sale of equity to the local partner. Such forced withdrawals can be avoided by continually emphasizing product line extensions and technological improvements. These contributions are critical inputs in successful joint ventures. Emphasis on continuing transmission of these resources to foreign affiliates is essential in maintaining a global network of affiliates. These activities are also critical elements in successful ongoing licensing activities.

Licensing Agreements

Many of the issues that are important in joint venture formation and management affect licensing agreements also. Although licenses are used to formalize agreements pertaining to the transmission of products between parent firms and wholly owned subsidiaries as well as joint ventures, the term licensing refers here to agreements with independent foreign firms. Selection of the licensee and definition of the licensing agreement are critical functions in licensing management.

International licensing activity was pursued initially in agreements between large, dominant firms in different countries. The famous cross-licensing agreements between DuPont and Imperial Chemical Industries (ICI) typify arrangements of this sort.[25] These agreements granted each company exclusive rights to the other's technology within their own market areas, thus avoiding direct competition between the dominant firms on both sides of the Atlantic. Such activity continues today in a number of highly concentrated industries. Pilkington Brothers opted to license its radical float glass process to leading firms in foreign markets rather than exploiting the innovation through direct investment.[26] Licensing activity between leading firms has also been prevalent in the metal can industry, in the motor vehicle engines sector, and in the electrical power generation and industrial machinery areas. Licensing agreements between leading competitors pre-date World War II in each of these sectors. Activity in these sectors appears to be derived largely from oligopolistic concerns about market and industry stability.

Licensing activity has increased dramatically since World War II. U.S. receipts of royalty payments from independent licensees have increased from under $50 in 1950 to almost $1 billion in 1980.[27] Much of this growth comes from a new group of secondary, smaller companies with previous international experience. Many of these companies have used licensing as a means of increasing returns from their investments in research and development. Licensing generates positive returns with very low incremental cost and thus significantly increases returns on research programs.

Licensing is particularly attractive to smaller firms that lack the experience, inclination or resources to enter international markets directly. For such firms, licensing represents an ideal means of participating in international markets. Participation policies that emphasize licensing do entail a significant cost, however. The costs of licensing, as seen earlier in the Continental Can–Metal Box example, are not the incremental costs associated with entering and executing agreements but the opportunity costs involved in eliminating the option to invest in foreign markets. Many firms have used licensing agreements in the early stages of international expansion only to find that those agreements constrained further expansion. It is important to consider this issue in the initial selection of licensees and specification of contract terms.

Many global firms have acquired foreign licensees following the successful introduction of a product via a licensing agreement. This strategy permits the firm to evaluate prospects for its product while incurring little risk. Acquisition of a successful licensee then eliminates market development and distribution problems, manufacturing and legal start-up costs and personnel needs. This option is desirable, however, only if the licensee is not active in a wide range of unrelated businesses, is not too large relative to the global firm, and is not opposed to a takeover.

The terms of a licensing agreement also determine the feasibility of increasing participation at a later date. One of the most important variables in this regard is definition of marketing territories for foreign licensees. Many agreements grant the licensee exclusive rights for a product in a number of markets. It is common to include Far Eastern markets in agreements with Japanese firms, Commonwealth markets in agreements with British firms, Scandinavian markets for firms from any of the northern European countries and so on. Such agreements limit investment options. Definition of the product line scope of an agreement can impose a second type of constraint on investment options. Agreements that give the licensee exclusive rights to the full range of a company's product line can limit effective deveopment of foreign markets for the company's other products.

Several other clauses in licensing contracts also dictate the feasibility of increasing participation at a later date. Some licensing agreements specify that the licensee shall receive rights, specifications and know-how for all current and future technology in a given industry. Such clauses can lock the licensor into a long-term agreement that severely limits other participation options. Term, renewal and release clauses are very important in determining the feasibility of terminating a licensing agreement so that a higher level of participation can be achieved in a foreign market.

These issues are important, but licensing activity should not be viewed solely as the first stage in a gradual, low-risk market entry sequence. The principal purpose of licensing is to generate economic returns on proprietary resources. Licensing is warranted when the returns and risks of foreign investment do not satisfy corporate investment criteria, and when the returns, risks and resource requirements of licensing activity are clearly superior to those involved in otherwise acceptable foreign investment projects. Viewed from this perspective, the most important elements of a licensing contract pertain to the resources and services rendered to the licensee and payments received in compensation by the global firm.

Returns from licensing agreements are typically defined in several forms. Initial up-front payments are specified in most agreements. The royalty rate, generally expressed as a percentage of sales, is a second key variable. Many agreements also include a minimum annual royalty payment. Several other forms of compensation can be derived from licensing agreements. Management contracts can be included in licensing agreements to compensate for managerial and technical services. Clauses detailing reimbursement for expenses and costs associated with implementing the licensing agreement can also be included. In addition, puchases of components, raw materials and capital equipment from the licensor can be specified in the contract to provide an additional souce of revenues.[28]

Agreement about terms of compensation represents a difficult challenge in negotiating a licensing contract. Realization of payments specified within the contract poses a second challenge. One of the principal problems in licensing activity is measuring and monitoring the licensee's performance and the enforcement of payments. Circumvention of payment agreements is a potential problem once the licensee has acquired the know-how and expertise required to produce and market a product. An important issue in this regard is definition of the royalty base. Agreements that precisely specify the base as sales of individual product models can be circumvented by minor modifications in product design. Definition of the royalty base as the licensee's total sales in a given industry provides broader coverage but can be difficult to negotiate. The royalty rate in such cases will bear no relationship to the prevailing rate on other agreements. Licensees with established activities in an industry will often be reluctant to accept such a clause.

Key Elements in Licensing Agreements

Payments

Initial payment

Royalty rate

Definition of royalty base

Minimum annual payment

Components and equipment purchases

Management contracts

Reimbursement of expenses

Services

Personnel requirements

Installation and start-up role

Service and maintenance requirements

Training

Scope of Agreement

Term

Market territory

Products covered

Exclusivity

Relicensing rights

Rights to future technologies

Renewal and release clauses

Arbitration procedures

Specification of liabilities

Warranties

Enforcement of payment and purchasing clauses can prove to be a problem in managing licensing activity. Another problem associated with licensing activity is the enforcement of market scope agreements. Magee describes one of the principal risks of licensing as the possibility that a licensee's products will compete with the licensor's own product in markets outside the territory assigned to the licensee.[29] This problem becomes even more severe after the expiration of a license. Several of the Japanese color television producers that successfully penetrated the U.S. market are former licensees of RCA. Yamaha's entry into the U.S. musical instruments market followed the expiration of patents from leading U.S. companies. Westinghouse has lost a number of contracts for nuclear power plants to its former French licensee. These cases are indicative of the potential competitive consequences of licensing activity. In support of licensing activity, however, it can be argued that such competitors would emerge regardless of the licensing policies of the leaders in an industry. Technology can be acquired from other firms in an industry. Technology can also be imitated without authoritization through reverse engineering procedures. If diffusion of technology is inevitable, licensing can generate positive returns and provide some control over the activities of foreign producers.

Licensing is most appropriate for firms that cannot or do not desire to exploit a product directly in foreign markets. Licensing is also a suitable strategy for small, inexperienced firms or for secondary products outside a firm's principal business. Firms use licensing for such products because they cannot support long-term investments in industries outside their core areas of expertise and commitment. As noted earlier in this chapter, licensing rates for products outside of firm's principal industries are twice as high as for products in their core business. Within a core business, the use of licensing requires careful evaluation. In most cases, such an approach limits options for future expansion, stimulates the growth of competition, and requires monitoring and enforcement efforts by the licensor. These externalities represent significant costs that must be considered before entering licensing agreements.

Despite these factors, enforcement of the terms of a licensing contract can prove to be easier within a company's core business. Enforcement of contract terms is best accomplished by emphasizing continuing contributions to the licensee. The promise of future generations of technology, product line extensions and process improvements ensures adherence to the terms of contracts by foreign licensees. The global firm's ability to provide an ongoing stream of useful products, information and expertise will be greatest within its core business.

Ironically, firms that can best meet the expectations of continued contributions to licensees are least likely to enter licensing agreements. The most successful global firms are those that can generate and transmit a perpetual stream of proprietary resources to foreign affiliates. These firms can justify long-term investments in building a network of foreign subsidiaries, since the initial overhead costs will be spread across several generations of products. Such firms are most likely to emphasize wholly owned subsidiaries in participation decisions. The firms that are least capable of providing long-term contributions in any product line will be least likely to invest abroad. Licensing provides the best participation option for such companies and product lines.

The choice among licensing, joint venture and wholly owned subsidiaries is determined by both economic and strategic factors. Effective management of licensing activity requires sophisticated analysis of the relative costs and benefits of licensing and direct investment. Economic models can be developed to capture the opportunity costs and externalities associated with licensing activity.[30] However, strategic concerns are as important as economic analysis. A considerable portion of licensing activity can be attributed to oligopoly considerations and incremental market entry strategies. The level of a firm's strategic commitment to a product also has an impact on participation decisions. Strategic considerations, as opposed to narrowly defined financial implications, dominate participation decisions in many cases. The objective of participation policy is selection of the entry mode most consistent with the objectives, resources, plans and concerns of the parent firm. In some situations, the use of licensing will be inconsistent with the strategic posture of global firms; in others licensing will fit well with the firm's priorities. Definition of the firm's participation policy formalizes guidelines for licensing and other participation decisions.

A PORTFOLIO APPROACH TO PARTICIPATION DECISIONS

A portfolio framework offers one means of formalizing some participation guidelines. The choice among licensing, joint ventures and wholly owned subsidiaries can be structured within a portfolio perspective. Products can be classified into four basic categories that reflect each product's relationship to the firm's core business, the level of resources available to the product and the level of the firm's strategic commitment to each business. Products within a firm's core business are least likely to enter foreign markets through licensing agreements or joint ventures. Licensing and joint ventures can be expected more frequently for products that have no relationship to the firm's core business and that are not viewed as sectors with future promise. These general principles can be extended into a framework of participation preferences for a pair of global and host country firms. Firms in the host country will exhibit preferences highly similar to those of the global firm. Host country companies will seek to maximize their own participation in ventures within their core businesses and will accept lower levels of participation in other lines.

In approaching negotiations with any given firm in a host country, Figure 2-1 can be used to provide guidelines for participation agreements. Likely outcomes of negotiations between the two parties, expressed in terms of participation levels by the global firm, appear within each cell of the figure. Figure 2-1 presents areas of possible collaboration between a global and host country firm and the probable outcome of negotiations in any given case. Global firms are unlikely to accept local participation in foreign ventures within their core businesses unless the host firm is also highly committed to the industry. Even then, global firms will generally prefer a majority ownership position in the joint venture. The global firm's willingness to accept local participation increases for products outside its core business. The ability, if not the desire, of both global and host firms to maximize participation decreases as the internal strategic priority and the external competitive position of a product line declines.

These guidelines do not take into account differences in characteristics of the parent, product, industry, potential partner and host country. Each of these factors will influence each party's preferences and ability to achieve its objective. For example, as noted earlier, firms and businesses with strong marketing or technological emphasis exhibit increased preference for the use of wholly owned subsidiaries. Inexperienced firms, on the other hand, find lower levels of participation acceptable and even desirable. Other factors, such as host country investment policies, also influence participation parameters. Guidelines can be adjusted up or down depending on the net impact of these factors in any specific situation.

	HOST COUNTRY PARTNER			
	CORE	**RELATED**	**FUTURE**	**UNRELATED**
Unrelated or Declining Businesses	Exclusive Current and Future License	Standard License	Agent Contract	
Future Businesses	Minority Joint Venture	Co-Owned Joint Venture	Majority Joint Venture	
Related Businesses	Co-Owned Joint Venture	Majority Joint Venture		
Core Business	Majority Joint Venture			

Figure 2-1.   Participation preferences for global firms: guidelines for negotiations.

The chart in Figure 2-1 assumes that the identities of the two parties involved in the negotiating process are fixed. Such a framework is relevant in many cases, but a more realistic approach treats the identity of the partner as a variable and emphasizes the preferred mode of participation by each party. This chart can be useful in searching for and identifying potential partners. Host country preferences for licensing agreements or domestically controlled joint ventures can be achieved most readily by targeting firms whose principal activity is unrelated to the product in question.

Negotiating objectives and tactics also should be adjusted according to the positions of the two parties in Figure 2-1. Attempts by either party to maximize participation in unrelated businesses will be difficult to achieve if the venture is within the other firm's core business. Even if control were realized in such cases, the results could prove to be undesirable. Maximization of ownership and control should not represent the primary objective in participation policy for unrelated and secondary product lines.

The shaded section of the figure represents situations in which collaboration is unlikely. The occurrence of licensing and joint ventures declines for products inside the firm's core businesses. Wholly owned subsidiaries are more likely to be the preferred participation mode for such products. In such cases, strategic preferences for full ownership of a venture can be realized in two ways—through the formation of a new subsidiary or the acquisition and integration of an existing company

Acquisition Activity

Evaluation and execution of acquisitions is a key function in participation management. Acquisitions have played an increasingly important role in the expansion of global firms into foreign markets. Several motives for the increasing emphasis on acquisitions can be presented. One derives from the conglomerate strategy of business expansion cited in Chapter 1. Growth through acquisition became a vey popular strategy in the United States by the late 1960s. This strategy can also be pursued in international markets. Such an approach may account for a significant share of international acquisition activity, even though the leading conglomerates have themselves generally avoided foreign acquisitions. A second motive derives from a scarcity of trained management personnel within multinational firms.[31] Acquisition provides a means of overcoming the constraints imposed by personnel requirements. Such constraints can be severe during periods of rapid expansion. Oligopoly considerations can also influence acquisition activity. Waves of acquisitions are common within highly concentrated industries. For example, Ciba-Geigy purchased Funk International, an American agricultural seed company in 1974. Within one year, Sandoz, another leading Swiss drug company, purchased a U.S. seed company.[32] Other acquisitions of seed companies by drug firms followed quickly. A similar wave of foreign acquisitions also occurred in the construction equipment industry. U.S. firms acquired a number of European producers of construction equipment in the early 1970s. In addition to these follow-the-leader patterns of acquisition activity, Graham cites several cases in which exchange-of-threat concerns stimulated international acquisitions.[33] The 1974 Daimler-Benz acquisition of the Euclid division of White Motor Company has been interpreted in this light. The acquisition can be viewed as a response to Caterpillar's aggressive entry into engine manufacturing for the European truck industry.[34]

While acquisition activity has risen sharply, it is notable that companies with strong proprietary business resources rarely use acquisitions in entering foreign markets. Companies such as Caterpillar, IBM, Michelin and Sony rarely, if ever, acquire foreign companies in their principal line of business. These companies are examples of firms whose global strategy focuses on product differentiation through technical and marketing efforts. The proprietary technologies and strong brand names generated by this approach are exploited almost entirely through newly formed, wholly owned subsidiaries. Licensing and joint ventures appear to be highly unattractive participation

TABLE 2-14.   Acquisitions in the European Construction Equipment Industry 1969–1977

Acquiring Firm	European Acquisition	Country	Year
Babcock and Wilcox	Blaw-Nnox	United Kingdom	1969
Clark	Cosmos	United Kingdom	1970
J.I. Case	David Brown	United Kingdom	1972
International Harvester	Yumbo	France	1972
Ford	Richier	France	1972
J.I. Case	Poclain	France	1977
J.I. Case	Weller	Germany	1972
Massey-Ferguson	Hanomag	Germany	1974
J.I. Case	Calsa	Spain	1972

Source: Company reports.

options for such companies. Acquisitions also do not appear to be attractive to companies possessing strong proprietary business resources. Acquisitions seem to be motivated by objectives other than those associated with the internalization of international markets for technology, information and other business resources. Financial motives may be critical in stimulating international acquisitions.

Two types of financial motives contribute to acquisitions. The first derives from the strong currency effect cited by Aliber.[35] He argues that companies from countries with relatively low-cost capital will value foreign earnings streams higher than financial markets within the host country. Lower capital costs are reflected in lower discount rates, which result in higher net present value estimates for a business. This difference in valuation provides the incentive for acquisition activity. Although these financial factors could also motivate the formation of foreign affiliates, it can be argued that companies driven by such financial motives will be more likely to acquire than create foreign affiliates. Such companies will be less inclined to develop and operate foreign units because they realize no competitive advantage in such activities. If all the rents from their foreign activities accrue from cheap capital, they will not benefit from subsidiary formation activities. Rents can be realized simply by acquiring existing businesses.

It is important to note several issues in this regard, however. There is an underlying assumption in the argument that the cash flows of the company will not change following the acquisition. This will generally be true for financial assets, such as stocks, bonds and notes, and for some real assets such as real estate. For operating assets, cash flow results are less certain. Results depend to a large extent on the parent firm's role in managing the acquired company. A passive management style presumes the acquired company will continue to operate as before. Under such conditions, it can be argued that incentives for the affiliate to match its former performance are reduced.[36] Management may no longer have the same incentive to perform under the new arrangement as it did when the company was independent. Successful acquisition activity with a passive management approach requires careful construction of incentive schemes for acquired companies.

The alternative approach of replacing existing management with company personnel raises another issue. Can the company continue to perform with a new management team? To a large extent, this depends on the parent's ability to add value to the new affiliate. Effective contributions from the parent can increase the acquired company's performance. Successful acquisitions are those in which performance can be enhanced by contributions of product lines, technology, management, information and sourcing and distribution connections as well as capital.

Such involvement in an affiliate's operations reflects a separate aspect of the global firm's participation policy. Participation is generally defined as the level of equity ownership a global firm holds in a foreign affiliate. A second aspect of participation is also very important. The level of a global firm's direct involvement in the management of a foreign affiliate can vary sharply from its level of equity participation in the venture. Passive management participation frequently is associated with minority ownership positions, such as the Flick group's relationship with W.R. Grace, General Electric's investments in Allgemeine Elektrizitats Gesellshaft (AEG) and Toshiba or Ford's investment in Toyo Kogyo (Mazda). It is also not uncommon for firms to adopt a passive managerial approach in majority-owned affiliates and even in wholly owned subsidiaries. United Shoe Machinery's controller once stated that his company received no more information from its 70%-owned British Shoe Machinery affiliate than any public shareholder. The Hoover Vacuum Company permitted its wholly owned British subsidiary complete autonomy for many years. That policy appeared to be highly successful as the subsidiary grew to become larger than the rest of the company. The point is that passive management participation is not uncommon among global firms. Discussions with corporate managers and reviews of cases histories reveal that a surprisingly large percentage of foreign acquisitions are treated as passive investments.

One global strategy that justifies a passive managerial approach emphasizes the benefits of international portfolio diversification. These benefits have been cited by Lessard and Rugman.[37] Foreign acquisitions provide a stabilizing influence on reported earnings as a result of the variance in business cycles around the world. They also represent a hedge against fluctuations in the value of the home currency. These benefits stimulate the acquisition of foreign assets.

However, we must again note that these benefits could be gained by purchasing liquid foreign financial assets. Relative to such assets, the diversification benefits gained by acquisitions can be outweighed by the operating and political risks associated with direct investment. Why do firms acquire operating assets with their attendant risks when financial assets provide the same international diversification benefits, greater liquidity and the opportunity to diversify holdings within any given host country? Passive acquisitions appear to offer several benefits not available from investment in financial assets.

Information plays two roles in such acquisitions. First, the global firm has a distinct advantage in the market for operating companies because it is a well-informed buyer by virtue of its own industrial activities. It has no such advantage in markets for government securities or other financial assets. Second, the acquired company generates information about foreign markets and competitors that can aid existing operations. Other externalities also favor the acquisition of operating companies as opposed to investment in government or other securities. The acquired firm represents a potential market for the global company's products and services. Opportunities for royalty payments, component and equipment purchases and management contracts enhance acquisition activity. The greater the global firm's ability to engage in such transactions with the affiliate, the stronger the stimulus for acquisition. Acquired firms also represent a base for future operations if the global firm decides to increase its involvement at a later date. These benefits must be weighed against the operating and political risks and loss of liquidity associated with a direct investment diversification strategy.

The costs and risks of acquisition activity can be seen in the high rate of mortality for acquired affiliates. Table 2-15 reveals that the mortality rate for acquired companies is significantly higher than that for newly formed subsidiaries. Like joint ventures, acquisitions suffer a high rate of mortality. Of the 5,914 foreign companies acquired by 180 U.S. firms between 1951 and 1975, 22.5% had been liquidated or sold by the parent before 1975, and an additional 13% were merged into other affiliates. Mortality rates for newly formed affiliates are significantly lower.

Although acquisitions can provide financial, competitive and timing

TABLE 2-15.   Acquisition Activity by 180 U.S. Multinational Corporations

Method of Entry	Pre-1950 (net)	1951–1955	1956–1960	1961–1965	1966–1970	1971–1975	Total Entries 1900–1975	Total Exits* 1951–1975	Mortality Rate (Exits/Entries)
Newly formed	1,230	507	1,009	1,430	1,916	1,576	7,668	1,652	21.5%
Acquired	465	301	645	1,314	2,155	1,499	6,379	2,237	35.1%

Source: Compiled from Curhan, J.P., W.H. Davidson and Rajan Suri, *Tracing the Multinationals* (Cambridge: Ballinger, 1977), p. 21.
*Exits through sale, liquidation or merger.

benefits, several factors contribute to high mortality rates for acquired affiliates. Problems often arise in attempts to convert existing personnel, facilities and systems to conform to the global firm's standards. The retrofitting of an existing company can prove to be far more costly, time-consuming and problematic than development of de novo operations. The condition and quality of physical facilities is one consideration in this regard, but managerial issues are particularly important. Attempts to modify acquired companies often lead to resistance from management and personnel accustomed to established operating procedures. Implementation of information and control systems in acquired companies often proves to be a difficult process.[38] Similarly, the management attitudes and incentives in acquired companies are often less constructive than those that can be developed in newly formed companies. These considerations play an important role in determining the use of acquisitions in participation policy.

Determination of the role of acquisitions in participation policy is driven by the same general concern underlying all strategic choices in global management. What is the effect of a commitment to the use of acquisitions on the firm's relative strategic position? The effectiveness of acquisition activity depends to a large extent on the nature of the firm and industry in question. Many highly successful global firms have avoided foreign acquisitions. Others such as ITT, Unilever, and Siemens have successfully emphasized the use of acquisitions in foreign markets. Firms with narrow, focused product lines, strong proprietary technology and brand names and high levels of marketing expertise are less likely to use acquisitions in expanding abroad. Diversified firms possessing strong management and financial control systems are more prone to use acquisitions. Acquisitions are also more common outside of firms' principal industries. This pattern suggests a basic principle about the use of acquisitions. In general, the stronger the firm's position in a given industry, the less likely that it will rely on acquisitions in expanding abroad. For secondary firms, acquisitions appear to offer many of the same benefits as joint ventures. Firm's desiring foreign expertise in expanding abroad can purchase the needed resources directly through takeovers.

Other aspects of the firm's position in an industry also influence the use of acquisitions. Firms that are late in coming to global markets often use acquisitions in expanding abroad to reduce the amount of time required to establish a global presence. This strategy can be seen in the construction equipment and metal can industry examples cited earlier. Firms following Caterpillar into foreign markets relied heavily on acquisition to establish a foreign presence. In the can industry, Crown Cork and Seal relied almost exclusively on the formation of new subsidiaries in expanding abroad. Continental Can, once it decided to increase participation in foreign markets, acquired existing companies in Europe and South America. American Can Company, another follower, also chose to acquire foreign can producers rather than forming new subsidiaries in several countries.

Acquisition activity also varies across industries. High technology industries exhibit relatively low rates of takeovers. Acquisitions as a percentage of subsidiary formations are lowest in the chemical, drug, computer and electronics industry. Table 2-16 suggests that acquisition activity follows an industry life cycle. As industries mature and growth rates decline, mergers and acquisitions within the industry are stimulated by increasing emphasis on cost−volume relationships.[39] Acquisitions in mature industries provide the additional benefit of reducing direct competition and capacity relative to the option of developing new operations.[40]

Industries in the accelerating stages of internationalization also exhibit

TABLE 2-16.   Acquisitions Per New Subsidiary Formation for 180 U.S. Multinational Enterprises

	Foreign Acquisitions as a Percentage of New Subsidiary Formation, 1951−1976
Beverages	2.05
Food	2.09
Textiles	1.11
Paper	1.85
Chemicals	.70
Drugs	.73
Cosmetics	1.17
Glass and materials	1.14
Metals	1.44
Construction and farm machinery	1.38
Office machinery and computers	.97
Industrial machinery	1.78
Electrical	1.03
TV and appliances	1.07
Electronics	.75
Communication equipment	1.07
Motor vehicles	1.72

Source: Harvard Multinational Enterprise Project Data Base.

high levels of acquisition. The ratio of acquisitions over new subsidiary formations is closely correlated with the rate of increase in foreign activity in an industry, as seen in Table 2-17. For industries experiencing a 50% or greater increase in total foreign investment activity, the ratio of acquisitions to new subsidiary formations exceeded 2.0 in 19 out of 22 cases. For industries experiencing a greater than 50% decline in total foreign investment during a three-year period, the ratio of acquisitions to new subsidiary formations was less than 1.0 in 9 out of 12 cases. The observations in Table 2-17 support the argument that acquisitions are relied on most heavily during periods of increasing international activity in an industry. This relationship can be attributed to constraints on management personnel and the strategic urgency of establishing a global presence during periods of rising international activity.

Acquisition activity also appears to be correlated with foreign investment growth in the aggregate. It is important to note that total acquisition activity by this sample of U.S. firms receded in 1971–1975. Prior to that period, the use of acquisition had accelerated rapidly. Acquisitions accounted for only one quarter of U.S. foreign market entries prior to 1950, but over one half of all new entries between 1961 and 1970. The surge of acquisition in the 1960s can be attributed to the overvalued status of the dollar, the success of conglomerate expansion strategies and constraints on management resources

TABLE 2-17.   Relationship Between Rates of Expansion in Three Digit SIC Industries and the Relative Use of Acquisitions

Rate of Increase in Total Foreign Investment Activity for the Industry Over the Previous Three-Year Period (Number of Subsidiary Acquisitions Plus Formations)	Ratio of Subsidiary Acquisitions over Subsidiary Formation in the Industry (Number of Industry Observations)		
	0–.99	1.0–1.99	2.0 or more
-50% or less	9	2	1
-10–49%	15	12	8
-9–+9%	11	8	6
10–49%	2	8	7
50%+	1	2	19

Source: Harvard Multinational Enterprise Project Data Base.
*Rates of increase in total activity were measured for 36 SIC three-digit industries for the 1967–1969, 1970–1972 and 1973–1975 periods.

during a period of rapid foreign expansion. In contrast, the decline in the relative use of acquisitions in 1971–1975 can be related to the devaluation of the dollar, disenchantment with conglomerate acquisition strategies and fewer constraints on management because of lower levels of activity in those recession years.

Regardless of the level of activity, the geographic composition of acquisitions has remained highly constant over time. Canada, the United Kingdom and Australia accounted for 47.5% of all acquisitions completed in the 1951–1975 period by the sample of 180 firms. Acquisitions were used in over half of all market entries in these nations. Levels of acquisition in Latin America, Asia and Africa were considerably lower, accounting for less than one third of market entries. These data appear to reflect two important issues in acquisition activity. Greater reliance on acquisitions in the industrialized world stems from the presence of existing companies in industries of interest to the global firm. Established companies with the required facilities and personnel do not exist in many developing countries. Even where such companies do exist in developing countries, problems of transition and conversion can reduce the attractiveness of acquisition candidates. Existing companies in Canada, the United Kingdom and Australia are relatively receptive to U.S. management systems, marketing procedures and technology. Implementation of these systems in companies with a highly dissimilar orientation can prove to be a difficult and expensive proposition. In such cases, the option of forming a de novo company becomes relatively attractive, since acquisition would not eliminate requirements for infrastructure development in managerial, marketing and manufacturing areas. The geographic composition of acquisition activity can be attributed as much to

TABLE 2-18. Acquisitions as a Percentage of Total Subsidiary Entries for 180 Multinational Firms (1951–1976)

Nation	Percentage	Total Entries
Canada	69.5	1,566
United Kingdom	59.9	1,392
Australia	50.5	681
Continental Europe	45.0	4,686
South Africa	35.5	153
North Africa and Middle East	14.2	318
Other Africa	12.8	366
Asia	23.3	1,267

Source: Compiled from Curhan, Davidson and Suri, *Tracing the Multinationals*, p. 27.

this factor as to the existence of a pool of acquisition candidates in various host countries.

Country, industry and company characteristics play an important role in determining the use of acquisitions in entering foreign markets. They determine the attractiveness and effectiveness of acquisition activity. Acquisitions are particularly attractive in industrial countries, and in established industries experiencing an increase in international activity. Based on these and other characteristics of the firm's global activities, the role of acquisitions in participation policy can be defined. Management of the acquisition process itself poses an additional challenge. Identification and evaluation of acquisition candidates, negotiation and execution of acquisitions, and finally, integration of acquired companies into the parent's global system and strategy are crucial management functions. Each of these areas of management activity requires considerable expertise and specialization.

Factors Determining Acquisition Activity

Company

Diversity

Foreign experience

Position in industry

Time schedule for foreign expansion

Relationship of product to core business

Degree of decentralization

Industry

Rate of foreign expansion

Rate of growth

Technology content

Cost-volume importance

Prevailing use of acquisitions

Country

Legal restrictions

Securities markets

Availability of candidates

Negotiation and integration requirements

DIVESTMENT

The principal focus of this discussion of participation policy has been on modes of market entry. Divestment involves another aspect of participation policy and management. Decisions to reduce or withdraw a presence in a foreign market involve important and increasing challenges to management. There is a growing need for explicit policies regarding the divestment decision and process. Levels of divestment activity have risen rapidly in recent years. Much of this increase can be related to the wave of acquisition activity that began in the mid-1960s. Unsuccessful acquisitions represent a large fraction of all divestments by global companies. Joint ventures also account for a significant percentage of departures from the affiliate networks of global firms. Of the more than 3,000 subsidiary departures from the sample of 180 multinational systems between 1950 and 1976, over half were affiliates that had originally been acquired. One third of the departures involved joint ventures.[41]

These statistics suggest that the problems of integrating an affiliate into the parent system play a major role in divestment decisions. These problems often are reflected in poor financial and operating performance, but the fundamental causes of failure derive from an inability to integrate the operations and management of an acquired firm or joint venture into the global system. Franko relates how such problems in the areas of marketing and manufacturing, (for example) contributed to the mortality of joint ventures.[42] Failure to integrate an affiliate's operations into a global system represents one cause of divestment. Tornedon cites several others as common factors contributing to liquidation or sale of foreign affiliates.[43] The most frequent cause of divestment cited by management was "inadequate return on investment." Excessive management and capital requirements, host government pressure, and uncertainty were also cited as common factors in divestments. Such conditions are apt to develop in three distinct types of situations that are best explored by examining individual cases of divestment.

Raytheon in Italy

Markets for military equipment long provided the principal source of Raytheon's business. The company grew from annual sales of $3 million in 1939 to $148 million in 1945 solely on the strength of defense products.

Following World War II, the company attempted to diversify into the consumer radio and television market, but its inability to successfully market consumer goods led to the sale of its domestic consumer division in 1956. Six years later, Raytheon acquired a controlling interest in an Italian producer of television components. The objective of the acquisition was entry into the emerging color television industry in Europe.

The venture absorbed significant amounts of capital and management attention as the introduction of color broadcasting was delayed by European debates over transmission standards. The high degree of uncertainty surrounding the emerging industry, the extensive capital and managerial requirements necessary to remain within the industry, and the fundamental mismatch between the affiliates activities and those of the parent all contributed to the decision to liquidate the company in 1968.

American Standard in France

In contrast to Raytheon's new venture is the experience of American Standard in France. American Standard had established a manufacturing facility in France in 1901. The affiliate, named Ideal Standard France (ISF), produced cast-iron radiators and boiler heating units. It became the largest firm in the French heating industry at an early date and maintained that position into the early 1970s. ISF held close to 60% of the French cast-iron radiator market, and that product line had been highly profitable during the postwar construction boom in France. In 1974, sales volume declined sharply because of the OPEC-induced recession. In addition, price controls imposed by the French government restricted the company in passing on unit price increases.

The affiliate's deteriorating financial performance led the parent firm to reassess its commitment to the heating business. Much of ISF's plant and equipment predated World War II, and extensive capital investments would be required to modernize these facilities. Growth prospects for the market appeared to be limited because of fundamental changes in heating economics and technologies. In addition, French competitors appeared to be in a position to capture market share from ISF in the short run. These factors led the parent company management to decide to withdraw from the French market. The affiliate was liquidated under bankruptcy proceedings in 1974.

The Raytheon and American Standard cases typify two very common patterns of divestments. Raytheon's withdrawal from its Italian venture essentially represented an unsuccessful market entry in a volatile and undefined industry. Emerging industries characteristically suffer high rates of mortality as product standards and technologies change.[44] The risk of mortality in such industry settings is compounded when the affiliate operates in a foreign market as well. At the other end of the spectrum, American Standard's liquidation of its French affiliate typifies what Raymond Vernon has called "senescence" in international operations.[45] There is perhaps no better example of an industry in which a global strategy is inappropriate than the cast-iron radiator sector. This sector is strictly a mature industry with limited production scale economies, routine process technology, local design preferences and prohibitive transportation economics. Foreign affiliates operating in such sectors are serious candidates for divestment.

Induced Divestment

Affiliates operating in mature sectors of any economy are also prone to a third common divestment scenario. Host government pressure is a factor in many divestments. In countries with national policies emphasizing indigenous ownership of industry, affiliates of global firms in so-called mature sectors offer ideal targets for forced divestment. In extreme cases, government pressure can lead to expropriation of an affiliate. In many more cases, the global firm will respond to official pressures and withdraw in a less dramatic fashion.

The nature and effects of host government pressure on global firms to divest themselves of local affiliates are best documented in the extractive industries. Studies of the negotiations between Alcan and Guyana, Amax and Zambia, Exxon and Peru, Kennecott and Chile, and Rio Tinto Zinc and Papua-New Guinea are among the many well-documented cases of forced reductions in participation, divestment, or expropriation in the extractive industries.[46] Host government attempts to force divestment in manufacturing or service industries have also been documented. Expropriations or forced divestments such as the case of Coca-Cola in India or ITT in Chile have received extensive publicity. In addition to these extreme cases, host government pressures have also forced reductions in participation by many global firms. Time Inc. was forced to sell a majority share of its Canadian affiliate to Canadian shareholders in 1976.[47] More recently, the Canadian Foreign Investment Review Agency has played an active role in effecting the sale of U.S.-owned assets to national interests.[48] Mexicanization policies have forced many global firms to reduce their ownership in Mexican affiliates.[49] Peruvian law forces indigenization of foreign affiliates through required annual sale of shares to employees.[50] This process formalizes the belief that a foreign investor's contributions to the host country decline over time. Although older affiliates are more apt to exhibit the signs of maturity associated with obvious divestment targets, age alone is not the key determinant of senescence. Senescence or maturity simply reflects a failure to grow or progress. Affiliates of global firms that fail to upgrade, expand and improve their capabilities are prime targets for divestment. Pressures for divestment are most likely to appear when local nationals can perform the functions of an affiliate without assistance from a foreign parent. Pressures for divestment are unlikely to be severe if the global firm performs functions that cannot be duplicated readily by local entities. Maintenance of this performance edge is the best insurance against divestment pressures. Bradley cites several other approaches that can strengthen the position of foreign affiliates.[51] One approach involves the obvious compromise of finding a satisfactory local partner and accepting a lower participation level. Other approaches involve maximizing the dependence of the affiliate on the parent firm through research, sourcing and branding strategies.

Expropriations are relatively rare events, accounting for 5.5% of all divestments by the sample of 180 U.S. multinational firms between 1951 and 1976. A study by Chopra, Boddewyn and Tornedon involving 432 U.S. companies also found that expropriations accounted for between 4 and 5% of divestment in the 1967–1975 period.[52] Host government pressures do contribute to many other divestments recorded as the sale of an affiliate. However, government pressure does not appear to be a factor in the majority of divestments. Almost two thirds of all divestments by the sample of 180 firms occurred in Canada, Europe and Australia. Government pressures, if they exist in these countries, would generally discourage divestment, particularly through liquidation. Many U.S. firms have felt compelled to continue operations in European countries because of the adverse public and official response to divestment.[53] Divestments in these countries can be attributed to business pressures, rather than government pressures. An analysis of mortality rates in various areas and sectors can provide insight into the causes of divestment.

Mortality Rates

The relative importance of different causes of divestment can be examined by analyzing mortality rates for different types of affiliates. Wilson analyzed mortality rates for the sample of 180 firms used here.[54] Several trends emerge from these data that suggest the factors determining levels of divestment. The striking increase in the number of subsidiary departures over time appears to reflect an increasingly competitive and volatile environment. Mortality rates in Table 2-19 reveal that 3.6% of the foreign affiliates in existence at any time between 1951 and 1955 were sold or liquidated during that period. The rate of mortality increases to 9.6% for the 1971–1975 period. Affiliates engaged in extractive activities experienced the greatest increase in mortality, while sales, manufacturing and other affiliates exhibited roughly similar patterns of mortality.

As noted earlier, mortality rates are highest for acquired companies and minority joint ventures. It is interesting to note that majority-owned joint ventures are by far the most resilient of all types of foreign affiliates. Only 5.2% of all majority joint ventures formed by these 180 firms were sold or liquidated between 1951 and 1976. In contrast, 23.0% of all minority joint ventures and 17.4% of all wholly owned subsidiaries active between 1951 and 1976 were divested before the end of the period. The use of majority-owned joint ventures appears to help reduce government pressures in restrictive host countries and to overcome market pressures in the industrial nations.

Mortality rates rose in virtually all countries and industries over the 1951–1976 period, but several areas and sectors exhibited particularly high mortality rates. Countries with highly restrictive foreign investment policies exhibited sharp increases in mortality. The countries with the highest mortality rates in the 1971–1975 period were Chile (30.4%) and Peru (21.9%). Surprisingly, mortality rates were lowest for the 1971–1975 period

TABLE 2-19.   Mortality Rates for Affiliates of 180 U.S. Multinational Firms, 1951–1975

Activity of Affiliate	Percent of Active Affiliates Sold or Liquidated in Period					
	1951–1955	1956–1960	1961–1965	1966–1970	1971–1975	Total
Manufacturing	3.1%	2.9%	3.3%	8.4%	9.0%	17.5%
Sales	3.3	3.5	3.5	8.7	8.1	17.3
Extractive	1.8	5.7	6.2	7.2	15.8	25.7
Other	3.9	4.9	3.0	9.3	9.2	17.7
TOTAL	3.6%	4.1%	3.9%	9.5%	9.6%	19.7%

Source: Harvard Multinational Enterprise Project Data Base.

TABLE 2.20. Mortality Rates for Foreign Affiliates of 180 U.S. Multinational Enterprises, by Affiliate's Principal Industry

Industry	Percentage of Affiliates Active in Period-Sold or Liquidated During the Period					
	1951−55	1956−60	1961−65	1966−70	1971−75	Total
Beverages	40.6	3.2	2.1	3.4	15.3	26.5
Food	2.5	6.0	4.0	10.1	9.9	20.7
Textiles and apparel	0.0	0.0	2.0	14.1	33.1	41.5
Wood and furniture	0.0	6.3	3.1	10.3	8.1	17.1
Paper	1.9	2.9	3.3	8.2	9.3	18.4
Industrial chemicals	3.8	1.3	5.1	15.6	8.2	24.0
Plastics	2.4	0.0	4.9	18.5	6.7	23.0
Agricultural chemicals	9.1	5.9	4.7	11.3	21.7	32.5
Cosmetics	0.0	4.9	4.7	5.3	4.8	11.6
Drugs	0.9	1.0	1.2	5.7	1.9	7.8
Other chemicals	2.3	2.8	2.4	10.9	5.9	14.8
Fabricated plastics	0.0	5.0	7.3	13.8	15.6	25.8
Tires	1.9	4.8	4.1	6.3	6.0	17.7
Petroleum	6.4	2.9	2.0	7.5	8.4	17.9
Leather	0.0	0.0	7.1	19.0	12.5	27.6
Glass	5.6	7.4	2.6	3.3	7.9	14.6
Iron and steel	33.3	0.0	8.3	17.6	7.8	20.3
Nonferrous metals	0.0	3.3	3.0	5.6	11.4	17.7
Engines and turbines	0.0	0.0	4.0	8.1	9.8	17.8
Construction machinery	0.0	17.9	0.0	3.6	10.7	13.5
Farm machinery	0.0	0.0	0.0	0.0	7.3	7.3
Office machinery and computers	2.4	2.0	5.1	6.4	7.1	17.0
Industrial machinery	0.0	2.9	1.6	9.9	10.9	18.5
Electrical light and wiring	0.0	0.0	0.0	7.5	15.7	20.4
Electrical transmission	0.0	0.0	4.3	14.3	17.4	26.9
Radios, televisions, and appliances	0.0	0.0	5.2	1.1	10.7	21.7
Electronics	0.0	0.0	5.7	8.3	9.0	15.7
Other electrical	0.0	0.0	3.0	4.4	9.2	13.4
Communication	0.0	3.3	0.0	6.3	12.7	18.4
Motor vehicles	8.7	3.3	3.1	8.4	6.6	15.0
Scientific instruments	6.7	4.8	1.5	4.8	8.1	12.1
Miscellaneous	1.8	5.3	4.5	10.1	11.1	21.9

Source: Curhan, Davidson and Suri, *Tracing the Multinationals.*

TABLE 2-21. Mortality Rates for Foreign Affiliates of 180 U.S. Multinational Enterprises by Host Country

Country	Percentage of Affiliates Active in Period That Were Sold or Liquidated During the Period						
	1951–1955	1956–1960	1961–1965	1966–1970	1971–1975	Total
Canada	4.2%	3.3%	4.8%	9.0%	10.0%	21.4%
Mexico	1.5	1.9	3.4	10.4	6.9	17.3
Other Latin America	2.8	18.2	6.7	10.4	10.1	25.9
Chile	3.0	2.6	0.0	18.4	30.4	43.3
Columbia	8.0	0.8	3.3	11.5	7.5	21.6
Peru	0.0	7.5	1.0	18.6	21.9	38.2
Argentina	6.1	4.7	1.9	9.1	13.7	25.5
Brazil	0.0	1.9	2.9	10.9	10.0	18.9
Venezuela	0.0	1.6	6.2	12.3	12.5	25.1
Belgium	6.5	2.0	2.3	10.0	10.5	19.4
France	1.4	2.3	2.8	10.9	8.4	18.3
Italy	1.3	5.3	3.0	8.7	10.5	19.3
Netherlands	3.5	3.0	3.5	11.4	8.0	18.2
United Kingdom	7.8	3.2	6.0	10.2	9.7	21.2
Other Europe	2.4	4.0	3.1	10.0	9.6	18.9
North Africa/ Middle East	6.1	3.3	5.1	10.0	1.4	24.2
East & West Africa	4.2	1.4	2.7	3.6	7.7	11.8
India	7.1	0.0	2.3	10.2	7.2	18.3
Japan	5.0	1.3	1.4	4.5	7.1	11.0
Other Asia	2.2	2.0	4.4	7.6	6.1	13.0
Australia	1.5	1.7	3.1	6.9	11.0	18.1
South Africa	4.7	2.6	5.1	6.7	6.6	15.1

Source: Compiled from Curhan, Davidson and Suri, *Tracing the Multinationals.*

in Mexico (6.9%), Colombia (7.5%), the African area (4.6%), India (7.1%), and the Asian area (6.1%). Secondary markets generally exhibited lower mortality rates than the principal industrial countries. Market pressures can be cited for the relatively high rates of mortality in the highly competitive markets of Canada (10.0%), the United Kingdom (9.7%) and Australia (11.0%). There appears to be a relationship between the degree of saturation of a market by foreign affiliates and the rate of affiliate mortality. These trends suggest that market pressures are the principal cause of divestment. These patterns also suggest that the relationship between risk and return in foreign direct investment is different than what might be anticipated. Markets that appear to have low levels of political risk can actually have relatively high levels of overall business risk. The probability of failure in countries such as Canada and the United Kingdom is higher than in India, Africa or much of Latin America. This phenomenon may be due to competitive pressures that arise from the concentration of foreign investment activity in so-called low-risk countries.

Divestment Policy and Management

Policies with respect to divestment are an important part of a comprehensive participation policy. Formal criteria and mechanisms for identifying and analyzing divestment candidates represent one component of such policies. Criteria frequently used for such purposes include return on investment, cash flow, capital requirements, market growth, profit margins and market share. These variables, when analyzed within a portfolio planning framework, provide a means of identifying divestment candidates.[55] Portfolio planning systems generally emphasize product line comparisons, but they can readily be employed to analyze a set of geographic entities in the same industry as well.

The use of such an approach in identifying divestment candidates can be complemented by a consideration of other factors. Divestment decision rules based solely on financial and operating data neglect other important dimensions of the problem. Analysis of broader environmental considerations provides additional information of a strategic nature. Competitive factors and trends are one important input in this regard. Analysis of developments in the market and industry may suggest other solutions to short-term operating problems. The time frame of the evaluation process is also important. Short-term problems and long-term prospects often differ.

That is not only true for emerging markets. Many so-called declining industries contain highly profitable firms.[56] An effective divestment policy generates decisions only when short-term operating considerations and the longer-term strategic outlook both conclude that divestment is warranted.

Two other factors need to be incorporated in divestment policy. The first reflects the opportunity cost of staying in an operation. In some cases, divestment may be warranted even when short-term results and longer-term outlook are positive. It is important to identify instances where continued operation in an area effectively limits entry or expansion in another more promising area. Such situations arise when management, personnel, components or other resources are constrained. Amax's sale of a controlling interest in its aluminum division to Mitsui represents a case in which a successful and promising business was divested so that the parent firm could pursue other markets.[57] The second consideration in divestment policy involves externalities associated with the sale or liquidation of any unit. It is obviously important to consider overhead costs borne by the unit, purchases from other system units, and components and services provided by the divestment candidate to the rest of the system.

Formal decision rules, complemented by consideration of strategic factors, can aid greatly in developing an effective divestment policy. Formal analysis and evaluation is particularly valuable in this area of participation policy for several reasons. Many organizations and individuals exhibit a tendency to avoid, ignore or mask ongoing difficulties in the apparent hope that things will improve before attention is drawn to the problem. Many cases of such management paralysis have been recorded, and the implications of this approach are quite clear. Failure to address problem areas can yield disastrous results. The Rolls Royce bankruptcy stemmed entirely from management's refusal to recognize continuing problems in meeting technical requirements for its Lockheed aircraft engines.[58] In another aerospace disaster, management at B.F. Goodrich persistently refused to admit its internal difficulties with meeting performance specifications on a new air-brake system. Failure of the brake system resulted in several casualties.[59] Such disasters are not always directly tied to top management. Divisional managers often hide problems from their superiors in the hope that they can solve them unnoticed. This approach, when adopted by highly autonomous bank foreign exchange traders, has resulted in stunning losses and bankruptcy.[60] These same phenomena can easily occur in foreign affiliates. Foreign affiliates are much more difficult to control and supervise than domestic units. For these reasons, formal review of a foreign affiliate's operating results and strategic outlook is a critical function in global management. Formal mechanisms and guidelines for identifying and analyzing affiliate operations can greatly improve the quality of divestment decisions.

Divestment policy represents one of the most complex components of participation policy. Implementation of divestment decisions is also one of the most challenging management functions in international business. Tornedon found that it took an average of 25.5 months to implement divestment decisions fully.[61] Much of this time was spent determining how to divest, as opposed to actually implementing a divestment plan. The options and details involved in the sale or liquidation of an affiliate are extensive. The sale of an affiliate requires identification of potential buyers and extensive negotiations about the terms of the sale. These two requirements consume large amounts of time and management attention. Managerial involvement in this process can be reduced if agents such as investment bankers and lawyers can be used to represent the firm. Such services are not readily available in many host countries, however. Liquidation often involves greater managerial involvement than the sale of an affiliate. Labor laws pose a particular problem in many countries. Where layoffs are permitted, severance pay equal to a year's wages or more is required in most European nations.[62]

Management of the divestment process is an area that is widely overlooked by many companies. Once a decision is made to divest a unit, top management often does not want to involve itself further with the problem. The unit can cease to exist in the mind of top management. For this reason, it is unlikely that other managers within the company will seek to involve or associate themselves with the divestment process. Senior management attention to the process is required. It is important to recognize that proper management of this process can yield significant financial and public relations benefits. In some companies, specialists in managing the sale and liquidation of affiliates hold high-ranking management positions.[63]

One of the most widely recognized maxims of military strategy is the principle that the most difficult maneuver to execute is retreat. Withdrawal from foreign markets poses the same challenge to global product managers. Divestment is an increasingly important function in the management of a global business.

SUMMARY

Decisions with respect to ownership, licensing and divestment decisions determine one critical dimension of a firm's participation profile. These decisions focus primarily on the firm's level of equity commitment in any host country. A closely related set of decisions determines the nature and extent of the firm's operating involvement in the host country. The level of managerial, marketing and manufacturing involvement determines other dimensions of participation. The four major dimensions of participation are shown in the following list.

DIMENSION

LEVEL	Ownership	Managerial	Marketing	Manufacturing
High	Wholly owned	Complete responsibility by parent	Internal staff and sales force	Full production
	Majority	Strategic Operating Financial		Component production
	Co-owned	Specialized, limited responsibility by parent	Distributors	Assembly Import from parent
	Minority		Agents	
Low	Licensee	Passive parent role	Brokers	Indigeneous procurement

Managerial participation ranges from a fully passive role, with complete local autonomy, to full parent responsibility for strategic and operating decisions. Marketing participation extends from the use of independent brokers, agents and distributors to complete internal staff and sales force. Manufacturing participation ranges from the use of local external suppliers to full production within the market.

Any combination of approaches along these four dimensions can depict a participation profile for a global firm in a single host country. Cases can be cited that correspond to any combination of participation decisions along these four dimensions. In general, however, there tends to be a correlation between levels of involvement across these four spectra. Typically, participation increase sequentially in the ownership and managerial dimensions first, marketing next and, finally, manufacturing.

Determination of marketing and manufacturing profiles within a given market will be discussed extensively in Chapters 4 and 5. Before addressing these issues, a more basic issue requires attention. One of the most fundamental strategic choices facing a firm in developing a global business is market selection.

NOTES

1. The data resources of the Harvard Multinational Enterprise Project are used extensively in this chapter to reflect actual participation patterns for a large sample of multinational firms. Two distinct data bases are referred to in this chapter. A sample of 180 U.S.-based firms described in Curhan, J.P., W.H. Davidson, and Rajan Suri, *Tracing the Multinationals* (Cambridge: Ballinger, 1977) is used to document participation patterns with respect to joint ventures and wholly owned subsidiaries. This data base provides broad coverage on these issues as the sample is estimated to account for roughly 70% of all U.S. foreign investment. A smaller subset of this sample involving 57 firms provides greater depth of coverage. This sample is described in Davidson, W.H., *Experience Effects in International Investment and Technology Transfer* (Ann Arbor: UMI Research Press, 1980). This subset provides product-specific participation data, including licensing activity.

2. Stopford, J.M. and L.T. Wells, Jr. *Managing the Multinational Enterprise* (New York: Basic Books, 1972). p. 107.

3. See, for example, IBM World Trade Corporation ICCH 4-374-303 Harvard College, 1974; "IBM to Leave India to Avoid Loss of Control," *New York Times*, November 16, 1977, p. D1.

4. Dunning, J.H. and D.C. Rowan, "Inter-firm Efficiency Comparisons: U.S. and U.K. Manufacturing Enterprises in Britain," in J.H. Dunning (ed.), *Studies in International Investment* (Canada: Allen and Unwin, 1970).

5. Arrow, K.J., "Economic Welfare and the Allocation of Resources for Invention," in National Bureau of Economic Research, *The Rate and Direction of Inventive Activity* (Princeton: Princeton University Press, 1962).

6. Buckley, P.J. and M.C. Casson, *The Future of the Multinational Enterprise*, (New York: Holmes and Meier, 1976).

7. Davidson, W.H. and D.G. McFetridge, "International Technology Transactions and the Theory of the Firm," unpublished manuscript.

8. Stopford, J.M. and L.T. Wells, Jr., op. cit., pp. 125−132.

9. Davidson, W.H., *Experience Effects in International Investment and Technology Transfer* (Ann Arbor: UMI Research Press, 1980), p. 52.

10. Teece, D.J., "Technology Transfer by Multinational Firms," *Economic Journal*, 1977.

11. Davidson, W.H., op. cit., pp. 40–42.

12. See, for example, Furnish, D.B., "The Andean Common Market's Common Regime for Foreign Investments," in Sauvant, K.P. and F.G. Lavipour, *Controlling Multinational Enterprises* (Boulder: Westview Press, 1977); Balasubramanyam, V.N., *International Transfer of Technology to India* (New York: Praeger, 1973); Helleiner, G.K., "International Technology Issues: Southern Needs and Northern Responses," in Bhagwati, J.N. (ed.), *The New International Economic Order: The North–South Debate* (Cambridge: MIT Press, 1977). Such restrictions are widespread and predominant in nonindustrial nations.

13. The IMF's *Annual Report on Exchange Restriction* lists royalty regulations in principal host countries.

14. See Yoshino, M.Y., "Japan as Host to the International Corporation," in Frank, Isaiah (ed.), *The Japanese Economy in International Perspective*, (Baltimore: Johns Hopkins, 1975); *Business Asia*, April 27, 1973, pp. 129–130.

15. For an interesting example of the foreign investment approval process, see Barlow Corporation in India ICCH No. 9-370-092, Harvard Business School, 1972.

16. See Sklar, R.L., *Corporate Power in an African State, The Political Impact of Multinational Mining Companies in Zambia* (Berkeley: University of California Press, 1975); Faber, M.L.O. and J.G. Potter, *Towards Economic Independence: Papers on the Nationalization of the Copper Industry in Zambia* (Cambridge: Cambridge University Press, 1971); Moran, T.H., "Transnational Strategies of Protection and Defense by Multinational Corporations," *International Organization* 27 (Spring, 1973), pp. 273–87; Mikesell, R.F., "Conflict and Accommodation in Chilean Copper," in *Foreign Investment in the Petroleum and Mineral Industry* (Baltimore: Johns Hopkins, 1971), pp. 369–386; Gott, Richard, *Mobutu's Congo*, Fabian Research Series No. 266 (London, 1968).

17. Morris, Michael, F.G. Lavipour, and K.P. Sauvant, "The Politics of Nationalization," in Lavipour and Savvant (ed.), *Controlling Multinational Enterprises*, op. cit., pp. 111–143.

18. General principles and techniques of negotiation are outlined in Walton, R.E. and R.G. McKersie, *A Behavioral Theory of Labor Negotiations* (New York: McGraw-Hill, 1965); Schelling, Thomas "An Essay in Bargaining," *American Economic Review*, Vol. 46, June, 1956. For specific studies of host country negotiations, see Smith, D.N., and L.T. Jr., Wells, *Negotiating Third World Mineral Agreements* (Cambridge: Ballinger, 1975); Kapoor, Ashok, *Planning for International Business Negotiation* (Cambridge: Ballinger, 1975).

19. A study of concentration trends in a number of specific sectors is presented in Vernon, Raymond, *Storm Over the Multinationals* (Cambridge: Harvard University Press, 1977), p. 81.

20. Franko, L.G., *Joint Venture Survival in Multinational Corporations* (New York: Praeger, 1973).

21. See, for example, the experience of Firestone in India, cited in *The Economic Times*, Bombay, April 1, 16, 18, 19, 1969.

22. For U.S. companies associated with Ataka, see "Gleason Works," *Wall Street Journal*, May 17, 1972, p. 30; "Ataka-Grumman," *Japan Economic Journal* January 14, 1975, p. 8 and "Ataka Terminates Role as Japan Agent for Grumman," *Wall Street Journal*, August 11, 1976; "Georgia Pacific," *Wall Street Journal*, March 13, 1974, p. 6.

23. Curhan, J.C., W.H. Davidson, and Rajan Suri, *Tracing the Multinationals* (Cambridge: Ballinger, 1977) pp. 380–81.

24. Vernon, Raymond, *Storm over the Multinationals* (Cambridge: Harvard University Press, 1977), pp. 151–73.

25. Hexner, E., *International Cartels* (Chapel Hill: University of North Carolina Press, 1946).

26. This policy is described in Pilkington Brothers, Ltd. Centre d'Etudes Industrielles, 1977, pp. 11–13.

27. National Science Founcation, *Science Indicators*, 1981.

28. For an informative view of actual patterns of compensation, see Root, F.R. and F.J. Contractor, "Negotiating Compensation in International Licensing Agreements," *Sloan Management Review*, Winter 1981, pp. 23–32.

29. Magee, S.P., "Information and the Multinational Corporation: An Appropriability Theory of Foreign Direct Investment," in J.N. Bhagwati (ed.), *The New International Economic Order: The North–South Debate* (Cambridge: MIT Press, 1977).

30. See, for example, Contractor, F.J., "The Profitability of Technology Licensing by U.S. Multinationals," *Journal of International Business Studies* Fall 1980, pp. 40–63; Mirus, Ralf, "A Note on the Choice Between Licensing and Direct Investment," *Journal of International Business Studies*, Summer 1980, pp. 86–91.

31. Dubin, M., *Foreign Acquisitions and the Spread of the Multinational Firm* (New York: Arno Press, 1980).

32. *Wall Street Journal*, October 27, 1976, p. 47; *Wall Street Journal*, August 5, 1974, p. 22.

33. Graham, E.M., Oligopolistic Imitation and European Direct Investment in the United States, unpublished doctoral dissertation, Harvard Business School, 1974.

34. Owen, Geoffrey, "The World (Construction Equipment) Scene," *Financial Times*, October 31, 1977, p. 26.

35. Aliber, R.Z., "A Theory of Direct Foreign Investment," in Kindleberger, C.P. (ed.), *The International Corporation* (Cambridge: MIT Press, 1970).

36. Alchian, A.A. and Harold Demsetz, "Production, Information Costs and Economic Organization," *American Economic Review*, December 1972, pp. 777–95.

37. Lessard, D.E., "International Portfolio Diversification," *Journal of Finance*, June 1973, Rugman, A.M., "Risk Reduction by International Diversification," *Journal of International Business Studies*, Fall 1976.

38. Several examples of the problems encountered in this process can be seen in: Galvor Company, ICCH No. 9-313-035 IMEDE, 1967, Corning (A-C); ICCH Nos. 9-379-051-3 Harvard College, 1979; Sigma Corporation in Italy, ICCH Nos. 4-377-085-6, Harvard College, 1977.

39. Authors such as Baumol, Scherer and Penrose have hypothesized that growth and concentration trend will be negatively correlated. The finding that growth and concentration trends are inversely correlated has been cited by: Nelson, R.L., "Market Growth, Company Diversification and Product Concentration, 1947–58," *Journal of American Statistics Association*, December 1960, pp. 640–49; Shepherd, W.G., "Trends of Concentration in American Manufacturing Industries, 1947–58," *Review of Economics and Statistics*, May 1964, pp. 200–12; Ghosh, Arabinda, "Concentration and Growth of India Industries, 1948–68" *Journal of Industrial Economics*, March 1975, pp. 203–22. A related point supports the contention that growth rate and acquisition activity are negatively correlated.

40. Monroe and Simkowitz found acquired companies tend to have lower than average price–earnings ratios. Monroe, R.J. and M.A. Simkowitz, "Investment Characteristics of Conglomerate Targets," *Southern Journal of Business*, November 1971. A similar finding was reported by Firth, Michael, *Share Pricing and Mergers* (Lexington, Mass.: Lexington Books, 1976), pp. 59–64.

The role of mergers and acquisitions in increasing concentration has been cited by Muller, Jurgen, "The Impact of Mergers on Concentration," *Journal of Industrial Economics*,

December 1976, pp. 113–132. Muller concludes that "mergers are the most important factor in increasing concentration."

41. Curhan, Davidson and Suri, op. cit., pp. 167–68.
42. Franko, L.G., op. cit., pp. 53–68.
43. Tornedon, R.L. *Foreign Disinvestment by U.S. Multinational Corporations* (New York: Praeger, 1975), p. 129.
44. The shakeout process has been observed in a number of emerging industries, most recently in the cases of the electronic calculator and digital watch industries. See "The Great Digital Watch Shake-Out," *Business Week*, May 2, 1977, p. 78; "Rockwell International to Leave Consumer Calculator Market," *Electronic News*, June 14, 1977, p. 20; "Carving up the Calculators," *Management Today*, March 1977, pp. 86–88.
45. Vernon, Raymond, "The Location of Economic Activity," in Dunning, J.H. (ed.), *Economic Analysis and the Multinational Enterprise* (New York: Praeger, 1974) pp. 89–114; *Storm over the Multinationals*, op. cit., Chapter 5.
46. For discussions of these cases, see Morris, M. Lavipour, F.G. and Sauvant, K.P., op. cit., Sklar, R.L., op. cit., Pinelo, Adalberto, *The Multinational Corporation as a Force in Latin American Politics: A Case Study of the International Petroleum Company in Peru* (New York: Praeger, 1973); Moran, T.H., op. cit., Bougainville Cooper B–E ICCH Nos. 9-174-104, 175-071-2, 175-204, Harvard College.
47. See "Time Canada Turns More Canadian," *Business Week*, October 20, 1975, p. 52, *Wall Street Journal*, February 26, 1976, p. 13, and February 27, 1976, p. 16.
48. "Forcing Fire Sales of U.S.-Owned Assets," *Business Week*, June 8, 1981, pp. 70–71; "Report from Canada," *Barrons*, April 6, 1981, p. 10.
49. Wionczek, M.G., "Mexican Nationalism, Foreign Private Investment and Problems of Technology Transfer," in Ady, Peter (ed.), *Private Foreign Investment and the Developing World* (New York: Praeger, 1971), pp. 191–206.
50. Foreign investment in Peru is governed by a common Andean Pact Policy, which ruled that "foreign companies operating in Peru had to agree to the gradual acquisitions of shares by national investors to transform their companies into national or mixed (maximum 49% foreign ownership) companies over a maximum period of fifteen years." *Exchange Restriction*, (Washington: IMF, 1976), p. 367.
51. Bradley, D.G., "Managing Against Expropriation," *Harvard Business Review*, July–August 1977, pp. 65–84.
52. Chopra, Jasbir, J.J. Boddewyn, and R.L. Tornedon, "U.S. Foreign Divestment: A 1972–75 Updating," *Columbia Journal of World Business*, Spring 1978, pp. 14–18.
53. "American Standard Says Court Appoints Administrator for Unit," *Wall Street Journal*, July 29, 1975, p. 26; Boddewyn, J.J., et al., *Investment and Divestment Policies of Multinational Corporations in Europe* (New York: Praeger, 1980).
54. Wilson, B.D., *Disinvestment of Foreign Subsidiaries* (Ann Arbor: UMI Research Press, 1980).
55. Classification of business units into broad portfolio planning categories identifies divestment candidates formally. This process is explicit in all portfolio planning systems. See, for example, Channon, D.F., *Multinational Strategic Planning* (New York: AMACOM, 1978).
56. Harrigan, K.R., *Strategies for Declining Businesses* (Lexington. D.C. Health, 1980); Dhalla, N.K. and Sonia Yspels, "Forget the Product Life Cycle Concept!" *Harvard Business Review*, January–February, 1976.
57. Amax-Mitsui (B and C), ICCH Nos. 9-375-388 and -389, Harvard College, 1975.
58. The causes of Rolls Royce's problems are discussed in "Rolls Probe Pinpoints RB.211

Contract," *Aviation Week and Space Technology,* August 20, 1973, pp. 60−61; see also *Wall Street Journal,* August 3, 1973, p. 8.

59. The Aircraft Brake Scandal, ICCH No. 1-673-007, Harvard College, 1973.

60. See, for example, "The Collapse of the Franklin National Bank," *Journal of Bank Research,* Summer 1976, pp. 113−22; "What Really Went Wrong at Franklin National," Fortune, October 1974, pp. 118−21; Banque de Bruxelles," *Wall Street Journal,* March 26, 1975; "What Went Wrong at Herstatt," *Business Week,* August 3, 1974, pp. 13−14.

61. Tornedon, R.L., op. cit., p. 126.

62. The impact of foreign labor laws on disinvestment decisions is discussed in Jain, H.C., "Disinvestment and the Multinational Employer," *Personnel Journal,* March 1980, pp. 201−205.

63. For examples, see "Stauffer Chemical Company's Aggressive (Divestment) Strategy Boosts Fund to $225 Million" *Pension World,* May 1981, pp. 15−18; "Selling Off a Doggy Division" *Institutional Investor,* June 1980, pp. 23−26.

THREE

THREE

Market Selection

No element of global strategy can be viewed entirely in isolation. The determination of market priorities is particularly dependent on participation policies, for example. Participation policies determine the relative attractiveness of a joint venture in Mexico, a licensing agreement in Japan or a wholly-owned subsidiary in the United Kingdom. In allocating scarce corporate resources to foreign opportunities, participation preferences underlie any comparison of markets. In addition to this and other policy considerations, four broad factors will be present in all market selection decisions. These factors are competition, market characteristics, service costs and uncertainty. Each of these factors can be evaluated within a framework that seeks to prioritize foreign market opportunities. This approach to market selection does not emphasize financial analysis of individual projects within a capital budgeting process. Such an approach is discussed in Chapter 6. The framework presented here provides an alternative approach to market selection. When a manager is attempting to prioritize markets for a single product line or SBU, project attractiveness differs primarily as a function of country conditions and characteristics. The manager can prioritize markets, at least in the first stage of analysis, by assessing the four factors identified above.

COMPETITION

Competition affects market selection in a number of ways. Competitive factors within the firm's home market can be just as important as competitive factors within potential foreign markets. One pattern of foreign expansion observed by Knickerbocker corresponds to a "follow-the-leader" phenomenon.[1] This phenomenon occurs primarily in highly concentrated industries. Preservation of the competitive status quo is a principal motive behind such investment patterns. The entry of a leading firm into foreign markets is perceived as a threat to competitive stability in the industry. Only by also entering foreign markets can other firms ensure that relative positions in the industry will not shift radically as a result of foreign operations.

The firm initiating the international activity frequently perceives foreign operations as a principal means of improving its competitive position in a tightly knit industry. International operations can result in higher sales, earnings and cash flows that provide the firm with a means to improve its competitive position in its industry. An excellent example of such a strategy occurred in the banking industry. Citicorp's aggressive commitment to foreign markets was primarily responsible for its superior earnings growth among major U.S. banks during the last 25 years. Foreign earnings accounted for 65% of Citicorp net income in 1980, highest among all major U.S. banks. Foreign earnings permitted Citicorp to improve its competitive position vis-á-vis its principal New York-based competitors. Although the other five major New York banks maintained highly stable positions relative to each other, Citicorp clearly improved its competitive position in the industry. One result of Citicorp's success, however, was a large increase in international activity by other U.S. banks, particularly by the large New York banks that view themselves as direct competitors of Citicorp.

In its pure form, follow-the-leader behavior causes firms to invest in exactly the same countries as the initiating company. Knickerbocker found that there was a very high propensity for firms in closely knit strategic groups

TABLE 3-1.   Earnings of Major New York Banks 1955 and 1980 ($ million after tax)

Bank	1955	1980	% Foreign
Chase Manhattan	42.8	311.2	47
Citicorp	42.5	544.2	65
Morgan	30.8	288.3	52
Manufacturer's Hanover	27.6	211.3	49
Chemical	23.0	142.3	35
Banker's Trust	19.0	114.5	52

Source: Corporate report.

to invest in the same countries. This phenomenon can be observed in a number of industries. Foreign investment patterns in the tire industry provide a striking example of the power of this factor in market selection decisions.

Goodyear was the driving force behind international expansion in the U.S. tire industry, initiating activity in a number of foreign markets. Other tire companies exhibited a striking tendency to enter specific foreign markets immediately after entry by Goodyear. In cases where another company entered a market before Goodyear, as in the case of Portugal, West Germany or Chile, Goodyear responded by entering those markets as well. One result of this pattern of activity has been great competitive stability among the Akron-based tire companies. The observations in Table 3-2 do not cover all foreign investment activity in the industry, but they provide a clear picture of the impact of one type of competitive consideration on market selection decisions.

The prevalence of follow-the-leader behavior varies sharply by industry. In some cases, however, failure to follow a leading firm into foreign markets has profoundly affected the competitive status of an industry. In 1950, Caterpillar Tractor Company accounted for approximately 16% of the world

TABLE 3-2. International Expansion in the U.S. Tire Industry

| Country | Year of Entry | | |
	Goodyear	Firestone	Goodrich
Canada	1917	1919	1918
United Kingdom	1927	1928	1934
Argentina	1930	1930	—
Brazil	1938	1939	1953
Sweden	1938	1945	1939
Philippines	1956	1957	1975
Japan	1956	1962	1963
France	1959	1960	1967
Portugal	1960	1958	—
West Germany	1961	1960	1964
Italy	1963	1966	1972
Taiwan	1971	—	1974
Chile	1978	1975	—

Source: Company reports.

construction machinery market. Since its formation in 1925, the company had been an active exporter, but prior to 1950 it had not made any investments abroad. Its first foreign subsidiary was formed in Great Britain in that year, and 13 others were added by 1964. Foreign sales accounted for 45% of total revenues in 1964. By 1979, Caterpillar's share of the world construction equipment market exceeded 50%, and foreign sales accounted for the majority of Caterpillar revenues. Foreign sales, achieved largely through exports, provided economies of scale and cost reduction benefits, which enhanced Caterpillar's ability to compete in the domestic market. Caterpillar's dominance of the industry was ensured by the slow response of its competitors in expanding abroad. Acquisition of independent foreign firms by U.S. companies began in the 1960s, but no other U.S. firm has developed international operations that account for more than one-third of total revenues.

TABLE 3-3.   Construction Equipment Sales ($ million)

	1955	1979	% Abroad
Caterpillar	479.7	7,613.2	54
Clark	145.4	636.6	31
Komatsu (Japan)	40(e)	1,975.4	52
Fiat Allis (Italy−United States)	119.0	900(e)	n.a.
Int'l. Harvester	51.3	1,007.1	28
John Deere	8.1	976.6	27
J.I. Case	110.0	936.0	31

Source: Company publications.

Success in developing foreign markets was a key factor leading to Caterpillar's dominance of the world construction equipment industry. Only in the last few years has another significant global competitor emerged in this industry, and it is not an American rival. Komatsu, whose sales in 1965 were less than 10% of Caterpillar's revenues, has expanded abroad rapidly since that date. Foreign sales accounted for over half of Komatsu sales in 1979, and the company is now the second largest firm in the industry, with sales exceeding $2 billion.

A similar pattern occurred earlier in the razor and blade industry. Gillette, the inventor of the safety razor, faced significant new competition when its principal patent expired in 1921. Foreign operations represented one of the principal factors contributing to Gillette's ultimate domination of this market. Gillette's foreign revenues more than tripled between 1920 and 1923 to account for 30% of total sales. Foreign operations contributed more than half of total earnings by 1953. These cash flows were an important factor in achieving dominance of the world industry. Gillette's principal competitors failed to develop foreign operations and consequently did not attain the size, stability and flexibility that supported Gillette's position of leadership in the industry.

These individual cases suggest the importance of maintaining a market profile similar to that of the leading firm in an industry. Failure to follow a competitor's initiative into international markets can result in a dramatic change in competitive position. Such considerations are an important factor in market selection, influencing the identity and number of markets chosen for foreign operations.

A related phenomenon also tends to occur in highly concentrated industries. Graham documents a series of investment sequences that correspond to an "exchange of threat" pattern.[2] This pattern reflects the importance of foreign global competitors in market selection decisions. Foreign multinational companies often represent primary competitors for U.S. firms pursuing a global strategy. The construction equipment industry provides one example of such a situation. In such cases, the entry of a foreign competitor into a market can result in a response somewhat different from that commonly reserved for domestic competitors. A frequent response to such initiatives is entry or increased activity in the foreign competitor's home market. By establishing a presence in the competitor's home market, a means of maintaining competitive stability is established. In the event that the foreign competitor seeks to expand its activities in other markets, an immediate retaliation can be enacted in its home market. Presence in the competitor's home market serves to ensure competitive stability. Without such a presence, the foreign competitor could use resources from a stable domestic market to support an offensive strategy in other markets.

Such competitive issues play a major role in market selection decisions in highly concentrated industries. In such industries, competitors are well-known and highly visible. Any initiatives pose a threat to competitive stability and are likely to be met by direct responses from rival firms. Competitive constraints play a major role in market selection decisions under such conditions. Follow-the-leader and exchange-of-threat market selection patterns are typical responses in such industries.

These issues may not be relevant in all industries, but the status of competition within the foreign market should be reviewed in all market selection decisions. The extent and nature of local competitors will have an important bearing on choice of markets. The extent of local competition can be measured in several ways. Assuming a market for the product in question already exists, it is important to know the number and size of competitors serving the market. A fragmented market presents obvious opportunities. One broadly used measure of market concentration provides a useful indicator of the extent of fragmentation in a market. The Herfindahl index measures the squared sum of market share percentages for all major market participants.

$$H_{ci} = \sum_{j=1}^{n} S_j^{2}$$

$$s = \text{Market Share of Company J}$$

This index rises as the market shares of the leading firms in a market increase. Measures of market concentration for a range of products and countries appear in Table 3-4.

Low levels of market concentration suggest that local competition will be

TABLE 3-4.   Market Concentration Ratios, 1979

Market	Autos	Soft Drinks	TV	Tires	Computers	Cosmetics	Razor Blades
				Herfindahl Index			
United States	.27	.19	.12	.20	.50	.06	.41
United Kingdom	.13	.39	.15	.17	.22	.07	.39
Japan	.23	.42	.23	.22	.16	.11	
West Germany	.16	.16	.10	.22	.41	.08	
Italy	.31	.06	.12	.32	.40	.06	
Brazil	.35	.22	.10		.21	.24	.73
France	.25	.03	.21	.52	.36	.04	
Netherlands		.07	.90	.15	.26	.07	
Mexico	.24	.27		.19			

Source: Primary sources.

fragmented and less likely to respond directly to a new entry. Initiatives in highly concentrated markets are far more likely to be met with a specific response. A market concentration index above 0.40 indicates the presence of a dominant firm. Such firms frequently attempt to impose discipline on new entrants through product innovation, promotion campaigns, "bundling" of various products into a unified package, and other tactics.[3] The presence of a dominant firm in any market suggests that attempts to penetrate the market will be met by a specific response of this nature. Activities in such markets can be extremely costly. If everything else is equal, a low level of market concentration significantly increases the attractiveness of any market.

In many cases, markets for the product in question may not yet be developed. This poses both problems and opportunities. The absence of immediate competition counterbalances problems associated with primary market development. Competition is not the principal concern in developing a new market, but potential competition should be assessed before pursuing such a strategy. Firms active in related businesses represent potential competitors. European vacuum tube manufacturers, for example, represented significant potential competitors to U.S. electronics firms attempting to develop European markets for electronic components and semiconductors. Similarly, European black-and-white television producers clearly posed as potential competitors in the color television industry. In assessing potential competition in new markets, the most important issues to be addressed focus on firms active in related industries and in upstream and downstream sectors. How large are these firms? What is the probability of their entry into the new market? The presence of large competitors in closely related sectors will discount the priority given to a market.

Such considerations appear to have been important in delaying Michelin's entry into the U.S. radial tire market. Although Michelin's radial tire had been introduced throughout Europe in the 1950s, Michelin did not enter the U.S. market until 1972. The major U.S. tire companies introduced radials in their European affiliates in the 1960s, but they had not introduced them in the United States prior to 1972. Following Michelin's entry into the U.S. market, however, they immediately responded by introducing their own radial tires. Michelin, though supported by its dominant position in the mature and stable European market, has made slow progress in attaining market share in the United States. Its entry into the U.S. market has done much to disrupt the once highly stable tire oligopoly, however. Goodrich was withdrawn from the highly competitive original equipment tire market;

there is speculation that Uniroyal may withdraw partially from the tire industry; and several secondary producers have disappeared in recent years.[4]

The size and extent of current and potential competition in any market are important factors in market selection decisions. The nature of the competition is also very important. In evaluating competition in any market, three distinct types of competitors can be identified: affiliates of other global firms, local private companies and state-owned enterprises. The prevalent type of competitors will influence not only market selection but other elements of global strategy as well.

Strategies for Global Competitors

Market selection decisions will determine a critical dimension of a firm's posture with respect to other global competitors. Does the firm want to be active in the same markets as other global competitors? Similar market profiles will result in direct confrontation, and superior performance will then derive from the firm's ability to outcompete its competitors on a head-to-head basis. Industries often exhibit a clustering of foreign investment in time and space. Many firms apparently wish to maintain a market profile similar to that of their global competitors. An alternative strategy suggests itself, however. Avoidance of direct confrontation with other global competitors could lead to different market selection patterns. Dispersion of competitors into different foreign markets could reduce direct confrontation and permit each global firm to grow in a variety of markets, instead of competing intensely for a limited set of markets.

Avoidance Strategies in Market Selection

Avoidance patterns appear in a number of industries. The most extreme examples of avoidance patterns are those found in the market sharing agreements of the pre-World War II cartels. Agreements in the tobacco and chemical industries, for example, carefully defined market territories for individual companies and products on a global basis. These agreements ensured that direct competition would not occur between major companies in these industries. Similar competitive patterns appear to persist today in some industries. However, such a competitive equilibrium is extremely difficult to maintain. The entry of new competitors has a particularly powerful effect on competitive stability.   In industries such as tires, oil, paper, aluminum, copper and chemicals, new competitors have shaken what were once highly stable competitive conditions. These new competitors are often highly aggressive, foreign-based and sometimes state-owned. The resulting disruption of competitve stability leads to rising competition instead of cooperation in these sectors.

Collaboration in market-sharing agreements is obviously illegal under U.S. antitrust legislation. In some cases, however, market selection patterns that appear to reflect such motives may occur for quite different reasons. Competitors in any industry may rationally opt to avoid markets in which other firms are active. In the otherwise extremely competitive agricultural equipment industry, for example, the two leading firms exhibit relatively little overlap in their foreign operations. Where John Deere and International Harvester are active in the same market, there are few cases where entry dates are close together. These two companies exhibit distinct foreign expansion patterns, in sharp contrast to patterns observed in the tire industry. Deere and Harvester are closely matched in terms of size, product lines and commitment to international markets. These factors could be expected to contribute to a high degree of overlap in international markets. The resulting global profiles of these companies suggests that competitive

TABLE 3-5.   Market Selection Patterns in the Agricultural Equipment Industry

Country	John Deere	International Harvester
Canada	1912	1919
Venezuela	1955	—
Mexico	1956	1948
Germany	1956	1921
Argentina	1957	—
Belgium	1958	—
Australia	—	1940
Switzerland	1960	—
France	1960	1921
Spain	1961	—
United Kingdom	1961	1948
South Africa	1962	1965
Italy	1965	—

Source: Company reports.

intensity and visibility need not result in direct confrontation in international markets.

Avoidance patterns often occur when new entrants in an industry venture overseas in the face of established competitors. Control Data's first foreign markets were Israel and Hong Kong, and it later emphasized activities in Yugoslavia and other Eastern Bloc countries. These countries represented markets of secondary importance to leading firms in the industry. Chrysler followed a similar pattern to some extent in its international expansion, establishing assembly operations in a number of secondary markets such as Greece, Algeria, Venezuela, Peru, Morocco, Iran and Turkey. These markets were unique in that General Motors and Ford had not established operations prior to Chrysler's entry. Such market selection patterns reflect conscious decisions to avoid rather than confront competitors in foreign markets.

Avoidance and confrontation patterns reflect decisions by a number of firms. The choice between confrontation or avoidance rests on firms' assessment of their ability to maintain or improve their position in direct competition and the cost of doing so. Market selection patterns need not reflect conscious decisions to avoid or confront other global competitors. However, in industries where the principal competitors are other global firms, this consideration should play an important role in market selection decisions.

Strategies for Local Competitors

The absence of other global competiitors in a specific market raises several important questions. There are four principal reasons for the absence of global competitors; each has important implications. The absence of such competition could be due to the undeveloped nature of the local market. If this is the case, the principal issues facing the firm are assessment of potential local demand for the product and evaluation of promotion and distribution requirements. Second, if government restrictions are primarily responsible for the absence of global competitors, it may be impossible to enter the market without giving up control to local partners. Such restrictions are increasingly common and pose fundamental constraints on global strategies. The company's participation policy plays a critical role in market selection decisions under such constraints. Third, investment restrictions represent only one element of host government policy and administration.

Other government activities and policies, in addition to social, economic, cultural and political factors, are important in determining the overall business climate in the host country. A stringent or unstable business environment could also be responsible for the lack of foreign investment. Political risk can provide a strong deterrent to foreign investment.[5] Fourth, strong local competition also discourages market entry by global firms.

When the principal competition in foreign markets is expected to consist of local firms, market selection and entry strategies will be driven by different considerations than in cases where the principal competitors are other global firms. If local competition predominates in all foreign markets, the fundamental feasibility of a global strategy must be re-examined. Will the product in question support a global strategy? Commitment to a global strategy in an industry dominated by local firms must be supported by a strong belief that the firm possesses or will realize economic and strategic strengths relative to local competitors. The foundations of the global strategy must be examined and analyzed extensively before a global strategy is pursued in such cases.

Principal Reasons for Absence of Global Competitors in a Market

Reason	Issue	Problem
Undeveloped market	Market potential	Market risk
Investment restrictions	Entry constraints	Control risk
Business environment	System continuity	Political risk
Local competition	Competitive conditions	Competitive risk

In industries dominated by local competitors, greater geographic concentration of marketing activity can be warranted. The domestic orientation of the competition permits the global firm to focus all its resources on a single market without fear of response in other markets. This suggests that market selection choices will be driven by a desire to concentrate rather than diversify foreign operations.[6] Such an approach has several implications for market selection strategy. It is unlikely that simultaneous market entry activity will occur under such conditions. Rather, individual markets will be singled out to receive the full resources and attention of the entire firm until market share objectives are realized. Then emphasis will shift to a second market, where the sequence will again be played out.

If a strategy of concentrated activity is pursued, it becomes even more important to select the right markets. Beyond competition, three factors should determine the firm's choice of markets: market conditions, service costs and uncertainty. Market conditions determine the attractiveness of the market in terms of demand levels and trends as well as the attractiveness of the underlying business environment. Service costs measure the economics of supplying individual markets. Uncertainty reflects the firm's relative confidence about operating conditions and results in the market. Each of these factors will be examined briefly in the following sections.

MARKET CONDITIONS

Analysis of market conditions can be broken down into two specific exercises. One level of market research focuses on generating estimates of potential demand for a product. Typically, trade and demographic data are examined in order to understand the size and nature of the consumer base in a country. Assessment of demand for a specific product normally proceeds from estimates of total primary demand in a market. A second level of market analysis focuses on broader environmental conditions. Often termed simply "country analysis," the principal objective of such activity is assessment of environmental conditions, constraints and risks associated with the market. Both of these activities, demand analysis and environmental analysis, are important in assessing foreign market opportunities. Some discussion of the methods and techniques used in these analyses will be useful in understanding their role in market selection.

Demand Analysis

Potential demand can be measured in many ways. Trade sources exist for most established products. Demand analysis for such products can be based on such sources. In such cases, primary demand figures can be taken as given, and analysis can proceed to the level of the firm's product. For products not yet established in a market, demand analysis becomes a more important and difficult task.[7] Several variables are typically used to measure potential demand. For consumer goods, disposable income per capita provides an initial measure of purchasing power. Although consumer purchasing priorities obviously differ from country to country, every product's consumer base originates at some broadly defined income level. This income threshold serves as one constraint on market selection. Measurement of the average per capita income in a country and more importantly of the number of consumers above the product's threshold level, provide a broad measure of potential demand. Estimates of the potential consumer population, as defined by per capita income levels or any other criteria, provide only the broadest measure of potential demand. Further refinement is needed to estimate the probability of purchase among this population. Sampling techniques that could be employed in the United States may not be feasible at this stage of market analysis. Other measures are needed to provide a preliminary estimate of potential demand levels.

Two further levels of analysis can help to provide measures of potential demand. The first focuses on the product's broadly defined sector. For example, if the product in question is an electric appliance, the annual per capita consumption of electricity provides an important reference in prioritizing markets. The next level of analysis focuses on consumer priorities within the sector. One means of assessing potential demand for a specific product within a broad sector is the use of a consumer purchasing hierarchy framework. Studies of consumer preferences for durable goods reveal that purchasing hierarchies exist for such products.[8]

In the consumer appliance industry, knowledge of purchasing hierarchies can provide a meaningful estimate of market potential. If purchase of a product appears to closely follow purchase of other products, market selection can be highly responsive to consumer demand by observing the development of markets for certain other products. If purchase of the firm's product typically follows acquisition of other products, market potential can

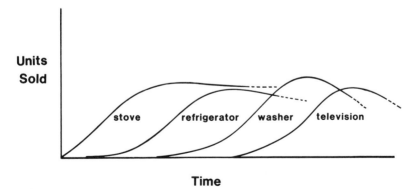

Figure 3-1. Typical purchasing hierarchy in consumer appliance industry.

be estimated by analyzing the number of units of the other products already sold in different markets.

   Purchasing hierarchies vary from country to country. Consumer priorities can be analyzed within this framework, however, to provide indicators of potential demand in different countries. If markets for the product appear to be developing more quickly or slowly with respect to other products in the hierarchy, market selection plans can be adjusted accordingly. The entire process, of course, is highly sensitive to disposable income trends.

Nondurables

Purchasing hierarchies are less useful in projecting demand for nondurable consumer goods. Sector size and trends can again be used as an indicator of demand within the broad category of goods in which the product competes. Per capita consumption of soft drinks provides a useful measure of primary demand for carbonated beverages, for example. However, consumer preferences within such sectors are often difficult to assess. Consumer preferences for nondurable goods are often a function of subjective factors. Consumer tastes for such products can vary sharply. Differences in taste must be assessed to provide realistic estimates of demand for a product. As Figure 3-2 suggests, the size and nature of markets for such products can vary sharply,

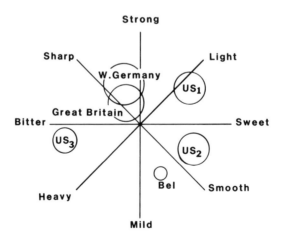

Figure 3-2.   Product attributes and market preferences for a nondurable consumer product. Circles denote the size and location of major market segments in terms of product attribute preferences.

with important implications for market selection and other elements of marketing strategy. To assess and understand differences in tastes, analysis of underlying social and cultural factors is imperative. Social attitudes vary considerably from country to country and have an important impact on consumption patterns. These social factors often correlate with the educational and religious characteristics of a market. High education levels are often associated with more receptive attitudes toward new ideas and products, for example.

Culture-bound beliefs and practices play an important role in all purchasing decisions, but they may be more important for nondurable goods than for other products. Culture includes a society's values, views, beliefs, accepted methods of interaction and communication, daily regimens, and, ultimately, behavioral patterns. Culture influences perception and use of products as well as buying behavior. The accepted role of women in society, for example, varies sharply. Such variances can have a dramatic effect on potential demand for a range of products. The practice of purdah still prevails in segments of the Hindu and Moslem world. Demand for cosmetics, hosiery and other products will be negligible under such conditions. Attitudes toward the use of cosmetics vary considerably even within the Western world.

Variances in cultural factors will be felt strongly in personal care and health aid markets. Personal care practices vary considerably in different parts of the world. In many markets the need for products such as Geritol, Sominex, Valium, Ex-Lax, and Carter's Little Liver Pills will often be met by products very different from those found in the United States. Traditional practices and products designed to serve the underlying needs of the consumer will vary sharply from those used in other markets. In such cases, it can prove difficult to convince consumers to use a radically different product. Changes in consumer beliefs and behavior are more difficult to achieve for personal care and health care products than for many other goods. Consumers will be unwilling to experiment with medications and grooming products unless a high degree of credibility for the product can be established. To assess the attractiveness of any given market for such products, the target consumer must be identified and analyzed in some detail. Constraints on consumer activity imposed by physical, social and cultural conditions must be recognized and factored into estimates of potential demand. The perception of the product from the local cultural perspective must be understood to predict receptiveness and potential demand in the local market. Test marketing based on such an analysis will provide a means of refining demand estimates and marketing strategies.

These additional levels of analysis can be used to estimate potential demand. After the number of potential consumers has been estimated on the basis of disposable income or other criteria, an initial probability of purchase based on domestic experience can be refined up or down based on sector and product priorities and indications of cultural receptiveness. The resulting estimate serves as a useful preliminary measure of potential demand in the market. This measure can be further refined through test marketing.

An additional dimension of potential demand should be taken into account. The rate of growth of the market is an essential factor in market selection. Rates of growth for established products can again be estimated from trade sources. Past rates can be refined to account for demographic and sectoral trends. Overall growth in disposable income provides a basic measure of growth, but will such growth add to the potential consumer base? How many new potential consumers will be created?

Growth in aggregate measures of income or economic activity need not result in an increase in demand for a product. Demographic trends alone can result in changes in demand. Dramatic reductions in birth rates and extension of average life expectancy are occurring in many foreign countries. Changes in consumer tastes can also radically alter market potential. Changes in the Japanese diet are closely associated with rising income levels, but they also reflect a fundamental shift in consumer tastes. The processed foods sector has grown sharply in many countries as a result of rising income and changing tastes. Such shifts in consumer tastes create major opportunities for perceptive market analysts. Effective demand analysis for consumer products requires not only identification of the potential consumer population and estimation of purchase probability, but projection of changes in the consumer population and its preferences.

Industrial Products

Estimates of market size and growth for industrial products can be derived from more precise econometric techniques. Capital expenditure trends and projections provide a useful aggregate measure of market size and growth for industrial products in general. Sector and product analysis can refine these estimates into measures of specific demand potential. A useful starting point for analysis of industrial products is an input–output table.[9] Given an expected level of final demand for consumer goods, input–output tables provide measures of demand for industrial and intermediate products. In Table 3-6, a simplistic eight sector economy is presented. Each sector uses inputs from the other sectors in its production process. The coefficients in the table represent the required inputs from each row industry per unit of output in the column industry. For example, it takes 1.10 units of steel to produce 1 unit of motor vehicles as appears in row 2, column 1. Each motor vehicle unit produced also requires .15 units of glass, .09 units of rubber, .21 units of plastic and .08 units of metalworking machinery.

These coefficients, when multiplied times expected output in each sector, provide an indication of total demand for industrial products. For example, total demand for metalworking machinery in this economy, given the expected demand in each sector, can be calculated using the following equation.

$$\text{demand} = .08(1,000) + .10(5,000) + .04(1,000) + .09(600) \\ + .08(500) + .01(898) + .20(500) + .15(500)$$

In this simplistic example, the motor vehicle industry is the only sector delivering its products to public consumers. The other sectors represent intermediate and industrial products purchased by other industrial sectors. Actual input–output tables cover the entire range of industrial and consumer goods and services.

Highly sophisticated input–output models and forecasting services are available for a number of economies outside the United States. These models offer demand forecasts for specific industrial sectors based on analysis of projected demand in other key sectors of the economy. This structure can be extremely useful in predicting demand for industrial and intermediate products. Levels of demand for user sectors can be used to predict demand for inputs. Demand for intermediate products, those that are incorporated into a final product, can be forecast as a function of demand in end-product sectors. Demand for industrial capital goods can be forecast on the same basis.

Several important considerations should be taken into account when attempting to employ this technique for market selection purposes. It is particularly dangerous to use coefficients from one market to estimate demand in another market. Input-output coefficients vary significantly from country to country. If the average motor vehicle is smaller in a foreign

TABLE 3-6. Input from Producing Sector per Unit of Output in User Sector

Producing Sector	User Sector								Total Inputs	Net Exports	Expected Final Demand Units	Total Output
	1	2	3	4	5	6	7	8				
1. Motor vehicles	—	.01	.01	.01	.01	.02	.02	.03	200	50	750	1,000
2. Steel	1.10	.10	.03	.04	.05	.30	.20	4.0	2,300	2,700	0	5,000
3. Glass	.15	.10	—	.01	.02	.01	.02	.01	730	270	0	1,000
4. Rubber	.09	.04	.02	—	.06	.02	.08	.01	495	105	0	600
5. Plastic	.21	.01	.03	.04	—	.11	.10	.05	540	−40	0	500
6. Metalworking machinery	.08	.10	.04	.09	.08	.01	.20	.15	900	0	0	900
7. Molding machinery	.04	.02	.04	.15	.40	.02	—	.02	500	0	0	500
8. Electricity-generating equipment	.02	.04	.06	.12	.04	.05	.05	—	500	0	0	500
9. Labor	1.15	.80	.60	.40	.30	.50	.50	.70				

country, input requirements per unit will be less than in the home market. Three other primary effects also lead to changes in input−output coefficients. The first is use of substitute products. Many inputs can be substituted for each other. Aluminum and plastic are used in varying degrees by different automobile producers. Differences in capital intensity also result in different coefficients. This is particularly true in regard to the use of capital equipment. Capital intensity varies substantially across countries in any given industry. The Japanese motorcycle industry, for example, exhibits a capital−labor ratio of $8,170 per worker. The U.S. ratio is $4,000, and the British ratio is $3,250 per worker.[10] Such differences reflect a fundamental issue in estimating demand in capital goods sectors. Differences in process technology also result in different input−output coefficients. The float process in the manufacture of glass and the direct-reduction process for steel making exhibit input requirements that are radically different from those of traditional technologies in these industries. Demand for inputs and capital goods will vary sharply according to the technology base and trend in a given market. Adjusted for these factors, macroeconomic analysis of this sort can provide an indicator of potential demand for industrial and intermediate products.

Estimates of demand for industrial products should also account for the user industry's projected role within the foreign economy. The future competitiveness of the host country's industry in world markets is a critical issue. National policies directed at the industry can provide insight into this issue. In many cases, formal industrial policies can be analyzed to gain an understanding of national plans and objectives for an industry. Current Japanese emphasis on the development and expansion of its semiconductor industry has created great demand for equipment used in circuit design and chip production. OPEC plans for downstream expansion into petrochemical sectors create huge demand for chemical plants and equipment. The French commitment to aerospace created opportunities in the specialty metals and engine sectors. On the other hand, low national priorities for a given sector should signal a warning to prospective investors.

Demand estimates provide one of the essential determinants of market selection decisions. Demand for consumer products can be estimated by assessing potential consumer population size, purchase probability, frequency and preferences. Econometric methods can be very useful in estimating demand for industrial products. Potential demand for a product can be measured quantitatively and used to rank markets in order of priority on this dimension alone. This factor can then be integrated with other determinants of market selection decisions. Analysis of the prevailing business environment represents another key aspect of market analysis.

Country Environmental Analysis

There is no substitute for intimate knowledge of operating conditions and realities in potential markets. Formal country analysis models represent an attempt to provide such knowledge in a systematic manner. The critical concerns that prompt country analysis are the nature of the local business environment and the probability of change in underlying legal, political, social or economic systems. These four areas comprise the principal elements of the business environment. Analysis of each element contributes to an understanding of the general business climate.

The first step in a country analysis is simple classification of the status quo along a wide range of descriptive variables. For example, legal conditions have a direct and immediate effect on activities in foreign markets. Existing legislation in a number of key areas can be examined to determine the attractiveness of the legal environment. The existence of property, patent and copyright laws will be of concern to all foreign investors. The absence of patent rights on pharmaceuticals in Italy has limited investment by foreign firms in that sector, for example. Legal restrictions on foreign investment and repatriation are also of primary importance. Restrictions on foreign investment exist in a wide range of countries. India and the Andean Pact countries are examples of particularly restrictive host countries. Repatriation restrictions are present in most countries. In Argentina, for example, 12% of registered capital can be repatriated annually free of tax. Any excess repatriations are taxed at a progressive rate commencing at 15% for remittances between 12 and 15% of registered capital.

The basic elements of country analysis can be divided into the categories on the following page.

Legal, political, social and economic conditions include an extensive list of variables of concern to the prospective investor. Analysis of these variables can absorb significant corporate resources, particularly if many countries are being examined. Adoption of a limited framework can reduce the time needed to produce a meaningful analysis.

Legal Conditions	Social Conditions
Property rights	Population trends
Patent and copyright	Life expectancy
Labor	Education
Consumer	Income distribution
Repatriation restrictions	Literacy
Foreign investment restrictions	Predominant religion
Court system	
Commercial codes	

Political Conditions	Economic Conditions
Type of government	Rate of growth
Age of system	Manufacturing/GNP
Number of political parties	Inflation
International relations	Unemployment
Nature of internal opposition	Balance of payments
Industrial policy	Industry structure
Trade policy	Disposable income
Monetary and fiscal policy	
Government role in the economy	

A Short Form for Country Analysis

One view of country analysis emphasizes the importance of national performance along five key dimensions. Performance is presumed to be the most important indicator of the health of the country. Sound economic performance in the areas of employment, growth, inflation, and trade suggests a firm foundation for foreign investment. Performance in meeting social objectives is often overlooked, however. Trends in education levels, income distribution, housing, medical care and social security provide critical indicators of the business climate. The following categories provide a working framework for country analysis:

Performance	Policies	Position	Politics
Employment	Monetary	Economic depen-	Parties
Growth	Fiscal	dencies	People
Inflation	Wage/Price	Economic assets	Type of system
Balance of payments	Trade	International rela-	Stability
Social objectives	Industrial	tions	Key issues
	Investment	Social foundation	Opposition
	Foreign exchange	Demographic	
	Social	trends	

Performance in these areas can be viewed as both a cause and effect of national policies, position and politics. Economic policies can be measured readily. The rate of monetary expansion is an important policy variable. Federal budgets provide indicators of fiscal policy and priorities. Trade policy has an important effect on employment, inflation and balance-of-payments results. Trade policy can be analyzed by examining tariff levels, quotas, currency regimes, import deposits and licenses, export subsidies and the role of state trading agencies. Broader policies with respect to import substitution and export promotion, both in the aggregate and for individual sectors, provides an important indicator for potential investors.

The position of the country in the international economic and political system provides an essential element in country analysis. Economic dependencies, such as reliance on oil imports or foreign debt to keep an economy going, must be analyzed. Measurement of annual debt payments or oil imports as a percentage of exports or exchange reserves provide a useful index of dependence. Economic assets, such as mineral or energy resources, also provide an important indicator of market attractiveness. In addition, the country's position in the world political system is essential in evaluating foreign markets. Participation in one or more blocs is an important indicator of local conditions and philosophies. The status of diplomatic relations with the firm's home country can be an important consideration.

Social and cultural foundations of the country often provide important insights into present conditions in a potential market. Former French colonies will differ in important respects from former British colonies. Countries based on Moslem cultures will differ from Christian countries, and the existence of mixed cultural and ethnic foundations provide another indicator of local conditions. Demographic data are also particularly important in understanding prospects for a market. As an example, advances in medical care in the 1950s resulted in a dramatic reduction in infant mortality in Iran. The resulting demographic pressures can be associated with subsequent political developments in that country.

Analysis of political conditions begins with classification of the system. Military dictatorships, parliamentary democracies, constitutional monarchies, and socialist states denote very different political conditions. The age of the system, frequency of change in administration and the nature of the transition process tell a great deal about the stability of the system. Political risk can also be measured by examining levels of terrorist or opposition activity.

Issue analysis can provide important insights into the political process in any country. By comparing the preferences of different parties on key issues and the priority each party places on the issue with actual political outcomes, a measure of power can be developed. The debate in the United States over imposition of import controls on Japanese automobiles provides an example of this technique. The outcome compares the power of broad consumer and international relations interests in the United States with specific labor and industry interests. A series of such analyses can be used to rank the political power and priorities of these parties. Such rankings are useful in understanding the political environment of the host country. This analysis also can be used on an ex post facto basis to examine coalition histories, to develop preference profiles for different groups, to measure power, and thus to predict outcomes for pending issues that will affect the business environment and ultimately the attractiveness of the market.

Issue: Imposing U.S. Import Quotas on Japanese Automobiles

Party	Position	Priority	Power
Labor: UAW	Pro	High	Low, increasing
Automobile industry	Pro	High	Low, increasing
State department	Con	High	High, decreasing
Consumer groups	Con	High	High, decreasing

Much emphasis is frequently given to the individuals who comprise the top management of the country. The character, personality, motives and interests of such people are critical in evaluating foreign business environments, particularly if their power can be measured. However, this approach often emphasizes the roles of technocrats and heads of state without accounting for labor, religious, social and opposition leaders. The issue analysis approach can be used to include all of the major parties and individuals within a country.

The general business environment can be evaluated along these primary dimensions. Specific aspects of the business environment will be important to any given product, however. The host government's investment and industrial policy with respect to individual sectors of the economy must be analyzed. Foreign investment is discouraged or prohibited in specific industries in many host countries. Restrictions on foreign investment represent only one aspect of foreign investment policy. Investment incentives are widely available to attract foreign investors in many countries.[11] These incentives include tax holidays, low-cost loans, grants, infrastructure and active political support. The availability of such benefits varies sharply by country and sector and plays an important role in investment decisions.

Industrial policy can be reflected in the education system, training programs, price controls, investment credits, import restrictions and research and development policies, among others. The role of specific state agencies and enterprises also varies sharply by country and sector. Regulatory agencies function in many sectors; state enterprises are often present as well. In other sectors, private competitors often possess excellent relationships with political figures and institutions. The history of such organizations and relationships reveals a great deal about public objectives, strategies and tactics with respect to a given sector and market.

The presence of a public enterprise in any sector generally limits the potential activities of private firms. However, an understanding of the objectives and plans of such enterprises can also reveal important opportunities. Public enterprises often require external sources of components and other inputs and can represent a significant market for the products of private firms. In addition, state firms' activities are often officially limited to certain segments of a sector. The scope and direction of state enterprise activities generally appear as a matter of public record.

Although many government officials view industries served by state enterprises as public property, niches within such industries can frequently be defined that will be approved by local officials. The French government welcomed Digital Equipment into the minicomputer segment of the computer industry at the same time it was attempting to establish a state enterprise at the expense of foreign subsidiaries in the existing mainframe segment.[12] The Brazilian state-owned chemical company has monopolized certain segments of the petrochemical industry, but has permitted a large number of foreign projects in other segments.

Government policies and activities at the sector level play a major role in determining the attractiveness of any market. General legal, social and economic conditions also have different implications for different sectors. Analysis of prevailing conditions in these key areas provides a measure of market attractiveness. Markets can then be ranked on a broad scale to reflect the relative attractiveness of potential demand and the local business environment.

Demand analysis attempts to measure the potential revenues associated with any market. Revenues are a function of unit volume, realized prices and currency conversion. Unit volume is a function of the size of the potential consumer population and the share achieved by the firm. Realized prices are influenced by inflation rates, exchange rates, price controls, price elasticity of demand and trade margins and terms. Each of these factors varies by country and should be evaluated accordingly. Measurement of the costs of serving a market is an important part of such an evaluation.

Service Costs

The cost of serving different markets varies sharply. Such costs include three broad categories of expense: entry costs, sourcing costs and sales and administration expense. Entry costs reflect the costs of establishing a managerial, manufacturing and marketing presence in the market. Each of these types of cost varies from market to market depending on a number of considerations. Unit marketing costs reflect logistic and distribution requirements, trade margins and promotion costs. Unit manufacturing costs reflect input costs, productivity and product quality. Unit managerial costs reflect the initial costs of market entry and ongoing administrative overhead.

Volume clearly plays an important role in determining unit costs, but other factors are just as important. Absolute initial entry costs will vary sharply by country. Entry costs include more than the legal expenses and consulting fees associated with establishing a legal presence. Entry cost also includes the management inputs required to initiate operations in a foreign market. Management inputs are required to negotiate entry into the market In some cases, many man-years of senior management time can be consumed in this process. This is not an insignificant expense, especially if such management resources are valued at their opportunity cost. Second, if the market is new to the company, there may be no qualified executive within the firm to manage the subsidiary. In such a case, the firm can train one of its officers to operate within the local business environment. Such costs do not simply include Berlitz sessions and tutorial fees. They also include the costs of inefficiency and ignorance as the manager learns about the local environment on location. An alternative approach can be used to solve this problem, but it may create a greater problem. The firm can hire a foreign national to run the subsidiary, thus avoiding the problems associated with lack of expertise in the local market. This approach, however, also bears significant costs. Although such a manager may function efficiently within the foreign environment, he or she will not function efficiently within the corporate environment. The foreign manager will not always follow corporate procedures or communicate with the appropriate personnel at headquarters regarding specific needs and issues, nor will he or she necessarily share corporate objectives, values and accepted modes of behavior. If the firm wishes to avoid these problems, it can train foreign nationals at headquarters for a year or more to acculturate them, but this also involves significant expense in time, money and management attention. These shortcomings result in significant inefficiencies and costs that are highly specific to individual foreign markets. Another dimension of initial entry costs also varies substantially from country to country.

The global strategy of any business represents the seed from which successful market entry and development proceed. This strategy includes the product's marketing mix, competitive interaction mechanisms, methods of internal organization, timing, and management objectives and incentives. This base is the firm's most valuable resource. When corporate strategies must be altered in order to enter a market, intangible but highly significant costs are incurred. These costs can be thought of in monetary terms, but they reflect consumption of the corporation's most valuable resource—its managerial talent. The need to alter an existing corporate strategy in order to enter a market varies considerably from market to market. A firm considering market entry in China, Yugoslavia or Nigeria must radically alter many dimensions of its basic strategy. An inordinate amount of senior management energy can be absorbed by such ventures. Entry into the United Kingdom or Canada would not require such extensive modifications.

These initial entry costs represent one element in the total managerial overhead associated with a foreign market. Ongoing administrative expense will also vary from country to country. Salaries and hiring costs determine part of this variance, but administrative requirements also vary. Government, labor, and public relations requirements differ sharply. Accounting and finance staff needs also vary as a result of regulations, inflation, currency volatility and tax and reporting requirements.

Manufacturing and marketing costs are more readily calculated. If the market is to be served from an existing plant in the United States or elsewhere, exact unit costs are known. These unit costs plus tariff and transport costs determine sourcing costs. If the firm intends to produce in the foreign market, unit costs must be estimated on a full absorption basis to include all manufacturing overhead. Although unit costs can be calculated using cost/volume relationships in existing plants, actual input costs, productivity levels and reject rates will vary by country. Marketing costs include promotion, distribution and sales expense per unit. These costs will also vary primarily as a function of volume, but basic costs in each of these areas vary sharply across countries. Media rates per capita vary as do media usage and availability. Distribution and logistic efficiency vary sharply. The cost per salesman call differs as a function of channel concentration, average outlet size, salary levels, working schedules, transportation costs, and other factors.

All these factors interact to determine the cost structure associated with serving a foreign market. High initial entry costs and ongoing administrative expense contribute to high unit costs and detract from a market's attractiveness. High marketing and sourcing costs also weigh against selection of an otherwise attractive market. In comparing service costs in different markets, it will be difficult to quantify all the factors presented earlier. An empirical approach cannot be supported with precision. The underlying concepts, however, can be incorporated into market selection decisions. The importance of service costs in different markets are presented conceptually in Figure 3-3.

Entry into the Canadian market entails very little initial expense in legal and consulting fees, negotiation requirements, management development or modification of existing corporate strategy. Entry into Japan involves substantial expense in each of these areas. The larger volume potential of the

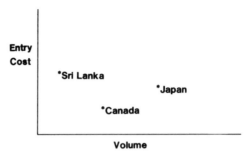

Figure 3-3.   Entry cost comparisons.

Japanese market can offset these expenses to bring unit costs down to favorable levels, but the high entry costs associated with the market reduce the attractiveness of the Japanese market.

An Integrated Framework for Market Selection Decisions

Competition, market conditions and service costs are primary factors in market selection decisions. Although these factors are difficult to quantify, countries can be ranked along a broad spectrum in each case. Quantitative measures can be used to represent the level of potential demand in different countries. Dollar figures can also be employed to represent estimates of unit service costs. The number, size, nature and sophistication of expected rivals in any market generates a broad indicator of the level of competition. Analysis of the various elements determining conditions in the business environment also provides a general indication of the degree of attractiveness of different markets. After these factors have been assessed for prospective markets, an integrated market selection framework emerges. Countries can be plotted along these four key dimensions to represent their overall attractiveness. The principal *economic* factors affecting market selection, potential demand and delivery costs, together determine a critical aspect of market attractiveness. Figure 3-4 presents the outcome of country plotting for a typical product.

Figure 3-5 could be used to plot countries along the two key *environmental* dimensions. The level of expected competition and the nature of the business environment serve as the axes for this chart. Several countries appear in the chart as they might appear for a given product in 1983. Of

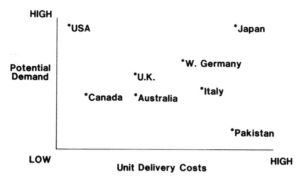

Figure 3-4.   Typical demand and delivery cost comparisons for selected countries.

course, the level of competition will vary considerably by product, and the overall business environment can also differ from product to product. In this framework, markets above the diagonal line appear particularly attractive to prospective investors.

The charts in Figures 3-4 and 3-5 can be overlaid to provide a comparison of economic and environmental attractiveness for different markets. A visual comparison provides an initial indication of relative attractiveness. Countries appearing in the upper left-hand corner of these charts exhibit the greatest

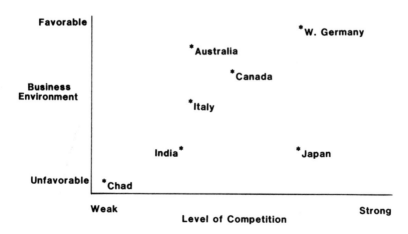

Figure 3.5   Environment and competition comparisons.

attractiveness under our criteria. A single scale could be developed to rank countries according to their proximity to the upper left corner of the chart. Such an approach would have to develop weights that exactly equalized the importance of each of these four factors, however. The weighting of different factors in market selection analysis is an internal issue for individual managers, firms and products. If this can be done to management's satisfaction, countries' positions in this chart could then be reduced to a single plot for each country with one axis measuring environmental attractiveness, the other economic attractiveness. Plots in such a chart could then be used to assign priorities in a market selection hierarchy.

The use of such rating scales in the market selection process can be integrated into the capital budgeting framework presented in Chapter 6. Once broad assessments of potential markets have been made, more precise economic and financial analysis can be accomplished at the project appraisal level. Environmental and competitive factors can also be analyzed in more detail for specific projects in markets perceived as attractive under this framework. Although this approach appears to be inconsistent with existing theories of finance, there is evidence to suggest that firms restrict the geographic area of their investment search prior to considering and pursuing individual projects.

Market selection patterns are extremely sensitive to the international experience level of the parent corporation. Aharoni found that firms in the early stages of international expansion typically make only limited searches for foreign market opportunities, restricting their analysis and activity to a small set of proximate markets.[13] Geographic investment horizons broaden over time as a firm's foreign activities expand. Perlmutter schematized this process by identifying four types of orientations toward international markets.[14] Market selection priorities appear to be closely related to the orientation of the firm toward foreign markets, as categorized in four broad groups: ethnocentric, polycentric, regiocentric and geocentric firms. The typical multinational enterprise is thought to evolve from a domestic orientation (ethnocentric) toward a global orientation (geocentric). The effects of this process on actual investment patterns have been observed and discussed by Vernon and Davidson[15]. The motives for such a process derive from fundamental uncertainty about international operations. Such uncertainty contributes to a gradual, incremental pattern of international expansion that has important implications for market selection decisions.

Uncertainty and Market Selection

Incremental expansion suggests a distinct pattern of market selection. Firms will move from environments in which they are most confident and comfortable toward more uncertain environments. Initially this process results in corporate preferences for markets that are most similar to their home market. Market similarity appears to play a very important role in market selection decisions. Actual market selection patterns suggest the importance of this factor. The Harvard Multinational Enterprise Project sample of 180 industrial multinational enterprises was employed to analyze market selection patterns.[16] This sample revealed sharp preferences for similar markets. An investment sequence matrix was developed to measure the relative priorities given to 20 principal host countries. This matrix shown in Table 3-7, measures the percentage of all the firm's product lines introduced into one host country before they were introduced into others. For example, the matrix shows that these 180 firms introduced product lines in Canada before the United Kingdom in 59.1% of all cases, and in the United Kingdom before Germany in 60.5% of all cases. These percentages provide measures of market selection priorities that can be used to analyze factors affecting such decisions.

The countries in the matrix are ranked in order of priority. Canada received the highest priority, occurring as the first foreign market selected by these firms in a majority of all cases. The United Kingdom received the second highest priority in market selection decisions. It is not because of market size that these two countries receive such preference. Canada is not a large market, and per capita income in the United Kingdom is significantly below levels in West Germany or France, but Canada and Great Britain are by far the largest recipients of U.S. foreign investment.[17]

Preferences for Canada, the United Kingdom and Australia appear higher than is warranted by an analysis of potential demand. Other factors explain this preference. Lower service costs encourage investment in these nations. The U.S. firms' managerial, marketing, and manufacturing capabilities can be readily transferred to these countries because of economic and cultural similarity. The ready transferability of these resources provides an economic incentive for selection of similar markets. In addition, firms face lower levels of uncertainty in such countries. The effects of uncertainty play an important role in the high priority awarded these nations. Initial expansion into similar

TABLE 3-7. Frequency by Which 180 U.S.-Based Multinational Enterprise Initiated Manufacturing for SIC 3-digit Industries in Country A Before Country B, 1900–1976

Country A										Country B											
	1	2	3	4	5	6	7	8	9	10	11	12	13	14	15	16	17	18	19	20	Total
1. Canada		.591	.693	.737	.740	.744	.782	.784	.826	.839	.853	.853	.892	.916	.884	.909	.976	.984	.986	.994	15.983
2. United Kingdom			.605	.666	.644	.667	.675	.703	.767	.769	.776	.808	.843	.876	.845	.888	.961	.972	.980	.992	14.846
3. West Germany				.545	.483	.550	.556	.576	.656	.722	.773	.717	.769	.817	.771	.798	.915	.967	.967	.972	13.256
4. Mexico					.513	.536	.568	.611	.689	.669	.669	.756	.776	.766	.812	.806	.967	.946	.972	.983	13.172
5. Australia						.500	.524	.579	.638	.647	.653	.784	.750	.772	.787	.813	.928	.944	.965	.971	12.794
6. France							.503	.557	.614	.631	.645	.700	.746	.813	.796	.796	.905	.945	.962	.962	12.578
7. Brazil								.552	.557	.612	.631	.678	.741	.748	.762	.802	.936	.949	.955	.974	12.353
8. Japan									.575	.573	.555	.672	.716	.702	.748	.757	.927	.951	.972	.993	11.779
9. Spain										.486	.505	.584	.643	.650	.673	.696	.801	.929	.945	.963	10.489
10. Italy											.515	.575	.638	.610	.617	.689	.872	.906	.941	.967	10.380
11. Colombia												.603	.664	.652	.687	.686	.891	.915	.941	.924	10.371
12. Belgium													.549	.580	.544	.593	.819	.886	.928	.927	9.026

							Total
13. Netherlands	.532 .527 .580 .678 .897 .897 .924						8.308
14. South Africa	.561 .568 .759 .882 .909 .895						8.140
15. Argentina	.537 .789 .877 .903 .903						8.117
16. India	.727 .842 .903 .941						7.534
17. Philippines	.656 .942 .731						4.286
18. Ireland	.750 .625						2.727
19. South Korea	.550 .500						2.005
20. Taiwan							1.856
							190.000

Source: W.H. Davidson, "The Location of Foreign Investment Activity," *Journal of International Business Studies*, Fall 1980.

The frequencies in the table are calculated by the following formula:

$$F_{ij} = \sum_{k=1}^{n} \left(\frac{A_{ij}}{A_{ij} + A_{jik}} \right)$$

where

F_{ij} = frequency by which products appeared in country i before country j.

k = product k.

n = number of products introduced in country i or j.

markets represents a means of reducing the uncertainties associated with foreign operations. If the firm has little confidence in its ability to estimate or predict costs, demand, competition or environmental conditions in various markets, it can minimize uncertainty in its selection decisions by choosing markets about which it has the best information. Canada, because of its geographic, economic and cultural proximity, represents an optimal choice for firms facing high uncertainty. If Canadian operations proceed in a satisfactory manner, the United Kingdom represents another market that U.S. companies can enter with relatively low uncertainty. Operations in these countries provide the firm with additional information, experience and confidence that contributes to a gradual broadening of horizons toward less similar markets.

Evolution toward a global orientation is a function of the experience accumulated at the firm level. Experienced firms exhibit market selection priorities that are significantly different from those of inexperienced firms. Experienced companies introduce products abroad more quickly and extensively, and they exhibit a lower preference for similar markets.[18] Such companies have greater confidence in the precision of their estimates for competition, service costs, potential demand and environmental conditions in various markets. Market selection decisions for experienced firms will be driven by these considerations and not by the desire to avoid uncertainty. Inexperienced firms are far more likely to emphasize market similarity in market selection. All firms, however, will exhibit preferences for the foreign markets in which they currently operate. Existing operations provide economies of scale, information and management expertise that dramatically alter the attractiveness of any given market.

The Marketing Mix and Market Selection

Marketing mix issues also play a very important role in the market selection process. The interrelationship between marketing mix issues and market selection decisions hinges on the importance of market similarities. Similarity to the home market ensures that existing product pricing, promotion and distribution strategies can be employed in the foreign market. The ability to utilize an existing marketing mix provides greater efficiency and permits immediate market entry. Similarity to the home market permits the firm to extend its existing operations into additional markets without making any significant change in its marketing strategy.

Realization of this potential benefit can be facilitated through the use of cluster analysis techniques. The process of clustering markets into common groups has important implications for market selection decisions.[19] Cluster analysis can be used to group countries according to economic, cultural, legal, social and political characteristics. Foreign markets identified as belonging to the home country cluster will benefit in terms of market selection priorities. These countries will exhibit low service costs, immediate entry possibilities and, just as important, lower uncertainty about consumer response to the firm's established marketing mix. The response of consumers in other countries to the firm's marketing mix is uncertain. However, by clustering markets into common groups, this problem can be addressed.

After clustering markets, the firm has several alternative market selection strategies. Market selection strategies will be based to a large extent on the perceived feasibility of global marketing standardization for the product. If a standard global marketing approach appears feasible, markets can be selected primarily on the basis of economic and environmental factors, with little regard for market similarity. If the feasibility of a standard approach is uncertain, however, two distinct expansion strategies are relevant.

The first approach follows a hierarchy based primarily on market similarity. The subset of countries within the home market cluster are selected first, with initial emphasis on those countries most similar to the home market. Although economic and environmental factors will be weighed in selecting markets, the general approach underlying such a strategy is expansion from the most similar market to the next most similar market. This incremental approach permits the firm to adjust its marketing mix at the margin in each market without a radical departure from the established marketing strategy. Incrementalism of this sort is a highly rational response to the uncertainties involved in the international expansion of a product line. Incrementalism permits the firm to gather information about operations at its periphery and adjust accordingly as it expands. This peripheral approach to information gathering can result in suboptimal market selection decisions in a competitive world, however. The firm that plods its way through Canada, the United Kingdom and Australia may find that its competitors have leapfrogged ahead to more desirable markets in countries like Germany, France and Japan.

Clustering of markets permits an alternative strategy. A sampling approach can be employed by introducing the product in representative countries within each cluster. This approach begs a very important question. Should the firm enter these markets with its established marketing mix or a modified configuration? In the absence of any solid rationale for modification, many firms choose to use the existing mix. Modification involves costs that need not be incurred unless a positive return is anticipated. If the standard mix is used, this sampling approach immediately confirms the feasibility or failure of a standardized marketing approach. Results in the sample markets can then be employed in two ways. If the existing mix appears to work well in a given cluster, that set of markets can be added to the initial selection subset. If modification is necessary, the development of an appropriate strategy can proceed immediately. Once an effective marketing mix has been developed, the firm can use this new marketing strategy as a second base for international expansion. Market selection decisions need not be based solely on extension of a single marketing strategy.

Marketing mix management plays an important role in market selection decisions. These two strategic choices are closely interrelated. Many of the factors that determine market selection decisions also influence marketing mix strategies. Yet the development and management of marketing mix strategy represents a second, distinct strategic element in global management.

NOTES

1. Knickerbocker, F. T., *Oligopolistic Reaction and Multinational Enterprise* (Boston: Division of Research, Harvard Business School, 1973).
2. Graham, E. M., Oligopolistic Imitation and European Direct Investment in the United States, unpublished doctoral dissertation, Harvard Business School, 1974.
3. The use of innovation to discipline competitors has been observed in the electrical equipment oligopoly. Sultan, Ralph, *Pricing in the Electrical Equipment Oligopoly* (Boston: Division of Research, Harvard Business School, 1974).
4. *Business Week*, July 14, 1980, p. 83; August 10, 1981, p. 76; *Barrons*, August 3, 1981, p. 29.
5. The impact of political risk on investment decisions is subject to some debate. Green and Bennett found that political instability did not affect foreign direct investment (FDI) activity. Green, R.T. and P.D. Bennett, "Political Instability as a Determinant of Direct Foreign Investment in Marketing," *Journal of Marketing Research*, May 1972, pp. 182–186. Kobrin also failed to find a significant relationship. Kobrin, S.J., "The Environmental Determinants of Foreign Direct Manufacturing Investment," *Journal of International Business Studies*, Fall 1976, p. 29.
6. This issue is addressed in Ayal, Igal and Zif, Jehiel, "Market Expansion Strategies in Multinational Marketing," *Journal of Marketing*, Spring 1979, pp. 84–94; Keegan, W. J., "Strategic Marketing: International Diversification versus National Concentration," *Columbia Journal of World Business*, Winter 1977, pp. 119–130.
7. The roots of demand analysis can be traced to prewar publications. See, for example, Brown, L. O., "Quantitative Market Analysis," *Harvard Business Review*, Spring 1937,

pp. 233−244; also, Moyer, Reed, "International Market Analysis," *Journal of Marketing Research*, August 1968, pp. 353−60; Armstrong, J. S., "An Application of Econometrix Methods to International Marketing," *Journal of Marketing Research*, May 1970, pp. 190−198; Rutchford, B. T., "Operationalizing Economic Models of Demand for Product Characteristics," *Journal of Consumer Research*, June 1979, pp. 76−85.

8. Kasulis, J. J., R. F. Lusch and E. F. Stafford, Jr., "Consumer Acquisition Patterns for Durable Goods," *Journal of Consumer Research*, June 1979, pp. 47−57.

9. Input−output analysis was developed by Wassilly Leontief of Harvard University. See Leontief, Wassily, *Input−Output Economics*, (New York: Oxford University Press, 1966); Carter, A. P. and A. M. Brady, (ed.), *Contributions to Input−Output Analysis* (Amsterdam: North-Holland, 1970).

10. The Boston Consulting Group, *Strategy Alternatives for the British Motorcycle Industry* (London: Her Majesty's Stationery Office, 1975).

11. See, for example, *Investment Incentive Programs in Western Europe* (Washington: Chamber of Commerce of the United States, 1978).

12. Gadonneix, M. P., *The Influence of the State of Industrial Strategies: A Study of the Computer Industry in France*, unpublished doctoral dissertation, Harvard Business School, 1974.

13. Aharoni, Yair, *The Foreign Investment Decision Process* (Boston: Division of Research, Harvard Business School, 1966).

14. Perlmulter, H. V., "Social Architectural Problems of the International Firm," *Quarterly Journal of AISEC International*, August 1967, pp. 33−44.

15. Vernon, Raymond, *Sovereignty at Bay* (New York: Basic Books, 1971) pp. 62−63; Davidson, W. H., *Experience Effects in International Investment and Technology Transfer* (Ann Arbor: UMI Research Press, 1980).

16. Davidson, W. H., "The Location of Foreign Direct Investment Activity," *Journal of International Business Studies*, Fall 1980.

17. *Survey of Current Business*, U.S. Dept of Commerce, June 1981, pp. 62−66.

18. Davidson, W. H. *Experience Effects*, op. cit., Chapter II.

19. Sethi, S. P., "Comparative Cluster Analysis for World Markets," *Journal of Marketing Research*, August 1971, pp. 348−54; Liander, Bertil, Vernon Terpstra, M. Y., Yoshino, and A. A. Sherbini, *Comparative Analysis for International Marketing* (Boston: Allyn and Bacon, 1967).

FOUR

Marketing Mix Management

Four well-known elements—product, pricing, promotion and distribution—are the key strategic variables in marketing mix management. The articulation of these elements into a cohesive and integrated marketing strategy is the goal of marketing mix management. Determination of an optimal marketing mix for a given product requires extensive analysis of market conditions. Market research and experimentation precede the creation of a marketing mix for the home market. The objective of these efforts is the correct combination of product, pricing, promotion and distribution policies to maximize consumer response and minimize marketing costs. The process of establishing a marketing mix is a continuous attempt to lock these elements into an integrated strategy that best meets market conditions. This process is widely discussed in marketing literature and need not be elaborated on here.[1] The important concern in this context is the international dimension of marketing mix management.

Strategies for foreign markets generally are addressed after a relatively stable marketing mix has been established in the home market. This established mix presumably represents the best configuration for home market conditions. Obviously, it may not be an optimal mix under conditions prevailing in a variety of foreign markets. The effectiveness of the established mix in foreign markets is a key issue in global marketing mix management. Concern about the effectiveness of an established marketing mix in foreign markets raises a basic question: Can international marketing be standardized?[2] The objective of finding the best marketing mix to match conditions in every market conflicts with a natural desire to standardize

123

global marketing strategy. Resolution of this conflict poses a fundamental issue in multinational marketing management.

Successful examples of highly standardized global marketing strategies can be found in many industries. Among consumer products, Bic's achievements in the writing instrument industry provide a classic case. Bic's marketing strategy built on a new product concept, the disposable ball-point pen. This pen was priced sharply below existing ball-points so as to be competitive with lead pencils. Extensive promotion emphasized the reliability and durability of this product and its remarkably low price. Television was used heavily for the first time in the industry's history to establish the Bic brand name in the public's mind. Innovations were also introduced in distribution of the product. Van salesmen were used to directly stock retailers' shelves. New outlets were opened. Volume discounts were given to retailers, and point-of-sale displays were placed to spur impulse buying for what had been a shopping item.

The success of this innovative marketing strategy in France led Bic to expand into foreign markets. The marketing mix employed in foreign markets virtually duplicated the strategy employed in France. The same brand name appeared around the world. Reliability and price were emphasized in the extensive promotion campaigns universally employed in the early stages of market development. Product design, packaging and pricing strategies were also highly standardized in all markets. Media usage and distribution policies proved more difficult to standardize, but the same fundamental strategy drove Bic's activities in all foreign markets. That strategy emphasized the creation of a new segment in the writing instrument market through aggressive promotion in the public media. The resulting primary demand was harvested through point-of-sale dominance in mass distribution channels. Retail visibility was achieved partially through the effects of Bic's pull strategy, but shelf space was secured because of the company's direct sales force, retail discounts and point-of-sale expertise. Channel acceptance ultimately hinged on unit sales volume, and volume depended on consumer acceptance of the new product concept. Consumer acceptance was ensured by price and product quality. All these factors come together in the success of the Bic strategy. The interdependence of products, pricing, promotion and distribution policies is vividly clear in Bic's marketing strategy. These elements of marketing strategy cannot be viewed as discrete strategic choices. The primary challenge of marketing mix management rests in finding the correct combination of these elements to match market conditions. Bic management performed admirably both in this regard and in meeting the challenge of multinational marketing.

The primary challenge of multinational marketing rests in duplicating the success achieved in a single market in other foreign markets. In some cases, success can be duplicated with identical marketing strategies in foreign markets. Bic provides an example of successful implementation of a standardized marketing strategy on a global scale. Bic executed the same basic strategy and achieved the same results in virtually every market it entered. Its ability to pursue a highly standardized marketing strategy followed from the nature of the market and industry in which it operated. A standardized strategy will not prove effective for all products. However, one of the first issues to be addressed in developing a global marketing strategy is the feasibility of utilizing a highly standardized marketing mix.

Marketing standardization provides many benefits. Economies of scale are realized in product design, promotion and other areas as a result of standardization, but perhaps the principal benefit is increased managerial efficiency. Execution of the basic strategy improves with experience, and each new market will contribute to the cumulative learning curve effect. Contingencies encountered in various markets will be factored into the marketing strategy and anticipated in new markets. Central administration of foreign affiliates will be enhanced because of standardization as well. It is far easier for the parent company to manage a set of cloned affiliates than it would be to manage a diverse group of subsidiaries. There will be few differences in objectives, strategies or problems among affiliates pursuing a standardized strategy. This permits the parent firm to comprehend and respond quickly to the needs of various affiliates. The parent company can support its affiliates more effectively if its strategy is highly similar to that pursued in the home market. The parent can also evaluate, control and coordinate foreign affiliates more effectively if strategies are highly similar.

INDUSTRIAL PRODUCTS

The benefits of marketing standardization are less applicable to industrial products. Industrial products are often sold on a highly customized basis within the firm's domestic market. The personal sales approach associated with most industrial products emphasizes response to individual customers' needs. Most manufacturers of industrial products produce a wide range of models and are prepared to modify their products to meet customer specifications. Delivery terms, installation and service contracts also vary considerably. The aerospace industry provides one example of such a customized marketing strategy. Many dimensions of product specification are determined by the customer. Airlines specify engines, flight control systems, avionics, seat and cargo configurations, pilot training, service contracts and other dimensions of the product. Customization of the product package also results in variable unit pricing and financing terms. The intense focus on individual customers in such industries does not permit standardization of product and pricing. However, firms in such industries may be able to employ highly similar promotion and distribution strategies in foreign markets. Personal selling requires extensive knowledge of foreign cultures and commercial practices, but this approach is employed on a global basis by many industrial product companies.

For most industrial products and many consumer goods, the benefits of global marketing standardization may not offset the costs of failure to respond to local market conditions in foreign countries. Attempts to standardize marketing can be counterproductive. The guiding principle of marketing mix management is to find that combination of marketing policies that best fits market conditions. That principle holds in global marketing mix management. The objective of finding the best marketing mix to fit market conditions applies to each foreign market in which the firm operates.

The ability to formulate effective marketing strategies for a range of markets is a key determinant of performance in international business. This process can be structured so as to maximize effectiveness in formulating marketing strategy. The most efficient means of designing marketing strategies for individual markets is not one which grants local autonomy in marketing mix management. Considerable benefits can be gained if central marketing managers can provide an explicit managerial model that structures and supports the formulation of marketing strategy in any given market. This support system provides a conceptual framework and information from a range of sources to be used to help define the best strategy in each new market. The development of a statistical information base can play an especially important role in this process.[3]

INFORMATION AND INTERNATIONAL MARKETING

The information essential to multinational marketing management details consumer response to various marketing mixes under a range of market conditions. Three distinct types of information are needed. The dependent variable, consumer response, is a function of market conditions, which are exogeneous variables, and the firm's marketing mix, a set of controllable variables. Each of these three variables can be broken down into lists of components. The relationship between these variables is the basis for the formulation of multinational marketing strategy.

The analytical starting point for any new market is estimation of consumer response to an established marketing mix. In formulating marketing strategies for foreign markets, management needs to know the effect of changes in market conditions on consumer response given an established marketing mix. The basis for such knowledge, ex ante, comes from experience and information from various markets. The effect of a 10% reduction in per capita income on consumer response can be estimated from experience in existing markets, for example. Regional variations in the home market provide useful inputs in estimating the effect of variation in individual market characteristics. Different parts of the home market exhibit varying market conditions along many of the dimensions listed in Figure 4-1. The effect of variation in these characteristics can be measured, and these observations can be used to generate the equivalent of a partial derivative for each market characteristic. By observing and recording variations in consumer response under a variety of market conditions, management's ability to predict consumer response under any given set of market conditions is enhanced. Regression analysis can then be used to estimate consumer response in any market, given observations for key market characteristics. The ability to estimate potential demand is useful in market selection decisions, but its true value comes in formulating marketing strategy.

Management wants to do more than estimate consumer response to a standardized marketing mix in a variety of markets. The objective is to create the marketing mix that will yield the best consumer response in any given market. Once the marketing mix is treated as variable, the full complexity of the global marketing mix management process can be seen. Effective management of this process requires sophisticated analysis of market information.

Although mastering this complex problem appears to be extremely difficult, this very process has been followed and mastered by a number of consumer product companies. Gillette's market information base in the razor blade business permits it to estimate precisely the effects of any changes in its marketing mix on consumer response in a variety of markets. Expertise of this sort often is not formally structured in sophisticated models, but such a

Market Conditions	Consumer Response	Marketing Mix
Per capita income	Awareness level	Product position
Literacy rate		Brand name
Education level	Trial level	Packaging
TV's per capita	Repeat-purchase level	Design
Radios per capita		Segment
Newsprint consumption per capita	Brand loyalty	Choice
Electric power consumption per capita		Price
		Assumed elasticity
		Premium or discount
		Penetration or skim
Predominant religion		Promotion
Average family size		Message
Life expectancy		Media
Average retail shop size		Distribution
		Sales force
		Trade margin
		Agents
		Outlet choice

Figure 4-1.   Factors in marketing strategy formulation.

conceptual structure frequently emerges from discussions with senior international marketing managers. Frameworks of this sort appear implicit in many multinational marketing decisions. Such expertise comes only with extensive experience. Firms just beginning international operations in a new product line face tremendous uncertainty in this regard. Uncertainty about the effects of variations in market conditions alone poses a major obstacle to international activity. The additional complexity imposed by the need to customize the marketing mix in individual markets can seem insurmountable.

The uncertainty surrounding multinational marketing management can be reduced through a systematic, efficient approach to developing a market information base. Data on characteristics of principal markets can be identified, measured and stored. Consumer response results can be gathered from all existing markets. Market research and testing results also feed into the information base.

Several different types of observations will be accumulated in the marketing information base. One type of observation details the effects of holding the marketing mix constant under a variety of market conditions. Such observations permit measurement of the effects of variance in market characteristics on consumer response. A second observation describes the effects of varying the marketing mix under constant market conditions. Results derived from these observations permit measurement of the effects of changes in marketing mix elements. The third type of observation details the results when both market conditions and the marketing mix vary simultaneously. Observations from such an approach contribute highly useful results to the central information pool, but may prove expensive to realize and difficult to analyze. Information of all three types will be accumulated and utilized in creating the information base used in marketing mix management. In any single company, however, it is likely that one of these three types of observations will provide the principal source of information. The predominant type will largely reflect the available means and cost of gathering information.

The cost of gathering market information depends primarily on market research capabilities. An effective market research capability permits the gathering of extensive information in a short period of time. If the firm possesses international market research capabilities or access to them, extensive information can be gathered prior to the commencement of foreign operations. Unfortunately, the role of market research in international marketing is in a relatively undeveloped state. Market research capabilities may not be readily available to many firms, particularly those that have the greatest need for such services. Market information for many firms accrues primarily as a result of operations. This fact will severely limit marketing options. If operations provide the principal source of market information, it is likely that many firms will pursue an incremental approach to international activities, emphasizing markets similar to home conditions in market selection decisions. Consumer response in similar countries to an established marketing mix will closely approximate the response in the home market. The great uncertainty surrounding the issue of determining the best marketing mix for a foreign market is minimized by such an approach. As noted in Chapter 3, U.S. firms exhibit a strong preference for similar markets in expanding a product line abroad. Canada, the United Kingdom and Australia receive very high priority as initial areas for foreign marketing activity.

Operations in similar markets provide additional information to marketing managers. Results in such markets provide measures of the effects of marginal differences in market characteristics. As the marketing mix is fine-tuned in these markets, the effects of marginal changes in product, pricing, promotion and distribution policies can also be assessed and used as input for marketing decisions in new markets. The incremental investment approach minimizes the possibility of an unexpected consumer response in any market. This approach is most appropriate for innovative new products, but it appears to have several disadvantages for established products. Extensive time will be required to develop a comprehensive market information base with this approach. The narrow set of observations will not be as broadly applicable as a wider range of data accumulated through other approaches. If the firm pursues a highly conservative, incremental expansion strategy, prime markets may be foregone and lost to competitors. It is crucial, especially for established consumer products, that additional sources of information be developed.

Operations need not be the sole source of market information. In addition to market research sources, the marketing strategies and experience of other firms in foreign markets can provide important inputs in developing marketing strategy. In the end, the more observations of the relationship between market characteristics, marketing policies and consumer response that are made, the more effective the firm is in determining its own marketing strategy. Effective information gathering permits answers to all the questions relevant to global marketing management. What happens if we cut prices by 10% in Argentina, in Canada, in West Germany? What happens if literacy rises by 10% in Indonesia, Turkey, or Mexico, and we make no changes in marketing policy? What happens if radio ownership in Brazil rises by 10%, and we increase radio advertising by 10%? An extensive information base and organized analytical structure provide the answers to these questions and a basis for effective global marketing mix management.

Cluster Analysis

An important assumption implicit in the preceding approach is that the same model of consumer behavior can be utilized in all foreign markets. This assumption clearly conflicts with many of the findings of cross-cultural research.[4] Consumers can respond to a product in very different ways.

Motorcycles represent primary modes of transportation in third-world countries and recreation vehicles in the United States and Europe. Beyond differences in perception of a product's use and purpose, consumer response to product attributes, promotional images, and distribution vehicles can vary substantially. The assumption that observed relationsips between marketing mix variables and consumer response are universally consistent is not likely to withstand actual experience for most products.

This assumption will not be prohibitive within certain sets of markets, however. Separate response models can be developed for carefully defined clusters of markets in which similar behavior patterns can be expected. The process of clustering markets into identifiable groups has been well developed. A 1967 study introduced the concept and rationale for clustering markets and provided a methodology for grouping markets.[5] Later studies have refined the methodology of clustering analysis[6] and expanded on the importance of this technique in international marketing.[7] The methodology for grouping countries can be drawn from any standard statistical package.[8] The objective is simply to separate countries into relatively proximate or homogeneous groups based on numeric or categorical observations for key market characteristics. The objective is not to explain differences in consumer response, but to identify groups of markets in which consumers are likely to respond to marketing policies in a homogeneous manner. Identification of such groups gives managers insight into the expected nature of consumer behavior in any market. Different consumer response characteristics will be reflected in the models for each group of markets. The partial derivative for radio advertising, for example, might be .06 in Group A markets and .15 in Group B countries. These estimates are useful in determining the core marketing mix for each cluster of countries.

After a core marketing mix has been developed for each cluster of countries, it can be used as the starting point in formulating more refined marketing strategies. Countries within the same cluster will vary sharply in social, economic and other characteristics. Further refinement will be necessary to match market conditions precisely.

If marketing strategy ultimately is to be customized for each market, what is the value of cluster analysis or consumer response analysis? Cluster analysis provides a starting point for the formulation of marketing strategy for any new market. It also generates economies of scale from standardization within market subsets. An international marketing strategy based on cluster analysis represents a compromise between pursuit of a standardized global marketing strategy and complete customization within individual markets.

However, market information can be accumulated and analyzed to support all three strategies. The only difference is that only one set of relationships between consumer response, marketing policies and market conditions is assumed in the standardized strategy. In a customized strategy, each country is assumed to exhibit a unique consumer behavior pattern. The use of cluster analysis assumes similar consumer behavior patterns will be exhibited in identifiable groups of markets. Regardless of the approach taken, however, the effectiveness of an international marketing strategy depends largely on the accumulation and use of market information.

Global marketing mix management is unlikely to be reduced to an exact science. The approach presented here represents a useful conceptual structure, but implementation of such a system may be unrealistic. Nevertheless, a systematic approach to marketing mix management will result in far greater effectiveness and efficiency than the principal alternatives. Decentralized customization of marketing policies will be less effective than an approach that both uses existing market information and contributes to a growing intelligence base. All sources of market information should be used both in creating marketing policies for new markets and in refining existing marketing activities.

The most basic approach in developing marketing strategies for foreign markets is to use the strategies employed in a company's existing markets as a starting point. The relative emphasis on each element of the marketing mix in the most comparable markets is taken as the initial mix for any new market. Specific product, pricing, promotion and distribution policies used in these markets are employed as the initial marketing strategy in the new market. Changes in relative emphasis on any element, and in the specifics of any policy, will be justified in terms of market characteristics and response. The process of adjusting emphasis on any element and refining or altering details of individual policies to best meet conditions in each market is the key function in global marketing mix management. Given a conceptual structure such as this as a starting point, the elements of the marketing mix can be examined individually, with emphasis on international considerations in each area.

PRODUCT DECISIONS

Determination of a product's position in the marketplace is the most basic decision in marketing strategy. The same framework applies to product decisions in foreign markets as at home, but many of the key factors influencing this decision will vary from country to country. In the personal and home care industries, for example, product design and formulation vary sharply by country. One example is the use of aerosol versus liquid or stick formulations for products such as shaving cream, personal and room deodorants, floor, furniture and car wax, insecticides and basic grooming aids. Product formulation is largely a function of consumer tastes as reflected in established practice and disposable income. In general, however, aerosol formulations have been considered premium products in most markets. Emphasis on aerosol formulations generally has been associated with markets exhibiting relatively high and growing disposable income. In markets with lower income, liquid or stick formulations could be used as initial product offerings, with aerosol formulations expected to penetrate the market at a later date.

The fit between market and product in such cases can be presented along a continuous line. Cheaper and less sophisticated offerings in a product category are emphasized in less sophisticated markets, while more expensive and sophisticated versions are emphasized in more developed markets. However, in analyzing foreign markets, a company may find that the competition already firmly controls the market for the traditional liquid or stick formulations. In such cases, the firm may choose to enter the market with an aerosol product even though analysis of consumer characteristics and market conditions suggest that a liquid formulation would best fit prevailing conditions.

The selection of product strategy depends on these key variables: segment analysis, assessment of competition and evaluation of strategic fit. The first step in segment analysis is identification of all key product segments. In addition to the type of user, the product may be characterized in terms of its size, color, flavor, formulation, range of function, type of input required, type of output produced, base technology used, useful life and, of course, price. Each of these product characteristics represents a dimension along which potential market segments can be identified. Some of these dimensions will be more important than others in determining consumer behavior. The first step in evaluating these segments is to assess how important variance in each characteristic is to consumers. This permits identification of key product dimensions. Key product dimensions are those that appear to correlate with significant variance in consumer response. Identification of these key product dimensions requires more than an analysis of existing products in the marketplace. Market research and test

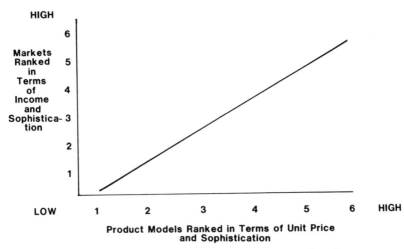

Figure 4-2.   Product line strategy in international markets.

marketing will be required to evaluate the effect of variance in certain product dimensions. Effective analysis of product segment potential rests on examining the response not only of existing consumers to each product dimension, but also of potential consumers who do not yet participate in the market. The objective of this analysis is to identify those dimensions that consumers think are important in order to position the product in the segments that will grow most rapidly. In such an investigation, the following product dimensions should be considered:

Size
Color
Flavor
Formulation
Range of function
Service requirements
Quality of performance
Type of input required
Type of output produced
Technology
Useful life
Configuration
Price
Compatibility

One of the most striking examples of effective market research in assessing the potential of a new market segment occurred in the motorcycle industry. American and continental motorcycle manufacturers had failed in several experiments to introduce small motorcycles.[9] Demand among existing motorcycle users was particularly focused on larger motorcycles, with key product dimensions being identified as quality of handling, acceleration and styling. The Japanese producers, however, identified an entire new consumer base that wanted small, reliable and inexpensive transportation, as well as recreation. Identification of this segment led to a complete revolution in the motorcycle industry.

Assessment of growth rates in individual segments follows identification of key product dimensions. Growth rates for aerosol versus stick deodorants, small versus large motorcycles, black-and-white versus color television, two-stroke versus four-stroke engines, and so on can then be estimated. These market growth rates provide one of the key inputs in determining product strategy. Assuming for the moment that the costs of entering given segments are roughly similar, product strategies in any market will be determined by the size and growth prospects for different segments, the competition in each segment and the firm's relative competence in the segment.

Product positioning can be presented as an exercise in selecting those segments with the best size and growth potential with the least competition and the best opportunity to effectively employ corporate resources and strategies. In the motorcycle industry, an analysis of market trends and competition in the European market can be presented graphically. As Table 4-1 indicates, the greatest growth is expected in the large motorcycle segment. At the same time, aggressive Japanese competitors dominate the market for smaller bikes. Product positioning decisions in such a situation generally would emphasize the larger size segments. Any firm entering the European motorcycle market would be likely to experience greater immediate growth and less immediate competition in this segment. This approach assumes that the firm's abilities are roughly equal in all segments. This consideration will also play a key role in product positioning.[10]

PRICING DECISIONS

Competition also has an impact on other elements of the marketing mix. Pricing policies in global marketing, in particular, are influenced by

TABLE 4-1.   EEC Motorcycle Markets (1975)

Size	Market Shares of Leading Competitors						EEC Total (Units)	Growth Rate (1974–1980)
	France		Germany		United Kingdom			
Small (<450cc)	Honda	37 %	Honda	39 %	Honda	54 %	307	6.4%
	Yamaha	19	Yamaha	20	Yamaha	19		
	Suzuki	13			Suzuki	13		
Medium (450–750cc)	BMW	32	BMW	55	BMW	12	58	14.4
	Honda	28	Honda	22	NV Triumph	48		
and large (750cc)	Kawasaki	14	Kawasaki	10	Suzuki	14	16	18.8
					Kawasaki	8		
TOTAL							381	8.5

*Source: A note on the World Motorcycle Industry, ICCH No. 9-578-210, Harvard Business School.

competitive conditions. The absence of competition permits a skimming price strategy. This approach is best documented for new products such as ball-point pens, calculators and digital watches. Prices for such products tend to fall over time as volume and competition increase. Initial high prices permit the firm to capture what is called the "consumer surplus" in economic theory.[11] By pricing the product initially at P_3 as in Figure 4-3, revenue equal to the shaded area in the graph is foregone. If an initial price of P_1 is set and gradually lowered to P_3, additional revenue and profit will be realized. This type of discriminatory pricing holds special significance in international marketing.

In the absence of competition, profits will be maximized by entering each new market with high initial prices. Prices would then gradually be reduced to equilibrium levels using a skimming approach to pricing. Utilization of such a strategy in a variety of markets raises several issues. Discriminatory pricing means that prices for the product clearly will vary from market to market depending on the stage of market development. International price variances can result in inquiries from government officials concerned with antitrust issues. Official inquiries into Hoffman-LaRoche's pricing for Valium and Librium resulted from information showing that prices for these products varied up to 400% from market to market.

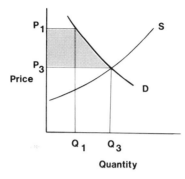

Figure 4-3. A discriminatory pricing strategy.

Pricing and the Public Authorities

Public authorities also play a role in pricing decisions. Hoffman-LaRoche, producers of Valium and Librium tranquilizers, followed a pricing policy for these products that led to sharp price differences across countries. In the United States, for example, Valium was priced at four times the price level in France. These pricing differentials were partially responsible for a series of overpricing cases in Great Britain, Holland, Germany and elsewhere. This litigation led to a £3.75 billion fine for overpricing in Great Britain in 1975. Shortly after the British finding, the Supreme Court of Ontario found the company guilty of predatory pricing on Valium.*

Variance in prices from country to country can also result in forms of arbitrage that undercut discriminatory pricing strategies. In some cases, a company's distributors in one market will opt to deliver products to customers in another market. Such activities can generally be controlled through active management of the distribution channel, but price differentials provide the motivation for a range of agents to perform highly profitable arbitrage activities. Arbitrage normally appears as a response to artificial price differentials created by governments. The same activity will appear in response to differential pricing policies pursued by businessmen.

The absence of competition is necessary to permit the use of a discriminatory pricing strategy. Such a strategy is clearly inappropriate in the face of competition. In facing competition, the basic pricing decision concerns the use of penetration, premium or passive pricing strategies.

A passive pricing strategy entails matching competitor's prices. Rather

---

Source: F. Hoffman-LaRoche and Co. A.G. ICCH 9-378-201, Harvard Business School, *The Economist*, February 16, 1980, p. 88.

than competing on the basis of price, this variable can be set to match the competition, and other elements of the marketing mix can be used to provide a competitive edge. Such a pricing strategy will be applicable if product quality, promotional skills or distribution strengths appear to offer the advantage needed to compete successfully in the market. Strengths in these areas could also contribute to a premium pricing strategy. If product quality is perceived to be high, or promotion and distribution strengths exceed those of competitors, a premium price can be justified. The success of a premium pricing strategy rests on a low price elasticity of demand. High price elasticity suggests that premium pricing will be inappropriate. In addition, premium pricing is rarely successful without some other means of product differentiation, and this consideration is important in developing such a strategy.

Penetration pricing strategies represent one of the most aggressive and risky options in marketing mix management. Such strategies are most effective in established markets exhibiting a high degree of price elasticity. Competitive response to such a strategy is just as important as market response, however. Penetration pricing follows a sequence almost the inverse of that employed in a discriminatory pricing strategy. Initial prices are set below the equilibrium level in order to maximize unit volume. By pricing below existing levels, the total size of the market is increased depending on price elasticity, and the firm acquires a significant share of the market. A classic example of a penetration pricing strategy occurred in the U.S. color television market.

Entering the U.S. market in 1967, Japanese color television manufacturers priced their product between $50 and $100 less per comparable unit than U.S. producers.[12] This pricing strategy helped Japanese producers achieve a rising share of this growing market. Japanese market share rose to over 40% by 1975. The effect of this strategy on the overall market was quite significant. Unit color television prices rose an average of only 3% between the Japanese entry in 1967 and 1978.[13] Volume levels, which appeared to be flattening out according to a classic product life cycle curve in 1967, abruptly rose again following the Japanese entry. A rising share of the reinvigorated market was captured by Japanese producers.

Penetration pricing strategies are frequently used by Japanese companies because of the powerful fit of this approach with other elements of their overall business strategy. Japanese firms in many industries exhibit extremely high operating and financial leverage. Automation and capital

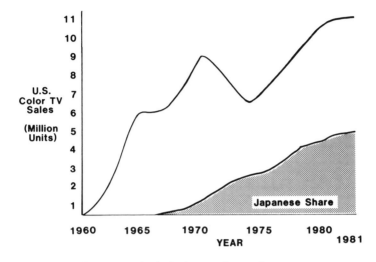

Source: Author's Estimates from primary sources.

Figure 4-4.   The U.S. color TV market and Japanese market share.

intensity in industries such as steel, motorcycle, automobile, and consumer electronics provide significant economies of scale, which are realized as unit volume increases. High financial leverage also provides incentives for increasing the volume of operations. Because of such production and financial strategies, unit costs decline sharply as volume increases. The best means of realizing high-volume levels and thus maximizing profits and competitive strength is through a penetration pricing strategy.

Old Masters

Penetration pricing is widely associated with recent successful strategies by Japanese companies in the automobile, consumer electronics and steel industries. The roots of this strategy are American, however. Henry Ford was perhaps the master at its use. He first developed automated, high-volume production facilities that turned out a standardized product of consistent quality—the Model T. The car was sold for $850 in 1906, when the average car sold for over $2,000. Ford sold 6,400 cars in 1907. By 1910, the price of the Model T had been reduced to $690 and volume was up to 34,500 units. In 1915, the car sold for $360, and 472,000 units were sold. Ford's market share rose from 15% in 1907 to 54% in 1913.

Ford used the same strategy in entering the tractor industry in 1917. The Fordson tractor was introduced at a price of $750. International Harvester's cheapest model sold for over $900 at the time. Ford quickly captured 35% of the market by 1920.

Then in January 1921, David Lewis reports, "the company reduced the price of the Fordson to $625, a figure below the cost of producing it, in an effort to expand output, lower per unit costs and earn long-term profitability." In February 1922, Fordson prices were cut further to $395. General Motors, which had followed Ford in entering the tractor market, dropped out in October with a $33 million loss. By the end of 1923, Ford unit sales had trippled the 1921 level and accounted for over 50% of the total market. Although Ford later lost its dominant positions in both the tractor and automobile industries to full line producers, Ford revolutionized both industries by realizing the potential of mass production and marketing. Henry Ford has been quoted as saying that "price cuts were by far the most important (factor) in merchandising the Model T."

The distinction between penetration and predatory pricing is subtle but significant. Predatory pricing generally involves discrete, short-term price cuts intended to financially weaken the competition rather than expand the market. After the price cuts produce their effect, competitors are acquired or eliminated, and prices are raised to monopoly levels. Such strategies were common in the age of the robber barons in the United States.

Pricing played a dominant role in the Ford and robber baron strategies. Although such strategies are now used with limited frequency in the United States, they remain very important in international business.*

Penetration pricing offers significant benefits in industries that yield significant unit cost reductions as volume increases. Realization of these cost reductions varies according to the type of technology employed by the firm, and the potential for unit cost reduction varies sharply by industry. In Figure 4-5, Industry 1 offers significant potential for a penetration pricing strategy. Attainment of higher volume levels provides a significant unit cost and profit advantage. In Industry 2, however, volume levels have very little effect on unit costs. Such industries are characterized by high variable costs and low capital intensity.

Penetration pricing strategies are most effective in industries with stable technology, established markets, high price elasticity and a rapidly declining unit cost structure. In the absence of these characteristics, such a strategy is less attractive. The elevator industry provides an example of an industry which does not exhibit these characteristics. An inability to fully standardize product lines because of national building codes and standards, a high

---

*Sources: Lewis, David L., The Public Image of Henry Ford (Detroit: Wayne State University Press, 1976), pp. 180−81; Epstein, Ralph C., The Automobile Industry (New York: Shaw and Company, 1928), Appendix A.

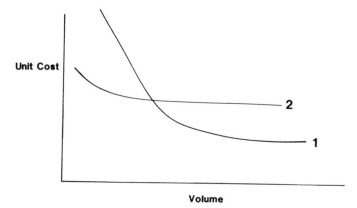

Figure 4-5.   Unit cost and volume relationship for standard process technology, minimum efficient scale facility in two industries.

variable cost structure (installation) and relatively inelastic demand for elevators reduce the effectiveness of attempts to dominate the market through such a strategy.[14] Even if the industry appears suited to penetration pricing, however, such a strategy invites potentially destructive responses from competitors. Competitors can force an aggressive firm to retreat from a penetration pricing strategy by matching prices and thus limiting revenue increases through volume gains. Bic's attempt to enter the razor blade market with such a strategy induced a preemptive price reduction move by Gillette.[15] As a result, both company's profit margins in this market were cut sharply. Penetration pricing invites such a response and can lead to a mutually destructive price war.

Competitors can respond to penetration pricing in four distinct basic patterns. First, they can match the price cuts. Second, they can cut prices below the new level. They can also maintain prices at prior levels, or they can attempt to segment the market into two distinct markets based on price. Nonprice responses can also be classified into four analogous categories. These categories reflect a matching approach, an aggressive response, a passive response and a concessionary response. In the parlance of the poker table, these are see, raise, hold and fold responses.

Many examples of each of these strategies exist. U.S. automobile producers followed the latter strategy in the face of rising imports in the

1950s. U.S. manufacturers effectively vacated the low end of the market and concentrated on the medium and high segments. One example of this can be seen by comparing the dimensions of a 1960 Chevrolet with a 1970 Chevrolet.[16] The size of General Motors' basic model increased in many dimensions by 25% or more over this period. The process of displacement in the face of competition is a phenomenon commonly found in population biology. When two rival species compete for the same niche, it is common to find what is referred to as "character displacement."[17] This process involves emphasis and magnification of the unique features of each competitor to minimize direct confrontation. In the auto industry that process can be documented in the 1960s. The U.S. auto producers opted to emphasize larger luxury cars in the face of direct competition in the low end of the market. This approach can be strongly justified for several reasons. First, it was the same approach that defeated Henry Ford in the first confrontation between these two strategies in the automobile market. Second, margins for small cars were only one-fourth the average unit margin for medium and high priced cars. If the American producers had successfully developed small cars, their profits would have eroded severely. Third, the small car segment did not appear particularly attractive in the pre-OPEC era. Subsequent developments have led to direct confrontations in a rising number of segments because of shifts in the marketplace and the natural tendency of the foreign producers to expand from the bottom segments of the industry to adjacent segments.

Penetration pricing will work admirably if the competition responds in such a fashion. This type of response effectively concedes a share of the market to firms pursuing a penetration strategy. Such responses have occurred in a surprisingly wide range of industries, including watches, writing instruments, motorcycles, and many areas of the consumer electronics industry. In many other industries, however, competitors have responded quite differently to penetration pricing. Assessment of potential competitor response to a penetration pricing strategy, or any other marketing initiative, is an important element in formulating marketing strategy. In highly diffused markets, this issue is less significant, but in most cases, one or more major competitors that can be expected to respond directly to any market initiative can be identified. The probable response can be assessed by examining historical events in the market. In most cases a meaningful history of competitive interactions can be developed and used to predict response. This information can then be used in a game-theory framework to structure potential competitive developments.[18] The simple two-party framework in Figure 4-6 provides an example of how such a structure can be used.

If Firm 1 cuts prices, what are the probabilities for each of the four possible competitive responses from Firm 2? Analysis of a rival's past competitive behavior provides insight into his probable response to any market initiative. This type of analysis generates information about competitor's priorities, objectives, sensitivities and time frame. The resulting profile can be used to support a plan of action, but projected responses to a market initiative cannot always be viewed with a high degree of certainty. A complete strategy includes contingency plans for all possible responses. These plans stipulate the best counter-response to any foreseeable reaction by competitors.

Each combination of actions generates a unique outcome for the two or more parties involved in the market. Assessment of the relative attractiveness of the outcome associated with each sequence underlies the formulation of competitive marketing strategy. The attractiveness of any combination of move and response depends on the firm's own resources, objectives and time frame. Firms with greater staying power and a long time horizon could prefer to see a rival match or even undercut an initial price reduction. In general, however, the preferred response to any price initiative would be a

Firm 2

		Cut	Match	Stay	Displace
	Cut				
	Match				
Firm 1	Stay				
	Displace				

Figure 4-6.   A game theory structure for competitive response.

displacement from the low end of the market by rivals. If this is viewed as a distinct possibility, displacement can be encouraged by the scale and scope of the market initiative.

If any initiative results in a displacement response, the initiating firm can choose to stay at its current price level. This outcome permits each firm to pursue a stable strategy, and a competitive equilibrium can be realized.[19] If a confronting response ensues, either firm can implement a second round of pricing moves. Such moves and countermoves, escalations and de-escalations, can continue indefinitely. Current confrontations between Bic and Gillette and Kodak and Polaroid reveal the complexity and duration of such competitive dynamics. The process of formulating a strategy in such dynamic competitive environments was first described by Chamberlain over 50 years ago.[20] This basic conceptual structure has been continuously refined since that time, and more detailed discussions of it can be found in a number of specific sources.[21] The important point in this context is the recognition that such a conceptual structure can play a vital role in developing and implementing marketing strategy. The model permits formal analysis of the competitive dynamics associated with any marketing initiative. It provides a framework that can be utilized in a wide range of markets to direct marketing strategy.

This basic structure applies as fully to initiatives in any other area of the marketing mix as it does to pricing initiatives. Pricing initiatives are particularly important in international business, however. Penetration pricing often fits nicely with the overall objective of building a dominant global position in an established market. The virtuous cycle of rising volume and falling unit costs starts with penetration pricing. Such benefits are particularly important in maturing industries. Cost leadership provides an increasingly important advantage as industries mature. The well-known experience curve effect dictates that cost leadership accrues to high-volume producers.[22] Volume can best be obtained by pursuing global markets with a strategy emphasizing penetration pricing.

Penetration pricing is particularly effective in industries dominated by nonglobal competitors. Globally oriented firms can use revenues from other markets to support a price initiative against targeted local competitors in selected markets. Such a strategy can be effective even in the absence of a strong volume/cost relationship. Penetration pricing will be most effective, however, in industries that exhibit several characteristics. The stage of industry maturation is a key issue. Industry maturation involves a number of processes. Abernathy and Utterback describe an increasing emphasis on cost reduction through refinement of the manufacturing process as industries mature.[23] This emphasis on cost reduction occurs primarily after product design becomes standardized and product technology stable. Mature industries provide a relatively stable environment for the large capital investments associated with a strategy built around the objective of attaining cost leadership. Mature industries exhibiting high price elasticity are ideally suited for a global strategy that emphasizes penetration pricing. Other industry characteristics that favor penetration pricing strategies are:

High unit volume
High price elasticity
Product standardization
Technological stability
Competitive fragmentation
Continuous process technology
Capital intensity

Pricing issues often dominate marketing mix management in industries exhibiting these characteristics. Product, promotion and distribution policies may play secondary roles in the marketing mix for such products. These other elements of marketing strategy tend to decline in importance, and price becomes the primary determinant of competitive performance as products mature.[24] This process can be arrested, however, through marketing strategies that emphasize product differentiation.

In the absence of effective product differentiation, performance will increasingly rest on the ability to deliver a standardized product at least cost. The most successful means of limiting this tendency involves continued technological change. Vernon describes how strategies emphasizing research and development forestall this process.[25] Other strategies can also limit severe price competition. The automobile industry invests billions of dollars each year in model changes to differentiate products in terms of style and option packages. Continual change in product design can limit or reverse the tendency toward strict price competition. As long as other differences are perceived between competing products, price differentials will not entirely determine consumption patterns.

A strategy of continuous change in product design works only as long as consumers are willing to pay for new or special features. In many cases, consumers will react negatively to changes in product design. Many consumers will resist changes in personal care, food and household products, for example. Successful product offerings are difficult enough to come by; changing them without thorough research is a risky and expensive proposition. Many of the most successful consumer goods, such as Crest toothpaste or Coca-Cola have changed very little over a long period of time. In such cases, the principal means of differentiating a product from other offerings involves the creation of a brand franchise. Such a strategy focuses less on changes in style or design and more on establishing a public image of quality and consistency. Success with such a strategy ultimately rests on the ability to deliver a product consistent with expectations, but the art of molding public opinion plays a key role in such strategies. Effective brand names are capable of leading consumers to prefer one product over otherwise similar products. Studies have shown, for example, that consumers cannot distinguish between brands of beer in blind taste tests.[26] Yet brand loyalty is quite high among beer consumers. Brand differentiation of this type can only be achieved through effective promotion.

PROMOTION DECISIONS

The first step in developing a promotion policy is assessment of the relative role of promotion in the marketing mix. Promotion issues dominate marketing strategy for many products. Promotion plays the key role in marketing strategies for many nondurable consumer goods such as tobacco, soft drink and liquor products. It also dominates the marketing mix for a wide range of personal care, household and processed food products. Success in these industries depends largely on effective promotion.

The prevailing level of promotion in the market provides an important input in determining promotion levels for a product. Aggregate advertising and promotion expenditures as a percentage of industry sales measure the relative importance of promotion in competitors' marketing strategies. This measure serves as an initial reference point in determining promotion policy. Decisions to match, exceed or undercut average promotion levels depend on a number of factors. The economics of promotion tend to favor firms with a large market share. The total cost of reaching the consumer population will be the same for all competitors, but the unit cost will be

TABLE 4-2. Industry Advertising Expenditures as a Percentage of Sales (United States, 1978)

Industry	Advertising Percentage
Meat products	1.2
Dairy products	1.7
Canned fruits and vegetables	2.3
Bakery products	1.6
Beverages	5.1
Cigarettes	6.2
Cigars	2.3
Clothing	1.7
Household furniture	1.7
Office furniture	0.9
Periodicals	3.9
Books	4.2
Drugs	6.4
Soap and cosmetics	10.4
Paints	1.8
Flat glass	0.8
Cement	0.1
Farm equipment	1.1
Construction equipment	0.8
Household appliances	3.9
Radio and TV	3.8
Motor vehicles	1.6
Jewelry	5.6
Toys	5.2
Retail stores	2.4
Insurance	1.0
Hotels and motels	2.5
Motion pictures	7.6
Engineering services	0.4

Source: Schonfeld and Associates Inc., cited in Advertising Age, July 23, 1979, p. 40.

lower for firms with greater sales volume.[27] Consequently, a small firm will have to spend more as a percentage of sales to match the promotion level of larger competitors. As a result of this relationship, large firms will prefer to compete on the basis of promotion activity and spend accordingly. On the other hand, a small firm could limit its promotion budget and attempt to exploit the primary demand created by larger competitors. It might choose to divert resources from promotion to product refinements, lower prices or trade margins. The success of such strategies depends to a large extent on consumer brand loyalty levels. If brand loyalty is high, consumers will be reluctant to experiment with unfamiliar product offerings. Such strategies will be more effective for goods with low brand loyalty and high price sensitivity, such as paper products. Where consumer uncertainty about product efficacy, quality or performance is high, however, reductions in promotion budgets could have a severely negative impact on market volume. Such uncertainty is a key factor in purchases of many products such as health care items, grooming aids and gasoline additives where product performance is difficult to measure. Consumer uncertainty is also high for major purchases because of the amount of money involved. Promotion for such products plays a key role in reducing consumer uncertainty and reinforcing purchasing decisions.[28] Similarly, promotion for industrial products is intended to prime customers for sales force visits and minimize the problem of establishing initial credibility.[29]

Continuous measurement of promotion effectiveness is essential in managing this element of the marketing mix. The effectiveness of various promotion strategies can be measured in discrete market tests. Response to varying promotion levels and programs in test markets can be used to generate estimates of the optimal level and thrust of promotion expenditure. Market testing also generates useful information about competitors' response to promotion initiatives. Market research of this sort is particularly important in industries exhibiting high levels of promotion activity. Management of such products requires deliberate and careful analysis of the role of promotion in marketing strategy.

Many global businesses have been built primarily on promotional activity. Coca-Cola, Johnny Walker and Rolex are brand names recognized around the world. These products are examples of the many successful global strategies based on brand promotion. However, global strategies emphasizing promotion will encounter major constraints and problems. Promotion requires perhaps the most customization of any element in the marketing mix. Even when its relative role can be made consistent across markets, the nature of promotion activity in each market will vary significantly.

Promotion Levels in Global Markets

The initial determination of promotional levels normally occurs in the home market. It may be unrealistic, however, to place an equal emphasis on promotion in all markets. Promotion levels vary significantly over different stages of market development.[30] For example, the process of building initial product and brand awareness requires higher promotion levels in the early stages of market development. Since different international markets will be in different stages of development at any point in time, promotion levels and programs will have to be tailored to specific market conditions. In addition, cost and availability constraints can limit a firm's ability to standardize promotion activities across markets. The effectiveness of a pull strategy depends to a large extent on media availability, cost and coverage. Variances in these factors influence the effectiveness of promotion in individual markets and suggest that promotion levels as well as programs need to be determined on a market-by-market basis.

Media availability varies sharply from country to country. Commercial television spots are not available in Norway, Sweden and Denmark, for example. British public television slots are sold through a sealed-bid auction process so that costs and advertising schedules are highly uncertain. Television broadcasting is controlled by the state in Italy and many nations in the third world. In such situations, advertising slots have to be reserved many months in advance and air-time is allocated primarily according to past utilization levels. Public ownership of television as well as other media is the rule in much of the world. Public ownership often imposes a number of constraints and uncertainties on advertising. These constraints affect the time schedules, coverage, content, frequency and costs of promotion campaigns. Such constraints can limit the role of promotion in marketing strategy.

Media cost and coverage also vary sharply across markets. Unit promotion costs are a function of media billing rates, audiences and yields. The cost per viewer or reader can be readily calculated and compared for most media alternatives in any market. The yield, or consumer response, for any media can vary significantly across markets, however. The percentage of television viewers representing prospective consumers of any product will differ in many markets. Mass marketing techniques employed in OECD countries will be less effective in third-world countries where potential consumers form only a small part of the population. The yield of mass promotion activities in such markets will be quite low, resulting in high unit promotion costs. Several options exist for markets exhibiting high unit promotion costs.

High unit promotion costs may dictate a diversion of marketing resources from promotion to pricing or distribution initiatives. These options could prove to be more cost-effective means of stimulating demand. For many products, however, promotion will remain the key competitive variable in the marketplace despite relatively high unit promotion costs. If success in the market ultimately rests on effective promotion, the question of cost-effectiveness becomes relevant primarily in relation to the competition's activities. All competitors in any market generally experience the same base costs for promotion, and effectiveness will depend on media selection and response to message content.

Media Selection

Mass media reach different segments of the population in different countries. Television ownership is almost universal in American homes, but under 30% of all the homes in Mexico have television. Literacy rates and newsprint consumption also indicate differences in the coverage of printed media. Media usage patterns also differ significantly by country. Television accounts for 30.1% of all advertising expenditures in the United States, but only 1.5% in India. Printed media account for 83.4% of all advertising in the Netherlands, but they play a minor role in Mexico. Such differences also appear for individual products across countries. Television is the dominant media for camera and jewelry advertising in the United States, accounting for 82% of total expenditures. In contrast, print media receive the bulk of promotion activities for these products in Australia. Comparison for a number of industries in the United States, Japan and Australia do suggest, however, that media usage patterns are highly similar in industrial countries. Recent research also suggests that similar media can be used to reach similar consumer groups in different markets. Urban found that women with college educations and higher incomes in both France and the United States watch less television and read more newspapers and magazines than women with less education and lower incomes.[30] Other media usage similarities for similar socioeconomic groups in different countries have been reported.[32] These similarities suggest that some standardization of media selection can be employed in global product strategies.

Prevailing media coverage and usage patterns play a key role in media selection decisions. The basic formula for effective promotion simply divides the total cost of promotion by the consumer response measured in unit purchases.

$$\text{unit promotion cost} = \frac{\text{media billing rate} \times \text{frequency}}{\text{audience} \times \text{yield}}$$

TABLE 4-3. 1977 Relative Media Usage ($ million)

Country	Total	% of Total Print	% of Total TV	% of Total Radio	$ US Per Capita
Argentina	382.2	47.5	31.6	13.4	14.67
Australia	1,186.4	50.1	28.6	9.3	84.32
Belgium	295.4	73.3	7.4*	0.3	30.05
Brazil	1,610.9	30.0	43.3	21.0	14.35
Canada	1,699.8	55.0	20.8	14.9	73.02
Columbia	167.8	21.7	54.2	17.3	6.70
Denmark	444.6	96.7	n.a.†	n.a.	87.35
Egypt	36.7	54.8	24.3	3.0	0.95
Finland	380.7	84.1	11.6	n.a.	80.32
France	1,720.0	56.5	16.3	10.8	32.40
Greece	71.9	48.4	43.5	6.3	7.76
India	143.8	61.6	1.5	6.4	0.23
Indonesia	63.3	56.1	12.5	7.3	0.45
Israel	81.3	76.4	n.a.	9.8	22.52
Italy	648.7	63.1	17.3	8.8	11.49
Japan	4,779.0	47.2	46.4	6.4	41.97
Kenya	10.7	57.0	1.9	18.7	0.75
Malaysia	45.6	67.8	17.1	5.3	3.63
Mexico	298.3	12.5	67.7	15.6	4.62
Netherlands	1,031.0	83.4	7.2	1.0	74.44
New Zealand	176.8	60.9	25.5	12.3	56.85
Nigeria	42.3	49.4	10.4	23.9	0.60
Norway	376.3	96.8	n.a.	n.a.	93.14
Pakistan	16.9	28.4	41.4	10.7	0.23
Philippines	81.4	42.4	27.5	20.3	1.81
Singapore	53.7	74.5	17.9	2.6	23.25
South Africa	307.1	76.1	2.2	13.7	11.40
South Korea	189.0	40.4	39.7	17.0	5.19
Spain	551.3	51.4	28.6	9.7	15.17
Surinam	1.9	36.8	21.1	42.1	5.18
Sweden	532.8	92.8	n.a.	n.a.	64.58
Switzerland	550.4	85.2	8.9	n.a.	86.95
Taiwan	118.4	38.3	44.3	8.7	7.18
Thailand	99.2	25.7	42.3	12.6	2.25
Trinidad & Tobago	12.7	36.2	39.4	20.5	11.34
Turkey	107.0	38.3	33.6	4.7	2.54
United Kingdom	2,568.9	66.5	27.3	1.8	46.00
United States	25,269.0	57.8	30.1	10.4	116.51
Venezuela	280.2	38.8	33.1	17.4	21.99
West Germany	3,148.9	78.9	12.3	3.5	51.29

Source: World Advertising Expenditures, Starch Inra Hooper, 1979.
*Includes TeleLuxembourg.
†Television and radio advertising commercials are not permitted in these countries.

Any media option that results in a reduction in billing rates or frequency, or increases in audience or yield, with everything else equal, offers a superior vehicle for promotion activity. Estimation of unit costs for various options requires sophisticated analysis of consumer and market data, but estimates for other products can often be used as references in this regard. Test marketing again serves a critical purpose in evaluating the effectiveness of various media options.

A key question in many media selection decisions is the use of mass or target media. Mass media campaigns on television or radio are effective when a significant percent of the general population represent potential consumers. The percentage of potential consumers among the general populace varies greatly from country to country for most products, so that mass media will be most effective in some countries, while target media will be superior in others. If the consumer base for a product starts at a per capita income well above the national average in a market, a more selective media strategy will be required. Printed media, especially selected magazines, are likely to play a more significant role in promotion efforts in such countries.

The use of target media is particularly important for industrial products. Where public media are used to promote such products, they tend to be highly specialized. Trade journals and business periodicals account for a significant share of public promotion activity for industrial products in most countries. Publicity at trade shows and conventions is also an important area of promotion activity for industrial products around the world.

Trade shows and conventions often attract an international audience. Other emerging international media offer access to similar consumer strata across a number of markets. International editions of magazines, posters and billboards in international airports and hotels and participation in international broadcasts of sporting events represent means of reaching potential consumers from a number of countries with a single message. Such media offer opportunities for centralization and economies of scale in promotion activity. The emergence of international media and converging media coverage patterns in different markets suggest that media selection can be increasingly standardized. Even when media selection can be standardized, however, it is unlikely that the message content of the promotion program can remain undifferentiated across markets.

TABLE 4-4. Advertising Levels and Media Usage by Industry in the United States, Australia and Japan, 1976

Product Group	United States			Australia			Japan		
	Total ($ million)	Print (%)	TV (%)	Total ($ million)	Print (%)	TV (%)	Total ($ million)	Print (%)	TV (%)
Food & beverages	1,913.3	24	76	66.4	23	77	646.1	19	81
Tobacco	383.8	95	5	9.2	57	43	(included in above)		
Clothing	203.2	39	61	14.6	29	71	110.0	50	50
Banking & insurance	n.a.			6.7	40	60	130.3	79	21
Government	n.a.			7.4	67	33	58.1	39	61
Automotive	836.2	42	57	34.1	52	48	n.a.		
Toiletries & detergents	1,197.2	12	88	33.6	13	87	277.1	26	74
Household furnishings	454.1	35	65	15.1	25	75	168.7	38	62
Entertainment	296.8	42	58	n.a.			278.5	58	42
Pet food & products	177.5	6	94	5.3	9	91	n.a.		
Pharmaceuticals	462.4	12	88	8.2	18	82	195.4	33	67
Publishing	76.8	34	66	9.5	20	80	n.a.		
Watches, jewelry, and cameras	95.6	18	82	3.1	54	46	n.a.		
Office equipment	n.a.			1.8	89	11	127.3	52	48
Electronic equipment	n.a.			14.6	33	67	161.1	44	56

Source: Australian data from Metwally, M.M., "Product Categories that Advertise Most," Journal of Advertising Research, February 1980; U.S. data from Statistical Abstract of the United States 1979, charts 1003–1007.

Message

Widespread debate exists over the feasibility and benefits of advertising standardization.[33] Many examples of dysfunctional promotion can be cited involving firms attempting to transfer a brand name, trademark, slogan, or an advertising theme from one market to another. Promotion programs do not readily transfer to dissimilar markets for a variety of reasons. Standardization of content neglects obvious differences in the stage of market development and cultural, demographic and socioeconomic conditions. The same message will not serve equally well in a market requiring emphasis on generating initial awareness of the product as it will in a static market dominated by repeat purchases. Comparison advertising is more appropriate in mature markets than in new ones, for example. Even if the stage of market development is similar, however, messages such as those explicit in comparison advertising may be perceived differently in various markets.

Some Examples of Dysfunctional Promotion

An American bank entering the Venezuelan market decided to use its traditional trademark of a squirrel hoarding nuts for the winter in its promotion campaign. Since Venezuela has no squirrels as we know them, and nuts are a cash crop there, the trademark was widely interpreted to represent a thieving rat. Ford Motor Company named its third-world truck the "Fiera," which means "ugly old woman" in Spanish. The slogan "Coke adds life" as originally translated into German was interpreted to mean "Coke resurrects the dead."[34]

Cultural differences play a key role in determining the effectiveness of advertising. A standardized message content runs the risk of missing or even offending consumer sensitivities in different markets. In some countries, the very act of publicizing a product could be dysfunctional. In Moslem countries, publicity for a wide range of products commonly advertised elsewhere would be inappropriate. Publicity for some personal care products could lead to negative reactions in a wide range of markets. Demand for these products exists, but public sensitivities preclude effective advertising. In less extreme cases, publicity itself will not be viewed negatively, but the message content could be.

Truly effective promotion requires an understanding of the values, emotions, expectations, aspirations and needs of the consumer population. The psychological dimensions of promotion activity are particularly important for consumer products. Consumers in many markets share common needs to affirm their identity through affiliation with symbolic products. These needs differ in nature and intensity, however. Many consumers prefer traditional products as symbols of their affiliation to a traditional culture. Males in some cultures relate more positively to products associated with the rugged individual or machismo image, such as Marlboro, than to product advertisements emphasizing bonhomie and comraderie, such as found in many beer commercials. Female consumers in different cultures respond very differently to images of the independent female or happy homemaker. Advertising designed to appeal to aspiring career women may be effective in the United States, but such a theme and image would be inappropriate elsewhere. On the other hand, some themes seem to be universally popular. The leading soft drinks are successfully promoted around the world with a theme and image emphasizing youth and vigor amid mixed social settings.

Such standardized approaches can be inferior to excellent locally-oriented promotions, however. The leading beer companies long employed typical male stereotypes in promoting their products in Puerto Rico. Schaefer's, a small regional producer, developed a series of ads featuring a local female vocalist. The vocalist later became a national entertainment celebrity and largely because of her identification with its product, Schaefer's captured over 80% of the beer market in Puerto Rico. Such anecdotes aside, sensitivity to prevailing attitudes, emotions and aspirations of the local consumer population is critical in developing effective promotion campaigns.

What's in a Name?

Most companies use their domestic name in international markets. This can lead to problems in international markets. Hoechst of Germany even built an entire advertising campaign around the difficulties of pronouncing its company name. One major company name, however, was selected with foreign markets in mind. Sony Corporation's chairman, Mr. Akio Morita, described how the company name was chosen.

> Sony derives from the Latin word sonus for sound, and we originally viewed ourselves as a producer of sound equipment. Also, Sony sounds like the American phrase, "sonny boy," and we associated very much with the idea of being a bright, young, promising and growing company.

Demographic differences also have an impact on the effectiveness of any message. Age, life expectancy, family size, education levels, rural versus urban population, and daily regimens all affect perceptions of any theme or image. Demographic differences generally can be accounted for through minor alterations of advertising content. Other modifications can also account for differences in buyer behavior or identity. An item viewed as a convenience item in one country can be seen as a luxury or shopping item in others because of economic conditions. The prevalent purchaser might be an adult male in one country and an adolescent or adult female in another. The problems of accounting for local variations in consumer characteristics poses problems for global firms. Complete customization and decentralization of promotion efforts is expensive and difficult to control and coordinate. Centralization of the promotion effort inevitably leads to a reduction in responsiveness to local market conditions. One means of maintaining some central control of promotion activities while retaining responsiveness to local markets entails the use of a global advertising agency or network.

Global Advertising Agencies

The leading U.S.-based advertising agencies today all generate at least one third of their earnings from foreign operations. The international orientation of the industry exceeds that of almost all other industries. The success of these advertising agencies abroad stems to a large extent from the critical needs of global firms to centralize some elements of promotion activity and to gain market research capabilities in foreign markets. The leading ad agencies operate offices in all major foreign markets. Ogilvy and Mather, for example, owns affiliates in 24 foreign countries and has formal associations with agencies in a number of others. The presence of these offices permits global advertisers to deal with the agency at a central location, while the agency performs much of the decentralized activity in each market. This type of relationship permits the global advertiser to centrally manage its programs while the agency in effect bears much of the burden of communication and coordination between foreign affiliates and headquarters. These agencies also provide creative services as well as valuable sources of information about media availability, cost and coverage, and cultural, socioeconomic and demographic conditions in individual markets.

Management of promotion activity in global marketing can be reduced largely to an oversight function through the use of an external agency. The benefits of relying on an external agency to manage this element of the

TABLE 4-5.   Foreign Earnings of the Largest U.S. Advertising Agencies

Agency	Gross Income (1979) ($ million)	Foreign Income as a Percentage of Total (1979)
J. Walter Thompson	253.9	53.4
McCann-Erickson	250.4	72.3
Young & Rubicam	247.6	39.5
Ogilvy and Mather	206.2	48.2
Ted Bars	181.0	45.6
SSCB	153.2	78.3
BBDO	144.8	36.9
Leo Burnett	141.1	33.0

Source: Annual reports.

marketing mix are great, but there are obvious risks and costs involved as well. Effective management of the agency relationship requires a great deal of interaction by central marketing managers with account managers at one level. Additional interaction between the client and the agency at the affiliate level is also needed, and both affiliates must communicate with headquarters. Successful promotion depends on the development of effective communications links along each of these dimensions.

Channel Promotion

This discussion of promotion activity has focused entirely on primary public media. Many other alternatives for product communications exist, including leaflets, billboards, T-shirts and other giveaway items, cinema, airplane banners, mobile loudspeakers and sponsorship of sporting, musical, and other events. Innumerable opportunities exist for creative communications managers to put their products in the public eye. However, promotion activity of this sort is of limited value for many products. Public promotion plays a secondary role in marketing strategies for most industrial products. Promotion activity for industrial products and some consumer products is largely embodied in the company sales force. The sales force provides information and generates product visibility to prospective customers. Personal selling, the most basic type of promotion, accounts for the bulk of communications with customers for many products.

The benefits of public communications are also closely tied to conditions in the channels of distribution. Pull strategies based on extensive public promotion can prove ineffective in markets dominated by closed-shelf retail outlets. In such outlets, the customer places his order at a counter rather than selecting products directly from shelves. Consequently, the retailer himself has a great impact on consumer brand selections. In countries where closed-shelf outlets dominate the distribution channel, public promotion often proves to be less effective in stimulating demand for a product than marketing strategies emphasizing channel promotion. "Push" strategies can prove highly effective in such environments. Promotion activities aimed at the channel itself are critical in such strategies.

DISTRIBUTION DECISIONS

Distribution issues can carry greater weight abroad than in the United States because of the nature of distribution channels in many countries. Fragmented distribution channels require distribution policies quite distinct from those used successfully in the concentrated channels found in the United States. Where distribution channels are difficult to access, such as in Japan, Eastern Block countries and many third-world markets, different distribution policies are required. In many cases a greater emphasis on channel relationships is needed to penetrate these markets. Even where the degree of emphasis on distribution conforms to its relative importance in the domestic market, distribution policies will need to be tailored to local conditions because of varying logistics requirements and channel structure.

Distribution includes a number of areas of activity. Transportation, storage, order processing, inventory management, packaging and customer service are basic functions necessary for effective distribution. Logistics are also very important in developing an efficient distribution system. Carrier selection, fleet management, facilities location decisions, inventory management, determination of delivery schedules and routes, and order and shipment processing all require sophisticated analysis and management. A wide body of literature addresses these decisions, and many models exist for determining optimal logistical systems.[35] These models can readily be used in foreign markets to analyze freight rates, delivery requirements, carrying costs, communications systems and geographic factors that occur in each foreign market. Logistical efficiency is the foundation for an effective distribution effort. Management of the distribution function also encompasses a range of decisions relating to trade margins, credit terms, use of agents, sales force management and channel promotion. The following functions and variables are critical in developing and maintaining effective distribution activities.

Logistics Management
Carrier selection
Facilities location
Fleet management
Inventory policy
Delivery schedules and routes
Order processing

Channel Management
Sales force management
Trade margins
Credit terms
Agent selection and use
Outlet selection
Channel promotion policy

Developing a Distribution Policy

Product characteristics play a key role in determining the level of emphasis on distribution issues in marketing strategy. Distribution issues dominate the marketing mix for industrial commodities such as bulk chemicals, metals, paper and cement. Sales force management dominates marketing activities for most industrial products. Distribution is also critical for consumer products such as gasoline and very important for a wide range of branded convenience items and other consumer products such as soft drinks, candy and related products. Success in these industries depends to a large entent on effective distribution. Prevailing distribution practices in existing markets again provide a valuable reference point in determining global distribution policies. However, distribution needs, problems and systems vary substantially in different markets. Variances in these factors contribute to the need for a high degree of differentiation in distribution policies and practices for international markets.

Differing participation levels also contribute to the need for a high level of customization in distribution policies. Licensees and local partners in joint ventures typically manage distribution activities in such arrangements. Local companies generally possess existing distribution networks, extensive contacts and knowledge of the channel. These resources eliminate the need for active management of distribution activities by the global firm. Global firms can largely function in an oversight capacity with regard to distribution issues in such arrangements. In the majority of cases, however, the global firm will seek to develop its own distribution network. In attempting to do so, the firm needs to take the structure of the existing distribution channel into account.

Channel Structure

The composition of outlets for any product can vary widely from country to country. The cosmetics industry provides one example of this issue. In the United States, drugstores account for 27% of cosmetics sales, department and discount stores handle 27% of total volume, and supermarkets are responsible for 25% of total sales. In Japan, specialty cosmetic outlets account for almost 60% of cosmetic sales and drugstores sell less than 10% of total cosmetics volume.[36] In Spain, department stores account for 55% of cosmetic sales, while such outlets represent only 7% of sales in West Germany. In Brazil, door-to-door sales account for over 50% of total cosmetics sales.[37] Similar disparities occur in other industries. Watches are still sold primarily through jewelry stores in most European markets, while discount houses dominate sales in the United States. Vending machines serve a significant share of soft-drink and candy markets in the United States, but play little or no role in the distribution of these products in most third-world countries. Specialized outlets, such as French Tabacs or American liquor stores, dominate distribution of products sold through general outlets elsewhere. These differences in distribution patterns clearly affect outlet selection and emphasis in different countries.

Distribution emphasis on chain, "mom and pop," supermarket and other outlets depends largely on the prevailing importance of each type of outlet in the larger distribution network. Supermarkets account for over 95% of all food retailing in the United States, but only 65% in West Germany. In Italy, small family-run *alimentari* account for over 50% of all food sales. The average food outlet in Italy is estimated to serve at most 30 families.[38] The number of such outlets is declining rapidly in many countries. The number of small (under 400 square meters) retail outlets in France declined by 75,000 outlets between 1961 and 1971. The number of retail outlets in the United Kingdom has been estimated to have declined from 600,000 in 1950 to 400,000 in 1980.[39] On the other hand, the number of small retail outlets in Japan doubled to 1,400,000 between 1964 and 1976.[40]

Markets dominated by many small outlets require a greater reliance on agents. The use of an internal sales force to serve such outlets involves tremendous costs. Several types of agents can be employed to distribute products to retail outlets. Brokers and jobbers represent one option. These agents distribute a wide range of products to other parties in the distribution channel. They generally do not actively promote a product but deliver in response to customer requests. These agents frequently carry competing brands of individual products. Although such intermediaries eliminate the need for transport and storage facilities, retail credit arrangements and an internal sales force, they exhibit little product loyalty and may not permit effective implementation of pricing or promotion initiatives.[41]

Exclusive distributors and dealers involve a higher level of commitment from both parties. These agents have exclusive rights to sell a product in a defined market. Arrangements with such agents normally are formalized in a legal contract outlining the responsibilities of each party and the terms of exchange between them. The manufacturer may be committed to provide training and service support, advertising funds and product line extensions. The distributor's responsibilities may be less explicit, but often entail specific capital investments and sales force development. Pricing terms and margins are also an important element in such arrangements.[42]

Distributors' or manufacturers' representatives are often used in the early stages of market development. Uncertainty about market conditions leads many firms to use independent agents to serve foreign markets initially. This approach often necessitates the renegotiation of agreements with distributors after the market has been developed. In many cases, the global firm acquires the distributor and takes direct control of the marketing and distribution effort.[43] Acquisitions of this sort are an extremely common form of international expansion. Many major multinational firms have acquired interests or taken control of existing independent distributors for their products in a number of foreign markets.

The relative importance and size of independent middlemen in any market also varies substantially. Brokers play a key role in the distribution of many industrial commodities. Trading companies such as Engelhard are major factors in metal markets, and Cargill and Dreyfus play important roles in the international grain trade. Trading companies are also very important in a number of countries. The 10 largest *sogo shosha*, or trading companies, account for over 50% of all Japanese imports and exports.[4] A similar pattern exists in Malaysia. "The "hong" trading houses of Hong Kong are also active in a wide range of industries. State trading agencies control monopolies on imports in all Eastern Bloc countries and in a number of third-world countries. These agencies, often called Foreign Trade Organizations, have exclusive authority to determine which products are imported in a specific industry.[45] Market entry and distribution in these countries depends entirely on the outcome of negotiations with state agencies.

The presence of dominant trading companies or state monopolies in an industry forces the firm to consider the use of such an organization as a marketing and distribution vehicle. In many cases, the distribution strength of these firms is so great that independent efforts to penetrate the distribution channel can prove fruitless. In Japan, for example, most major companies consider themselves members of an extended corporate family or *keiretsu* group.[46] These relationships are not based on equity ownership, but *keiretsu* membership has an important impact on distribution efforts. Distribution channels tend to be segmented into these groups, and it can be difficult to penetrate these channels without a formal arrangement with a Japanese firm belonging to such a confederation.

The use of independent agents appears most useful when outlets are highly fragmented, where existing channels are dominated by large trading companies or state agencies, and in the initial stages of market penetration. Relationships with independent agents often prove unsatisfactory, however. Implementation of marketing strategy is hindered greatly by the need to work through independent agents. Most major multinationals limit reliance on such agents to small, peripheral or restricted markets. However, middlemen in the form of wholesalers, brokers and jobbers play important roles in most markets exhibiting fragmented retail outlet structure.

Fragmented outlet structure also affects other distribution decisions. Small outlets often carry low inventory levels and require frequent restocking. This increases the need for storage facilities and delivery trucks. Higher inventory levels can be required in markets with fragmented distribution channels. Small outlets are also particularly sensitive to credit terms because of their limited financial resources. Credit terms are particularly important in achieving effective distribution in markets dominated by small outlets. As a result of liberal credit policies, accounts receivable can also be high in such markets. Trade margins may also have to be adjusted for such outlets. The channel values a product strictly in terms of unit margin times volume, or total contribution. Small outlets by nature are not volume oriented, so they will generally prefer a high margin product over a lower one. This preference can limit the effectiveness of a penetration pricing strategy if the channel resists the lower margin product.

The development of a positive relationship with participants in a distribution channel depends to a large extent on such issues as inventory policy, credit terms and trade margins. Ultimately, however, relationships with channel members will hinge on profitability and integrity in distribution practices for a product. Integrity implies consistency in terms, schedules and interaction patterns. Even if the company itself enforces integrity in its own actions, control over other agents in the channel can prove difficult to achieve and maintain.

Channel Control

Control of distribution practices is one of the most important objectives in building an effective distribution network. Distribution programs can be disrupted if control over terms and supplier linkages is lost. Independent agents often offer varying prices, terms, and service to different customers within a channel. As a result, some outlets may receive different price quotes from different distributors. Outlets that learn of the better terms offered elsewhere will react negatively to existing distribution efforts. A similar problem can occur if certain retailers are allowed to source directly from the company rather than through the wholesaler. Inconsistencies of this sort reduce the effectiveness of distribution efforts. Control over terms and service patterns is a key objective in management of the distribution function.

Consistency at the wholesale level is not the only problem facing the company. Similar problems can arise at the retail level. Competition among types of outlets can disrupt marketing activities. Discount chains, for example, can quickly undermine selective distribution networks. Discount outlets can undercut existing outlets developed and maintained at great expense. Once discount outlets achieve dominance in any channel, the level of service, product image and the manufacturer's control of marketing strategy will diminish.

Discrimination against any participant in a distribution channel is illegal in the United States under the Robinson-Patman Act. In many foreign markets, however, activities by specific parties can be limited or reduced by varying distribution policies. Selective terms, rebates, quotas, delivery schedules or prices are important means of retaining control of the composition of any distribution channel.

Despite these options, attempts to discriminate against selected outlets can run afoul of public legislation in other countries as well. The maker of Rossignol skis refused to sell its products to an aggressive French discount retail chain in the early 1970s, and the European commission ruled that such discrimination against individual customers was illegal.[47] Fair trade laws and resale price maintenance requirements exist in many countries to ensure equal terms to all distributors. Such laws can constrain selective distribution strategies.

Independent agents and discount houses are not the only parties guilty of circumventing existing channels. The temptation to circumvent existing distribution middlemen is universal. An American soft drink distributor in Nigeria found that his delivery truck drivers were selling direct to the consumer at slightly above the wholesale price and pocketing the difference. Such leakage from one level of the distribution channel can seriously hinder efforts to develop an effective distribution network.

These issues are particularly important in countries that rely on turnover taxes as a principal source of revenue. Turnover tax revenues are the single most important source of government revenue in most of the world's nations. Turnover taxes are effectively a sales tax imposed as a percentage of companies' sales at each level of the channel. The presence of these taxes can provide further incentives for product leakage out of formal distribution channels.

The circumvention of formal distribution channels is common within many countries around the world. One source estimated that over 40% of all cigarettes sold in New York City are smuggled in from southern states, which do not have a state excise tax on cigarettes. Arbitragers are quick to take advantage of the price differentials that result from such situations. International arbitrage, or the illicit movement of goods across national boundaries, assumes far greater proportions.

Invisible Agents

Gillette's Argentine subsidiary experienced record results in 1976, increasing its blade sales by more than 50% over the prior year. This increase in volume was not gained at the expense of competitors, since Gillette already controlled 98% of the razor blade market in Argentina. Blade quality had recently been upgraded with the expected result of increasing the number of shaves per blade. The increase in unit volume was puzzling. One explanation focused on blades becoming a "poor man's gold" in the face of the world's highest inflation rate. Were razor blades being sewn into mattresses as a hedge against inflation? Perhaps, but the principal cause of the sales increase soon became clear when Gillette's Chilean subsidiary reported a dramatic decline in its sales. The Argentina peso had been devalued by 55% with respect to the Chilean peso, and Argentine blade prices were significantly below those in Chile. Argentine blades had flowed into Chile as a result of the price differential.

Most opportunities for international arbitrage are created by government regulations, taxes and subsidies. Arbitrage, or smuggling, is particularly powerful in Latin America, India and the Middle East. A significant volume of goods is distributed through invisible agents in these and other areas. Uruguay, for example, has the highest per capita consumption of Scotch whiskey in the world by a factor of three times according to the shipment data of the Scotch Whiskey Manufacturer's Association. Much of this product ultimately ends up in Argentina and Brazil. The "errors and omissions" entry in Uruguay's balance of payments exceeded 25% of its reported imports in the early 1970s. Underground or invisible channels of distribution probably account for an even greater percentage of economic activity in the Soviet Union and other Eastern Bloc countries.[48] Underground activities of this sort disrupt distribution efforts and lead to a loss of control over marketing strategy. Many companies go to great lengths to avoid selling their product to underground distributors around the world, simply because it is difficult to predict where that shipment will turn up.

Corporate pricing policies can also stimulate the development of uncontrolled distribution activity. Differential pricing can lead distributors to ship the product from a low-price country to a higher-priced market. Although most governments would applaud efforts to retain product movements within normal distribution channels, attempts to restrict such leakage can lead to problems with public authorities. Japan's Pioneer group was fined $9.9 million in December 1979 for restricting exports of its consumer electronics products from West Germany to France.[49] The EEC found that Pioneer's West German subsidiary refused to sell hi-fi equipment to another German firm without an assurance that the equipment would not be exported out of Germany. The products in question were priced an average of 27% cheaper in West Germany than in France. Johnson and Johnson was fined in May 1980 for restricting British wholesalers and retailers from exporting its Gravindex pregnancy test kits to West Germany, where their price was nearly twice as high.[50]

When such activity is suspected, some companies have used coded packages to identify the distributors responsible for exporting the product. Other companies use varying packages, designs, brand names and formulations from country to country to insure channel integrity. Leakage from low-priced countries to high-priced countries continues to be a problem in the drug industry, however, where price differentials of up to 300% are not uncommon between adjoining countries. Differences in national laws, public medical services, marketing and prescription practices result in wide price differentials that stimulate leakage from distribution channels. Control of the distribution network is a key issue in any industry, particularly when a differential pricing policy is being followed in a number of adjacent markets.

Distribution Objectives

Channel control is only one objective of distribution management. Other principal objectives include coverage, cost, continuity, consistency and capital costs.[51] Each of these issues has to be considered in formulating distribution policy.

Coverage reflects the level of penetration of distribution channels achieved for a product. Coverage is greatly influenced by the decision to rely on agents or an internal sales force. Agents can provide breadth of market coverage, but often they cannot provide the intensity or duration of penetration to have a significant impact in the marketplace. The use of agents has an important bearing on other objectives as well. Agents involve little or no capital investment, resulting in low unit distribution costs. On the other hand, agent relationships can be highly unstable. Independent agents frequently shift allegiance to competitive brands if their incentives or margins look more promising. Ironically, when the agent performs well, the multinational firm may wish to alter its distribution arrangements in order to participate more directly in the market. Consistency will rarely be achieved or maintained with independent agents. Pricing, margins, delivery schedules, and other elements of marketing strategy will be determined largely by agents who react to an entirely different set of incentives than the manufacturer. Channel control also becomes a more difficult issue when agents are used as primary distributors. An internal sales force permits far greater consistency, control and continuity in distribution and marketing activity. The capital investment and unit distribution cost associated with the use of an internal sales force are important considerations, however.

Distribution costs are primarily a function of overhead costs associated with storage and transport facilities and equipment, personnel and the computer system used to record and process orders and shipments. Distribution facilities requirements can vary sharply from country to country. Distribution of refrigerated goods in many countries can be extremely expensive because of the climate and inadequate public transportation systems and retailers storage facilities. The lack of a basic delivery and storage infrastructure can prohibit activity in some markets.

The important variable with regard to these fixed distribution costs is unit volume. Market size and concentration are key factors in estimating whether sufficient volume will be generated to bring unit distribution costs down to a satisfactory level. In some cases, the cost factor will discourage firms from attempting to penetrate an entire market and lead them to focus on one area within a market. Over one half of the Brazilian population resides in greater São Paulo and Rio de Janeiro, for example. The cost of reaching this share of the market is significantly less than would be required to distribute to the other half of the population scattered throughout one of the world's largest countries. Estimates of unit distribution costs are an important factor in determining many dimensions of global strategy, including market selection and, within any market, segment emphasis, pricing, agent selection and market share objectives.

TABLE 4-6. Distribution Costs as a Percentage of Sales Dollar (United States, 1976)

	Outbound Transportation	Inventory Carrying	Ware-housing	Adminis-tration	Receiving and Shipping	Packaging	Order Processing	Total
All manufacturing companies	6.2%	1.3%	3.6%	0.5%	0.8%	0.7%	0.5%	13.6%
Chemicals and plastics	6.3	1.6	3.3	0.3	0.6	1.4	0.6	14.1
Food manufacturing	8.1	0.3	3.5	0.4	0.9	—	0.2	13.4
Pharmaceutical	1.4	—	1.2	0.7	0.5	0.1	0.5	4.4
Electronics	3.2	2.5	3.2	1.2	0.9	1.1	1.2	13.3
Paper	5.6	0.1	4.6	0.2	0.3	—	0.2	11.2
Machinery and tools	4.5	1.0	2.0	0.5	0.5	1.0	0.5	10.0
All other	6.8	1.0	2.9	1.2	1.4	0.4	0.4	14.1

Source: Herron, D.P., "Managing Physical Distribution for Profit," *Harvard Business Review*, May–June 1979, pp. 121–132.

Consistency is particularly important in maintaining effective relations with wholesalers and retailers and, through them, with ultimate consumers. Consistency involves the development of a distribution system with a high degree of stability and integrity. A clear definition of responsibilities for distribution territories, standardization of terms and margins and avoidance of confusion about distribution activities all contribute to consistency in distribution. Stability in sources, prices and terms contributes to wholesaler and retailer commitment to the distribution system. Channel commitment is the first step in building a distribution franchise, the ultimate objective of distribution activity. A distribution franchise is built by establishing a profitable and positive relationship with wholesalers and retailers in the channel. The establishment of such a relationship requires effort and attention. The channel responds to promotions, credit terms, margins and unit volume. These variables play a key role in acquiring channel acceptance of a product, but to be successful, the firm must also build relationships and its reputation.

COMPETITION

The value of a distribution-based push strategy in markets with fragmented channel structures has already been noted. In such markets, emphasis on distribution rather than promotion can be warranted. The relative emphasis on distribution versus promotion must be viewed within a competitive framework. The use of pull strategies is widely associated with multinational, especially American, companies. In many cases, a global firm will find itself competing against a local firm whose principal strength is in its distribution network. There are many documented cases where global firms entering a foreign market have used extensive promotion as part of their strategy to gain market share. Bic doubled the existing advertising expenditure of the entire writing instrument industry in many of the markets it entered.[52] Honda spent over $30 million on advertising in its first 10 years of activity in the U.S. motorcycle market while U.S. competitors spent under $5 million in the same period.[53] In many cases, however, promotion activity will not dislodge a competitor from its position of strength in the channel. Greater emphasis on distribution will be needed when competitors dominate existing channels.

In addition to promotions, point-of-sale activity, terms and margins, another means of gaining channel acceptance involves increasing service levels. For consumer products, service can be enhanced by direct, frequent delivery, faster response to orders, personal and rapid attention to requests or complaints and the provision of storage facilities for key customers. The leading Japanese supplier of stationery paper, for example, recently installed an on-line computer system with terminals in over 400 distributors to improve order processing and inventory management services. For industrial products, service includes installation, maintenance, training and design. These factors represent a critical element in marketing strategy for many industrial products. The delivery of such services involves costs in administration, field personnel, inventory carrying costs, special freight rates and facilities investments. However, a reputation for personable efficiency and reliability can be a tremendous resource in a close-knit business community.

Competitive considerations have an important impact on decisions to emphasize distribution activities. In making these decisions, management must consider the relative emphasis placed on different marketing activities by principal competitors. How have they deployed their marketing resources with respect to the product, pricing, promotion and distribution dimensions of marketing strategy? The effective deployment of marketing resources requires that management view individual marketing decisions both within a competitive and comprehensive framework. The preceding sections have focused on discrete decisions in each principal area of the marketing mix. These decisions cannot be made in isolation. A comprehensive approach to marketing mix management results in the most effective use of marketing resources.

INTEGRATED MARKETING MIX MANAGEMENT

Any marketing initiative represents the allocation of scarce marketing resources into a specific area of the total marketing mix. The commitment of resources involved in a series of product, pricing, promotion and distribution decisions fixes the competitive posture of the firm in the marketplace. This posture can occur as a de facto result of a series of discrete decisions, or it can result from an integrated analysis of all areas of the marketing mix. Every

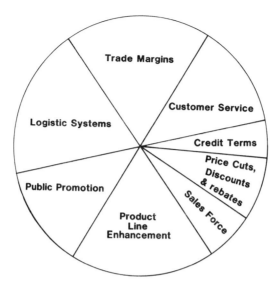

Figure 4-7.   Deployment of marketing resources: a possible configuration.

marketing decision should be evaluated within a context that emphasizes the optimal allocation of total resources. Each of the many product and market characteristics cited in the preceding sections plays a critical role in determining the deployment of marketing resources. It is imperative to estimate the cost effectiveness of investments in each area of the marketing mix and to relate the overall pattern of marketing activity to that of competitors.

Marketing decisions must also account for the interrelationships between different elements of the marketing mix. Initiatives in any area of the marketing mix may be inconsistent with strategies in other areas. For example, Bulova pursued a global expansion strategy for its watch business in the 1960s. Product policy for its wide network of foreign subsidiaries emphasized complete customization of product design within each market. At the same time, however, the company enforced a standardized pricing policy for each category of watch across all markets.[54] One of the benefits of a customized product line is the ability to pursue a differential pricing policy. On the other hand, the problems that arise from pursuing a variable pricing policy for standardized products have been documented in the Hoffman-LaRoche and Pioneer cases.

Other marketing strategy combinations that represent suboptimal allocation of resources can be cited. It may be inappropriate to initiate pricing discounts or rebates on a product while expanding service activities, for example. If the product is being sold on the basis of price, service initiatives would appear to be unnecessary and vice versa. Investments in product line extension or modification may be inconsistent with a penetration pricing strategy. Penetration pricing is most effective when a product line is converging and becoming standardized. Efforts to broaden and differentiate a product line are inconsistent with a penetration pricing strategy.

An understanding of competitors' level and deployment of marketing resources also plays a critical role in determining marketing strategy in international markets. Competitors in any given market will place different emphasis on individual areas of the marketing mix. As a result, global firms will find that adjustments in resource deployment are sometimes necessary because of competitive factors alone. The exact nature of the adjustments required can be determined only through a sophisticated analysis of consumer, channel and competitor response to any alternative marketing mix. The ultimate problem of multinational marketing is the deployment of marketing resources in each country to provide the best possible marketing mix for each market given its consumer, channel and competitive conditions.

NOTES

1. Kotler, P., Marketing Management (Englewood Cliffs: Prentice-Hall, 1980); Webster, F. E., Jr., *Industrial Marketing Strategy* (New York: Wiley, 1979).

2. Buzzell, R.D., "Can You Standardize Multinational Marketing?" *Harvard Business Review*, November–December 1968, p. 102; Sorenson, R.Z. and V.E. Weichman, "How Multinationals View Marketing Standardization," *Harvard Business Review*, May–June 1975, pp. 38–00.

3. For references in the area of consumer psychology and market research studies, see Brith, S.H., *Psychological Principles of Marketing and Consumer Behavior* (Lexington: Lexington Books, 1978); Green, P.W., *Multidimensional Scaling and Related Techniques in Marketing Analysis* (Boston: Allyn and Baron, 1970); Green, P.E. and D.S. Tull, *Research for Marketing Decisions* (Englewood Cliffs, N.J.: Prentice-Hall, 1978).

4. Munson, J.M. and S.H. McIntyre, "Developing Practical Procedures for the Measurement of Personal Values in Cross-Cultural Marketing," *Journal of Market Research*, February 1979, pp. 48–52; Hoover, R.J., R.T. Green, and J. Sargent, "A Cross-National Study of Perceived Risk," *Journal of Marketing*, July 1978, pp. 102–08; Hornik, J., "Comparative Evaluation of International vs. National Advertising Strategies," *Columbia Journal of World Business*, Spring 1980, pp. 36–45.

5. Liander, B., et al., *Comparative Analysis for International Marketing*, op. cit.
6. Sethi, S.P., "Comparative Cluster Analysis for World Markets," *Journal of Marketing Research*, August 1971, p. 350.
7. Wind, Y. and S.P. Douglas, "International Market Segmentation" *European Journal of Marketing*, Vol. 6, No. 1, 1972, pp. 17–25; Vogel, R.H., "Uses of Managerial Perceptions in Clustering Countries," *Journal of International Business Studies*, Summer 1976, pp. 91–98.
8. See, for example, Nie, N.H., et al., *Statistical Package for the Social Sciences* (SPSS) (New York: McGraw-Hill, 1975), pp. 434–468.
9. AMF–Harley-Davidson Motor Company, Inc., ICCH No. 9-579-153; Note on the Motorcycle Industry, ICCH No. 9-578-210.
10. For an application of a corporate strategy framework to marketing issues, see: Abell, D.F., and J.S. Hammond, *Strategic Market Planning* (Englewood Cliffs, N.J.: Prentice-Hall, 1979).
11. Mansfield, F., *Microeconomics: Theory and Applications* (New York: Norton, 1979), pp. 93–97.
12. *Business Week*, April 21, 1973, p. 26.
13. Nevin, J. J., "Can the United States Survive Our Japanese Trade Policy?" *Harvard Business Review*, September–October 1978, p. 173.
14. DAAG Europe, ICCH No. 9-374-037.
15. "Gillette Takes the Wraps Off," *Fortune*, February 25, 1980, pp. 148–150.
16. For a comparison of internal and external dimensions for American cars in 1960 and 1970, see *Consumer Reports*, April 1960, p. 177; April 1970, p. 222.
17. Bossert, W.H. and E.O. Wilson, *A Primer of Population Biology* (Stamford: Simaner Association, 1971).
18. Luce, R.D. and H. Raiffa, *Games and Decisions* (New York: Wiley, 1958); Schelling, T.C., *The Strategy of Conflict* (Cambridge: Harvard University Press, 1960); Von Neumann, J. and O. Morgenstern, *Theory of Games and Economic Behavior* (Princeton: Princeton University Press, 1949).
19. Scherer, F.M., op. cit., pp. 131–144; Fellner, W., *Competition Among the Few* (New York: Knopf, 1949).
20. Chamberlin, E.H., *The Theory of Monopolistic Competition* (Cambridge: Harvard University Press, 1933), Chapter III.
21. Davis, K.R., "Increasing Model Usage in Marketing: A Gaming Approach and Case Situation," *Industrial Marketing Management*, 1977, pp. 113–18.
22. A Note on the Boston Consulting Group Concept of Competitive Analysis and Corporate Strategy, ICCH No. 9-175-175; A Note on the Use of Experience Curves in Competitive Decision Making, ICCH No. 9-175-174.
23. Abernathy, W.J., and J. M. Utterback, "A Dynamic Model of Process and Product Innovation," *OMEGA*, Vol. 3, No. 6, 1975, pp. 639–55.
24. Wasson, C.R., *Dynamic Competitive Strategy and Product Life Cycles* (St. Charles, Illinois: Challenge Books, 1974).
25. Vernon, Raymond, "The Location of Economic Activity," in Dunning, J.H. (ed.), *Economic Analysis and the Multinational Enterprise* (New York: Praeger, 1974), pp. 89–114.
26. Allison, R.J. and K.P. Ohl, "Influence of Beer Brand Identification on Taste Perception," *Journal of Marketing Research*, August 1964.
27. Comanor, W.S. and T.S. Wilson, *Advertising and Market Power* (Cambridge: Harvard University Press, 1974).

28. See, for example, Cox, D.F., *Risk-Taking and Information Handling in Consumer Behavior* (Boston: Division of Research, Harvard Business School, 1967).

29. Webster, F.E., Jr., *Industrial Marketing Strategy*, op. cit.

30. Farris, P.W., "Determinants of Advertising Intensity: A Review of the Advertising Literature," (Boston: Marketing Science Institute, 1977).

31. Urban, C.D., "A Cross-National Comparison of Consumer Media Use Patterns," *Columbia Journal of World Business*, Winter 1977, pp. 53−63.

32. Thorelli, H. B., "Concentration of Information Power Among Consumers," *Journal of Marketing Research*, November 1971, pp. 427−32; Engledow, J., H.B. Thorelli, and H. Becher, "The Information Seekers—A Cross-Cultural Consumer Elite," in Schlinger, M.J., *Advances in Consu(Atlanta: Association for Consumer Research, 1975)*.

33. Green, R. T., W. H. Cunningham and I.C.M. Cunningham, "The Effectiveness of Standardized Global Advertising," *Journal of Advertising*, Summer 1975, pp. 25−30; Donnelly, J.H., Jr., and J.K. Ryans, Jr., "Standardized Global Advertising: A Call As Yet Unanswered," *Journal of Marketing*, April 1969, pp. 57−60; Hornik, J., "Comparative Evaluation of International vs. National Advertising Strategies," *Columbia Journal of World Business*, Spring 1980, pp. 36−45; Colvin, M., R. Heeler, and J. Thorpe, "Developing International Advertising Strategy," *Journal of Marketing*, Fall 1980, pp. 73−79.

34. These anecdotal incidents are cited from Davis, S.M., "Trends in the Organization of Multinational Corporations," *Columbia Journal of World Business*, Summer 1976, p. 61; Cateora, P.R. and J.M. Hess, *International Marketing* (Homewood: Irwin, 1979).

35. Wentworth, F., and M. Christopher, *Managing International Distribution* (New York: AMACOM, 1979); Ballou, R.H., *Basic Business Logistics* (Englewood Cliffs: Prentice-Hall, 1978).

36. Slater, A., "International Marketing: The Role of Physical Distribution Management," *International Journal of Physical Distribution*, Vol. 10, No. 4, 1980, pp. 160−84. For the United States, see "Cosmetics Distribution," *Chemical Marketing Reports*, February 25, 1980, p. 38. For Europe, see "Cosmetics Distribution Indicators," *Consumer Europe*, 1977, p. 123; for Japan, *Japan Marketing Advertising*. Dentsu, July 1978 (selected products, pp. 49−54).

37. Sterling Windsor, a case analysis (Lausanne, Switzerland; 1 Mede, 1976).

38. Drine, E., "Italian Supers: Up Against the Little Guy," *Advertising Age*, September 1977.

39. For France, see Carrefour S.A., ICCH No. 9-273-099. For the United Kingdom, Cateora, P.R. and J. M. Hess, *International Marketing* (Homewood: Irwin, 1979) p. 593.

40. See Kanabayashi, M., in Cateora, P.R. and J.M. Hess, op. cit., pp. 606−10.

41. Terpstra, V., *International Marketing* (Hinsdale: The Dryden Press, 1978), pp. 443−51; Cateora, P.R. and J. M. Hess, op. cit., pp. 553−75; Keegan, W.J., *Multinational Marketing Management* (Englewood Cliffs: Prentice-Hall 1980), pp. 331−53.

42. An example of such an arrangement is described in Autodraft Corporation, ICCH No. 9-329-019.

43. For the Harvard Multinational Enterprise Project sample of 180 firms, over 900 foreign distributors were acquired between 1950 and 1976.

44. Tsurumi, Y., *The Japanese are Coming* (Cambridge: Ballinger, 1976), pp. 128−30; Young, A.K., *The Sogo Shosha* (Boulder: Westview, 1979), p. 4.

45. Hill, M.R., "International Industrial Marketing into Eastern Europe," *European Journal of Marketing*, 1980, pp. 139−64; Lauter, G.P. and P.M. Dickie, *Multinational Corporations and East European Socialist Economics* (New York: Praeger, 1975); Lange, I., Government Agency and East−West Trade, ICCH No. 9-376-975. For a case example, see Alfa-Laval (A&B) 9-578-198, 99.

46. Yoshino, M.Y., *The Japanese Marketing System* (Cambridge: MIT Press, 1971), p. 114.

47. "Marketing in Europe: Steering Clear of German Anti-Trust Rules," *Business Europe*, December 24, 1976, p. 414.

48. Feifer, G., "Russian Disorders," *Harpers*, February 1981, pp. 41–58.

49. *Electronic News*, December 31, 1979, p. 17; *Financial Times*, December 18, 1979, p. 26; *Wall Street Journal*, December 17, 1979, p. 8.

50. *Business Europe*, December 5, 1980, p. 387.

51. This framework is adopted from Cateora, P.R. and J.M. Hess, op. cit., pp. 577–605.

52. An example of Bic's advertising strategy and tactics appears in Scripto Pens Ltd., ICCH No. 9-505-057.

53. See A Note on the Motorcycle Industry, ICCH No. 9-578-210.

54. See Bulova Watch Company (B), ICCH No. 1-374-051.

FIVE

Sourcing Strategy

Sourcing strategy includes a number of basic choices firms make in deciding how to serve foreign markets. One choice relates to the use of imports, assembly or production within the country to serve a foreign market. Another decision involves the choice of technology used to manufacture a product. A third issue involves the use of internal or external suppliers of components or finished goods. An even more fundamental issue is the decision to manage sourcing activities on a market-by-market basis or from a centralized, system perspective. System choices involving the degree of rationalization of a manufacturing network, capacity location decisions and the extent of integration of production can conflict with more discrete sourcing preferences in individual markets. Resolution of this conflict is a key issue in developing a sourcing strategy.

The most basic sourcing strategy for global markets involves a single world-scale manufacturing facility. This approach is often utilized by Japanese companies. Capital-intensive, volume-oriented facilities in Japan manufacture standardized products for shipment to world markets. The success of this strategy can be seen in the consumer electronics, automobile, steel and other industries. The Japanese approach to manufacturing emphasizes capital intensity and maximum scale. For example, one large plant provides the chassis units for all black-and-white televisions produced in Japan. Nippon Steel operates the three largest steel facilities in the world; its largest, with a capacity of over 20 million tons, exceeds the total steel output of all but four countries. These facilities exhibit the highest levels of automation in their industry. This approach attempts to achieve low unit costs through volume production in highly capital-intensive facilities. Automation and centralized quality control also ensure consistent product quality. The combination of low cost and high quality generated by such a

177

sourcing system has been a powerful force in many world markets. Similar sourcing strategies have been employed by multinationals from the United States and elsewhere.

In pursuing such a strategy, the plant need not be located in the firm's home market. Centralized offshore sourcing of components has become common in industries where labor costs are significant. The use of Asian or Mexican sources of supply is widespread in the electronics, textile and appliance sectors, for example. Companies such as General Motors, General Electric, GTE and many others have established foreign affiliates in the Far East or Mexico to manufacture products to be sold in the United States and elsewhere. General Electric employs over 12,000 workers in Singapore alone. Such offshore plants are used as central sources of supply for company affiliates around the world.

Sourcing South of the Border

When low-wage manufacturing sites are discussed, countries such as Taiwan and South Korea immediately come to mind. Less attention is given to the role Mexico plays in the foreign sourcing activities of U.S. corporations. There are now over 600 foreign-owned plants operating in the Mexican border zone, a sector of the Mexican economy that exists because of Mexican incentives and U.S. tariff regulations. Under U.S. law, if the components of a product are imported from the U.S. and the product is re-exported to the United States, duty is paid only on the value added by foreign assembly. With typical wage rates of $1.00 to $1.50 in 1981, the border zone offers substantial savings. U.S. companies, as well as Japanese and European firms, are increasingly using Mexico as an assembly base for products sold in the United States. The following U.S. firms are typical of those operating border plants:

U.S. Firm	Product
Ampex	Electronics assembly
Certron	Tape cassette assembly
Litton	Transformer assembly
Mattel	Toy assembly
Motorola	Semiconductors assembly
Kayser-Roth	Women's wear

For a description of the early history of the Mexcian border zone, see Baerresen, D.W., *The Border Industrialization Program of Mexico* (Lexington: Heath, 1971); Walker, H.O., Jr., "Border Industries with a Mexican Accent," *Columbia Journal of World Business*, January–February 1969, pp. 25–32.

The alternatives to a central sourcing strategy entail management of production facilities distributed in a number of locations. Two principal forms of distributed sourcing systems can be identified: One emphasizes integrated system sourcing; the other emphasizes indigenous sourcing. The integrated form of distributed sourcing involves a system exhibiting a high degree of rationalization. In such a system, each facility tends to specialize in one component or product, producing most or all of the system's requirements for that good. Rationalization, a term often used to mean consolidation, here refers to the streamlining of the number of products manufactured within each facility.[1] These goods are then transshipped between affiliates to meet individual sourcing requirements. A good example of such an integrated manufacturing network is IBM, whose principal European affiliates each export a significant percentage of their sales to each other.

Rationalization of sourcing systems occurs frequently in Europe. U.S. companies with established operations in a number of European countries have found that system sourcing costs can be reduced by specialization. Rather than having each subsidiary produce a full line of products for its own market, each affiliate produces only one product line for the entire European market. The former approach was successful prior to the formation of the Common Market, but elimination of internal tariff barriers created an environment in which larger and more efficient production facilities could serve the entire European market. Rationalization along these lines achieves greater efficiency for the sourcing system. Specialization permits longer runs, economies of scale and, consequently, lower unit costs. These benefits can be significant, but the interdependence of operations in such systems

TABLE 5-1. Exports and Intrasystem Transactions of Foreign Affiliates of U.S. Multinational Firms in Relation to Affiliation Sales

Affiliates Sales (1975)	Percentage of Affiliates with	
	Exports > 10% of Sales	Intrasystem Transactions > 10%
Under $1 million	10.3%	8.7%
$1−10 million	24.0	15.0
$10−25 million	36.0	21.5
$25−100 million	42.4	26.3
Over $100 million	48.7	36.4

Source: Compiled from Curhan, J.P., W.H. Davidson, and Rajan Suri, *Tracing the Multinationals* (Cambridge: Ballinger, 1977), p. 389.

requires extensive coordination and integration by central planners and managers. In such rationalized sourcing systems, two-way flows of products between sister affiliates are typical. In an indigenous sourcing system, by contrast, transactions between members of the parent network are very limited.

U.S. firms typically emphasize indigenous sourcing within individual markets. Of 3,733 foreign manufacturing subsidiaries reporting intrasystem transaction levels in the Harvard Multinational Enterprise Project study, 9.4% reported that such transactions accounted for more than 50% of their revenues.[2] Although an additional 11% of these subsidiaries reported intrasystem transactions between 10 and 50% of their turnover, the data suggest that most foreign affiliates of U.S. multinational firms are largely self-reliant when it comes to sourcing.

One important exception to this generalization is the fact that larger foreign affiliates tend to exhibit higher rates of exports and intrasystem transactions. These larger affiliates are primarily responsible for the observation that intrasystem sales, on a dollar basis, represent a significant share of world trade. Most U.S. foreign affiliates, however, source and sell the bulk of their products within their own market.

This indigeneous sourcing strategy differs from the central strategy used successfully by many Japanese competitors. There is a marked contrast between the typical sourcing strategy of U.S. and Japanese global competitors. Many U.S. companies perceive this as a weakness and are moving to modify their manufacturing networks. Ford has pursued a strategy of global manufacturing rationalization that attempts to achieve some of the benefits of centralized sourcing.[3] International Harvester completely overhauled its manufacturing network in the late 1970s to create single worldwide sourcing locations for many principal components and final products.[4] Many other U.S. firms have attempted to reduce unit costs by emphasizing centralized sourcing. Despite such activities, the majority of U.S. firms appear still to rely primarily on a distributed, decentralized approach to product sourcing. Is this a strategic error? Probably not: There are a number of very good reasons for employing such an approach.

The use of a centralized, single plant sourcing strategy is a common response to the increasing cost pressures and competition facing U.S. companies such as Ford and International Harvester. Yet this approach does not always improve manufacturing and sourcing efficiency. International Harvester had just completed its transition to single-plant global sourcing when it was crippled by a prolonged strike.[5] Centralized sourcing leaves a company extremely vulnerable to transportation disruptions as well as labor problems. A central sourcing strategy also increases a firm's vulnerability to host government import restrictions. Japanese firms have been unable to penetrate many European and other markets because of their emphasis on the use of imports to serve those countries.[6] Even when access can be gained, markets served by imports can often be captured by competitors willing to assemble or produce locally. This process occurs even in the most technologically advanced industries.[7] The pressing balance-of-payment problems faced by many host governments as a result of rising oil bills will lead them to increase pressures for local sourcing. With the number of global competitors rising in every industrial sector, host governments will not find it difficult to find firms willing to enter into arrangements that guarantee a protected market in exchange for local sourcing. Central sourcing is unlikely to be a successful strategy in such an environment.

The benefits of central sourcing may also be limited in duration. Centralization can provide an optimal production configuration for a static set of products and markets. However, market shifts can occur with dramatic speed, leaving existing facilities outmoded. A shift in markets can alter the transportation and tariff economics that dictated the use and location of a central sourcing facility. A shift in products can change the cost structure assumed in the decision to source centrally; projected economies of scale may not be realized. A centralized manufacturing strategy is essentially less flexible and mobile than a multi-plant strategy. Such concerns were cited by Philip Caldwell, chief executive officer (CEO) of Ford Motor Company, in reviewing Ford's experience with world sourcing of car components.[8]

An additional factor also affects the performance of a central sourcing strategy. Currency revaluation can dramatically affect sourcing costs. In many cases, the equilibrium relationship between currency value and cost indices assumed in the purchasing power parity model will not be realized over extended periods of time.[9] This is particularly true of labor costs. The Swiss watch industry is a case in point. Switzerland was Bulova's principal source of watches, movements and components in 1973.[10] Revaluation of the Swiss franc had a severe effect on the company's performance in the late 1970s. Revaluation is not the sole foreign exchange issue to affect central sourcing. Mere fluctuation in foreign exchange rates create variances in costs and margins that cause pricing, planning and financial problems for management. Competitors who source locally do not face this additional element of uncertainty. Their costs and revenues are denominated in the same currency. This particular problem has become increasingly important in recent years. The effects of foreign exchange fluctuation on a central sourcing strategy can be examined in the disguised case of Chandler Home Products.[11]

Chandler served its U.S. aerosol products market through a single facility in Peoria, Illinois. In entering European markets during the 1960s, Chandler decided to employ a central sourcing strategy. Such an approach appeared attractive at the time, since internal tariff barriers had been eliminated in Europe and the EEC could be viewed as a single market. The central facility, located in Holland, assured quality control and economies of scale in production, purchasing, product design and personnel.

The facility was established in 1967, and it immediately realized all the expected benefits associated with the central sourcing approach. However, these benefits were realized at a time when foreign exchange rates were fixed. When foreign exchange rates began to be adjusted in the early 1970s, and later when they were permitted to float freely, the benefits of the central facility were called into question by several managers of Chandler's European marketing subsidiaries. One manager complained that unit sourcing costs were going up more quickly than their unit revenues as a result of the Dutch guilder's appreciation. As a result, cutbacks in sales force and advertising were required to meet the unit's financial budget. Other managers stated that they could not properly plan their marketing activities because of frequent fluctuations in sourcing costs. In addition, all complained that transport costs were rising because of gasoline price increase. As a result, they were losing market share to competitors who sourced locally. Chandler's biggest competitor in Europe used local contract fillers in each market as its source of supply. The loss of market share resulted in a decline in production volume at the central facility, which further increased unit costs. Chandler's central sourcing strategy, which had contributed greatly to its initial success in Europe, became a competitive liability in a world of floating exchange rates.

These factors argue against the use of a central sourcing strategy. Yet central sourcing will be a superior strategy in certain situations. The success of such an approach depends on the degree to which increased production efficiency outweighs the obvious costs associated with central sourcing. The benefits of increased efficiency are primarily a function of the cost structure of the product and the firm's choice of process technology.

MANUFACTURING COST STRUCTURE

The effectiveness of a distributed or centralized sourcing strategy depends greatly on the underlying economics of manufacturing for a product. The most important relationship in this regard is that between unit manufacturing costs and production volume. Products that exhibit rapidly declining unit costs are prime candidates for centralized sourcing. Figure 5-1 reflects a

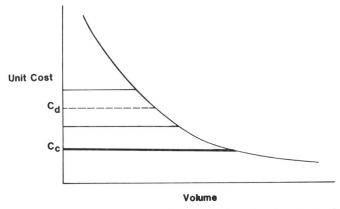

Figure 5-1.   Factory unit costs associated with distributed and centralized sourcing strategies.

cost structure that is highly sensitive to manufacturing volume. The importance of sourcing strategy can be seen by examining the average unit costs resulting from both a centralized and a distributed approach to serving foreign markets. The centralized approach results in an average factory unit cost of C_c, while the distributed approach yields a much higher average production cost. The greater efficiency of centralized manufacturing in this case can outweigh the additional transport, tariff and other costs associated with this approach. If the product in question also exhibits a high value to bulk ratio and is subject to modest import tariffs, central sourcing can offer the most efficient means of serving world markets. Products with relatively flat cost curves, low value to bulk ratios and high average tariffs are poor candidates for central sourcing.

These criteria for determining sourcing strategy are largely predetermined for any product. A quick evaluation of these criteria need not preclude either a centralized or distributed sourcing, however. Firms can exercise some degree of control over each factor. Tariff regulations generally encourage local assembly, so that subassemblies and knockdown units can be exported from central plants with minimal tariff changes. Such practices are common in the motor vehicle, pharmaceutical and many other industries. Honda operates over 30 motorcycle assembly plants in the third world, for example. This approach also permits local sourcing of those components subject to the highest tariffs and transport costs. Separately, design and material modifications can reduce the weight and area of a product. More importantly, the manufacturing process employed by the firm can be designed to yield a factory cost curve quite different from the prevailing structure in an industry. The cost or supply curve in Figure 5-1 represents only one manufacturing process among a number of possibilities. Other manufacturing technologies that offer very different cost structures can be employed. Capital-intensive production processes offer significant reductions in unit costs as volume increases. Labor-intensive processes reduce fixed costs and increase variable costs, resulting in a flatter cost curve. The availability of such technological options gives the firm some latitude in the choice between central and distributed sourcing regardless of the prevailing cost curve for a product.

CHOICE OF TECHNOLOGY

Various cost curves exist in most industries, reflecting alternative manufacturing processes and scale options. Highly capital-intensive technologies generally permit the highest volume production and the steepest cost curve. Intermediate processes involving lower levels of capital investment possess a lower break-even volume and total capacity but provide some economies of scale. At the labor intensive end of the spectrum, cost curves are flat, break-even is low and capacity is limited.

One example of the availability of various manufacturing technologies can be found in the semiconductor industry. Semiconductor production and assembly have been pursued largely through labor-intensive processes. Facilities in the Far East and Mexico have been used heavily to provide low-cost labor in the manufacturing process. The cost of assembling a typical integrated circuit in Taiwan was about $.30 in 1980; if the same process were employed in the United States, assembly costs would exceed $2.00 per unit. Recently, however, new capital equipment that offers greater precision and highly competitive unit costs has been developed. These capital-intensive direct bonding technologies provide a means by which U.S. and other semiconductor companies can reduce their reliance on offshore sourcing. Another example of the economics of alternative semiconductor fabrication technologies appears in Table 5-2. The availability of such technologies permits the firm to choose a manufacturing process that is consistent with its preferred sourcing strategy. In most cases, such options are available. As a result, sourcing strategies need not be dictated by the prevailing cost structure in an industry.

Choice of technology is closely related to preferences for central or distributed sourcing systems. Capital-intensive technologies are associated with centralized sourcing. In distributed sourcing systems, choice of technology can be approached in two distinct ways. The most basic approach to technology selection involves use of a standard manufacturing process in all facilities. In most cases, the standard process employed around the world would not be the most capital-intensive process available. The use of standardized facilities helps to ensure consistent quality and offers multi-plant economies of scale in the areas of capital equipment purchases, service and reserve parts.[12] In addition to such economies of scale, learning benefits can be realized in installing and operating standard production facilities. Experienced installation teams can efficiently duplicate a standard facility. Operation of the facility will benefit from the use of refined work procedures and systems associated with the established manufacturing

TABLE 5-2.   A Comparison of Alternative Semiconductor Patterning Processes

	Technology		
Characteristic	Projection Printing	Mann Direct Step	E-Beam Direct Step
Working resolution	2 microns	1.5 microns	1 micron
Machine cost	$250,000	$750,000	$1,500,000
Factory cost/bit	$.0039	$.0024	$.0023
Labor cost/bit	.0029	.0016	.0004

Source: Integrated Circuit Engineering Corporation.

process. The potential benefits of standardization are perhaps even greater in the area of manufacturing than in the area of marketing. However, the use of a standardized manufacturing process neglects variances in factor costs across countries. Factor costs are the relative costs of labor, material and capital in different countries. Variations in factors costs have an important effect on the choice of manufacturing technology. Clearly, a capital-intensive technology is less appropriate in a low labor cost site than in a high labor cost country.

Relative Factor Costs

Many authors have addressed the issue of selecting so-called appropriate technology for foreign operations.[13] Much of this literature is written from the host country point of view with emphasis on the observation that capital-intensive techniques do not seem appropriate in countries with low wages and high unemployment. It is important, however, to consider this issue from a corporate as well as a country perspective. The costs of labor are viewed quite differently by corporations than they are from a social cost–benefit analysis perspective. From the host country perspective, the social cost of labor is zero when unemployment exists.[14] Training costs and productivity rates are important considerations to corporations. In addition, the availability of skilled and supervisory workers may preclude a labor-intensive approach. Even if these problems do not arise, corporations are not indifferent about alternative technologies. Significant costs are involved in deviating from a standard manufacturing process. These considerations help explain why multinational companies often appear to be unresponsive to local conditions and factor costs.

Multinational corporations' sensitivity to variances in factor costs is subject to wide debate. Strassman and Yeoman have observed that many multinational firms rely heavily on standardized manufacturing processes in foreign production facilities.[15] Morley and Smith and Amsalem observe that some firms are responsive to factor cost differences in the selection of production processes for foreign affiliates.[16] Leaving social issues aside, sensitivity to factor costs in the choice of technology is important only when differences in factor costs have a significant effect on manufacturing efficiency. In many cases, variations in factor costs will not result in major variances in total manufacturing costs.

The impact of factor cost variances on production costs depends primarily on three variables: the percent of total costs accounted for by each factor under a standard process at normal output levels, the ratio of factor costs in a country to those in other countries, and production volume levels. The principal focus in examining the factor cost structure of a product normally concerns its labor content. Material and capital costs are unlikely to differ sharply from country to counqry. Under the purchasing power and interest parity theories, the cost of materials and capitals are assumed to be equal in all countries. Of course material and capital costs will vary because of tariffs, transport costs, currency restrictions and other market inefficiencies. In general, however, materials and capital are highly mobile across national boundaries, so that costs for these factors tend to equalize in different countries. The principal source of variation in factor costs will be wage rates. Thus the principal issue in technology decisions will be the relative use of labor and capital in the production process. The optimal capital/labor ratio employed in the manufacturing process will vary directly with labor costs in any location.

Actual opportunities for substituting labor and capital depend primarily on the technological options available in an industry. The ability to substitute labor for capital will vary from one industry to another and, within a given industry, by volume levels. The feasibility of substituting labor for capital can be determined by measuring the number of units of labor required to offset one unit of capital while maintaining constant output. This relationship can also be reflected by measuring the marginal product of capital divided by the marginal product of labor for any production function.[17] If that ratio is high in a given situation (i.e., when many workers must be added to replace capital equipment), the feasibility of adopting a more labor-intensive technology will be low. Cost savings will be greatest when the number of units of labor required to offset a unit of capital is low. Industries with this characteristic can benefit greatly from sensitivity to labor cost variances in their choice of manufacturing process.

A more precise framework can be developed to specify the opportunities for adopting labor-intensive technologies. Two critical relationships determine the feasibility of adopting alternative production processes. The first is the cost of labor at home over that in the foreign country, adjusted for any variance in productivity under constant conditions. The second is the number of units of labor required to equal the output of one unit of capital in a given process at a given volume level. By analyzing these two relationships, the range of feasibility for modifying production processes can be defined. Figure 5-2 shows that opportunities for adopting labor-intensive techniques are greatest when foreign labor costs are low, and capital can be readily replaced by labor in the manufacturing process. Host country labor conditions are critical in identifying situations in which labor-intensive techniques are justified. However, the benefits of adopting more labor-intensive techniques depends greatly on the characteristics of the industry. One variable is particularly important. The degree and rate at which labor can be substituted for capital in manufacturing depends largely on the product's position in what might be called the process life cycle.

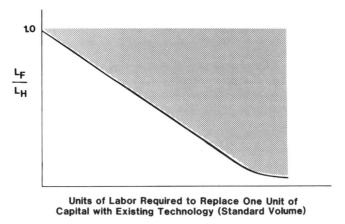

**Units of Labor Required to Replace One Unit of
Capital with Existing Technology (Standard Volume)**

L_F : Labor Costs in foreign country

L_H : Labor Costs in home market

Figure 5-2. Specification of the feasible range for adoption of labor-intensive techniques. The shaded area represents the region where labor can not be substituted for capital at efficient rates.

Industry Process Technology Cycles

In evaluating technology choices, it is important not only to consider alternative techniques in terms of labor or capital intensity, but also to consider the evolution of process technology within an industry. Labor content is largely a function of the type of manufacturing process employed in an industry. Woodward describes a continuum of manufacturing processes, from unit, small-batch, large-batch, mass and continuous-flow production systems to fully automated process production.[18] Building on the work of Kuznets and others, Abernathy and Utterback propose that prevailing production techniques in an industry progress from one end of the spectrum toward the other as products and industries mature.[19] New products tend to be produced by labor-intensive techniques, which explains the relatively high labor content in the computer, electronics and communications industries. As products become more standardized and market volume rises, there is an increased feasibility and need for automated, volume-oriented facilities. Industries with continuous process production exhibit extremely low labor content. The best examples of such process technologies are the petroleum refining and chemical industries. Metal cans and motor vehicles are also examples of industries dominated by continuous process technology.

As industries progress from unit to continuous production processes, the principal considerations in sourcing strategy are likely to change signifi-

TABLE 5-3.   Labor Content in Various Industries

Industry	Labor Cost as a Percent of Sales
Cookies and crackers	18
Clothing	32
Wood furniture	31
Industrial chemicals	13
Pharmaceuticals	17
Petroleum refining	5
Tires	20
Metal cans	16
Industrial machinery	36
Computers	42
Electric transmission equipment	35
Home appliances	23
Communication equipment	36
Electronic components	40
Motor vehicles	10
Aircraft	32
Optical products	40
Watches	25

Source: Compiled from *Census of Manufacturers*, U.S. Department of Commerce, (Washington, D.C.: U.S. Government Printing Office, 1971).

cantly. Unit production processes are highly sensitive to labor costs, but skill requirements in such industries can prohibit foreign sourcing. There is often a need to maintain production facilities near research and development centers for such products.[20] At the continuous process end of the spectrum, proximity to markets and materials take on increased importance. The principal objective in operating a continuous facility is capacity utilization. Location near markets and materials supplies helps ensure continuous operation without large inventory requirements. Logistics costs are also reduced by locating near markets and supply centers. At the same time, minimum scale requirements for such facilities are so high that a distributed sourcing strategy often will be infeasible.

These various stages of process evolution represent alternative technologies for foreign production facilities. Capital intensity increases from one stage to the next, so that "outdated" processes offer labor-intensive options for foreign production. As a result, a process which has become outmoded in the home market can often be used in foreign markets to realize cost savings based on its greater labor intensity. The benefits of such an approach can include the recapitalization of outmoded plants and equipment. This approach also avoids problems associated with learning unfamiliar production techniques.

The various options developed here suggest the importance of technology management in international business. The existence of technological alternatives permits the firm some discretion in choosing between a centralized or distributed sourcing strategy. Fundamental economic realities in factory production, transport and tariff costs dictate sourcing strategy, but these variables can be managed to some extent. The choice of technology is a central issue in this regard. The conditions facing the firm play the primary role in the selection of a distributed or centralized sourcing strategy. However, because the firm has some flexibility in the area of process technology, a consideration of the pros and cons of each approach is important regardless of the characteristics of the industry. A list of considerations is presented in Table 5-4. Note that the benefits of each approach reflect costs of the other.

The decision to pursue a centralized or distributed sourcing strategy, or some intermediate form, should be based on an assessment of existing technological options and trends in process evolution, as well as tariff and transport considerations, competitive developments and broader concerns involving trends in the international trade and monetary systems. Once a

TABLE 5-4.   Costs and Benefits of Two Sourcing Strategies

	Distributed	Centralized
Benefits	Responsiveness to local needs Multiple sourcing flexibility	Factory scale economies Quality control
Costs and risks	High unit factory costs High management requirements Lower product consistency	Tariffs Transport Foreign exchange risk Import restriction risk Labor strike risk
Favorable conditions	High tariff charges Host country preference for local sourcing Import restrictions Labor-intensive production	High value/bulk ratio Declining cost structure Continuous process manufacturing Host country export incentives

basic sourcing strategy has been selected, efficient implementation and management of the system requires emphasis on several unique variables. For distributed sourcing, the key concerns involve international technology transfer. For centralized sourcing, the critical issues arise in location decisions.

Distributed Sourcing

The basic principle behind a distributed strategy is a commitment to serve markets from indigenous sources. Underlying that strategic commitment is a need to maximize the efficiency of the sourcing system. The efficient management of a distributed international system is closely related to operating a multi-plant network in a domestic setting. Much of the literature on multi-plant domestic operations can be applied to international operations.[21] Scherer et al. found that optimal plant size is determined not only by manufacturing process economics but also by market size, density and growth, seller concentration and tariff and transport costs.[22] These concerns are of primary importance in developing a distributed international sourcing system. All these factors must be considered in seeking to minimize production plus physical distribution costs for foreign markets. A principal strategic decision facing the firm in pursuit of this objective is the question of when to establish production facilities in a foreign market. Management of distributed sourcing focuses on a single issue: the comparative costs of serving a market from external and internal production facilities. Analysis of comparative costs is the first step in managing distributed sourcing; the second step is the execution of international technology transfers.

International Technology Transfer

The international transfer of technology refers to the process by which the manufacturing capability for a product is established at a foreign location. The key issue in technology transfer decisions under a distributed sourcing strategy is timing. The economics of international technology transfer hinge on identification of break-even volume levels for indigenous sourcing plants. The establishment of a indigenous production facility to serve a foreign market is warranted economically only when the unit costs of importing exceed the unit costs of local production. Depending on process economies, production will be warranted only after the foreign market achieves a certain unit volume sufficient to absorb the overhead associated with a new plant. Consequently, technology transfer generally follows the development of a foreign market. In Vernon's well-known product cycle model, technology transfer occurs after the development of the foreign market through export activity.[23] This sequence will apply to most technology transfer decisions. Cases will occur, however, in which technology transfer precedes local market development. Such cases will include the establishment of export-oriented facilities and licensing arrangements with independent foreign firms. In most other cases, it can be assumed that technology transfer will follow market development. In such cases, initiation of production within the market will be determined primarily by two factors. The first factor is unit volume within the market. Production will be warranted only when unit sales reach the break-even level for the preferred production process. In Figure 5-3 production within the market will not be warranted until the unit cost of local production falls below the unit cost of serving the market by importing from an existing plant abroad. Once this actual volume level is exceeded for the preferred manufacturing process, local production repre-

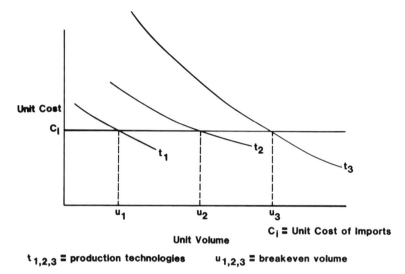

Figure 5-3. Break-even volumes for three production processes for a given product.

sents the least-cost sourcing option. Technology transfer generally will not occur until after this minimum sales level is achieved. Figure 5-3 identifies the break-even volume for three alternative production processes. Foreign production generally will not occur until at least a minimum volume level u_1 is reached.

Satisfaction of a minimum sales volume can be viewed as a necessary but not sufficient condition for technology transfer. The effects of competition on transfer decisions are also important. In a detailed study of nine foreign production decisions, Stobaugh found that the initiation of foreign manufacturing occurred only after an export market was threatened by competition.[24] Such defensive behavior is attributed to the uncertainties associated with the transition to foreign production. The economics of foreign production are uncertain because of potential variances in productivity. Logistic, legal and technical uncertainties associated with the start-up of foreign operations discourage investment. Political risks are also incurred by investment in foreign facilities. These uncertainties can lead firms to postpone production within foreign markets until competitive threats trigger the transfer of technology. Such behavior is often referred to as defensive foreign investment activity. Defensive behavior occurs most frequently for products with strong proprietary characteristics. Firms possessing such products can ignore the dictates of production economics because of their competitive strength. Buckley and Pearce found that research-intensive firms relied far more heavily on exports to serve foreign markets than firms with lower levels of research activity.[25]

This paradigm applies primarily to transfer decisions for entering a new foreign market. A quite different type of behavior can be expected by firms entering markets in which they are already established. Two factors distinguish such transfer decisions from decisions to produce within a new foreign market. First, the economics of such decisions are more favorable. Existing manufacturing facilities, distribution channels, administration systems and personnel can be utilized at a much lower unit cost. Economies of scale from overhead resources are complemented by the learning benefits accumulated in the existing operation. Start-up costs are reduced significantly in established markets. The volume levels needed to warrant local production in such situations will be much lower than requirements in new countries. In addition, the effects of uncertainty will be quite different for firms considering production in an established market. The management of the existing affiliate can specify the legal requirements and costs associated with technology transfer. Productivity rates, logistic conditions and many other details can be factored into a decision with relatively high degrees of confidence. As a result, the firm will be more likely to act on its assessment of production economics for a product in an estabished market.

The different economics associated with transfer decisions to established affiliates appears to be a primary cause of a dramatic acceleration in international technology transfer. My study of 954 products introduced in the United States between 1945 and 1976 reveals that the speed of transfer has increased steadily. Of the 174 new products first introduced in the U.S. between 1945 and 1949, only 8.0% were produced abroad within one year of their U.S. introduction. Over 32% of the 121 products introduced domestically between 1970 and 1975 were manufactured abroad within one year. The overall rate of transfer activity has also increased over time. These trends suggest that U.S. firms are placing increasing reliance on the use of indigenous facilities to serve foreign markets. Production is initiated more quickly in more markets for recent products. A principal cause of this acceleration in international technology transfer activity appears to be the growing experience of U.S. firms in foreign markets. Experience reduces overhead costs, increases the efficiency of implementing transfer projects, and eliminates uncertainties associated with foreign production.

Teece found that the cost of implementing a technology transfer project

TABLE 5-5. Initial Transfer Lag, Transfer Ratio and Average Transfer Rate for 954 Products: By Period of U.S. Introduction

Period of U.S. Introduction	Number of Products	Initial Transfer Lag % of Products First Transferred Abroad in:					Transfer Ratio Total % Introduced Abroad as of 12/77	Average Annual Transfer Rate from Year of First Foreign Productions to*:	
		1 Year or Less	2–3 Years	4–5 Years	6–9 Years	10 or More Years		3 Years Thereafter	1977 year-end
1945–1949	174	8.0	9.2	8.0	16.7	46.6	88.5	.843	.212
1950–1954	151	8.6	9.3	12.6	25.8	28.4	84.1	.919	.236
1955–1959	153	8.5	15.7	17.6	23.6	19.6	85.0	.901	.205
1960–1964	185	23.2	19.4	14.6	13.5	9.9	80.6	.941	.314
1965–1969	170	28.2	16.5	11.8	7.1	—†	63.6	1.018	.433
1970–1975	121	32.2	18.1	—†	—†	—†	50.3	1.311	.718
TOTAL	954	17.7	14.1	11.7	14.7	18.1	76.3	.952	.308

Source: Reprinted from Davidson, W.H., *Experience Effects in International Investment and Technology Transfer* (Ann Arbor: UMI Research Press, 1980).

*Average annual transfer rates are compiled for individual products by dividing the number of transfers in a period by the total number of years since the first case of foreign manufacturing for the product. These individual rates are then averaged to yield annual rates for subsets of the data base. In compiling this average rate, products that were not manufactured abroad have been excluded.

†Not applicable.

declines as the number of projects already completed for a product rises.[26] My own analysis found that the speed and rate of technology transfer was positively related in cross section to the firm's number of prior transfers for a product, in an industry, to a host country and in total.[27] Realization of experience effects in technology transfer projects is an important benefit and objective for firms pursuing a distributed sourcing strategy. Management of the technology transfer process is a critical function for such firms.

CENTRALIZED SOURCING

The same objective of minimizing sourcing costs applies to centralized strategies. Efficiency in such systems again depends on choice of technology, but the principal decisions facing firms under this approach involve the location of production facilities. In examining location patterns for export-oriented facilities, there appears to be recurrent emphasis on a few well-known countries. Mexico, Ireland, Taiwan, Hong Kong and Singapore accounted for 22.1% of the 362 pure export plants identified by the Harvard Multinational Enterprise Project.[28] Surprisingly perhaps, another group of five OECD countries accounted for 33.1% of the total. These countries were Canada, Belgium, Netherlands, the United Kingdom and Italy. Each of these countries offers substantial incentives to qualified foreign investors. The Italian development programs for the Mezzogiorno are perhaps the most well-known, but the United Kingdom and Canadian regional development programs are also highly developed. Despite the emphasis on a few selected locations for export plants, less well-known sites can also serve as effective locations. Panama, the Virgin Islands and Puerto Rico are widely used as sourcing centers. Haiti supplies over two thirds of all baseballs and softballs sold in the United States.[29] Hoffmann-LaRoche uses Uruguay as a central sourcing point for Western Hemisphere markets.[30] Examination of logic boards for minicomputer reveals that many components are assembled in El Salvador, Indonesia and Malaysia.

Location Decisions

The extensive management literature on facilities location provides a well-developed framework for international location decisions.[31] Given a specified process cost structure, the principal factors in domestic location decisions are proximity to consumer and factor markets. International facilities planning also requires consideration of tariff rates, factor costs, foreign exchange relationships and the role of governments in location decisions.

Given a static set of markets, tariff costs can still vary depending on the location of production facilities. Preferential tariff agreements are applicable for imports to the EEC from nations with associate status. The United States grants preferential tariffs to a number of Caribbean and Latin American countries. Such arrangements can offer opportunities for cost reductions and should be factored into location decisions.

Factor costs are, of course, an important concern in facilities planning. Centralized sourcing plants in Taiwan, South Korea, Mexico and elsewhere in the third world confirm the importance of relative wage rates in location decisions. Costs of other inputs are also important. Location decisions in the aluminum smelting sector are highly sensitive to the cost of electric power.[32] Smelters located in areas such as Norway, Switzerland, and the Haut Savoie utilize inexpensive hydroelectric power to process aluminum for export to foreign markets. Direct reduction pig iron plants tend to be located near supplies of iron ore and natural gas, the principal material inputs for the process.[33] Such facilities are operating or under construction in Mexico, Venezuela, Nigeria, Indonesia, Iran, Iraq and Saudi Arabia. Pulp and paper plants are generally located within a radius of forest land or cellulose supplies. Proximity to material inputs is also important in most agribusiness sectors. Unless material inputs are renewable resources, location near material sources can result in increased costs over time as supplies are depleted. This problem was solved in the early U.S. steel industry by moving pig iron plants to a new location whenever local supplies of wood for charcoal gave out.[34] A similar approach pioneered by Japanese firms in Brazil involves the construction of marine production facilities. A pulp-processing plant installed in a tanker is one of several floating factories that range up and down the Amazon River. Shipboard processing is increasingly used in the fishing industry as well.

One of the most important considerations in facilities location for export-oriented plants is the role of potential host governments. Export-oriented facilities are highly attractive to host governments because of the benefits of employment, direct and indirect tax revenues, balance-of-payments consid- erations, growth, externalities in training and technical spin-off effects. These benefits lead host governments to offer highly attractive terms to global corporations interested in establishing export plants within their borders. Investment incentives are available in virtually every nation of the world. The federal and provincial governents of Canada budgeted over $500 million in 1980 to provide grants and assistance to new industrial projects. Many states in the United States provide similar incentives to industrial investors. Abroad, extremely attractive packages are offered to export-oriented foreign investors. Ireland's industrial development program is typical of the benefits available to foreign investors, although its success in attracting foreign investors exceeds that of many other host countries.

Industrial Promotion in Ireland

The Industrial Development Authority (IDA) is the principal government agency involved in stimulating industrial development in Ireland. Under the Industrial Development Act of 1969, the agency's charge is:

> To provide and administer grants and other financial facilities to industry; to develop, construct, maintain and administer industrial estates; to provide and arrange housing for employees in industry; in order to foster the national objective of regional industrial development.

The agency provided grants to 893 projects in 1976. These projects involved a total capital investment of $400 million. Grants from the IDA accounted for $140 million of this total. The IDA is authorized to provide up to 60% of total fixed assets involved in projects located in designated areas. In addition, other agencies offer grants to cover the full costs of employee traninng programs, export incentives, low cost loans and guarantees, tax exemptions on export earnings, and full immediate depreciation of capital investments.

In exchange for all these benefits Ireland seeks investors in industries that meet the following criteria:

Rapid world market growth

Advanced technology

High value-added

Export feasibility

Low capital investment per job

Linkage of spin-off effects with local industry

In order to identify and inform prospects of these benefits, the IDA maintains representative offices in London, Paris, Stuttgart, Cologne, Amsterdam, Milan, Copenhagen, New York, Los Angeles, Chicago, Houston, Toronto, Tokyo and Sydney. Because of these benefits and its membership in the European Common Market, Ireland provides a particularly attractive sourcing center for European markets. Products are exported duty-free to Western European countries. In 1980, there were 215 U.S. affiliates operating in Ireland. These affiliates account for about 50% of the $4 billion of foreign investment in Ireland.*

The availability of investment incentives permits firms to be extremely selective in choosing a location for export-oriented plants. In this area of international business, the bargaining power of the global corporation has risen steadily over time. More and more governments are actively bidding for export-oriented facilities. As a result, the negotiating position of firms has increased, and the terms and benefits realized in establishing foreign sourcing plants have improved.

Investment incentives can dramatically affect the pattern of international sourcing activity pursued by global corporations. Corning Corporation provides an example. Corning introduced its photochromic lenses in the United States in the mid-1970s. Although foreign markets for these lenses are not yet highly developed, Corning established its first foreign manufacturing facility for this product in Brazil in 1979. This export-oriented facility was located in Brazil principally because of the investment incentives offered by the government.

Investment incentives offer important benefits to global corporations, but they can greatly distort the underlying economics of plant location decisions. Overemphasis on incentive benefits can be harmful if it leads management to neglect fundamental economic and operating realities. The political foundations of the export plant is as important as its underlying economic base. Although export-oriented plants generally need not fear expropriation, political stability is obviously a desirable feature in location decisions. The disruption of manufacturing activities during political unrest in Portugal posed major problems for several U.S. companies using that country as a sourcing center. Lebanon was a highly popular sourcing and logistics center just prior to the eruption of civil war in that country. Political turmoil in South Korea raised similar concerns for many U.S. companies in 1980.

Export plants are also sensitive to political developments in the markets they serve. In several recent cases, countervailing duties have been imposed on imports from highly subsidized export plants. One of the most famous incidents involved Michelin Tire Company's attempt to import radial tires

---

*Sources: Investment Incentive Programs in Western Europe (Washington, D.C.: Chamber of Commerce of the United States, 1978); "Ireland's Success," Industry Week, May 12, 1980, pp. 57–65.

into the U.S. market.[35] A number of sourcing options were available to serve the North American market. Michelin initially chose to produce one critical component, steel tire cord, and one product from its full line, steel-belted radial truck tires, in North America. It also announced that it planned to begin production of passenger radials within three years. The remaining product line would be imported initially from France. This partial sourcing solution is a common incremental approach to supplying a foreign market. What was unusual about Michelin's sourcing strategy was its choice of location for its production facilities. Michelin announced in July 1969 that it would establish production facilities in Nova Scotia, Canada. The location appeared to be inconsistent with Michelin's obvious emphasis on the U.S. market for radials. Over 80% of the plant's output was expected to be sold in the United States.

The selection of the Nova Scotia site was "induced by major grants and other forms of assistance from federal, local and provincial governments." The $85 billion project was financed entirely by Canadian agencies through grants and low-cost loans. Michelin's entry into the U.S. market was met by an immediate and stiff response from the U.S. government. In 1973, the U.S. Treasury department imposed a 6½% countervailing duty on all Michelin imports from Canada to offset the subsidies granted by Canadian agencies. This rapid response and the additional costs involved in importing tires from Canada convinced Michelin of the need to produce tires within the United States. A manufacturing facility for radial tires was established in Anderson, South Carolina, in 1975. Two additional plants are now in operation in Lexington, South Carolina, and Lubbock, Texas.[36]

The risk of such responses from importing countries is a principal vulnerability of centralized sourcing. The likelihood of such a response is compounded by the presence of incentive benefits. One means of limiting this political problem while maintaining economic efficiency involves developing a distributed sourcing system with specialized plants that transship to each other. This approach reflects a compromise between indigenous and centralized sourcing. Such an approach can minimize the threat of import restrictions while realizing economies of scale in production.

INTEGRATED SOURCING

An integrated sourcing system need differ from an indigenous sourcing system only in the product lines manufactured within individual facilities. In its pure form, production facilities will be located within each foreign market served by the company. Each plant will specialize in one or more products or components. These goods will be shipped to sister affiliates to serve markets in foreign countries. The intrasystem transactions will be subject to the same tariff and transport costs and foreign exchange risks of a centralized sourcing system, but political risks can be reduced by such an approach. Host countries are unlikely to impose import restrictions on a local affiliate that exports a large percentage of its own output. Although many host countries attempt to measure the net balance of trade for firms operating within their market, the presence of export-oriented manufacturing facilities in the host country places the global firm in an entirely different perspective in its relations with public officials.

Integrated sourcing alleviates political pressures while maintaining the efficiency associated with centralized sourcing. Although this approach appears to offer the best of both worlds, such sourcing strategies will be most effective only when the underlying economics of manufacturing justify centralized sourcing. In addition, most of the costs and risks of reliance on centralized sourcing apply to integrated sourcing. Vulnerability to strikes, transport disruptions and foreign exchange fluctuations still exist. A lack of

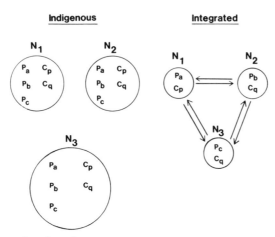

Figure 5-4.   Two distributed sourcing systems. Integrated and indigenous sourcing systems reflect two different approaches to distributed manufacturing. In the indigenous system, plants in Nations 1, 2 and 3 each manufacture products a, b and c as well as components p and q. In the integrated system, each plant produces one product and one component and trades with the other affiliates. Many variations on these basic schemes can be envisioned.

flexibility and mobility in response to shifts in products and markets continues to be present in such systems. The additional constraint of matching facilities to markets arises in development of an integrated system. This constraint can neglect lower-cost sites in countries not served by the parent firm. As a result, an integrated system, in its pure form, will not achieve the efficiency of a centralized system.

These considerations are some of the principal reasons why actual sourcing systems rarely approach pure integration. Partial integration is the rule in most multinational corporations. Multiple sourcing points will exist in most cases. Individual products and components will be produced in a number of sites, the number and location depending primarily on factory cost structure plus physical distribution costs and the level of market development in various countries. Production facilities will not always appear within markets served by the parent. Not all products will be produced in export-oriented facilities. Some products and components will be sourced indigenously. The result can be called a mixed sourcing system. Some products are sourced centrally, others locally. Some affiliates actively engage in transshipment, others rely primarily on central or local sources. Sourcing patterns are tied closely to product and market characteristics. Sourcing patterns also depend on the product's stage in what can be called the sourcing cycle. The sourcing approach used to serve a foreign market appears to follow an identifiable cycle (see Figure 5-5).

Markets are invariably served initially through exports. Local content typically evolves gradually over time as assembly operations are assumed within the market. Extensive local production follows, with the slope and peak of the local content curve determined by market size and growth, competition, government import restrictions and old-fashioned production and distribution economics. In many cases, local content declines from this peak as production of individual models or components is rationalized on a global basis. The presence of a variety of products with different characteristics and a variety of markets in different stages of the sourcing cycle results in a mixture of sourcing approaches at any point in time.

Actual sourcing systems for most global coprorations reflect such a combination of factors. Most systems include elements of all the principal sourcing options: centralized, indigenous and purely or partially integrated sourcing. Such results are due in part to the need to specify sourcing strategy on a product-by-product basis. Product-specific characteristics in the areas of factory cost structure, transport and tariff costs, degree of standardization

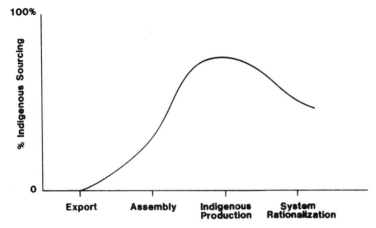

Figure 5-5.   Stages in the sourcing cycle.

and technological stability are the principal determinants of sourcing strategy. Even for individual products, however, sourcing systems often reflect a combination of approaches. Market size, competition and political factors can dictate deviation from a specified sourcing strategy. Responsiveness to these factors results in the mixed sourcing approaches evident for many products.

Such sourcing systems appear to be inefficient in many cases, but they represent optimization under the constraints imposed on management. A senior Gillette official stated, "It would be far easier and more efficient for the company to produce razor blades for all world markets in one facility. Political and competitive realities prohibit us from doing so." Existing sourcing systems reflect the dictates of environmental realities.

Sensitivity to the unique characteristics of individual products and markets is critical in sourcing decisions. Failure to respond to individual product characteristics and market conditions in order to adhere to a specified global sourcing strategy can be disastrous. Adherence to an indigenous strategy will prove inferior in small, open markets like Norway and Venezuela. On the other hand, adherence to central sourcing clearly will not succeed in protected markets. Rather than avoid such markets because of their inconsistent fit with a stated strategy, most firms will adapt to local conditions. Rigid sourcing strategies can lead to failure in certain identifiable environments. The problem becomes one of identifying the most desirable sourcing option within the constraints imposed by external forces.

At the other end of the spectrum, complete customization of sourcing systems for individual markets represents an extremely vulnerable strategic stance. A decentralized approach to sourcing can neglect important scale economies and other benefits. When individual foreign affiliates determine which products and components are manufactured where, when and how, the resulting de facto global system can be highly inefficient. Coordination at the system level is necessary to ensure that the network as a whole takes advantage of the benefits of specialization and internal transactions. In addition to promoting efficiency in this manner, a principal objective in coordinating a global sourcing system is efficient capacity utilization and management.

GLOBAL CAPACITY MANAGEMENT

There are three principal reasons for coordinating global capacity management. Decentralization of capacity management can result in duplication of manufacturing overhead and shorter production runs, which raise system sourcing costs. In addition, a decentralized approach can result in a suboptimal level of capacity utilization by the system as a whole. Finally, without central coordination, capacity additions can occur in the wrong place at the wrong time. Capacity utilization can be improved significantly through central coordination of production schedules and capacity expansions. In a system with several plants operating at or near capacity, decentralized management might order capacity expansions at each facility. Centralized management of such a situation provides three benefits. A central capacity coordinator can identify the single least-cost site for capacity expansion; unit cost savings can be achieved by adding a larger chunk of capacity at one facility, and system capacity utilization can be improved because the reserve capacity buffer for the system need not be as large as the sum of reserve capacities for decentralized plants. The realization of these benefits depends primarily on the ease of transshipment of the product. Ease of transshipment depends on the degree of product standardization across markets and tariff and transport costs.

The benefits of central capacity management are not entirely dependent on the ability to ship the product from one market to another, however. Capacity management is essentially an exercise in resource allocation. Decisions to expand capacity for any given product or country are the most fundamental determinant of a firm's business position. These decisions must not be made on a decentralized basis. The positioning of the organization in terms of products and markets is the primary strategic responsibility of top management. Central capacity management is a critical function in the deployment of corporate resources. The strategic importance of capacity decisions requires that central managers play a major role in capacity management decisions.

Conflicts between central and local management often arise in the area of capacity management. One of the best documented cases of such a situation occurred in the N.V. Philips organization.[37] Philips Electrical Ltd., a British affiliate, was an active participant in the emerging United Kingdom color television market in the early 1970s. Faced with a rapidly growing market and a plant operating at full capacity, local management pushed for an immediate, major plant expansion. The British market had grown at a rate in excess of 50% each year between 1968 and 1973. Despite the rapid rate of growth, management of the Central Video Group at headquarters in Holland opposed expansion of television manufacturing capacity in the United Kingdom affiliate. This group, which held responsibility for worldwide TV product policy, was charged with evaluating opportunities for expansion in all foreign markets. From their perspective, the British market was less promising than other markets for several reasons. First, color televisions were not sold to the final consumer in Great Britain. Instead, they are sold to leasing companies, which charged users an installation and monthly rental fee. The absence of the typical wholesale and retail structure did not permit Philips to employ its well-developed marketing and distribution strategy in Great Britain. Second, the British market was highly regulated. Government regulations were principally felt in a tax on TV purchases and in a deposit requirement on rental contracts. Both regulations varied sharply over time since the government used them as principal tools of macroeconomic policy. The purchase tax ranged from 0 to 60%, while the rental deposit varied from a minimum of nine-month charges to no charge. As a result, demand for color televisions was subject to frequent, unexpected change. Third, British color television standards were quite different from those in other markets. In addition to technological differences, the leasing companies demanded utilitarian, nonbranded sets with minimum service requirements. Also, the chassis and components used in the British sets were distinct from those used elsewhere. As a result, British sets and components could not be readily exported. Finally, the British market was one of the few European markets in which Philips was not the leading producer. Thorn's market share was more than double that of Philips. These factors discouraged capacity expansion in what was viewed as an extremely attractive market by United Kingdom management. Rather than expanding in the United Kingdom, Philips opted to utilize excess capacity in a continental factory to meet British demand. Efficient system capacity utilization was a principal objective of the Central Video Group. In addition, the Group determined that any major new capacity expansions would be located in the Far East in order to realize lower system sourcing costs.

The role of central management in such situations is to compare opportunities and conditions in different markets to ensure that incremental expansions occur in the most favorable location. Central managers can incorporate the total system's perspective into such decisions, while local managers often cannot. In the case of Philips, the Central Video Group was responsible for deploying its limited resources on a global scale. Higher up in the organization, the emphasis on the television market relative to other products was subject to the same type of review. These concerns are closely tied to the planning process to be addressed in Chapter 8. The important issue in this context in recognition that global capacity management is a critical strategic activity for multinational firms. The implications of capacity decisions extend far beyond the concerns of sourcing efficiency into the area of the fundamental business and market profile of the organization.

INTERNAL OR EXTERNAL SOURCING

The fundamental make-or-buy decision framework underlies the choice between internal and external sourcing for global firms. The economic analysis involved in such a framework can also be supplemented by contributions from the theory of the firm and the theory of vertical integration. Only slight modifications of these concepts and frameworks are needed to address the international dimensions of this basic issue. Make-or-buy decisions depend primarily on the relationship between a user's volume requirements and the minimum efficient scale of operations in the industry in question. Generally, user volume requirements in excess of minimum efficient scale levels are necessary to justify internal sourcing. Comparison of unit costs from internal and external sources is an important issue in sourcing decisions, but other factors play very important roles as well.

Reliability of supply is a prime concern in many cases. The availability of an assured supply is particularly important when one product is a major input in a user's finished product. Such is the case in a number of vertically integrated industries such as petroleum refining, steel and nonferrous metals and, to a lesser extent, chemicals, computers and communications equipment. Reliance on critical inputs creates major dependencies and vulnerabilities that stimulate firms to develop captive sources of supply. Where captive sources are not acquired, long-term contracts are often used to serve the same purpose without direct investment.[38] The need for internal sourcing is strengthened if the supply side of the market for a key input is highly concentrated. The presence of an efficient, atomistic market for an input reduces or eliminates the need for internal sourcing. Food processing firms rarely integrate backwards to internalize sources of supply.

Other characteristics of the supplier and user industry also affect pressures to internalize sources of supply. Users with a wide range of input requirements will be less likely to source internally. The range of activities, investments and expertise required can overwhelm a firm pursuing an internal sourcing strategy. Automobile manufacturers are an excellent example of the effect of input proliferation on sourcing strategy. While relying heavily on external sources, these firms rarely permit any single supplier to account for more than 50% of their requirements for any input. The automobile industry also provides an example of the effects of buyer concentration. Highly concentrated user industries can rely more heavily on external sources because the buyer's market power ensures conscientious attention and delivery by suppliers. The relative size of buyers and suppliers also works in favor of the buyers in the automobile industry. Japanese trading companies, partially by virtue of their size, are particularly effective at developing supplier relationships.[39]

The nature of the manufacturing process in the user industry also plays a role in decisions to source internally or externally. Reliability of input supply is particularly important in industries with capital-intensive, continuous process technology. Since capacity utilization is critical in such industries, disruptions in the supply of inputs have severe consequences. The petroleum refining and chemical industries are prime examples of industries with continuous, capital-intensive manufacturing processes. Firms in such industries have strong incentives for securing assured supplies of inputs. If sufficient arrangements cannot be secured in external markets, internalization of supply sources can result.

The stimulus for internal sourcing can be reduced if the input sector exhibits frequent technological change. Technological change can discourage users from committing themselves to internal sourcing because of research and development requirements and the uncertainty of future sourcing needs and economics. However, a number of semiconductor firms have recently been acquired by large firms interested principally in securing a captive source of chips.[40]

The criteria in Table 5-6 can be used to analyze the costs and benefits of internal sourcing. Cases can be cited that run counter to the relationships specified. However, consideration of all these factors will provide a framework for evaluating alternative sourcing strategies. These characteristics can help to explain prevailing sourcing patterns for a company or industry. Within any given industry, different approaches to sourcing can often be attributed to factors such as firm size and volume requirements. IBM and ATT, for example, rely heavily on internal production for electronic components. Other companies in these industries use external suppliers. In the automobile industry, Chrysler and American Motors rely more heavily on external suppliers than Ford and General Motors. In some cases, differences in approach do not appear to be directly related to size. In the color television industry, RCA, Zenith, General Electric and GTE Sylvania produced color TV tubes internally while other large manufacturers such as Motorola and Magnavox purchased tubes from independent suppliers. The choice between internal and external sourcing for these companies was not

TABLE 5-6.   Conditions Favoring Internal and External Sourcing

	Preferred Sourcing Strategy	
Characteristic	Internal	External
User volume/Minimum efficient scale	High	Low
Supplier concentration	High	Low
Number of inputs in user industry	Low	High
Percent of user total costs represented by input	High	Low
Level of technological change in input sector	Low	High
Capital-intensity of input sector	Low	High
Degree of process evolution in user industry (unit, job shop, continuous process)	High	Low
Rate of growth of user industry	High	Low
Buyer concentration	Low	High

dictated by company or industry characteristics but by managerial preferences.

Differences in sourcing strategies also appear in foreign companies. Japanese companies often appear to exhibit a greater reliance on external sources of supply than their American counterparts. However, there are often powerful nonequity ties between customers and suppliers.[41] These ties permit Japanese firms to source externally with less concern for quality, delivery or inventory problems. In other cases, Japanese firms collaborate in owning a common producer of components. Fijitsu and Hitachi jointly own a captive producer of computer peripheral equipment, for example.

In Europe, reliance on internal sourcing is evident in the industrial giants such as Philips, Siemans and Istituto Ricostruzione Italiano (IRI). Large, diversified corporations will tend to exhibit a greater reliance on internal sourcing than smaller, fast-growing companies. Because European industry tends to be dominated by large established firms, a greater general reliance on internal sourcing can be expected. An excellent example of this phenomenon can be seen in the European electronics industry. While new, dynamic companies emerged to dominate the U.S. electronics industry, established companies like Siemens and Philips dominate the European electronics industry. These firms place a greater emphasis on internal sourcing and internal sales than smaller, fast-growing competitors.

Philips and Siemens represent a special case in that they produce components not only for internal use but also for external sale. Philip's Elcoma division sells electronic components to its sister manufacturing divisions as well as outside customers. The internal transfer price for such transactions is established at standard cost plus a 10% change.[42] In many cases, external customers provide a better return, creating a problem of allegiance for the components division. Such problems arise for any firm that treats an internal sourcing division as a profit center.

Most of these factors apply in a domestic setting as well as in a global context. When the choice between internal and external sourcing is considered primarily from a global perspective, however, several other factors take on added importance. The degree of standardization of the product can play an important role in decisions to produce internally or purchase externally. Standardized products are better candiates for internal sourcing. Another important concern is the extent of international activities by suppliers. If suppliers are widely active abroad, suppliers selling to the parent at home can also serve foreign affiliates. In many cases, suppliers are willing to follow their customers into foreign markets in order to better meet their needs. Auto parts manufacturers provide an excellent example of this process. In other cases, the absence of existing suppliers in foreign markets forces global firms to integrate backwards. Gillette, for example, opened its own plastic molding facility in Argentina in the early 1950s to supply parts and packaging for its razor business even though the present company had no prior experience in the industry. Many firms have established foundries in foreign countries to produce precision castings necessary for assembly of their end product. In such cases, transport economics ruled against purchasing components from existing suppliers in the home market.

The international dimension of the make-or-buy decision is seen most clearly in the development of captive offshore sourcing facilities. Foreign investments in Taiwan, the Mexican border zone, Ireland and other countries primarily represent the internalization of supply sources.[43] There are, for example, over 150 electronics plants in Malaysia owned by U.S. firms.[44] The entire output of most of these plants is sold to the parent firm. Why did the parent firms not choose to buy their components from independent foreign suppliers? When offshore sourcing of inputs is dictated, decisions to produce internally may be driven by concern for quality control, reliability and availability. Rather than accept dependence on relatively unknown and unproven foreign suppliers, many firms will choose to develop their own internally controlled sources of supply in low-cost locations. In order to realize the cost savings associated with foreign sourcing, the user may be required to establish its own manufacturing or assembly facility abroad.

International Inventory Management

An issue related to the internal or external sourcing decisions is the firm's inventory policy. At the most basic level, foreign sourcing requires an increase in inventory levels because of the greater length of the delivery system. More product will be in the pipeline at any point in time. In addition, because of greater perceived risks of disruption of supply, firms relying on external sources may choose to carry higher inventory levels. With internal foreign suppliers, the user can carry lower lower levels of inventory than might be the case with independent foreign suppliers. Control of the source of supply eliminates some of the need to hedge against the potential stoppage of flow from foreign sources.

Source of Supply	Usage Level	Delivery Lag	Pipeline Inventory
Domestic	100 units/day	2 days	200 units
Foreign	100 units/day	10 days	1,000 units

International operations require not only higher levels of inventory, but also higher levels of complexity in inventory management. International operations generate an unavoidable proliferation of models, products and components. In some cases, variations reflect only differences in electric power requirements or size. In others, local needs require complete modification of products and components. As a result, the number of items produced and stocked in inventory expands rapidly when firms enter foreign markets. This process can be managed and limited by strong central control over production and inventory systems, but such control is generally lacking in the early stages of international expansion. In the early stages of global growth, most firms' activities are dominated by concern for market development. Responsiveness to markets requires customization of products to local needs. Only later in the firms' operations does concern for rationalization of product lines become important.

An interesting example of this phenomenon can be seen in the case of the International Harvester Company. In its initial push into foreign markets, International Harvester designed virtually unique tractor models for each

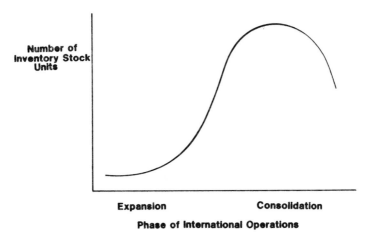

Figure 5-6.   Inventory stock units and international operations.

market in which its products were sold. By the early 1970s this policy had resulted in an inventory system that listed over 300,000 products and parts. The burden of maintaining production, supply and inventory stock lines for each of these items began to severely affect the company's operations. Pressure for rationalization of product lines led the company to move toward standardization of parts and product models, but the need to service existing products meant that inventory units could not be eliminated for many years. Similar problems have affected virtually all multinational manufacturers of consumer durables. Most have attempted to control the proliferation of models and parts, but only after that process reached large proportions.

The nature of inventory management largely follows the sourcing strategy employed by the firm. Central sourcing facilities permit centralized inventory management; distributed sourcing generally implies decentralized inventory management. Firms that transship between affiliates require extensive coordination of production and inventory management. A centralized approach also requires sophisticated production scheduling and inventory management systems. Production lines will have to be scheduled separately for each market or formulation for the product. In some cases, this may only involve changing the packaging or the container for a product. In others, the product itself will require modification. In the simple example in Table 5-7, a central sourcing facility in Puerto Rico produces a men's cologne for sale to marketing affiliates in Western Hemisphere countries. Each market requires a unique combination of product formulation, container and packaging. Production scheduling and inventory management needs are assisted by a stock unit identification system.

TABLE 5-7.   Inventory Management and Production Scheduling in a Central Sourcing Facility

| | Stock Identification Numbers | | | | | |
	Mexico	Colombia	Brazil	Argentina	U.S.A.	Canada
Cologne	101	102	103	104	104	104
Container	201	201	203	202	204	204
Package	301	301	302	304	305	306
Finished product	11	12	13	14	15	16

Central inventory management can reduce system inventory levels, control the proliferation of inventory units, reduce the costs of procurement from outside suppliers and achieve consistent quality control. This approach is most valuable when components and products are highly standardized and when the firm employs a central sourcing strategy. On the other hand, decentralized inventory management is most appropriate when products are not standardized and economics dictate distributed sourcing. If markets are served by indigenous facilities, the benefits of central inventory management will be minimal. Reporting and control relationships will still be required to ensure compliance with the firm's inventory policy, however.

Strategic Emphasis

The strategic importance of sourcing efficiency will vary sharply for different firms. In industries with relatively large gross margins, manufacturing efficiency is less important than in other industries. If the prevailing gross margin in an industry is 60%, a 10% reduction in unit sourcing costs will have less competitive significance than in an industry where gross margins are 20% of sales revenue. The key to success in most industries with high gross margins is not production efficiency but research and development and marketing activities. In such cases, the firm's strategic emphasis on sourcing operations will take a secondary position. Quality control will often be as important as unit costs in such industries.

Emphasis on sourcing activities will be greatest in situations where price competition is high. Generally, the importance of price as a competitive variable is greatest in markets exhibiting high elasticity of demand and undifferentiated products. Products in advanced stages of the product life cycle are most likely to exhibit these characteristics. Emphasis on sourcing efficiency is also warranted when the cost structure of an industry pemits the realization of significant economies of scale. If cost curves with respect to volume are relatively steep, sourcing strategy can be a critical competitive variable. The same relationship holds true when production costs vary sharply in different locations. If a product or part can be produced at a significantly lower cost in certain foreign locations, sourcing decisions assume great strategic significance. The following considerations are important in determining the level of strategic emphasis for sourcing activity.

Conditions Prompting Sourcing Emphasis	
Consumer price sensitivity	High
Level of price competition	High
Slope of production cost curve	High
Manufacturing costs as a percent of revenue	High
Stage in product life cycle	Advanced
Firms scope of international activities	Extensive
International production cost differentials	High
Degree of product differentiation	Low

These factors help determine the relative importance of sourcing decisions in global strategic management. In many cases, sourcing activities will play the dominant role in a company's global strategy. In others, sourcing will play a secondary role. In any event, the strategic importance of sourcing issues is likely to rise as a firm expands its international operations, as a product matures, and as competition increases in world markets.

NOTES

1. See, for example, Doz, Y.L., "Managing Manufacturing Rationalization Within Multinational Companies," *Columbia Journal of World Business*, Fall 1978.
2. Curhan, J.P., W.H. Davidson and Rajan Suri, *Tracing the Multinationals*, op. cit., p. 394.
3. "Ford Fiesta," *Dun's Review*, August 1977, pp. 62−64; *Wall Street Journal*, February 7, 1977, p. 6; Ford Bobcat (Al) ICCH No. 9-380-093.
4. "Five International Harvesters in One," *Forbes*, April 15, 1977, p. 60.
5. "The Strike that Rained on Archie McCardell's Parade," *Fortune*, May 19, 1980, pp. 91−99; "International Harvester: When Cost-Cutting Threatens the Future," *Business Week*, February 11, 1980, pp. 98−99.
6. See, for example, "Philips Fiddles With Controls in European Television Market," *The Economist*, June 28, 1980, pp. 81−82.
7. A classic example is the role of Burroughs Corporation and International Computers Ltd. in the Indian government's policy towards local ownership and sourcing requirements in the Indian computer industry. See Encarnation, D.J., The Behavior of Political Elites: The Organization of the Janata Coalition, Chapter 6 of A Ratioanlist Theory of Collective Action and the Policy Process, unpublished doctoral dissertation, Duke University, 1981. pp. 240−243; *Economic Times*, January 11, 1978, p. 1.
8. From remarks of Philip Caldwell at the Harvard Business School, May 1980.
9. Almost all studies of this relationship note that the equilibrium relationship is subject to significant distortions. See, for example, Aliber, p. 7 and Stickney, C.P., "Accounting Measure for Foreign Exchange Exposure," *Accounting Review*, January 1973, pp. 44−57;

Hackerman, D., "The Exchange Risk of Foreign Operations," *Journal of Business,* January 1973, pp. 42–48; Westerfield, J.M., "Empirical Properties of Foreign Exchange Rates Under Fixed and Floating Rate Regimes," *Journal of International Economics,* June 1977, pp. 181–200.

10. Bulova's international sourcing system is described in Bulova Watch Company Inc. (B) ICCH No. 1-374-051. See also "Japanese Heat on the Watch Industry," *Business Week,* May 5, 1980, p. 103.

12. The benefits of multi-plant operations are developed and covered in considerable detail in Scherer, F.M., et al. *The Economics of Multi-Plant Operation* (Cambridge: Harvard University Press, 1975).

13. See, among others; Jequier, Nicholas (ed.), *Appropriate Technology: Problems and Promises* (Paris: OECD, 1976); Robinson, Austin (ed.), *Appropriate Technologies for Third World Development* (New York: St. Martin's Press, 1979).

14. Social cost-benefit analysis techniques utilize a linear programming approach to determine the "shadow cost" or marginal product of labor. If the supply of labor is not an acting constraint on output, the social cost of using labor is zero. See Wells, L.T., Jr., "Social Cost-Benefit Analysis," *Harvard Business Review,* March–April 1975; Roemer, Michael and J.J. Stern, *The Appraisal of Development Projects: A Practical Guide to Project Analysis* (New York: Praeger, 1975).

15. Strassman, W.P., *Technological Change and Economic Development* (Ithaca: Cornell University Press, 1968); Yeoman, W.A., Selection of Production Processes for the Manufacturing Subsidiaries of U.S.-based Multinational Corporations, unpublished doctoral dissertation, Harvard Business School, 1968; See also Lecraw, D., Determinants of Capital Intensity in Low Wage Countries, unpublished doctoral dissertation, Harvard Business School, 1976.

16. Morley, S.A. and G.W. Smith, "The Choice of Technologies: Multinational Firms in Brazil," *Economic Development and Cultural Change,* January 1977, pp. 239–64; Amsalem, Michel, Technology Choice in Developing Countries, unpublished doctoral dissertation, Harvard Business School, 1978.

17. This relationship is described within the framework of the Cobb-Douglas production function in Smith, W.L., *Macroeconomics* (Homewood, Ill.: Irwin, 1970), pp. 404–419.

18. Woodward, Joan, *Industrial Organization: Theory and Practice* (Oxford: Oxford University Press, 1965).

19. Kuznets, Simon, *Economic Change* (New York: Norton, 1953), p. 266; Abernathy, W.J. and J.M. Utterback, "A Dynamic Model of Process and Product Innovation," *Omega,* Vol. 3, No. 6, 1975, pp. 639–656.

20. This point is developed in Vernon, Raymond, "The Location of Economic Activity," in Dunning, J.H. (ed.) *Economic Analysis and the Multinational Enterprise* (New York: Praeger, 1974), pp. 92–93.

21. Bain, J.S., "Economics of Scale, Concentration and the Condition of Entry in Twenty Manufacturing Industries, *American Economic Review,* March 1954, pp. 15–39; Bain, J.S., *Industrial Organization* (New York: Wiley, 1967).

22. Scherer, F.M., et al., *The Economics of Multi-Plant Operations,* op. cit., pp. 63–170, especially pp. 98–108.

23. Vernon, Raymond, "International Trade and International Investment in the Product Life Cycle," *Quarterly Journal of Economics,* May 1966, pp. 190–207.

24. Stobaugh, R.B., *Nine Investments Abroad and Their Impact at Home* (Boston: Division of Research, Harvard Business School, 1976).

25. Buckley, P.J. and R.D. Pearce, "Overseas Production and Exporting by the World's

Largest Enterprises: A Study in Sourcing Policy," *Journal of International Business Studies*, Spring 1979, pp. 9–20.

26. Teece, D.J., *The Multinational Corporation and the Resource Cost of International Technology Transfer* (Cambridge: Ballinger, 1976).

27. Davidson, W.H., *Experience Effects in International Investment and Technology Transfer* (Ann Arbor: UMI Research Press, 1980).

28. Curhan, Davidson and Suri, op. cit., pp. 398–99.

29. *New York Times*, April 12, 1981, Business Section, p. 1.

30. F. Hoffman-LaRoche and Co. A.G. ICCH No. 9-374-201.

31. Many credit Losch as the founder of the field of location economics. For more recent sources, see Smith, D.M., *Industrial Location* (New York: Wiley, 1971); Collins, Lyndurst and D.F. Walker *Locational Dynamics of Manufacturing Activity* (New York: Wiley, 1975); Rosenthal, R.E., J.A. White, and Donovan Young, "Stochastic Dynamic Location Analysis," *Management Science*, February 1978, pp. 645–653; and Carroll, T.M. and R.D. Dean, "A Bayesian Approach to Plant-Location Decisions," *Decision Sciences*, Vol. 11, 1980, pp. 81–89.

32. Brubaker, S., *Trends in the World Aluminum Industry* (Baltimore: Johns Hopkins Press, 1967) pp. 153–55.

33. "Smoke Stack Steel is Aging," *Economist*, February 14, 1981, pp. 85–86; "The Sponge in Iran's Steel Future," *Fortune*, January 1971, pp. 106–113; "The New Economics of Steel Making," *Business Week*, August 3, 1974, pp. 34–39.

34. Temin, Peter, *Iron and Steel in the Nineteenth Century* (Cambridge: MIT Press, 1964), pp. 82–86.

35. Michelin Tires Manufacturing Co. of Canada Ltd. (A&B) ICCH No. 9-378-668.

36. *Business Week*, December 1, 1980, pp. 119–121; *Wall Street Journal*, June 9, 1980, p. 28; *The Economist*, November 3, 1979, p. 62–63; *Wall Street Journal*, November 3, 1981, p. 7.

37. Philips, N.V., ICCH No. 1-378-096.

38. The use of long-term contracts to secure buyer-seller relationships is particularly prominent in extractive sectors. See D'Cruz, J., Quasi-Integration in Raw Material Markets, unpublished doctoral dissertation, Harvard Business School, 1970. For a discussion of the use of long-term contracts in the textile industry, see Arpan, J., The Pacific-Basin Textile Apparel Complex, unpublished paper.

39. Yoshino, M.Y., *Japanese Multinational Enterprises* (Cambridge: Harvard University Press, 1976); Tsuromi, Y., *The Japanese are Coming* (Cambridge: Ballinger, 1976), Chapter 5; Lifson, T., Strategy and Structure of a Large Trading Company of Japan, unpublished doctoral dissertation, Harvard University, 1978; Young, A.K., *The Sogo Shosha* (Boulder: Westview Press, 1979).

40. Some recent acquisitions include General Electric-Intersil, *New York Times*, November 20, 1980, p. D5; Philips-Signetics, *Electronics*, June 7, 1979, p. 42; "Siemens-Advanced Micro Devices," *Wall Street Journal*, November 5, 1979, p. 7; "United Technologies-Mostek," *Electronic News*, December 3, 1979, p. 16.

41. Japanese suppliers and their relationships with customers are described in Vepa, R., *Small Industries in Japan* (Mystic, Conn.: Verry Press, 1967; Yamanaka, T. (ed.), *Small Business in Japan's Economic Progress* (Tokyo: Asahi, 1971); Abbegglen, J.C., *Business Strategies for Japan* (Tokyo: Sophie University Press, 1970), pp. 162–65.

42. Philips, N.V., ICCH No. 1-378-096.

43. This phenomenon is described in Buckley, P.J. and M.C. Casson, op. cit., Chapter 2.

44. *Business Week*, April 13, 1980, pp. 68–73.

SIX

Financial Policies

The principal challenge to the global firm in the financial management area is the formulation of effective structures, methodologies and decision rules for dealing with international financial transactions and functions. In addition, the assignment of responsibilities for international financial decisions and functions poses a major challenge. An effective international financial management system provides policies and structures for dealing with a number of distinct issues and activities. The following elements of international financial management are interrelated but distinct areas of activity.

Capital budgeting

Funding

Cash management

Intracompany transactions

Repatriation

Exposure management

Tax

Financial reporting (public and management)

Operating policies and structures need to be defined in each of these areas.

Operating structures for these finance functions are subject to a fundamental choice between centralized and decentralized responsibility. Certain financial management functions demand greater centralization than others. Kimber found that capital budgeting, repatriation and subsidiary capital structure decisions generally are managed centrally, while cash management and working capital management were managed locally.[1] A wide range of approaches was reported for exposure management and tax planning. Despite these general patterns, the degree of centralization varied significantly from firm to firm. Robbins and Stobaugh found that centralization of financial management typically increases as firms expand and refine their international operations.[2] However, in large, diversified corporations, significant financial management responsibilities often revert back to foreign affiliates because of the complexity and volume of the transactions involved. Regardless of the choice between headquarters or affiliate responsibility for finance functions, however, financial management is one area where the corporate headquarters typically imposes strong standards, procedures, policies and controls. Even in companies that assign virtually all financial management responsibilities to foreign affiliates, these guidelines and controls reflect the importance of headquarters' involvement in the finance function. This involvement is perhaps most pronounced in the capital budgeting process.

CAPITAL BUDGETING

Capital budgeting reflects far more thhan the allocation of a firm's financial resources. The objetives of capital budgeting include maximization of return and minimization of risk, but more importantly, capital budgeting determines the firm's strategic direction and deployment of resources. Capital budgeting decisions cannot be separated from larger strategic decisions concerning the firm's goals, objectives, strategies and structure. Within this broader framework, however, financial analysis procedures provide a means of evaluating the attractiveness of a variety of alternative investments. Standardized procedures for evaluating these options are essential, particularly at the level of operating management. Formalized project analysis policies and procedures are an important element in an effective global management system.

Several issues are important in defining capital budgeting procedures. The location of decision-making responsibility is one important issue. Most firms use formal criteria based on project size to determine where investment decisions will be made. In one typical company individual projects under $50,000 can be executed at the level of the foreign affiliate, subject to a predetermined total discretionary budget and return criteria contained in the annual plan and budget. Regional or divisional approval is required for projects involving investments larger than $50,000, again subject to discretionary budget and return criteria. Corporate approval is necessary for all projects involving investments larger than half a million dollars. Such criteria formalize the degree of central involvement in investment decisions. Even for projects selected at the affiliate or divisional levels, however, headquarters plays an important role by specifying discretionary budgets, return criteria and methods for evaluating and selecting projects.

Specification of project analysis procedures is an important area of international financial policy. Many different project analysis models can be used to evaluate investment projects. Most require discounted cash flow analysis in one form or another, although the importance of this analysis in the actual decision-making process can vary substantially. At one extreme, with extensive emphasis on quantitative analysis, capital budgeting procedures can be formalized within the framework of the capital asset pricing model. This model is widely used in designing and managing portfolios of liquid securities; it is being increasingly applied to direct investment decisions as well.[3]

The Capital Asset Pricing Model (CAPM)

This approach to capital budgeting seeks to allocate funds to projects on the basis of risk-adjusted returns, where returns are calculated from discounted cash flows. Risk reflects the beta or unsystematic variance of the project with respect to average returns on all investments.[4] In stock markets, a security with a beta of 1.0 would experience the same variance in return as the market as a whole. Although this framework is most relevant in the area of portfolio investment (i.e., for passive financial investments such as stocks or bonds), it is also relevant in analyzing direct investment projects controlled and operated by the investor. This framework can be useful in analyzing foreign direct investment decisions, but its limitations must also be recognized.

The calculation of cash flows for foreign projects is a complex task. In order to measure returns, foreign currency costs and revenues can be calculated on the usual pro forma basis. However, the resulting cash flows must then be translated back into dollars before they can be discounted to yield the required net present value or internal rate of return for the project. Future exchange rates must be assumed in converting foreign currency cash flows into dollars. A common method for estimating future exchange rates involves the use of the familiar purchasing power parity model. Under the usual assumptions of this model, the problem of estimating future exchange rates can be greatly reduced. Assuming that project revenues and costs each increase at the general rate of inflation and that exchange rates reflect inflation differentials between the home and host country, project cash flows will be unaffected by exchange rate fluctuations. In Table 6-1, there is assumed to be no inflation in the United States, and the exchange rate exactly offsets the inflation differential between the United States and Mexico. Unfortunately, it is highly unlikely that project revenues and costs would experience identical inflation rates. Although researchers report a high degree of correlation between exchange rate changes and inflation differentials, exchange rates will also deviate from expected levels.[5] Such deviations will result in increased variance and distortion of estimated returns.

The problem of estimating returns is further complicated by the problem of repatriation. Project returns can be translated into dollars readily, but conversion into dollars and actual repatriation often involves additional taxation and transaction costs. In some cases, repatriation is restricted. Few global corporations would measure project returns strictly on the basis of repatriated funds flows, but this issue must be considered in evaluating foreign investments.

Several significant problems are encountered in measuring returns within a capital asset pricing model framework. The measurement of risk proves to be even more difficult. Risk is defined within the CAPM framework as the expected variance in project cash flows. For direct investments an estimate of expected variance would be made by examining the past history of the

TABLE 6-1. Project Economics Under Purchasing Power Parity

		Inflation Rate		
	Year 1	10%	20%	30%
Project revenues (pesos)	1000	1100	1200	1300
Project costs (pesos)	600	660	720	780
Cash flow (project revenues plus project costs, in pesos)	400	440	480	520
Exchange rate	10/$1	11/$1	12/$1	13/$1
Cash flow (dollars)	40	40	40	40

firm, other firms in the same business, or aggregate statistics for the relevant industry. This estimate provides a measure of the expected volatility of the cash flows to be derived from the project. The application of such measures to foreign direct investment projects raises several concerns, however. It is easy to question the ability of a variance measure derived from past domestic operations to capture the risks associated with a future project in a foreign country. Even a variance measure for the project's industry from the prospective host country will not capture the full risk facing the firm. The risks associated with foreign direct investment tend to be associated more with default than with variance in cash flows. Assessment of default risks primarily requires qualitative analysis of economic and political conditions within a host country.

Several means of refining the measurement of risk can be envisioned. A traditional approach to this problem involves adjustments in the discount rate to include a risk premium associated with foreign projects.[6] This technique has been refined by practitioners to reflect specific risk premiums for individual countries derived from economic and political host country analysis. Projects would then be evaluated using a variance measure drawn from the project's domestic or host country industry and a discount rate reflecting the premium associated with the prospective host country. A second common practice involves the adjustment of cash flow estimates to reflect levels of risk higher than those associated with a domestic investment. Rather than using the expected value or most likely outcome figure for project cash flows, a lower figure could be used to reflect the risk involved in the project. Robinchek and Myers and Eitemann and Stonehill propose a formal method for adjusting cash flows to reflect risk.[7] They advocate reducing project cash flows to certainty equivalents and discounting these figures by the firm's risk-free cost of capital. Such an approach raises an important issue in measuring risks in international business. Certainty equivalents are not the expected value or mean of a projected cash flow estimate. They represent the risk-adjusted value of a stream of future payments to the investor. In other words, in examining a project's estimated future cash flows and weighing the attendant risks, the certainty equivalent is that stream of risk-free payments equated in value to those to be derived from the project by the investor in question.[8] In Figure 6-1, two certainty equivalents are presented. The first project, p_1, reveals a relatively low discount for risk. The investor's certainty equivalent, or stream of risk-free cash flows equal to the estimated value of the project, is only slightly below

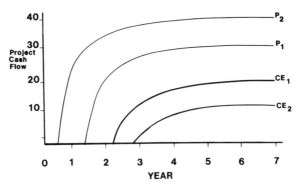

Figure 6-1. Certainly equivalents for project cash flows.

the expected revenues of the project. Project 2 is reduced to a far lower risk-free revenue stream, indicating a high degree of risk inherent in the project.

Uncertainty

The typical approach to measuring risk in terms of expected variance does not correspond to the realities of the risks involved in international direct investment decisions. In many cases, the most important element of risk in a foreign project is uncertainty. Knight distinguished between risk and uncertainty in that risk was a known variance pattern that could be reduced to an expected value in a probability distribution.[9] Uncertainty reflects ignorance of the actual parameters and dimensions of variance. In other words, the shape of the distribution curve for an outcome is unknown. Uncertainty is far more important to many investment decisions in international business than measurable variance. Since both risk and uncertainty play roles in investment decisions, it is important to speak in terms of the overall confidence levels involved in a foreign project.

Uncertainty, as distinct from measurable risk, has been shown to play a key role in actual international investment decisions. Reductions in uncertainty result in increased foreign investment activity.[10] It is important to incorporate uncertainty into formal investment models, and it is important to distinguish between uncertainty and risk in measuring the overall variance levels associated with estimated returns. This can be accomplished through redefinition of the variance associated with individual projects. The measurable variance involved in a project can be approximated through the use of corporate or industry standards, preferably for the host country in question. The beta or standard deviation of the project can then be divided by management's confidence level in the estimate in order to reflect the effects of uncertainty. If management's confidence level in the estimate is high, then the variance of the project will approximate its measurable risk or beta. If management confidence is low, the effects of uncertainty on investment decisions will be significant. The result of the division provides an overall measure of risk, including risk and uncertainty for the project.

Regardless of the method used to evaluate foreign investment projects, actual investment patterns indicate that firms facing high uncertainty heavily discount foreign investment projects. Firms with limited international experience typically exhibit highly risk-averse investment behavior. Investment patterns for the firms in the Harvard Multinational Enterprise Study reveal a powerful relationship between foreign investment experience and foreign investment behavior. Experienced firms are more likely to pursue foreign projects than inexperienced firms, with everything else equal. [11] As a firm gains experience, uncertainty levels decline, and the firm is better able to assess the returns and risks associated with a project. Firms with little experience and high uncertainty about international operations are likely to exhibit highly defensive, conservative investment patterns. Even within a specific firm, different experience and uncertainty levels for individual product lines and host countries correlate highly with levels and rates of foreign investment activity. [12] Formal means of assessing uncertainty in investment decisions can be useful in focusing attention on the impact of this factor and the value of uncertainty reduction in capital budgeting.

The role of uncertainty in investment decisions can be shown graphically. In Figure 6-2, three firms are evaluating the same foreign investment project. The first firm has extensive experience in the industry and country in question, the second has experience in the industry but not the country, and the third firm has no experience in either the country or the industry. These differences in experience levels will generally translate into differentials in estimated returns because of scale economies and learning curve benefits. They will also be revealed in the different levels of total uncertainty associated with the project by each firm. Total uncertainty is defined as the project's estimated variance or beta divided by the firms confidence factor in the variance estimate. The confidence factor in the denominator ranges from .01 to 1.0. The graph reflects total uncertainty for each firm. Firm 1 has a

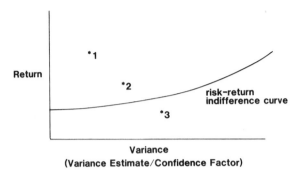

Figure 6-2.   Experience and project evaluation.

high degree of confidence in the pro-forma projections, Firm 2 has a lower level of confidence and Firm 3 has the lowest confidence about project return estimates. This same relationship can be seen within a single firm over time as well as for several firms in cross-section.

Formalization of project analysis procedures within a CAPM framework, whether it involves customization of discount rates or cash flows to reflect risk and uncertainty or the graphing of return and uncertainty estimates, provides a standard method for evaluating investment projects and allocating capital. However, complete reliance on such procedures will neglect critical environmental and strategic factors in project analysis. Incorporation of these factors into project analysis is a principal challenge to managers of global corporations.

Environmental and Strategic Factors

Various country analysis services rank host countries on numerical scales according to perceived levels of risk. These rankings can be used to weight or discount return or variance estimates. Identification of these factors is extremely hazardous, however. Country risks vary substantially from sector to sector, and the use of an overall numerical rank can fail to capture such subtleties. Even more importantly, the risks associated with foreign invest-ment projects should not be equated with the traditional concept of risk as variance. Volatility and fluctuation in returns is certainly a concern in foreign investment projects, perhaps more so than in a domestic setting. Other types of risk may be more important for such projects, however. The risk of expropriation, formal or informal, is an important consideration. Insurance can be purchased to offset formal expropriation risk, but the more prevalent mode of expropriating returns and not assets is far more subtle. Political risk, in its full sense, reflects the possibility that project returns or assets may be confiscated in whole or in part through various political agencies. Rather than incorporating estimates of the likelihood of partial or complete expropriation into the variance estimate, separate criteria can be adapted to qualify rather than quantify the nature of such risks. A strong case can be made for evaluating the environmental attractiveness of a project separately from its financial attractiveness. In many companies, separate cases must be made for both the financial attractiveness of the project and the environmental attractiveness of the host country before a project is approved. Assessment of environmental conditions, as described in Chapter 3, can be just as important as financial analysis in foreign investment decisions. One need only cite the many financially attractive projects initiated in Iran in 1978. Country analysis is largely a qualitative art; much of its power is lost by incorporating it in a quantitative model.

Foreign Investment Evaluation Procedures

A recent survey of 105 U.S. multinational enterprises outlines the actual procedures used to evaluate foreign investment projects. The criteria used for evaluating projects varied significantly among these firms. The following six criteria were cited as the most important measures for selecting foreign investment projects.

Criteria	Percentage of Firms Placing Premium Emphasis on This Criteria
Payback	21.9
ROI	31.4
Return on sales	8.6
Internal note of return	46.7
Net present value	13.3
Contribution to earnings per share	18.1

Total exceeds 100% because of multiple responses

The definition of the income stream also varied sharply for this sample of firms. Earnings after foreign taxes were cited by over half of the firms sampled, but cash inflows to the parent after foreign and domestic taxes were used by over one third of the firms in evaluating projects. The third most frequently cited measure of income included cash flows to the parent plus reinvested earnings.

On the investment base, 52% of the parent firm measured investment solely in terms of the parent's net contribution in the form of equity and direct debt. Total capital employed was used by 45% of the firms to measure the investment base.

The majority of the firms in the sample reported that their evaluation of project risk was primarily subjective. However, based on risk assessment of any sort, over 80% of the firms reported that they did adjust their evaluation procedures to reflect business risk. The following risk adjustments were made by different percentages of the firms:

Method	Percentage of Firms
Vary hurdle rate of return	60.0
Vary cost of capital	25.7
Vary pay-back period	28.6
Adjust cash flows	5.7
Make no adjustment for risk	18.1

Total exceeds 100% because of multiple responses

A similar response was reported when the firms were questioned about political or foreign exchange risk alone, although a larger percentage of the firms—29 and 37%, respectively, reported that they made no adjustment for political or exchange risks in their financial analysis.*

Strategic factors can also outweigh financial considerations in project evaluations. Otherwise attractive projects may be rejected because they divert energies from the company's grand design. A strategic commitment to expansion in a given sector can also cause firms to accept projects with unattractive financial prospects. Projects must fit with the stated goals, objectives and values of the corporation. Lucrative projects involving severe exploitation of labor or requiring questionable business practices will be rejected by most firms. There are also many cases where externalities such as use of management resources, the initiation of a relationship with another party, market access, or spillover effects on existing markets could outweigh immediate financial considerations.

It is particularly important to consider global competitive dynamics in capital budgeting. Firms using strict financial criteria in capital budgeting are highly susceptible to targeted, concentrated competitive activity. Imagine two global competitors operating in the same industry and same set of

*Source: Wicks, M. E., A Comparative Analysis of the Foreign Investment Evaluation Practices of U.S.-based Multinational Companies (New York: McKinsey and Company, 1980)

countries. One firm concludes that fundamental political, demographic and economic trends in Spain warrant expansion of its existing operations there. This leads to an expansion of advertising and increased investment in distribution, leading to an immediate increase in market share. As a result, the second firm's Spanish affiliate fails to meet its budgeted financial objectives. Since this firm allocates capital principally by financial criteria, investment in Spain is reduced and the Spanish affiliate fails to grow and expand. Firms that rely on financial results and projections are highly vulnerable to competitive strategies involving price cuts, increased promotion, improved product quality, credit terms or other benefits in targeted markets. Competitors pursuing such a strategy can selectively and sequentially cripple the foreign operations of a finance-driven company. Capital budgeting decisions must always be viewed within a strategic perspective.

Effective capital budgeting combines financial analysis, environmental analysis and strategic assessments. Responsibility for these functions will typically exist within separate and distinct parts of the organization. Within the financial analysis function alone, affiliate managers might be responsible for estimating pro forma cash flows in local currency, while central staff estimate the relevant exchange rates, discount rates and variance factors applicable to a project. Environmental analysis, if done internally and formally, might be conducted within a planning group at regional or corporate headquarters. Assessment of the fit between potential investments and the strategic posture of the firm must occur at senior management levels. Strategic posture includes the objectives, goals, and policies of the firm; existing and planned programs of action and direction; and the firm's relationships with principal competitors, customers, suppliers, internal and external constituencies and public institutions. Effective capital budgeting systems possess mechanisms for incorporating each of these factors into project analysis.

In practice, capital budgeting systems typically involve extensive negotiation and bargaining. Political processes, track records and the charisma of project champions can play key roles in determining capital investment patterns. The balance between qualitative and quantitative analysis and between formal and informal decision processes are important variables in designing effective capital budgeting systems. These issues will be addressed further in Chapter 8.

Once a project has been approved, regardless of the nature of the capital budgeting process, functional considerations come to the fore. Legal, logistical, personnel and financial concerns dominate this early stage of

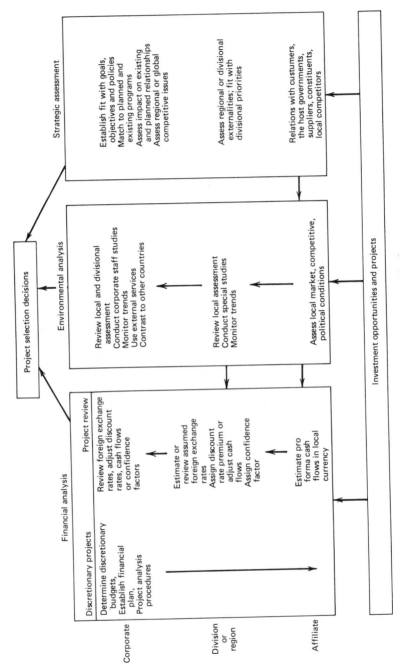

Figure 6-3. Elements of the capital budgeting system.

228

project implementation. Many of these concerns need not be addressed at the corporate level if the project is implemented by an existing affiliate. Even in such cases, however, financial issues will generally require corporate involvement. Delivery of funds to the foreign affiliate responsible for the project is of primary importance.

FUNDING OF FOREIGN AFFILIATES

The capital budgeting and planning processes formalize the net funding requirements of each foreign affiliate. These formal requirements can often be supplemented by capital needs that arise and are approved outside the scheduled budgeting cycle and process. Separate mechanisms for dealing with irregular funding requirements are important, but the bulk of the funding schedule presumably falls within the formal capital budgeting and operating plan cycle. Given a set of specified funding requirements and a timetable, the treasurer's function is to deliver funds in a form such that a number of funding criteria are optimized. Cost minimization is probably the principal criterion for determining how affiliates are funded. In addition, the effect of funding decisions on liquidity, political risk, tax and repatriation factors, exchange risk, capital structure and institutional relationships are also important. Assessment of these factors is an important process in evaluating different funding options.

The range of options available in funding foreign affiliates can be extensive, but three fundamental variables largely determine the principal alternatives. Choices between debt and equity, internal and external sources and local or foreign currency determine the key dimensions of a funding package. These are not the only variables of concern to management, nor are they binary variables. Additional issues can be addressed within a broad framework that focuses on these three factors. The use of short- or long-term debt, fixed or floating rate loans, or guarantees can be aaddressed within the context of determining the overall role of debt in the funding package.

The process of evaluating all funding alternatives with reference to a set of funding criteria is a complex and demanding task. Many firms rely on decision rules or guidelines to simplify funding decisions. Stipulation of such policies is a basic step in addressing the funding function. At one extreme, universal decision rules can be used to dictate funding patterns. Policies specifying the maximum use of host country debt provide one example. A

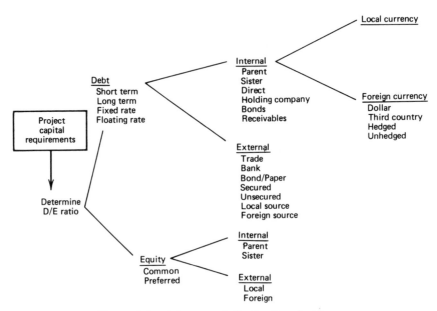

Figure 6-4.   A framework for funding decisions.

more selective approach specifies distinct funding policies for different types of projects. Under such an approach, host country debt would be maximized for projects in inflationary or politically unstable countries, while dollar debt might be used in low inflation environments. At the other extreme, analysis of individual funding programs can be approached on a case-by-case basis. Under the latter approach, the management focus falls on standardizing the analytical process rather than the decision rule. Regardless of the broad approach taken, trade-offs between different funding options must be factored into funding policies and analytical procedures. Assessment of the costs and benefits of different funding options can begin within the framework presented above.

Funding Options

The trade-offs between debt and equity are widely discussed in the international finance literature. Much of this discussion focuses on the relative cost of debt and equity to the firm. The issue of determining the relative cost of debt and equity is not a key concern in international funding activities if the affiliate is wholly owned by the parent firm. In such cases, the choice between providing funds in the form of debt or equity has no direct impact on the cost of funds to the parent. The relevant cost of funding is simply the parent's opportunity cost of capital.[13] Costs to the system will always be the parent's cost of capital regardless of how funds are provided to the affiliate. The choice between debt and equity can be made on grounds other than cost under such conditions.

If external markets are used to sell equity in the venture, the comparison of costs for debt and equity becomes essential in weighing this choice. However, the usage of public equity markets by U.S. affiliates is extremely rare. Less than 3% of all U.S. foreign affiliates have publicly traded stock.[14] In many such cases, the stock is traded because of legal requirements for local ownership. Despite exceptional cases, such as ITT's Standard Elektrik Lorenz $300 million equity offering in 1977,[15] public external equity markets do not represent a principal option for funding foreign affiliates. Outside of public equity markets, foreign affiliates do raise funds from joint venture partners. It would be hazardous, however, to apply funding motives to the use of joint ventures. Funding issues are very important in structuring joint ventures, but such considerations are rarely cited as the principal motive for entering such arrangements.[16] To a large extent, the choice between debt and equity hinges on other considerations.

In terms of the funding criteria cited earlier, debt offers advantages in several dimensions. The nature of the advantages differs depending on the currency of denomination. Debt can be used to reduce repatriation barriers, since interest and principal payments typically are not subject to restrictions. In order to realize this benefit, however, the lender must be located outside of the affiliate's host country, and the loans will have to be denominated in a currency other than that of the host country. The benefits of repatriability must then be weighed against the costs and risks of foreign currency funding. Host currency debt does not offer repatriation benefits. In fact, heavy reliance on local debt can reduce a firm's ability to remit funds. Repatriation laws generally permit firms to remit a fixed percentage of their registered capital annually.[17] Registered capital typically is based on the amount of equity invested in the affiliate. Host currency debt does offer several distinct advantages, however. Since the affiliate's cash flow will be realized in local currency, no exchange risk will be encountered in payment of interest and principal. Reliance on host currency debt provides substantial reductions in exposure to political risk. In the event of confiscatory action, the parent's direct exposure is limited to its net capital infusion. This benefit can be foregone if the parent extends guarantees to the affiliate's creditors, but reliance on host country debt can provide a major deterrent to confiscatory political action. By establishing working relationships with local financial institutions, the affiliate can gain political as well as commercial assistance.

The use of host country debt can reduce political risk and exposure, but it should not be viewed as a means of reducing economic risk and exposure. Even in the absence of direct guarantees, most multinational firms would not be able to divorce themselves from their affiliates' operations and obligations. Reliance on local debt reduces the direct exposure of the parent, but the best measure of the parent's gross exposure in any host country is the sum of its affiliates' liabilities.

Debt can be used to achieve benefits in the areas of political risk and institutional relationships (host country debt) and repatriation (foreign debt). Both forms of debt provide tax advantages. Interest payments are tax-deductible in virtually all host countries, while dividend payments are generally not tax-deductible. In some countries, however, interest payments to foreigners are subject to withholding taxes, discriminatory exchange rates and holding periods, [18] so that the tax advantages of foreign debt are reduced.

The advantages of debt relative to equity are less clear in examining capital structure issues. If equity is used to fund a foreign affiliate, a capital structure is created with significant debt capacity. Initial funding in the form of equity is consistent with a decentralized philosophy of financial management. Given a large equity base, affiliate managers can establish local funding relationships to meet ongoing financial requirements. The use of internal debt in initial funding is more consistent with tight operating controls. Another aspect of capital structure is its impact on reported earnings. At the affiliate level, returns on equity for debt-heavy affiliates can be misinterpreted by government or public figures, raising the issue of monopoly profits. On the other hand, the heavy use of equity can result in significant fluctuations in the parent's reported earnings and net worth as a result of the reporting requirements of FASB No. 8 and its successor.

In the absence of any analysis of the actual costs of different funding options, the choice between different funding options can be made by weighing the relative importance of different funding criteria. Where political and exchange risk are important factors, host currency debt offers distinct advantages. Where repatriation is the key concern, internal foreign

Pros and Cons of Different Funding Mechanisms

Principal Funding Approaches	Principal Advantages	Costs & Risks
External local debt	Low political risk Tax deductions	Availability of funds Repatriation
	Eliminate affiliate exchange risk Institutional relationships	Capital structure (debt capacity, financial ratios)
External foreign debt	Tax deductions Access to low-cost funds	Affiliate exchange risk
Internal foreign debt	Repatriation Tax deductions Economics of central borrowing Access to low-cost funds	Affiliate exchange risk
Internal equity	Debt capacity Managerial flexibility Economies of central borrowing Access to low-cost funds	Translation exposure Repatriation Expropriation

debt is the best option. Internal equity represents the best option for rapidly growing affiliates in firms with decentralized management.

These generalizations do not take into account differentials in cost for these options. It cannot be assumed that costs will be equal for all options. Internally provided funds are likely to be less expensive than funds received by the affiliate from external sources. If the parent corporation raises funds centrally and distributes them to individual affiliates, economies will be realized. In addition, the parent will probably be able to access funds at lower cost than affiliates. Even if an affiliate could tap the Eurodollar market or another low-cost source of funds because of parent guarantees, the cost of a series of such financing arrangements will be greater than one large central offering.

Although cost considerations may weigh in favor of internal funding of foreign affiliates, there are also cost-related factors that appear to favor funding in the currency of the host country. In theory, currency denomination should not affect estimates of financing cost. The interest parity model holds that any differentials in interest costs will be exactly offset by charges in currency exchange rates, ex ante.[19] Consequently, the expected cost of financing will be the same in all currencies. Calculations of ex post facto borrowing costs in different currencies can differ, but costs tend to be roughly equal for major currencies. If expected costs are equal, a common characteristic of host country tax codes acts to favor the use of local debt.

Many foreign countries, such as Australia, Indonesia, South Africa and West Germany, do not tax gains or losses arising from most long-term foreign exchange transactions. In many other countries such gains or losses would be subject to preferential tax rates or reserve treatment.[20] These tax conditions act to increase the after-tax effect of foreign exchange gains or losses relative to interest costs. Interest costs are generally deductible in full. An example of this effect is the following:

Analysis of Funding Options

	Dollar	Peso
Interest rate	20%	40%
Exchange rate (t_o)	p10/$	
Predicted devaluation under interest parity	$\dfrac{x_{t1} - x_{t0}}{x_{to}} = \dfrac{i_{US} - i_{Mex}}{1 + i_{US}} = -13.3\%$	
Future exchange rate (t_1)	11.33 pesos/$	

Cost of Funding to Affiliate (in millions of pesos)

Dollars:	Principal	Interest	Total
1. Convert $1 million to 10 million pesos			
2. Repay $1 million = 11.33 million pesos	11.33		11.33

	Principal	Interest	Total
3. Pay monthly interest installments of $16,667.00 at average rate of 10.75p/$		2.15	
4. Pre-tax cost			13.48
5. After-tax cost [13.48-(.5)2.15m]			12.405

Pesos:

	Principal	Interest	Total
1. Borrow 10 million pesos			
2. Repay 10 million pesos	10.0		10.0
3. Pay 4 million pesos interest		4.0	
4. Pre-tax cost			14.0
5. Tax cost [14.0-(.5)4.Om]			12.0

If foreign exchange gains and losses are not taxable, the after-tax cost of the dollar option is significantly higher than the peso debt. This effect will tend to favor host currency financing, but its ultimate effect is determined by the ratio of tax rates for exchange gains or losses relative to those for interest costs, and the nominal interest rate in the host country. The higher the interest rate relative to the dollar rate, the more powerful the after-tax effect in favor of host currency debt. This example assumes that foreign exchange results are not tax-deductible, while interest costs are deductible at the 50% corporate tax rate. As a result, the after-tax cost of the host currency option falls below the cost of the dollar option on an after-tax basis. This effect will encourage financing in local currency whenever nominal interest rates exceed those in the United States, and when tax codes treat exchange effects as nontaxable or preferential items. The decision rule that emerges from this analysis is as follows: Given interest parity cost expectations and preferential tax treatment of exchange gain and losses, the least-cost financing option will be denominated in the currency with the highest nominal interest rate.

When cost differentials do not appear to be significant for principal options, funding decisions can be based on other criteria. It is important, however, that financial officers attempt to identify those cases in which significant cost differentials may exist. Procedures for calculating expected financing costs in different currencies are an important part of an effective funding system. In many cases, expected financing costs can be measured with great precision for different funding options. Where future markets or forward facilities exist, the expected costs of borrowing in different currencies can be determined with perfect accuracy. Future rates provide both a measure of expected financing costs, and more importantly, an opportunity to lock in a fixed financing cost for any option. Total financing costs for each currency will be interest costs plus any exchange gains or losses incurred in the forward transaction.

In Table 6-2, each of the currencies except the French franc is expected to appreciate relative to the dollar. If a firm borrows in any of these currencies and converts the proceeds into dollars, it will take more dollars than were initially realized to repay the loan. Futures markets permit the firm to fix the exact number of dollars required to repay the loan. In the case of the Swiss franc, the firm would need to borrow 2,084,202 Swiss francs to realize proceeds of $1 million. To repay the 2,084,202 Swiss francs in one year, $1,052,571 will be needed at the given future exchange rate. By entering a futures contract to buy that number of Swiss francs one year from today at that exchange rate, the exchange risk of the transaction is removed and the exact borrowing cost can be computed. These costs can then be compared to expected costs of borrowing for other currencies. If major cost differences are found for different options, funding decisions can be based on cost alone.

TABLE 6-2   Financing Costs in Different Currencies (August 1981)

| Currency | Exchange Rates ($/x) | | | Exchange Cost* | Total Cost |
	Prime Rate	Spot	One Year Forward		
United Kingdom pound	13.0%	1.8745	1.9267	2.8%	15.8%
French franc	15.9	.1732	.1694	(2.2)	13.7
Danish mark	14.25	.4155	.4277	2.9	17.15
Yen	6.5	.00434	.004697	8.2	14.7
Swiss franc	7.0	.4798	.5139	7.1	14.1

*Forward spot/spot, (For example, the United Kingdom: (1,9267−1,8745)/.8745=2.8%).

If major cost differences do not appear to exist, several approaches can be taken. One of several possible decision rules can be applied. If management believes that central sourcing of funds provides significant economies and controls, dollar debt could be used in all such cases. If the benefits of host currency debt are seen as offering greater benefits, local funding can be emphasized for all indeterminate funding programs. A decision rule emphasizing the use of the debt option with the highest nominal interest rate could also be justified. A fourth approach involves additional analysis and screening before determining which option is best for the project. This analysis could focus on underlying economic trends, such as inflation, real interest rates and exchange rate determinants, as well as political and managerial conditions, to determine the best funding option given the needs of the affiliate, the risks involved and projections of economic conditions.

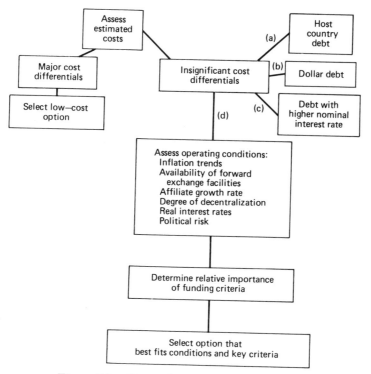

Figure 6-5. Cost analysis for principal options.

CASH MANAGEMENT

Once affiliates have been initially funded, several ongoing financial functions require attention. One of the most important is cash management. Cash management is closely related to funding activity in that it can involve international transfers of funds within the corporation. Excess cash reserves within one part of the global company can be used to fund the requirements of other affiliates, so that cash management and funding can be closely related. The most important aspect of cash management, however, does not involve international transfers. In developing foreign affiliates, the implementation of basic financial management systems is a critical concern. Perhaps the most important of these systems revolve around the cash management function. Accounting and EDP systems are an important foundation for this function and are needed to ensure effective cash management. Given these foundations, the cash management system monitors the receivable and payable position of the company, payroll and overhead expenditures and other transactions. The resulting data can be used to project cash balances and needs. Other functional areas will use the underlying system for their purposes as well. Marketing, inventory and cost accounting functions, in particular, are closely tied to the cash management system.

Once cash needs and balances can be determined with a high degree of accuracy, affiliate financial officers can determine the long-term funding and short-term financing needs of the affiliate. Any net long-term requirements can be entered into the parent's capital budgeting process for approval before funding decisions are made. Short-term financing needs might be handled by the affiliate itself.

Once an effective cash management and reporting system is in place in all affiliates, an additional dimension of cash management activity can be pursued. International cash management structures the short-term use of surplus cash accrued by foreign affiliates. There are several different approaches to this aspect of international cash management. One dimension is the degree of central involvement in the process. Some companies require that all affiliates' surplus cash balances be transferred to a central account. The management of the central pool can be given several possible mandates. The unit can be structured much as a money market fund, where affiliates can withdraw funds on demand. The pool would probably be invested in short-term liquid securities under such circumstances.

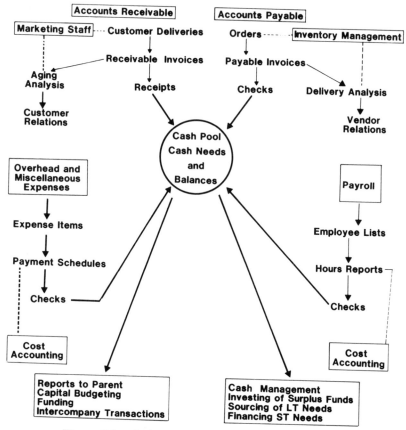

Figure 6-6. Cash management system for affiliates.

Central management of surplus funds is likely to have several distinct advantages. First, there are the benefits of specialization of management. Second, there are economies arising from the larger pool of funds available to the central manager. The larger pool permits the central manager to extend the term of a portion of his or her assets to realize higher returns. Affiliate managers might be less willing to lock up funds for longer time periods. The size of the pool also may permit investment in securities not available to individual affiliates. Central management provides an opportunity to restructure the currency denomination of the firm's cash assets as well. Centralized management permits greater control over the currency and asset composition of the portolio.

Decentralized management does offer several advantages, however. Local control of cash surpluses results in an automatic diversification of assets. Local managers have knowledge of and access to local security markets, which will often be closed to a central manager. The returns on surplus cash balances realized by affiliate investment of those funds could equal or exceed the returns realized through central investment. If the advantages of decentralized management appear to justify such an approach, a third option can be valuable: central cash managers can be given an option to use affiliate funds if they can exceed local returns available to the affiliate. If the central unit believes it can exceed local returns, it will ask the affiliate to deposit funds in a New York or other bank in its name. The affiliate is then paid interest at its opportunity cost. Any return over and above that rate will be the net contribution of the central management unit. If the central unit cannot equal or exceed any affiliate's return, it will prefer to relinquish responsibility for its funds. Such a system would permit flexibility in management of surplus cash and would work to maximize returns. It would not, however, optimize the currency, risk and term composition of the aggregate cash pool.

These approaches represent different means of structuring liquid cash investment activity for a global corporation. As mentioned earlier, cash surpluses can also be used to fund direct capital investments. A central approach to such a system would create an internal bank available primarily for intrasystem loans. Under such an approach, affiliates' contribution to the pool would not be treated as demand deposits. Access to the funds would be achieved only through approval of the capital budgeting system. Many firms do use surplus cash in one affiliate to finance the needs of others.

There are several benefits to such an approach. The parent will not wish to borrow external funds to finance an affiliate if surplus cash is internally available, since the return on cash balances will be below the cost of raising additional debt or equity. When surplus cash accrues in a foreign affiliate, it could be remitted to the parent and then loaned directly to another affiliate. However, by remitting funds to the parent in the usual form of interest, dividends or fees, tax liabilities will be incurred. By loaning the funds directly from the surplus affiliate to the affiliate in need of capital, the tax issue is eased. Such transactions are one of many forms of intracompany financial transactions managed by central financial officers.

Intracompany Transactions

Intracompany transactions provide vehicles for both funding and cash management activities. Some intracompany transactions are executed solely for such financial purposes. Others occur as a result of operating ties between members of the corporate network. Intracompany payables and receivables result from the movement of goods and services between units. Such transactions can be substantial and will require corporate supervision, guidelines and often active management. One of the most important issues in managing intracompany transactions, domestic or international, is transfer pricing. Transfer pricing guidelines range from strict arm's-length approaches such as found in ITT to strict cost-plus formulas in companies such as Philips.[21] Both approaches have obvious disadvantages. With the cost-plus system, there may be an incentive to discriminate against internal customers. With arm's-length sales, there may be an incentive for affiliates to purchase from external, rival suppliers. Sourcing policies that require internal sourcing or permit outside purchases are an important dimension of intrasystem transactions policy. For global corporations, any rigid sourcing or transfer-pricing policy has an obvious drawback. Such policies neglect the potential to use intrasystem transactions for funding, cash management and taxation benefits. The following example illustrates this potential.

A company's French affiliate requested and received approval for a $1 million working capital injection. This injection could be accomplished through adjustments in the terms of intracompany transactions. The affiliate purchases $4 million in components from the parent and exports $6 million to sister affiliates annually. By reducing transfer costs on component by 10% and increasing export prices by 10%, the entire working capital requirements can be funded. Such an approach seems to offer a tidy solution to the affiliate's funding requirements, but several issues must be addressed. First and foremost, such practices can violate tax laws. Transfer pricing adjustments have been used in the past to shift profits from high tax jurisdictions to tax havens. Tax authorities around the world are very sensitive to such practices.

In the preceding case, even where transfer pricing shifts funds to non-tax haven countries, tax authorities in the United States would view a reduction in export prices as evasion of U.S. taxes. Second, adjustments in transfer prices raise enormous managerial and business unit evaluation problems. Sales and profitability figures cannot be used for evaluation, planning and capital budgeting purposes without readjusting to show the effects of the original modifications. The problems associated with such a process can be significant. Third, active use of transfer pricing and intracompany transactions for financial purposes can result in deviation from line management priorities and prerogatives. For example, financial managers could recommend that an affiliate in need of funds supply existing export markets at the expense of other established suppliers within the corporation. Most companies would be unwilling to permit funding requirements to dominate operating activities of this sort.

In addition to transfer pricing adjustments, payment terms can be manipulated to shift funds from one affiliate to another. The use of leads and lags in payments is an effective means of increasing an affiliate's working capital. By accelerating payment on the intracompany sales of an affiliate while simultaneously delaying payment on it bills, significant increase in working capital can be achieved. In the preceding example of the French affiliate, a 20-day increase in its export receipts and a 45-day delay in its import payments results in an injection of $958,000. Other details of payment terms can also be utilized to shift funds. Billing dates, currency denomination, and payment of insurance, shipping and customs costs are among the variables that can be used for this purpose.

The extent to which operating transactions are used to shift funds within a global corporation depends on management's willingness to superimpose such activities on operations. Many companies adopt policies restricting the use of operating transactions for such purposes. Others use such transactions extensively to shift funds. A compromise policy might require operating units to report all scheduled intracompany transactions to a central financial unit. That unit can then serve as a clearing house to net all transactions and facilitate payments. In a more active approach, the schedule of transactions dictated by operating managers can be scanned to identify opportunities for meeting financial management's objectives and requirements. Under this approach, financial managers would not be able to influence the direction of operating transactions, but some control over prices and payment terms could be exercised.

Financial managers' control over the terms of operating transactions varies considerably. In many cases, they have relatively little power to use these transactions for their purposes. However, financial managers typically play a more important role in determining intracompany payments of interest, fees, royalties, dividends and principal. These payments are used, within certain legal and operating constraints, primarily to meet financial management objectives and requirements. Such financial transactions can be used to support funding and cash management activities. The intrasystem purchase and sale of financial instruments provides an effective means of shifting funds. Specification of interest rates and payment schedules on intracorporate bonds and paper can be used to fine-tune these activities. Fees and royalties offer additional vehicles for these purposes. Dividend payments are another important tool in managing intracompany transactions. Funding and cash management objectives are important in determining schedules for these transactions, but liquidity, reported earnings and repatriation issues are also important.

Repatriation Policy

Fees, royalties, interest and dividend payments are largely subject to the firm's repatriation policy. Firms wishing to achieve pay-back as soon as possible in a foreign investment will maximize initial payments of fees and royalties. Repayment of intracompany debt and dividend payments could also be initiated early in the affiliate's existence. The emphasis on immediate pay-back would be greatest in high-risk ventures, most notably in extractive sectors or politically unstable countries. In more typical affiliates, the need for working capital to finance growth will require minimal net repatriation in the early stages of the affiliate's life. Repatriation will increase after the affiliate becomes established in the market. Mature affiliates represent the cash cows within the parent's portfolio of foreign units. In addition to growth rates, levels of repatriation depend on political and exchange risk, affiliate cash flows and parent needs.

The actual means of repatriation depends on tax, legal and structural considerations. Interest and fees are taxable at U.S. corporate tax rates if they are remitted directly to the parent. Credits for foreign income taxes are applied to dividend receipts, but significant tax liabilities can still be incurred if foreign tax rates are less than the U.S. rate. Holding companies based in countries that do not tax dividend receipts can be used to handle such payments. In addition to the usual tax havens, many Western countries such as Holland and the United Kingdom do not tax foreign dividend receipts for holding companies.[22] The holding company, which often exists

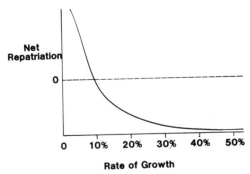

Figure 6-7.   Repatriation and affiliate growth: a theoretical relationship.

within a regional administrative entity, can then act as a bank to fund affiliates and as a cash management center for surplus funds. It is important to note that the use of such entities can be viewed as tax evasion by U.S. authorities. The United States is relatively unique in that it does not tax the foreign earnings of U.S. companies until the earnings are remitted to the parent in the form of dividends or liquidations. The accumulation of retained earnings in foreign holding corporations can be viewed as a means of avoiding U.S. taxes. Such activities are subject to review by tax authorities. U.S. tax authorities can "impute" a transfer of earnings to the parent if retained earnings accumulate in offshore holding companies.[23] This process makes foreign earnings taxable whether or not they are actually paid to a U.S. corporation.

Interest payments are frequently routed through similar legal structures to minimize taxes. Finance affiliates "located" in such places as the Netherlands Antilles, Bermuda, Luxembourg and Switzerland float Eurobonds under the parents' guarantee. The proceeds are loaned to operating affiliates by the finance unit. Interest payments are accumulated by the finance affiliate at extremely low tax rates. These payments and principal repayments can be made available for use by central financial managers through banking mechanisms. In other cases, the offshore finance affiliate can serve as a working internal bank.

Legal intermediaries can also be used to collect management fees and royalties. Such practices are somewhat less common for these transactions because of the operating services associated with their payment. Some companies do create technical assistance affiliates in countries such as the Bahamas or elsewhere, however. The use of fees and royalties to transfer funds is limited by regulations in many host countries.[24] These payments must reflect actual services and assets rendered to the affiliate, so that their use for financial purposes will be limited.

Repatriation policy formalizes the process of determining the level and timing of remittances from individual foreign affiliates. The use of different repatriation mechanisms under different conditions can also be specified. Finally, repatriation policy affects the legal and organizational structure of intrasystem transactions.

TAX AND FINANCIAL REPORTING

Tax factors play a key role in determining the level, legal structure and form of repatriation activity. These factors play a broad role in virtually all functions of international financial management. Tax accounting for a global business carries highly demanding requirements. It is very difficult to attain and maintain mastery of a single national tax code. Differences in national tax codes are remarkable, considering the degree of global standardization in other aspects of financial management. Tax codes change with annual frequency, requiring continuous study and updating of tax planning and management. The letter and spirit of tax codes can also differ sharply. Given this type of environment, it would be understandable if many firms opted for a passive, decentralized approach to tax management. Under such a policy, taxes would be handled by local management who would be evaluated on an after-tax basis. Affiliate managers would have the option of developing internal expertise or relying on local legal and accounting services. In either case, there are some strong arguments in favor of local tax management. Most importantly, relations with tax authorities will require local expertise. Relations with host government agencies cannot be centralized. The use of local tax management also enables the firm to keep abreast of tax code revisions and rulings.

There are several obvious problems with such an approach. One is the firm's inability to coordinate tax planning with other elements of central financial planning. The system tax implications of various options in funding, cash management, repatriation and other functions will be difficult to estimate without central tax expertise. Second, minimization of taxes on a country-by-country basis may not achieve the same results as central tax management. Actions taken to reduce taxes in one country may increase

TABLE 6-3.   Income and Withholding Tax Rates (1980)

	Income Tax		Withholding Tax	
		Dividends	Interest	Royalties
Argentina	33%	17.5%	11.25%	18%*
Australia	46	30	10	46
Brazil	35	25†	25†	25†
Canada	46	25	25	25
Cayman Islands	0	0	0	0
Colombia	40	20	0†	47
France	50	25	25−42	33
India	55	25	75	75
Mexico	42	21	42	42
Netherlands	48	25	0	0
Spain	33	15	15	15
United States	46	30	30	30

Source: Compiled from Ernst and Whitney International Series for Selected Host Countries
(New York, Ernst and Whitney.)
*Rates applicable if payment is approved by government agencies. Nonapproved payments are taxed at a 45% rate.
†Remittances in excess of 12% of official registered capital is subject to an additional tax commencing at 40% for remittances of 12−15% of registered capital.
‡Rate of 40% applied to nonapproved payments.

taxes for the system as a whole. Opportunities for system tax savings will be missed.

Effective tax management requires both a solid local capability and a central coordinating and planning unit. The integration of these two managerial units poses a challenge to financial managers. One means of achieving this objective is through the use of an external multinational accounting firm. The accounting firm can provide many of the same benefits that global advertising agencies provide. Accounting affiliates in foreign countries can meet the local needs of the global firm while providing a useful vehicle for international integration and coordination of tax planning and management. The accounting affiliates help meet the system problems of standardization, consolidation and coordination while providing responsive service at the host country level. Reliance on such accounting firms for financial reporting and tax management services is increasing rapidly. The big eight U.S. accounting firms have expanded abroad to meet the needs of their global customers. These firms are also active in designing and implementing management information systems, cash management systems and other management systems for multinational corporations.

In addition to tax accounting and management, financial reporting requirements are also very important. Although management has relatively few

Key International Tax Terms, Structures and Concepts

Domestic International Sales Corporation (DISC)	Purpose: Export sales from the United States. Principal benefits: Tax deferred earnings are not taxed until distributed or deem distributed. Also, transfer price latitude is permitted between the U.S. parent and its DISC.
Foreign tax credit	U.S. recipients of interest, dividends or royalties can claim a credit for any foreign taxes paid against U.S. tax liabilities. For example, a foreign subsidiary with eearnings of $1,000,000. paid $400,000 in host country taxes. U.S. tax liability on the $1 millon in earnings would be $480,000 at the 48% corporate tax rate. By applying a credit of $400,000 for foreign taxes paid, the U.S. tax liability is reduced to $80,000. When the host country tax rate exceeds that in the United States, the credit is limited to the U.S. tax liability. Firms can elect to pool all earnings and credits against aggregate U.S. taxes, however.
Offshore insurance activity	Insurance premiums paid to an affiliate are not tax-deductible in the United States. Payments to offshore insurance affiliates can be. Such offshore insurance units have become extremely popular. They have appeared, most notably in Bermuda, to permit self-insurance and deduction of premiums.
Subpart F	Tax code enacted in the Revenue Act of 1962. Subpart F permits U.S. tax authorities to tax foreign earnings under certain conditions even if they are not remitted to the United States. The code permits taxation of a foreign affiliate interest and dividend income, income from sales of services to affiliated companies, or sales of goods for affiliated companies. Under this code, gains realized in the liquidation of foreign affiliates engaged in such activities would be taxed as ordinary income rather than capital gains.

Possession corporation	A company incorporated in the United States but operating in a U.S. possession. Such companies are not taxed by the U.S. unless earnings are remitted. Such companies are not subject to Subpart F regulations if 50% of their revenues is derived from an active business in the possession itself.
Western hemisphere trading corporation	Domestic companies engaged in export activities in the Western Hemisphere receive a 30% reduction in tax liability.
Withholding tax	A tax applied by host countries to payments of interest, dividends and royalties to foreign parties. Such taxes typically range between 15 and 50%.
Value-added tax	Most countries of the world rely on indirect taxation rather than direct income taxation for fiscal revenues. The value-added tax is a principal means of applying indirect taxes. It is essentially a sales tax imposed at every level of the distribution channel for a product. Notably, most countries provide rebates of all indirect taxes when a product is exported.

policy options with respect to tax and financial reporting, effective management of these functions is a major challenge to global corporations. The development of personnel and mechanisms for managing these functions is a key responsibility of financial management.

Financial reporting practices vary depending on participation levels in the affiliate. For affiliates in which the parent system owns less than 20% of the equity, the cost method of consolidation is required. The investment appears on the balance sheet under the heading Investments in Foreign Affiliates. The entry appears at cost or market value, whichever is lower. Earnings from the affiliate are not reported in financial statements unless they are actually remitted to the parent. This practice permits manipulation of reported earnings by active management of dividend payments. Nonconsolidated foreign affiliates provide an earnings buffer for financial reporting purposes. Dividend policy can be used to determine the reported earnings of the parent company. Affiliates owned between 20 and 50% appear on the balance sheet under the equity method of consolidation. The value of the investment is recorded as initial cost plus the parent's share of accumulated earnings. The parent's share of annual earnings or losses are reported on its income statement. Honeywell reduced its stake in its French affiliate, CII-Honeywell-Bull, to 19% in the spring of 1982 so as to avoid reporting losses from this unprofitable but heavily subsidized subsidiary.

For subsidiaries owned more than 50% by the parent, standard accounting practices dictate that the affiliates balance sheet and earnings statement be consolidated with the parents' on a line-by-line basis. However, the parent has the option not to consolidate the affiliates financial statements if "significant political or repatriation uncertainties are present." Nonconsolidation provides several benefits. First, flexibility in reporting earnings is gained. Second, the liabilities of the affiliate will not affect aggregate financial ratios for the parent. Such affiliates will tend to have high debt-equity ratios, which might reduce the parents' debt capacity. Third, volatile translation gains or losses associated with Financial Accounting Standards Board (FASB) requirements can be avoided. Fourth, consolidated financial reporting requires a standardized format that can be difficult to superimpose over accounting practices and realities in foreign countries. Management has relatively little discretion with regard to financial and tax reporting requirements. Systems must be designed to meet the demands of external regulatory bodies. However, the design and management of financial reporting systems is very important for another reason. These reporting systems represent the first step in developing effective channels of communication and control between the parent and affiliate.

The design and implementation of a financial reporting system represents but one dimension of a larger management information system. In most cases, the financial reporting system precedes development of a broader management accounting system. Financial reporting systems can be used as a foundation for the implementation of broader management information systems. Consequently, design and implementation of financial reporting systems should be managed in such a way as to permit and promote expanded information collection, processing and transmission. Standardization of format, procedures and schedules is essential for effective information systems. Implementation and management of such reporting systems is an essential function in global strategic management.

Exposure Management

Exposure management is one of the most important responsibilities of international financial officers. Two different types of exposure are important in international business. All international transactions involve what can be called conversion or transaction risk. One of the parties to an international transaction must exchange its domestic currency for the currency of the other party. During the time lag between invoicing and payment for an order, currency values can shift, resulting in an increase or decrease in the cost or value of the transaction. This possibility represents the conversion risk inherent in all international transactions. Means of minimizing and managing such risks are an important element in international financial management systems. The second form of exposure is translation risk. In the process of consolidating financial statements, affiliates' asset and liability balances are translated from local currency into dollars at exchange rates in effect at the time of consolidation. Exchange rate changes can cause the asset and liability values reported to increase or decrease, resulting in changes in the book value of the parent system. Management of translation exposure is a second key responsibility for financial officers.

Management of transaction or conversion exposure generally requires a significant level of central management activity. Centralized management of transaction exposure offers the benefit of netting exposures in different currencies before engaging in any hedging activity. If each affiliate reports its payables and receivables denominated in local currency to a central unit, liabilities and assets will be offset to yield the net exposed positions in each currency for the system as a whole. The central manager responsible for transaction exposure management monitors corporate positions in each currency on a daily basis.

Two types of computer-based schedules derived from detailed accounting data are helpful in monitoring transaction exposure. One schedule records open positions in all foreign currencies for the system as a whole. An example of such a schedule appears in Table 6-4. All units report receivables and payables denominated in currency other than that of their host country to the exposure monitoring and management unit. The exposure manager then measures net exposure positions in each currency for the system as a whole. By computing dollar values for each payable or receivable at the time of entry and comparing these values with dollar values at present exchange rates, potential gains and losses can be monitored. In addition to potential gains and losses, actual gains and losses can be recorded in a separate schedule documenting the results of completed transactions. This schedule records actual gains and losses for the relevant periods and permits comparison with previous periods.

TABLE 6-4. Net Transaction Exposure Record (in local currency)

Currency	System Receivables	System Payables	Net Position	Change from Previous Day	Dollar Value at Initial Booking Date	Present Dollar Value	Net Gain (Loss)
Australian dollar	63,101	11,311	51,790	0	59,698	59,485	(213)
British pound	191,212	96,009	95,203	16,101	174,983	180,219	5,236
Canadian dollar	201,013	108,311	92,702	9,303	78,592	77,666	(926)
Dutch guilder	19,431	112,353	(92,922)	0	37,168	35,110	2,058
French franc	81,633	196,413	(114,780)	(6,311)	22,956	25,252	(2,296)
German mark	176,211	85,308	90,903	44,211	36,361	34,543	(1,818)
Italian lir	13,345,000	0	13,345,000	0	11,087	10,265	(822)
Mexican peso	491,652	0	491,652	0	19,825	19,825	0
Swiss franc	9,806	118,315	(108,509)	65,313	50,413	51,346	(933)
TOTAL							286

251

Hedging Activity

The use of such information in an exposure management program depends on corporate policy. An active approach would entail significant hedging activity to reduce exposure. Hedging policy in most cases incorporates some attempt to estimate prospects for individual foreign currencies. Although prediction of future foreign exchange rates is a hazardous business, the probable direction of the movement in rates can be projected with high degree of accuracy in many cases. It is highly unlikely, for example, that the Brazilian cruzeiro or Argentine peso would ever appreciate relative to the dollar. Relative interest and inflation rates and trends in trade balances and capital flows are widely used to predict foreign exchange rate movements.[25] Forward market rates can also be used as estimates of future exchange rates.[26] Foreign exchange advisory services are widely available to assist in the analysis of currency movements. Classification of currencies into three basic categories provides a framework for specifying hedging policy. In the following example, hedging policy may dictate that hedging is applied only when a net receivable position occurs in a weak currency or when a net payable position occurs in a strong currency. Such guidelines serve to define the responsibilities of the exposure manager.

Hedging Policy

Exposed Position	Foreign Currency Prospects		
	Strong	Neutral	Weak
Net receivable	Hold/ postpone payment	Hold/ regular payment	Hedge/ encourage payment
Net payable	Hedge/ prepay	Hold/ regular payment	Hold/ postpone payment

Definition of the exposure manager's responsibilities and authority is a key element in financial policy. The exposure management unit can be defined as a profit center, at one extreme, or simply as an information-processing unit. If the exposure manager has profit responsibility, he or she will be evaluated on the net gain or loss recorded on the transaction schedule

(Table 6-5), adjusted for the results of any hedging transactions. Alternatively, the exposure manager's mandate could reflect a management belief that gains and losses from the firms' portfolio of international transactions will offset each other over time. In such a case, a passive exposure management system might be used to simply record and monitor gains and losses. A slightly more active approach would require hedging only for large positions in a single currency.

Passive approaches to exposure management permit decentralization and avoid managerial costs. However, there are several drawbacks to such approaches. The composition of the portfolio of payables and receivables can become a problem over time. Natural forces will tend to ensure that receivables get billed in weak currencies, for example. The average life of receivables in strong currencies will tend to be less than that of receivables in weak currencies. Monitoring and compensation for such trends is important. One refinement of a passive approach gives the exposure manager responsibility to engage in hedging activity whenever indexes of portfolio quality reach certain levels. A measure of weak versus strong currency exposure for payables relative to receivables serves this purpose. One reference index would measure the ratio of weak over strong currency payables relative to the ratio of weak over strong currency receivables. The higher this index, the better the quality of the transaction portfolio. If, for example, payables denominated in currencies considered weak account for 10% of all payables at a given time, while payables in strong currencies account for 50% of the total, the numerator of the quality index would be .1/.5 or .2: the denominator would be calculated from a similar ratio for receivables. If weak currencies account for 40% of all receivables and strong

TABLE 6-5.   Transaction Portfolio Quality Index (Payable Weak/Strong Ratio) Over Receivable Weak/Strong Ratio)

			Receivables (Weak/Strong)				
Weak Currency (% of total)		Strong Currency (% of total)	.1/.5	.2/.4	.3/.3	.4/.2	.5/.1
PAYABLES .1	/	.5	1.0	.4	.2	.1	.04
.2	/	.4	2.5	1.0	.5	.25	.1
.3	/	.3	5.0	2.0	1.0	.5	.2
.4	/	.2	10.0	4.0	2.0	1.0	.4
.5	/	.1	25.0	10.0	5.0	2.5	1.0

currencies 20%, the denominator is 2.0, and the index is .2/2.0 or .1, indicating an unhealthy composition of payables and receivables. Decision rules can be developed that would require exposure managers to maintain the quality index above certain levels. Whenever the index falls below .8, for example, the exposure manager could be required to reduce exposure in weak receivables or strong payables to bring the index back to an acceptable level.

Guidelines for hedging policy can vary sharply. The mandate given to exposure managers can permit extensive latitude, even to the point of encouraging speculative activity. Such aggressive approaches often bear spectacular results. Defensive approaches to exposure management appear to be more common. In such cases, hedging is used primarily to protect against losses and to minimize exposure. Regardless of the nature of corporate policy, hedging activities are an important aspect of international financial management. Several mechanisms exist for hedging international transactions.

Hedging Techniques

Forward and future markets provide important mechanisms for hedging foreign exchange exposure. Futures markets exist for about half a dozen major currencies. These markets offer contracts of fixed amounts for each currency valid for exchange on a fixed date. Contracts for currencies traded on the Chicago Board are available for September, December, March and June delivery. Contracts for the British pound (£25,000) Canadian dollar (C $100,000), Japanese yen (Y 12.5 million), Swiss francs (125,000 S.F.) and German mark (DM 125,000) are traded on this exchange and others. To enter into a futures contract, the exposure manager places a deposit with his or her broker and takes a short or long position in the currency. The initial deposit typically represents 5 to 10% of the contract value. Additional margin deposits will be required if the value of the position declines.

Futures markets have several advantages over other forms of hedging. They are highly liquid and can be closed out at virtually any time. They do not involve interest costs other than the interest foregone on the margin deposit. Futures contracts are rarely exercised. Any gains or losses are realized upon liquidation of the contract. In a perfect hedging exercise, the gain or loss on the futures contract will exactly offset any loss or gain on the underlying transaction. In the following example, a U.S. exporting firm expects to receive 1,250,000 Swiss francs in six months. In order to hedge its transaction exposure, the firms sells 10 futures contracts at a rate of $.525 per Swiss franc. The spot rate at the time the receivable is recorded and the futures contracts opened is $.50 per Swiss franc. By entering into the futures contracts, the firm has guaranteed the dollar proceeds of the exchange transaction regardless of fluctuations in the dollar–franc exchange rate. In six months, the firm will receive the 1,250,000 francs and exchange them for dollars at the prevailing rate (Table 6-6). At the same time, the short futures position will be closed by buying 10 Swiss franc futures contracts at the market rate, which will be equal to the spot rate on the final day of the contract. The net proceeds from these two parallel transactions will be constant regardless of the spot exchange rate.

Such an example shows how futures markets can be used to cover transaction exposure. It should be noted that the closing date of the futures contract and the actual date of receipt of foreign currency rarely match perfectly. The results of the spot and future transactions will not perfectly offset each other in many cases, leading to some deviation from expected proceeds. Futures contracts do not provide flexibility in the time period or amount of coverage. Net exposure positions will differ from futures unit contract values. More importantly, efficient futures contracts exist for only a handful of major currencies. For other currencies, forward markets can be utilized. Forward markets provide greater coverage and flexibility than

TABLE 6-6.   The Effects of Future Market Hedging on Transaction Results

	Actual Exchange Rate at Closing Date				
	.45	.50	.525	.55	.60
Opening value of futures position	$656,250	$656,250	$656,250	$656,250	$656,250
Closeout value of futures contracts	562,500	625,000	656,250	687,500	750,000
Gain or loss	93,750	31,250	0	(31,250)	(93,750)
Opening value of receivable	625,000	625,000	625,000	625,000	625,000
Proceeds of franc receivable	562,500	625,000	656,250	687,500	750,000
Gain or loss	(62,500)	(0)	31,250	62,500	125,000
Net proceeds (gain or loss)	31,250	31,250	31,250	31,250	31,250

public futures markets. Forward markets are organized by the same major banks that form the bulk of the spot currency market. Forward contracts differ from futures contracts not only in institutional nature, but also in the form of contract. Forward contracts can be specified for any amount and time horizon. In contrast to futures contracts, delivery will normally be made on such contracts. Thus, when the firm described earlier receives 1,250,000 Swiss francs, it will give those francs to its bank in accordance with the forward contract. Such an approach has several advantages. Customized coverage is gained, and the need to engage in parallel spot and future closing transactions is removed. Much of the management responsibility can be assumed by the bank. The principal drawback of such an approach is the cost of the contract. Forward contracts may be less efficient than futures contracts, as measured by comparing spreads and charges on forward contracts with commissions and margin deposits interest for futures. Futures markets are likely to be more efficient than forward markets because of greater transaction volume. In many cases, the bank offering a forward contract will lay off its own risk in the futures market, so that the use of a forward contract essentially involves the use of an intermediary, with higher hedging costs the result. When both options are available, direct cost comparisons can be made. Where futures are not available, cost comparisons with other options are valuable in selecting hedging techniques.

Prior to the development of forward and futures markets, treasurers often created hedges by establishing offset loans. In this procedure, a loan is secured in the currency of the receivable. Continuing with the same example, the treasurer would borrow 1,250,000 Swiss francs from a bank. The francs would be immediately converted into dollars. When the Swiss francs were received, they would be used to pay off the loan. Exchange risk is eliminated because dollar proceeds are realized immediately. A Swiss franc payable has been established to offset the receivable. The cost of such a procedure can be calculated as the differential between interest paid on the franc loan and the interest earned on the dollar proceeds. To offset a payable position in a similar fashion, the firm would buy Swiss francs upon placing an order. The cost of such a hedge would again be the differential earned on Swiss francs versus dollar deposits.

A slightly more complex form of such offset loans is the swap or back-to-back facility. Back-to-back loans usually involve an intermediary, typically but not always a bank, and two parties planning foreign exchange transactions. One firm is planning to convert pounds into dollars in six months to make an interest payment to its parent; the other plans to convert dollars into pounds to fund a capital investment project in Great Britain. Rather than entering forward or futures contracts, the two parties can simply agree to trade directly at a specified rate and date. Each of these techniques provides a means of eliminating foreign exchange. By locking in exchange rates for futures transactions, the possibility of loss or gain is removed. Each technique involves costs that can be measured. Selection of hedging technique can be based largely on cost and convenience factors.

Speculation

Definition of and policy toward speculation is a key part of exposure management. Technically any unhedged payable or receivable involves speculation. Most firms are willing to carry certain types and amounts of unhedged positions resulting from operating transactions. Very few firms are willing, however, to enter short or long positions for financial speculation purposes. There are numerous examples of disastrous losses incurred as a result of uncontrolled speculation by foreign exchange managers. Many of these examples have occurred in financial institutions, but they are also common among global manufacturing firms.[27] The degree of latitude given to exposure managers typically permits a certain amount of speculation simply in the decision whether or not to hedge an open position in a currency. Some firms go beyond that to permit marginal speculation activity above and beyond hedging in unusual circumstances. Success in such a limited program often leads to expanded speculative activity. More typically, top management adheres to policies reflecting the general principle that "this company makes its profits in the manufacturing business, not in foreign exchange trading."

Translation Exposure

The design of a translation exposure management system poses severe philosophical and policy issues. Translation exposure does not result directly in realized exchange gains or losses. Translation results report accounting changes in the net value of affiliates' monetary assets and liabilities. These items include cash and securities and receivables on the monetary asset side and all payables and debt on the liability side. Translation results can be viewed as "paper" gains or losses with no effect on the value of affiliates' present and future cash flows. Many firms approach translation exposure management from such a philosophical base.

The assumption underlying such an approach is the going concern concept from basic accounting. Translation results reflect changes in the net sum that would be realized if an affiliate's monetary assets were liquidated and the proceeds converted into dollars. However, if foreign affiliates are viewed as going concerns, many managers believe translation exposure results should be discounted and management of such exposure downplayed. Under this approach, the sole purpose of translation exposure management might be simply recording and reporting consolidated translation results.

Several reasons encourage a more active approach to translation exposure management. The inclusion of translation gains and losses in reported earnings can have a dramatic effect on earnings per share and other measures of financial performance. The impact of such results on security prices has not been substantiated. However, one survey of chief financial officers indicates that 41% of those queried believe that security analysts consider translation gains and losses part of a firm's normal earnings stream.[28] At the bottom of such opinions may lie the basic concept that investment returns are typically composed of two components: annual cash flows plus gains or losses in the liquidation value of the underlying capital asset. Foreign affiliates are not liquid assets that can be bought and sold like securities. However, the high rate of turnover among foreign affiliates seen in Chapter 2 suggests that measures of liquidation value have some validity. Investors may also discriminate in favor of the firm that performs better in managing translation exposure in the hypothetical case where everything else is equal.

Translation results can have a dramatic impact on reported earnings. In the first year after the introduction of FASB No. 8, earnings of leading multinational consumer product companies were particularly affected. Exchange losses exceeding 50% of foreign net income were reported by several companies. Consumer companies with operations in weak currency countries are particularly vulnerable to translation losses. Consumer companies tend to carry relatively high receivable positions relative to payables because of high gross margins. The resulting net asset exposure will generate translations losses upon devaluation of the host currency unless corrective exposure management steps are taken.

Surveys of multinational corporations reveal a widespread use of hedging techniques to manage translation exposure. Evans, Folks and Jillings interviewed executives of 152 miltinational corporations and found that over

TABLE 6-7.   Foreign Exchange Losses by Consumer Product Companies (1976)

Company	1976 Exchange Loss (in Thousands of Dollars)	Exchange Loss As a Percent of Foreign Net Income
Gillette	19,081	57
Eastman Kodak	61,000	55
Philip Morris	15,520	47
Bristol-Myers	17,014	43
American Cyanamid	15,700	28
Avon	14,272	28
Cheseborough-Ponds	3,242	28
American Home Products	20,113	24
Warner-Lambert	20,800	20

Source: Annual reports.

80% followed the practice of increasing foreign borrowing in currencies with net exposed asset positions.[29] Future or forward contracts are also used periodically by a majority of these firms to cover accounting exposure. A majority of these firms also indicated that management of dividend payments, leads and lags in intracompany payments and receivables, and rescheduling of internal debt also are used to reduce exposure. Participants in the survey cited a lack of explicit company policy toward exposure managements as a pervasive problem. However, the principal objective of exposure management reported by a majority of the participants was "protection of the dollar value of foreign currency-denominated assets."

Monitoring Translation Exposure

Most global firms monitor translation exposure regardless of their exposure management policies. Reporting standards and procedures can vary significantly, but the objective is the same in all cases—measurement of net exposure positions in different currencies. One global company interviewed requires a monthly exposure statement from each of its foreign affiliates. The statement is structured as follows:

Country: _____

Month: _____ Year: _____

Local currency   *Dollar value*

Total current assets

Less: Intrasystem receivables

	Local currency	Dollar value
Plus: Deferred assets		
SUBTOTAL		
Less:		
Amounts in foreign currencies		
Amounts denominated in cash and securities		
Net receivables		
Other (specify)		
TOTAL ASSETS EXPOSED		
Total current liabilities		
Less:		
Intercompany payables		
Dividend payable		
Advance advertising provision		
SUBTOTAL		
Add:		
Deferred taxes		
Long-term debt		
Other liabilities		
SUBTOTAL		
Less:		
Amounts denominated in foreign currencies		
Loans payable		
Accounts payable		

	Local currency	Dollar value
Accrued liabilities		
Other (Specify)		
TOTAL EXPOSED LIABILITIES		
NET EXPOSURE POSITION		

Another company interviewed consolidates basic financial information into a summary statement for review purposes. The summary statement lists translation exposure positions in each currency, gains and losses in each and total profit/impact for different periods. Sample entries from the system appear below.

Daily Accounting Exposure Analysis
(in $000)

Currency	Balance Sheet Position As of (Date)	Profit/Loss Last Quarter	Profit/Loss Year to Date	Translation Last Quarter	Impact Year to Date
Italian lira	26,242	3,411	12,413	613	2,109
Mexican peso	−17,311	4,561	17,432	0	0
Spanish peseta	−21,202	3,945	16,319	291	952
South African rand	6,312	913	2,415	−809	−737
Swiss franc	12,915	7,632	21,723	415	1,150

	Current Quarter
TODAY'S TOTAL IMPACT	191
YESTERDAY'S IMPACT	431
PRESENT CUMULATIVE TOTAL	9,802

Regardless of how translation exposure is defined and reported, many firms make a significant effort to reduce or eliminate its effect. This objective is difficult to achieve without compromising operations, however. Tension between operating and financial objectives is a universal problem in exposure management. One means of reducing this problem is specification of the conditions under which exposure management activities can influence operating decisions. Rather than attempting to achieve balance in all affiliates, exposure management can focus on situations where potential losses are significant. In the following chart, affiliates with net asset positions in weak currencies or net liability positions in strong currencies pose particular problems. Guidelines for exposure management activities can also include a threshold reflecting the total value of asset or liabilities exposed.

Effects of Exposure on Earnings

	Currency Trend	
FASB Position of Affiliate	*Devalue*	*Revalue*
Net asset	Loss	Gain
Net liability	Gain	Loss

FASB No. 8 Reform?

FASB No. 8 has been subject to extensive debate and decision ever since it was first adopted in 1976. A recent study of over 100 companies by the Conference Board found that 51% favored the repeal of the standard. As a result of such criticisms the Financial Accounting Standards Board established a panel to review FASB No. 8 and recommend revisions. In August 1980 an Exposure Draft on Foreign Currency Translation was released. The draft recommends changes in the measurement of exposure and the reporting of translation gains and losses. Under the proposed system exposure would reflect all financial assets and liabilities, including inventory. Such a system would not eliminate exposure; if anything it would increase exposure for affiliates with net asset positions. More attractive to most managers is the recommendation that gains and losses not be reported on the income statement. Under the proposed system, translation gains and losses are entered into on equity account. This approach is highly similar to the reserve treatment used in the United States prior to FASB No. 8 and in many other foreign countries today. Actual transaction gains and losses would continue to be reported on the earnings statement.

Reaction to the exposure draft has been highly mixed. The FASB panel itself approved the revision by only a 4−3 vote. Corporate treasurers appear to hold roughly the same opinion of the proposal.[28] The nature of the public response to the exposure draft has led the FASB to reconsider its position. Reform of FASB No. 8 remains an uncertain proposition.*

For affiliates with potential translation exposure problems, the treasurer can utilize funding and cash management tools to reduce exposure. Net asset positions in weak currencies can be reduced by accelerating payment of dividends, royalties and fees. Declines in cash positions through repatriation or investments in capital equipment will reduce accounting exposure. As the preceding survey indicates, the most popular means of reducing asset exposure involves increasing host currency debt. An offset will be realized, however, only to the extent that the proceeds of the debt are used to fund repatriation or investment in inventory or capital equipment.

A selective, active exposure management policy involves significant managerial time and expense. An alternative approach involves reliance on general guidelines and policies in a decentralized management mode. Policies specifying the use of local debt in combination with capital structure guidelines can accomplish exposure management objectives. Capital structure guidelines can simply specify that monetary assets and monetary liabilities should always be within 10% of each other, for example.

Decentralized treatment of exposure management immediately raises conflicts between operating and financial objectives. Affiliate managers often are inclined to favor operating objectives when conflicts arise. For example, extension of credit terms and expansion of receivables improve sales and earnings performance, but can also result in an increase in asset exposure. Affiliate managers may also prefer to fund capital investments through loans or equity from the parent because interest payments or dividend requirements on such sources are often lower than the cost of raising funds locally in external markets. As a result, funding decisions and capital structure will deviate from exposure guidelines. The only means of ensuring effective decentralized exposure management involves making affiliates accountable for exposure gains and losses.

---

*Sources: Conference Board; "Why FASB No. 8 Reform Isn't Easy," Business Week, December 22, 1980; "FASB No. 8 in Transition," Business International, February 13, 1981; Exposure Draft on Foreign Currency Translation, Financial Accounting Standards Board, August 1980.

Accountability

Assignment of responsibility for translation exchange gains or losses poses a major challenge. At one extreme, the corporate treasurer can be made accountable for all translation results. To be effective in such a mode, the treasurer needs the authority to determine affiliate capital structure and capital budgets in addition to funding decisions. Given such authority, the treasurer could limit translation losses with a high dgree of reliability. The benefits of such an approach would easily be outweighed by the costs, however. Interest costs could increase sharply under such an approach. Preference for local debt, especially in high inflation countries, could add significantly to the firm's interest burden. The following example points out the potential impact of such a policy.

Gillette Corporation operates extensively in Latin America, notably in high inflation economies such as Brazil, Argentina and Chile. Razors and blades account for approximately 80% of Gillette's business in Latin America. This product line is distinguished by extremely high gross margins and relatively low capital intensity. As a result, the typical capital structure for a Gillette affiliate includes high cash and receivable positions and low payables. The resulting net asset exposure is highly vulnerable to devaluations. In 1976, for example, Gillette experienced translation losses of $1.2 million in Argentina, $2.9 million in Brazil, $.7 million in Chile, $2.8 million in Mexico and $.6 million in Peru. These reported losses caused Gillette's earnings per share in 1976 to fall below the 1975 level. In response, emphasis on host currency borrowing was increased in these countries. Gillette reported that it paid an average pre-tax interest cost of over 23% on short-term debt totaling $114.3 million in 1977. Gillette's 1977 consolidated financial statements also included cash and securities of over $130 million on the books at the end of 1977. Such an approach can result in a reduction in foreign exchange losses.

The most meaningful measure of accountability, given a centralized approach to exposure management, would require the treasurer to minimize the sum of after-tax foreign exchange losses plus interest costs. In assigning such an objective, it is important to distinguish between translation and transaction results. The two generally are distinct and can be managed separately with one exception. If forward contracts are used to offset translation exposure, actual foreign exchange gains and losses will be reported. A fundamental question to be addressed involves the comparison of transaction results with translation results: Are the two equivalent? Regardless of the policy adopted on this issue, it is important to note that transaction results are taxable in the United States, while translation results are not.

Measurement and comparison of central exposure manager's performance under such a system proves to be a highly complex problem. It is not appropriate to contrast net interest costs plus foreign exchange results over time or across companies. Differences in the geographic location of affiliates makes cross-company comparisons misleading. A company whose operations are principally in Germany and Switzerland could report net interest costs of 3% and a substantial foreign exchange gain. A similar company with principal operations in Brazil and Israel would report net interest costs of 50% or more and a substantial exchange loss. In addition, differences in prevailing capital structures across industries and companies makes comparison difficult. Unless the treasurer has control over capital structure and capital budgeting decisions, any attempt to define performance in absolute or comparative terms cannot be supported. Perhaps the only meaningful way of measuring the treasurer's performance is to compare actual net interest costs and foreign exchange results with those that would have been realized had the firm followed one of several fixed policies towards exposure management. Actual results can be contrasted with those that would have resulted under policies which (1) took no action to address translation exposure, (2) covered all exposures in the forward market (3) increased local or foreign debt to offset all net exposures, (4) covered only those positions with significant loss potential. Any savings above and beyond the results of these simulated policies could be used to measure the exposure manager's performance. Such man versus machine contests are not easy to design and execute, but they are virtually the only way to measure effectiveness in this and other areas of international management.

Few companies are willing to give central treasury managers the authority they need to justify complete responsibility for interest cost and foreign exchange results. Most global firms hold affiliate managers responsible for interest costs, and many include foreign exchange results in performance evaluation of foreign units. Shank, Dillard and Murdock interviewed 25 leading global corporations and found that 8 held foreign affiliate managers responsible for exchange results.[30] The remainder, however, did not hold affiliate managers responsible for exchange effects. The philosophies behind these two approaches differ in two crucial respects. The argument for local accountability is largely based on the premise that returns and performance are relevant to the parent only as measured in the home currency. The counterargument emphasizes that the role of the affiliate manager is to run the unit in accordance with the demands and conditions of its operating environment. ITT Corporation provides a useful example of how one company resolves these arguments.[31]

ITT's management strongly emphasizes earnings per share results, and this variable is very important in the internal evaluation of operating units. ITT's legendary performance evaluation system focuses on formal earnings targets. Actual results are compared every month with targets formalized in the operating plan and budget for each of 235 profit centers. Since foreign sales account for roughly half of ITT's total revenues, translation results can have a significant effect on reported earnings. In fact, translation losses in 1978 totaled $139 million after tax, or ($.98) per share. Translation losses in the third quarter of 1981 alone reduced quarterly earnings by almost $250 million or $1.41 per share.[32]

ITT's approach to exposure management prior to 1977 held unit managers responsible for exchange gains and losses. In preparing annual budgets, affiliate managers specified expected foreign exchange rates in defining performance targets in dollars. Actual results were translated at prevailing rates, so that any deviation in exchange rates from projection would affect unit performance. ITT's experience with this system proved to be unsatisfactory for several reasons. Unit managers felt they were being held accountable for a variable beyond their control and expertise. Corporate management also believed that the system "diverted subsidiary management from focusing on operating variances and variables they could be expected to control, such as volume, mix, price and costs."[33] As a result of these problems, a new accountability system was introduced in 1977.

The new system placed operating units in one of three categories: Foreign Exchange Exempt, Latin America, and Foreign Exchange Reporting Units. Foreign Exchange Exempt Units included all profit centers that had never reported more than a $50,000 foreign exchange gain or loss. These units were primarily located in the United States or in countries with rates tied to the dollar and had minimal involvement in international transactions. These units were evaluated in actual dollar results, so that technically management was responsible for foreign exchange effects on earnings. These effects were deemed to be negligible, however, if they did not exceed $50,000 per year. Once such a unit recorded an exchange loss in excess of

$50,000, however, it entered a second category of Foreign Exchange Reporting units.

The majority of the profit centers, 175 in all, were categorized as Reporting Units. These units reported a monthly statement detailing balance sheet positions and income statement trends in local currency. The "local currency equivalent" approach was used to monitor performance for these units. By measuring performance solely in terms of local currency results and budgets, affiliate managers were not held responsible for exchange fluctuations. In converting local currency results into dollars for evaluation purposes, a fixed, predetermined rate was used to finalize budgets and to translate actual results. ITT's decision rule used the rate prevailing on October 1 of each year for this purpose. The resulting system emphasized operating variance alone; foreign exchange effects would not be incorporated for performance evaluation purposes.

Foreign exchange variances would be generated for top management review by contrasting budgeted results at the fixed rate with actual results at prevailing rates. These effects were monitored, but no active management efforts were pursued to reduce translation exposure at the corporate level. ITT's policy toward translation exposure management was based on the belief that exposure as defined under FASB No. 8 did not reflect economic realities. Furthermore, the size and shape of ITT's foreign operation were considered too large to permit meaningful hedging and exposure management. ITT did not use leads and lags or intercompany transaction to reduce exposure. Company policy did encourage affiliates to manage assets and use local debt to balance economic exposure, which was defined as FASB No. 8 exposure plus inventories. Subsidiary managers could use forward contracts to hedge transactions involving foreign currency, but a strictly antispeculative policy limited the aggressive use of exposure management techniques. Despite this basic policy, a third group of unit managers was held responsible for exchange results. Latin America units were treated as responsible for exchange results. Latin America units were treated as responsible for exchange results because exchange rates in those countries were believed to closely parallel interest rate and inflation differentials with the United States. Exchange rate movements were assumed to be highly predictable in terms of direction and magnitude. In evaluating these units, actual exchange rates were used to translate results. Managers of these units were held responsible for exchange effects.

The ITT approach is appropriate primarily for companies that heavily discount the effects of translation exposure. Passive, decentralized approaches to exposure management will not control translation gain and losses. On the other hand, active, centralized exposure management can have undue effects on operations and capital budgeting. The solution to these problems must be resolved at the level of the individual firm. Explicit policies with respect to exposure management are an essential part of international financial management. These policies must specify the degree of importance attached to exposure management, the tools and technique to be used in exposure management, conditions dictating their use, and responsibility for exposure effects.

SUMMARY

The various functions of international financial management cannot be viewed as discrete areas of activity. They are all closely interrelated. Cash management activities cannot be determined without reference to repatriation policy, exposure manaagement objectives and capital budgeting

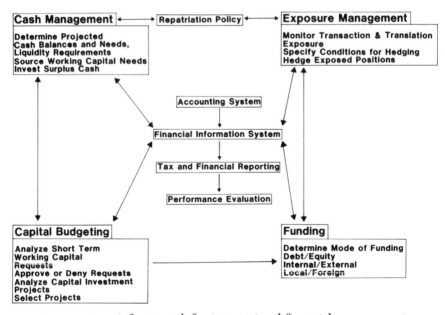

Figure 6-8.   A framework for international financial management.

schedules. Funding decisions must take exposure management considerations into account. Tax issues underlie all aspects of international financial management.

Articulation of an effective financial management system requires a number of basic policy decisions. Accountability for exchange effects poses a fundamental issue. The relationship between financial and operating objectives and functions also requires definition. Specification of conditions under which different objectives take primacy is an important part of financial policy. Decision rules can be formulated to determine when and how steps are taken to address financial issues. At a more basic level, procedures and standards for reporting must be established to ensure global consistency in capital budgeting and performance evaluation. The effective integration of all these elements into a working international financial management system is one of the greatest challenges to global corporations.

NOTES

1. Kimber, J.C.S., Financial Planning in Multinational Corporations, unpublished doctoral dissertation, Manchester Business School, 1976.
2. Robbins, S.M. and R.B. Stobaugh, *Money in the Multinational Enterprise* (New York: Basic Books, 1973).
3. For a review of foreign investment evaluation procedures used by multinational firms, see Wicks, M.E., *A Comparative Analysis of the Foreign Investment Evaluation Practices of U.S.-based Multinational Companies* (New York: McKinsey, 1980).
4. The capital asset pricing model is formulated in Vintner, J., "Security Prices, Risk and Maximal Gains from Diversification," *Journal of Finance*, December 1965, pp. 587−616.
   Sharpe, W.F., "Capital Asset Prices: A Theory of Market Equilibrium Under Conditions of Risk," *Journal of Finance*, September 1964, pp. 425−42.
5. Rogalski, R.J. and J.D. Vinso, "Price Level Variations as Predictors of Flexible Exchange Rates," *Journal of International Business Studies*, Summer 1977, pp. 77−81; Giddy, I.H. and G. Dufey, "The Random Behavior of Flexible Exchange Rates," *Journal of International Business Studies*, Spring 1975, pp. 1−32.
6. The concept of a risk premium is developed in Fisher, I., *The Rate of Interest* (New York: MacMillan, 1970), p. 215; see also Hirschleifer, J., "Risk, the Discount Rate and Investment Decisions," *American Economic Review*, May 1961, pp. 112−30.
7. Myers, S.C., "Interactions of Corporate Finance and Investment Decisions," *Journal of Finance*, March 1974, pp. 1−26; Eitemannn, D.K. and A. I. Stonehill, *Multinational Business Finance* (Reading: Addison-Wesley, 1979).
   See also Lessard, D.R., "Evaluating Foreign Projects: An Adjusted Present Value Approach," in Lessard, D.R. (ed.), *International Financial Management* (New York: Warren Gorham and Lamont, 1979) pp. 577−592.

8. The concept of the certainty equivalent is an integral part of Bayesian decision theory. See Hamburg, M., *Statistical Analysis for Decision-making* (New York: Harcourt Brace Jovanovich, 1977), pp. 575–87; Schlaifer, R.S., *Analysis of Decisions Under Uncertainty*, (New York: McGraw-Hill, 1969).

    For an applied view, see Hammond J., "Better Decisions with Preference Theory," *Harvard Business Review*, November–December 1967.

9. Knight, F.M., *Risk, Uncertainty and Profit* (New York: Harper and Row, 1965).

10. The role of uncertainty in foreign investment decisions is described in Aharoni, Y., op. cit.; Perlmutter, H.V., op. cit. Johanson, J., and J.E. Vahlne, "Internationalization of the Firm," *Journal of International Business Studies*, Spring 1977, pp. 23–32.

11. My research indicates that measures of firm-specific experience correlate highly with propensity to invest abroad: Davidson, W.H., *Experience Effects*, op. cit., Chapter 2.

12. Propensity to invest abroad rises significantly as the firm's experience in industry increases: ibid., Chapter 2.

13. For further discussion, see Modigliani, F., and M. H. Miller, "The Cost of Capital, Corporation Finance and the Theory of Investment," *American Economic Review*, June 1958, pp. 261–77; Nartell, T.J., and C.R. Carlson, "The Cost of Capital as a Weighted Average," *Journal of Finance*, December 1975, pp. 1343–55; Rodriguez, R.M., and E. E. Carter, *International Financial Management* (Englewood Cliffs: Prentice-Hall, 1979), Chapter 11.

14. Curhan, J.P., W. H. Davidson and Rajan Suri, op. cit., p. 374.

15. *New York Times*, September 13, 1980, p. L29.

16. Franko found that access to capital was not a principal factor in multinational firms' decisions to enter joint ventures. Franko, L.G., *Joint Venture Survival in Multinational Corporations* (New York: Praeger, 1971), p. 33.

17. Legislation for different host countries can be examined in *Annual Report on Exchange Restrictions* (Washington: International Monetary Fund, 1981).

18. For a good survey of tax codes in Europe, see *Corporation Taxation in Europe* (London: Alexander Grant Tansley Witt, 1980).

    For other countries, see Ernst and Whinney, *International Series*, Annual.

19. Giddy, I.H., "An Integrated Theory of Exchange Rate Equilibrium," *Journal of Financial and Quantitative Analysis*, December 1976, pp. 883–92.

20. Brief descriptions of national tax codes with respect to foreign exchange results can be found in: Business International Corporation, *Investment, Licensing and Trading Conditions Abroad*. Country reviews include statements such as the following, which are typical of the three main categories of tax treatment of foreign exchange results.

    Indonesia (8.03) "There are no provisions for deduction of exchange losses."

    Taiwan (8.03) "In calculating taxable income, the following deductions may be made . . . reserves held against foreign exchange fluctuations up to an annual limit of 7% of outstanding foreign currency debt used to purchase production equipment."

    Italy (8.03) "Actual (foreign exchange) gains must be reported and are taxed, while actual losses are deductible."

    Preferential tax treatment varies considerably. France, for example, permits reserve treatment of foreign exchange results, but only to a limited extent. Short-term gains are subject to treatment as ordinary income in a majority of countries. Long-term gains are also taxable as ordinary income in many countries, but more often at preferential capital gains rates. The conclusion is that foreign exchange gains or losses are never taxed at greater rates than ordinary income, and quite frequently they are taxed at significantly lower rates.

21. Company transfer pricing policies are described in ITT International Finance, ICCH No. 9-380-045; Philips, N.V., ICCH No. 1-378-096.

22. Ernst and Whinney, Netherlands and Great Britain Reports, International Series, 1980.

23. Eitemann, D.K. and A.I. Stonehill, *Multinational Business Finance* (Reading: Addison-Wesley, 1979), Chapter 7.

24. For a review of regulations in different host countries, see *Annual Report on Exchange Restrictions* (Washington: IMF, 1981).

25. Folks, W.R., Jr., and S.R. Stansell, "The Use of Discriminant Analysis of Forecasting Exchange Rate Movement," *Journal of International Business Studies*, Spring 1975, pp. 33–50; Rogalski, R.J., and J.D. Vinso, op. cit.; Murenbeeld, M., "Economic Factors for Forecasting Foreign Exchange Rate Changes," *Columbia Journal of World Business*, Summer 1975, pp. 81–95.

26. Amihud, Y., and T. Agmon, "The Forward Rate and the Effective Prediction of the Future Spot Rate," Working Paper, Tel Aviv University, 1978; Bradford, C., "Spot Rates, Forward Rates and Exchange Market Efficiency," *Journal of Financial Economics*, August 1977, pp. 55–66; Kohlhagen, S., "The Forward Rate as an Unbiased Predictor of the Future Spot Rate," Working Paper, University of California—Berkeley, 1974.

27. A list of major foreign exchange losses in financial institutions appears in footnote 58, Chapter 2. It is also important to note that foreign exchange trading generates substantial profits for many banks.

Foreign Exchange Trading Profits (1980)*

Bank	Amount ($ million)
Citibank	$164.0
Chase Manhattan	96.0
Manufacturers Hanover	8.9
Chemical	34.8
Continental Illinois	32.3
Bankers Trust	33.6
First National of Chicago	21.8

Source: Company reports.

28. Stanley, M.T., and S. B. Block, "Economic Consequences of FAS 8," Working Paper, Texas Christian University, 1977; see also Dukes, R.E., *An Empirical Investigation of the Effects of Financial Accounting Standards Statement Number 8 on Security Return Behavior* (Stanford: FASB, 1978).

29. Evans, T.G., W. R. Folks, Jr., and M. Jilling, *The Impact of Statement of Accounting Standards No. 8 on the Foreign Exchange Risk Management Practices of American Multinationals*, (Stanford: FASB, 1978).

30. Shank, J.K., J. F. Dillane and R.J. Murdock, *Assessing the Impact of FASB 8* (New York: Financial Executives Research Foundation, 1979).

31. "How ITT Evaluates the Performance of its Foreign Operations," *Business International*, April 24, 1981, pp. 131–35; ITT International Finance, ICCH No. 9-380-045.

32. *Wall Street Journal*, October 28, 1981, p. 56..

33. ITT International Finance, ICCH No. 9-380-045.

SEVEN

Organizational Design

The design of organizational formats consistent with the nature of a firm's global operations and strategy poses a growing challenge to top management. In the early stages of international expansion, organizational issues typically do not present severe problems. As a firm's foreign operations expand and mature, and as competition becomes more severe, organization design becomes a primary problem. Different structures will be needed to address the key problems facing a firm as its international operations evolve. This pattern has been described by Stopford and Wells in terms of an evolutionary "stages" theory of international organization.[1] Under this paradigm, firms initiially manage foreign operations through the creation of a separate export unit in a marketing division. As markets grow, the firm enters into foreign licensing agreements, joint ventures and subsidiaries. The increasing scale of participation in foreign markets requires new types of management skills and sensitivities. Responsibility for these new international operations generally is placed outside the firm's traditional structure because of their unique managerial requirements. Often, the first foreign operations are watched very closely by the CEO and the Board of Directors. These ventures tend to be viewed as autonomous entities that report directly to the highest levels of management. After foreign operations become more established and more routine, most companies create an international division to manage all international operations. The international division in most cases operates as a highly independent unit.

As international operations grow in size and complexity, new organizational pressures and requirements will lead to adoption of more integrated global structures.[2] Global structures based on product lines represent a principal option for firms choosing to adopt a new structure. Area, matrix or mixed structures also provide alternative means of organizing for international operations. According to the stages theory of multinational organization design, firms will progress from an international division to more global structures as the percentage of sales received from foreign operations rises. The firm's degree of diversity will play a key role in determining which option is chosen to displace the international division.[3]

In examining the actual record of organizational change among leading U.S.-based multinationals, the trend suggests that such an evolution does occur. Of the 180 firms examined in the Harvard Multinational Enterprise Project, 163 initially created a separate international division to manage foreign operations. Over time, a significant number of these firms have displaced the international division with global product, area or matrix structures. Examination of those companies that have gone through such a transition suggests that several factors provide most of the stimulus for their move.

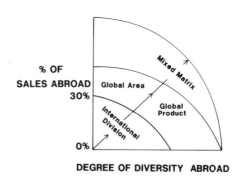

Figure 7-1.   A view of organizational evolution.

PRESSURES FOR ORGANIZATIONAL CHANGE

The displacement of an existing international division typically stems from a combination of expected benefits and internal forces. Several types of benefits are widely cited in justifying adoption of a global product or matrix structure. These benefits all derive from the increased integration of domestic and foreign operations in these global structures. The move to a global product or matrix structure is seen as a means of integrating international operations with domestic activities. The benefits of integration are expected to appear in marketing, manufacturing, technology transfer and competitive strategy areas.

In marketing, integration supports coordination of pricing, product design, specifications, and delivery terms across markets. Such coordination is essential in businesses serving multinational customers. In manufacturing, the move to a global structure is expected to facilitate the rationalization of manufacturing operations to improve cost efficiency. Cost efficiency on a global basis has become the key competitive imperative in a growing number of industries. Rationalization of manufacturing to achieve economics of scale is a principal goal behind many reorganizations. Centralized global capacity management is expected to facilitate this process.

Another benefit associated with global structures is improved communication and transfer of resources, especially technology, between domestic and foreign units. The lifeblood of many U.S. multinationals is the flow of technology from the parent to its affiliates. By providing closer ties between these units, it is presumed that both development and transfer of technology will become more effective and efficient. The problem was stated clearly by the president of North American Operations in a leading multinational company:

> Our business is to develop and apply new technologies to markets. Dissolving the international division will remove a major barrier to the transfer of technology from our domestic product divisions to our markets abroad.

The integration of domestic and international operations contributes to another benefit associated with global structures. The most important advantage of such structures is the development of a global strategic focus. The global competitive environment has changed dramatically in the last decade. From a series of individual matches against local competitors in single markets, most multinationals now find themselves competing against other U.S., European and Japanese multinationals on a global basis. This environment creates a great need for sensitivity to global competitive developments. As globalization of industries and markets continues, the need for distinction between domestic and foreign operations will diminish. Organization along global lines permits a better perception of competitive developments and a more integrated posture with respect to global competitors.

In addition to external pressures for marketing coordination, manufacturing rationalization, improved technology development and transfer, and improved global strategic focus, several internal forces also promote the transition to a global structure. One of these forces can be the use of a formal portfolio planning system. A recent survey revealed that 48% of all Fortune 500 companies had adopted such an approach by 1979.[4] Although only 19% considered portfolio planning central to their management process, this latter group consisted primarily of larger and more international companies. The definition of strategic business units (SBU's) is central to all portfolio planning approaches. The definition of these SBU's tends to promote adoption of a global structure for several reasons. The definition of SBU's typically breaks down many of the distinctions between domestic and foreign operations. SBU's are defined to include all businesses that utilize common resources and share common competitors. When foreign operations and domestic operations are grouped together into SBU's for planning purposes, a strong pressure is created to acknowledge these units' commonality in the formal organizational structure. Although this process can stimulate reorganization along either global product or area lines, it is more likely to promote emphasis on global product lines. Most portfolio planning systems emphasize the definition of SBU's along business as opposed to market lines.

Closely related to the effect of adopting a formal planning system is the impact of developments in management information and control systems. These systems tend to be poorly developed in the early stages of international expansion. Often, highly informal procedures are followed to accomplish these functions. As international operations expand, the need for formal information and control systems rises rapidly. In many cases, pressures from the parent to implement such systems are resisted strenuously by affiliate managers within the international division. These managers, who are often highly entrepreneurial, resent any reduction in autonomy. Such conflict, along with the need for consolidation of decentralized operations, can contribute to the pressures for adoption of a global structure.

Another internal force also favors reorganization along global product lines. Advocates for the transition to a global structure typically emerge from the ranks of the domestic product managers. These managers perceive an opportunity to claim control over international revenues, earnings and growth opportunities within their line of business. International divisions often exhibit the highest rate of growth within a firm and frequently the highest profitability as well. This success can be attributed to use of the domestic divisions' technology, marketing and managerial resources.

Domestic division managers seek to gain control over foreign operations by promoting a transition to a global product structure. A possible compromise between these pressures and the desire of affiliate managers to retain their autonomy can be found in the global matrix structure.

All these motives and forces contribute to pressures for reorganizing international operations. Awareness of the need for reorganzation typically leads to evaluation of the major alternative structures employed by multinational corporations. Each of these structures offers particular costs and benefits that can be related to the particular needs of the company in question. Selection of a new structural format requires comparison to the characteristics of the firm with those of different organizational structures.

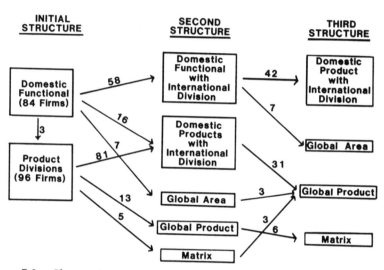

Figure 7-2. Changes in organizational structure for 180 U.S.-based multinational enterprises. *Source:* Update from Stopford, J.M. and L.T. Wells, Jr., *Managing the Multinational Enterprise* (New York: Basic Books, 1972).

SELECTING A GLOBAL STRUCTURE

At the most basic level, the problem of organization design can be reduced to three closely related issues. The first involves the definition of organizational subunits based on the key functions and dimensions of the firm's operations. The second involves the choice between centralization and decentralization of individual functions.[5] The third involves the assignment of reporting and responsibility relationships between units.[6] The result of these exercises determines the structure of an organization at the macro level.

Definition of subunits can vary sharply. The most basic issue in this regard is the relative degree of emphasis placed on the product, area and functional dimensions of the organization. Several factors influence this decision. A variety of forces serve to emphasize the area dimension in defining organizational subunits. Many firms consolidate their activities in individual countries under an area-based manager because of the unique nature of the local business environment. Most companies with international divisions tend to break down their foreign activities along regional lines before considering other dimensions of organization. Figure 7-3 presents a

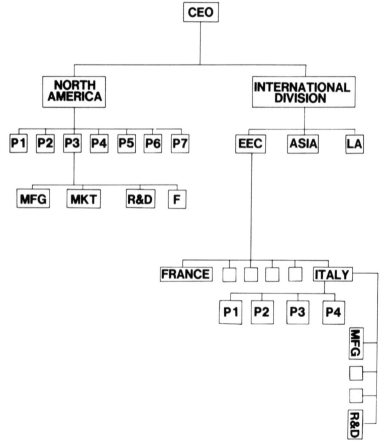

Figure 7-3.   A typical international division structure.

typical organization pattern for firms with an international division. The organization chart differentiates by area first and then within each area by product and function. Product-based structures differentiate first by product divisions then by area and function within each division.

Forces favoring product-oriented structures have been cited above. Pressures for marketing coordination, manufacturing efficiency and effective technology development and transfer, lead firms to place priority on product-based subunits. This tendency is reinforced by the use of portfolio planning systems. In only 7% of the Fortune 500 firms using such systems do formal organization units differ from the underlying planning units.[7] The tendency to define planning units along product lines and the increasing use of planning systems promote a product emphasis in organization design.

The third building block of organization design is the functional dimension. Subunits can also be defined along functional lines. Manufacturing, marketing, finance, technology, control, personnel and other functions tend to receive greater organizational emphasis in companies with very narrow product lines.[8] In most companies, functional subunits appear below area and product divisions in the organization chart.

Definition of subunits along these dimensions begs an important question. Which dimension takes precedence over the other two? A large part of organization design is involved in assigning priorities to these three dimensions.

ESTABLISHING DIMENSIONAL PRIORITIES

Determining priorities for product, area and functional elements of the organization requires careful analysis of the characteristics of the business. The issue of centralization versus decentralization plays a major role in this assessment. Generally, businesses requiring centralized management will be organized primarily along product or functional lines. In most cases, global product divisions are the basis for centralized structures. Central product managers will be responsible for area and functional activities around the world. Businesses requiring decentralized management will place greater emphasis on an area-based orientation in which product and functional managers report to local country managers. The issue of centralization versus decentralization is an old, basic theme in international management.[9] It has been involved in each of the preceding chapters of this book. It can also be used to help determine organizational design priorities.

One means of assessing a firm's need for centralization is to examine the characteristics of its market and industry. A wide range of criteria can be used to make this assessment. In Table 7-1, market and product characteristics are examined for three businesses. The criteria used to assess these businesses reflect the potential benefits of centralization in organization design.

Products that are highly standardized in world markets in terms of design, usage, buying behavior and distribution mechanisms can realize benefits

TABLE 7-1.   A Business-Based Analytical Approach to Organization Design

	Benefits of Centralization		
Criteria	Semiconductor	Bakery Products	Watches
Market Characteristics			
Degree of standardization in:			
Product design	High	Low	Low
Product usage	High	Low	High
Buying behavior	High	Low	Low
Distribution	High	Low	Low
Nature of customers:			
Global/local ratio	High	Low	Low
Nature of competitors:			
Global/local ratio	High	Low	High
1/ Advertising rate	High	Medium	Low
Product Characteristics			
Rate of technological change	High	Low	High
Manufacturing:			
Minimum efficient scale	High	Low	High
Scope of cost curve	High	Low	High
1/ Tariff rate	Medium	n.a.	Medium
Value/weight	High	Low	High
Capital intensity	Medium	Low	High
Financial Characteristics			
Fixed assets/Sales	Medium	Low	Medium
R&D sales	High	Low	Medium
Cost of goods sold/Sales	High	Low	Low
Value-added/sales	High	Medium	High
Inventory/sales	Medium	Low	High

from centralization of management. If the principal customers for the product are multinational firms, centralization of marketing management to ensure coordination of prices, design specifications, terms and quality is essential. The presence of multinational competitors in an industry requires centralized management to guarantee an integrated global strategic posture. The benefits of centralization are substantial and the cost of decentralization significant in businesses with rapid rates of technological change. Innovation and manufacturing are performed more efficiently at central locations in such industries.[10] The economics of manufacturing also play an important role in organization design. Businesses with high economies of scale, low tariffs and high value-to-weight ratios benefit from centralized management.

Some indication of the need for centralized management can be drawn from financial statistics of the industry. Generally, businesses with high R&D/sales ratios will often benefit from centralization. Many industries with high cost of goods sold ratios tend to be candidates for centralization, if high unit volume, continuous process technology and capital intensity are also present.[11] Success in such businesses can rest on the realization of lower production costs through automation and rationalization of production. These activities require centralized management in either functional form for companies in narrow lines of business, or product form for more diverse firms.

Examination of these characteristics for different businesses can provide an initial assessment of the need for centralization. The semiconductor industry provides a perfect example of a business that benefits greatly from centralized management. Standardization of products is quite high around the world. The principal competitors in the business tend to be firms with global activities. Customers also tend to be larger firms with multinational activities. Advertising is not a factor in semiconductor sales. At the manufacturing level, the rate of technological change is extremely high, requiring close contact between central research activities and the manufacturing function. Despite the frequency of technological change, the economics of production are increasingly capital-intensive, as can be seen in Chapter 5.[12] The value-to-weight ratio for semiconductor chips exceeds that of virtually any other industry, permitting shipment from a central factory. The cost curve is volume-sensitive, and the minimum efficient scale of production is rising sharply. All these factors contribute to a need for centralized management of such a business.

In contrast, the bakery products industry presents the opposite conclusion. Product standardization is not pervasive across markets. Tastes, buying behavior and distribution channels vary widely in different markets. Customers for such products are locally oriented, as are competitors. Production of bakery products is not a capital-intensive business. Even more importantly, shipment and storage of baked goods is limited because of freshness and handling requirements. The financial characteristics of the bakery products business also suggest that centralization will not provide significant benefits in this business. Asset-to-sales ratios are relatively low, R&D is nonexistent and the cost of goods sold is low. Wherever production costs are low as a percent of sales, and there is little technological content in the product, pressures for centralization will tend to be low. In addition, the high inventory turnover found in this industry requires local responsiveness to market demand. The bakery products business is one that requires decentralized management.

The watch industry provides a third perspective on the issue of centralization versus decentralization. The level of product standardization in this industry is not high. There is a great deal of variety from market to market in preferences for digital versus hour-hand faces, frames, size, price and power supply. Distribution channels and buying behavior also vary sharply in this industry. Yet the rate of technological change is very rapid in this industry, and production economics are increasingly capital-intensive and volume-sensitive. Value-to-weight ratios are also very high in this industry, encouraging centralized production. The watch industry does not provide a clear-cut answer to the issue of centralization in organization design. While semiconductor and bakery products clearly demand a specific structural approach, watches present a more complex picture. One way to design an organization to fit the needs of the watch industry is to emphasize the role of functional dimensions in the centralization issue. We have been using the product and area dimensions to reflect the two poles of the centralization spectrum. When the functional dimension is added, more design options become available. In the case of watches, it is clear that the marketing function requires a decentralized approach to ensure sensitivity and responsiveness to unique local conditions. On the other hand, this industry requires a centralized manufacturing approach. By defining a centralized manufacturing unit and decentralized market units, an organization can be designed to meet the needs of this business.

Such an approach to organization design can be adopted by diverse firms in organizing each business division. When a unique organization is designed to fit the needs of each business, the result can be called a "mixed" structure. The problem with this approach is its emphasis on differentiation. Lawrence and Lorsch describe organizational design in terms of two processes—differentiation of subunits along functional, product or area lines and integration of those subunits through assignment of reporting and responsibility relationships or other administrative mechanisms.[13] A business-by-business approach to organization design can readily accomplish the first process. Each business reveals a unique pattern of subunit definition and dimensional priority. Coordination and integration across divisional lines, both at the affiliate and headquarter levels, can be extremely difficult to accomplish in such cases. Integrating mechanisms are required to coordinate divisional activities.

Integrating Mechanisms

Primary integration needs are addressed in the initial definition of organizational subunits. By creating and emphasizing area, product or functionally oriented units, integration is maximized along one dimension. Area-based structures promote integration of different functional and product activities at the affiliate level. Global product structures promote integration of area and functional activities on a global basis. In each case, another dimension of integration is lacking. Area structures do not promote integration of product and functional activities across different countries. Product structures do not encourage integration across products at the country level. Functionally based structures involve similar trade-offs. Effective organization design requires integration along all three dimensions. The most important axis can be emphasized in selecting the primary dimension along which to organize activities. The other dimensions can be integrated through other mechanisms. The term "administrative overlays" has been used to describe the addition of committees, planning forums and coordinating agents designed to integrate the secondary dimensions of an organizational structure.[14] Figure 7-4 presents one such mechanism for coordinating product-related activities in an area-oriented firm. Definition of secondary reporting and responsibility relationships can be used to promote integration. In companies organized by area, product managers can coordinate activities through a second layer of reporting channels to a central product coordinator. Manufacturing and marketing activities can be coordinated in a similar fashion. Such activities lead to what can be called a de facto or latent

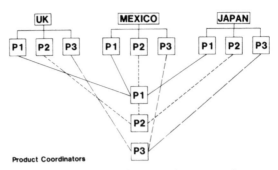

Figure 7-4.   A product coordinator overlay.

matrix structure.[15] Even though the organization places priority on a particular dimension, the integration requirements of the other dimensions are also addressed. The result of such efforts is not only to improve integration across secondary dimensions but to increase the role of these dimensions in organizational decision making. Several examples can be used to highlight the need and results of this process.

In pure area-based structures, individual country managers will determine manufacturing and marketing activities for each affiliate. As a result, product lines will proliferate, product standardization will deteriorate and competition for export markets between affiliates can occur. The manufacturing configuration resulting in such a structure can be highly inefficient as each affiliate produces the same products at low volume levels. Coordination needs will rise as these problems grow. Coordination of marketing and manufacturing activities across affiliates will result in improved consistency in sales to global customers and a more efficient manufacturing configuration.

The same problem can occur in product-based structures. Divisionalization along global product lines can result in duplication of overheads at headquarters and at the host country level. The duplication of staff resources, facilities, sales force and management can significantly increase the costs of foreign operations. More importantly, divisionalization fragments the expertise and experience of the company, which can result in failure to learn from mistakes, embarrassing inconsistencies in divisional activities and reinvention of procedures. Coordinating mechanisms can be developed to reduce these problems. These problems can be addressed through the use of area functional coordinators, through a planning system or through direct communication at senior management levels. Top managers in many firms spend a great deal of their time performing coordination functions. Although this often occurs more by default than design, such an approach can be formalized in a company's management system. ITT offers an extreme example of this approach. Its profit center managers meet as a group every month to review unit performance, activities and plans.[16] These meetings provide, among other things, a top-level forum for resolution of coordination problems. This approach to this problem stands in sharp contrast to the means by which coordination problems are handled in many other multinational companies.

The planning process can also be used to promote resource sharing and consistency in operations. General Electric's planning group emphasizes the formation of "internal joint ventures" between product divisions in foreign markets.[17] At the affiliate level, the largest or most experienced division in each country can take a leadership role in coordinating national activities. One division can plan an "innkeeper" role in each country by handling major overhead items such as legal and accounting staff, government and labor relations and corporate communications. Facilities such as manufacturing, warehousing and distribution channels can also be shared on this basis.

Structural Strengths and Weaknesses

Consideration of the strengths and weaknesses of various structured approaches is important in deciding which dimension to emphasize in designing and organization. Product-oriented structures offer the ability to realize manufacturing rationalization, sourcing efficiency, marketing consistency and strategic coordination. However, such structures are less effective in managing relations with host governments, responding to local market conditions, in avoiding duplication of overheads at the affiliate level, and in responding to local threats and opportunities. Area-oriented structures, in contrast, are highly effective in performing these latter functions. The strengths of the area structure are largely the same as the weaknesses of the product structure and vice versa. One means of determining which orientation to emphasize in organizational design is to assess which set of functions is most important to the ultimate success of the company.

Characteristics of Different Structures

Organizational Needs	Product	Area
Manufacturing rationalization	Strength	Weakness
Sourcing efficiency	Strength	Weakness
Marketing consistency	Strength	Weakness

Characteristics of Different Structures

Organizational Needs	Product	Area
Global strategic coordination	Strength	Weakness
Effective host government relations	Weakness	Strength
Responsiveness to local markets	Weakness	Strength
Efficient use of affiliate infrastructure	Weakness	Strength
Perception of local opportunities and threats	Weakness	Strength

In developing integration and coordination mechanisms to deal with the secondary dimensions of an organization, the distinction between formal and informal structure is important. Formal structures never fully capture the actual reporting and responsibility relationships and the patterns of interaction between managers and units within a company. Informal relationships develop in response to the needs, opportunities and interpersonal dynamics of the organization. Quinn has observed that most business planning decisions occur outside formal planning systems.[18] Formal hierarchies are extremely important in shaping the activities of managers and in forcusing attention on key functions and relationships. However, informal relationships and processes also contribute substantially to the actual pattern of management and decision making. Although some autonomy in this area is healthy, the informal elements of structure can also be managed in the organizational design process. Informal relationships can be used as integrating mechanisms. In the simplest cases, congregation of managers in a semisocial setting can result in important integration results. Physical proximity contributes significantly to integration requirements. Other informal mechanisms for achieving organizational design objectives can also be utilized.

THE OBJECTIVES OF ORGANIZATIONAL DESIGN

The preceding discussion has focused on selecting a formal structure that best fits with the characteristics of the business and its environment. Although this is the principal objective of organizational design, the importance of integrating secondary dimensions is also seen as a central objective. Several other objectives are also universally important in selecting a structure for a global company. Besides coordination, other key objectives of organizational design are communication, control and culture definition.

Communication

One school of thought on organizational design emphasizes the information-processing requirements of the organization in selecting a structure. Galbraith views organizational design primarily as an exercise in matching capacities, channels and requirements for information processing.[19] Applying this framework to multinational firms, Egelhoff distinguishes between four different types of information processing requirements.[20] Different structural formats possess varying abilities to handle each type of information processing. Functional organizations, for example, permit extensive information processing between the parent and foreign subsidiary on tactical matters and on some strategic matters that involve only one function. On the other hand, communication on multifunctional strategic issues will be more difficult to achieve. Each structure permits information processing or communication in certain dimensions and inhibits it in others. Product structures permit effective treatment of tactical and strategic product-related matters, but less effective treatment of country matters. Area structures exhibit the opposite tendency in evaluating structural alternatives. Selection of a structure can be based on the information-processing characteristics of different structures.

The information-processing approach to organizational design is highly compatible with design methodologies derived from existing differentiation—integration models. Its emphasis on information flows and decision-making requirements provides additional refinement to this approach. As with coordination requirements, communication needs can and

TABLE 7-2. Information Processing Modes

Nature of Information Processing	Content of Information Processing	
	Country	Product
Tactical	Example: Affiliate financing	Example: Price levels
Strategic	Example: Participation policy	Example: R&D budget

Source: Derived from Egelhoff, William, An Information Processing Approach to Multinational Organization Design, unpublished doctoral dissertation, New York University, 1979.

are met through secondary layers of structure as well as through primary, formal organizational design.

Control

The distinction between primary and secondary levels of structure is particularly important in the area of control. Controls take two principal forms, strategic and operating. Operating controls tend to be embodied in discrete management systems rather than in formal structures. Strategic controls are more likely to exist and function within the primary structure. Operating control systems are generally part of a broader management information system that overlaps with operations planning, budgeting and performance evaluation functions. Development of annual operating plans provides the basis both for budgeting resources and performance evaluation. Deviation from plans and budgets triggers the operating control system.

The function of a control system raises an entirely different perspective on organizational design. Management systems, as opposed to structural hierarchies, represent another dimension of organizational design. Systems require a micro approach to design, with less emphasis on hierarchies and more on process and function. Systems interact closely with macro structures, and consistency between these two dimensions is a principal objective in designing an organization. Systems can be used to shore up some of the secondary coordination and communication needs of a company, but these systems must also support the existing macro structure. When profit and responsibility centers are defined for control purposes differently than those specified in the formal hierarchy, problems will develop. The management information system (MIS) must interact with the formal hierarchy to ensure appropriate feedback, control responses and relationships.

In many cases, control and other management systems dictate primary structure rather than the reverse. Problems in implementing control systems often are associated with transitions from an international division format to a global product or other structure. Implementation of control or other management systems is particularly challenging for global corporations, especially those that expand abroad through acquisition.

A Portfolio of Basic Management Systems

Management systems play a rapidly growing role in the administration of all organizations. The design and implementation of these systems are critical activities in molding the decision environment within an organization. Systems can be applied to virtually all aspects of management activity to provide information and decision support and focus. Such systems include:

Manufacturing Operations
    Yields
    Standard cost variances
    Payroll

Fixed Assets
    Depreciation

Facilities Planning
    Construction schedules

Inventory
    Product line analysis

Marketing
    Pricing
    Product line composition
    Market share
    Regional sales analysis
    Outlet sales analysis

Cash Management
    Billing
    Receiving
    Financial accounting
    Balance sheet ⎱
                   ⎰ by unit
    Income statement ⎰

Capital Budget
    Capital investments
    Cash flow

Debt
    Balances
    Rates
    Schedules

The design of these systems is principally a concern of central management. Implementation of such a portfolio of systems at the level of the foreign affiliate is one of the major challenges to global corporations.

Most global businesses are built by men and women with strong entrepreneurial instincts. The management style of such individuals often de-emphasizes formal management systems. In other cases, where expansion occurs primarily through acquisition, it is often difficult to integrate existing management systems and styles into the affiliate. In both cases the affiliate managers, who have built the business, will resist the implementation of central control systems because of the potential loss of autonomy.[21] Such resistance can contribute to pressures for reorganization on international operations. Design and implementation of control and other management systems for global corporations should account for such political concerns. Such concerns are the focus of another key function in organizational design—culture definition.

Corporate Culture

Culture can also be described in terms of corporate context, climate or style.[22] In basic terms, culture reflects acceptable modes of interaction, typical responses to specified conditions, expectations of support, constraint and autonomy, and other behavioral qualities of organizational life. Culture includes the assumptions, beliefs and values of corporate management. It represents the unspoken contract between a manager and an organization. It communicates the shared objectives, experience and weltanschauung of the organization. Culture or context can be determined and shaped by the philosophy, ideology, style and values of top management. In the absence of active culture definition by senior managers, either a de facto culture reflecting these qualities can develop or a culture can arise out of lower management ranks.

Corporate culture is reflected in modes of behavior, dress, work hours and habits, communication patterns and many other dimensions of organizational life. These distinctions are important in dealing with organizations as an employee, competitor, supplier, customer or analyst. More importantly, culture affects organizational performance, and most importantly, culture can be designed and controlled.

Pascale and Athos describe style, one of their seven S's of management, as a critical variable in corporate performance.[23] Ouchi's extension of theories X and Y into a theory Z typology of management style also assumes that culture affects performance.[24] Although the relationship cannot be readily tested and measured, it is relatively easy to differentiate between elements of healthy and unhealthy corporate cultures. These variables are often controllable. Top management can seek to influence or manage culture to improve performance by addressing these elements of culture. Culture can be thought of as reflecting a set of informal elements of structure. Formal structures and systems are useful only to the extent that they promote the right types of managerial responses, focus, interaction and relationships. Informal elements of structure can have an important effect on these managerial activities as well.

Elements of Corporate Culture

Companies vary substantially across a wide range of formal and informal variables that reflect aspects of corporate culture. Some of these aspects can be seen in the way companies perform certain functions, others can be seen in prevalent attitudes and modes of behavior, and others in some of the operating activities and results of the company. The following list outlines the principal variables of corporate culture for two extreme organizations.

Comparative Corporate Cultures

Company A	Company Z
Personnel	
Turnover	Tenure
Multiple entry points	Single entry level
Emphasis on financial compensation	Emphasis on personnel development
Discrete relationship to individual	Familiar, paternal attitudes
Output demanded	Loyalty demanded
External Relations	
Social responsibility is profit maximization	Civic & social participant
Political system is viewed as a marketplace	Corporate citizen
Power Relationships	
Monolithic	Diverse
Strong superior-subordinate emphasis	Collegial
Emphasis on formal hierarchy	Informal hierarchy
Closed policy forums	Open forums
Vertical communications	Horizontal communications
Clear authority and responsibility	Group responsibility

Comparative Corporate Cultures	
Company A	*Company Z*
Single decision maker	Group decision making
Darwinian conflict resolution	Parliamentary conflict resolution

The Manager's Role	
Executive	Entrepreneur
Diversity discouraged	Diversity permitted
Watchdog	Gardener
Explicit, discrete objectives	Implicit, broad objectives

Controls	
Direct	Indirect
Strong	Weak
Formal	Informal

Performance Evaluation	
Formal	Informal
Frequent	Infrequent
Regular	Periodic
Quantitative	Qualitative
Objective	Subjective

Operating and Investment Emphasis	
Efficiency	Excellence
Short term	Long term
Financial results	Quality

It can be argued that corporate culture is largely a reflection of the values, ideologies and style of the chief executive officer. Through effective communication of these qualities to the organization, the CEO can direct and manage corporate culture. Symbolic actions can also be used to alter or influence culture. All management actions, whether intentional or unintentional, send important messages to the rest of the organization about how and why things are done, about priorities, objectives and values, and about expectations. Management of this process is a key dimension of organization design. Effective organization design includes emphasis on informal culture management as well as on primary macro structures and management systems.

Levels of Organization Design

	Formal	Informal
Macro	Unit definition Dimensional priorities Reporting and responsibility relationships	Culture definition Secondary structural relationships
Micro	Management systems: Control Budget plan MIS systems Personnel development	Unwritten contracts Work environment

COMPARATIVE STRUCTURES

Different companies place very different degrees of emphasis on macro, micro, formal and informal organization design. U.S. corporations place by far the highest degree of emphasis on the macro, formal dimensions of organization design. Japanese companies, by contrast, emphasize the informal and micro dimensions of structure. Yoshino points out that Japanese companies place great emphasis on "shared implicit understanding" and exhibit an aversion for explicity in decision making.[25] The bottom-up nature of the decision-making process, the emphasis on group responsibility, employment security and other elements of Japanese corporate culture all diverge sharply from typical practices in the United States.

Examination of Japanese corporate structures at the formal, macro level reveals relatively simplistic structures. It is very common in Japan to find multibillion dollar global companies organized along functional lines. The number of formal profit and responsibility centers in these companies often is dramatically below the number found in comparable American firms. Japanese firms appear to be extremely simplistic, if not unsophisticated, in approaching organization design. This impression stems from the typical American emphasis on formal, macro structure. Examination of other dimensions of organization design in Japan reveals levels of sophistication far more advanced than anything to be found in the United States. Japanese firms certainly place greater emphasis on the cultural and behavioral dimension of organization design. These dimensions provide the principal tools by which Japanese companies focus management and mold and control behavior. The power of these tools to meet organizational design objectives is very great. However, it would be misleading to attribute the effectiveness of the Japanese corporate form to this factor alone. Two other characteristics of Japanese companies are very important.

Japanese companies appear to share a relatively greater level of emphasis on information collection, communication and processing than American companies. This propensity is seen in the widespread intelligence networks of the *sogo shosha*, in the high degree of emphasis on market research by many exporters, and in the internal emphasis on meetings and group office spaces. Japanese office spaces tend to be small for obvious reasons, but they also are open and normally contain a number of adjacent desks. Proximity encourages interaction. Studies show that Japanese spend more time in meetings than their American counterparts. Finally, the process of *nemawashi*, or informal after-work discussion in bars, cafes, or restaurants deserves emphasis.[26] These factors stimulate communication/coordination and information processing activities, as does an emphasis on group decision making.

The second dimension of Japanese emphasis that deserves attention can be called a micro element of organization design. In fact, it represents an alternative conception of organization design that derives from the bottom-up orientation of the Japanese management philosophy. Although Japanese organizations tend to be relatively simplistic when viewed from a top-down perspective, they are very rich when viewed from the bottom up. This point can be seen clearly in the following analysis of small group activity within a Hitachi semiconductor facility and profit center.[27] Small group activity, from a Western perspective, might be considered a labor relations management system. An understanding of the Japanese use of such systems provides insight into an alternative approach to organization design.

Small Group Activity at Musashi Semiconductor Works

The implementation of a small group program at Musashi Works began in 1971. Hitachi Corporation had already initated programs at 14 other factories, and procedures for designing and implementing small group systems were well-established. As will be seen, small group systems are introduced at both the managerial and worker levels. Hitachi calls the initial stage of implementation the enlightenment period. This period focuses almost entirely on orientation of management. Between 1971 and 1975, Musashi management was trained and oriented in the philosophy, principles, structure and function of small group activity. The small group concept was introduced to the rest of the organization in 1975. At the worker level, the small group program was introduced as part of a broader campaign designed to dramatically improve the status and productivity of Musashi Works. This program, called the MMM movement, entailed no specific organizational or managerial innovations. It was intended to provide broad goals and a continuing theme throughout the process of initiating the small group program. The MMM movement refers to three words: *muda, mura, muri*. These terms were used to symbolize a new guiding theme for Musashi Works. They can be translated as waste, inconsistency and fear of the impossible, respectively. The theme of the MMM movement was to eliminate these three evils from Musashi Works.

Several phases of the MMM movement at Musashi can be identified. In the first phase, the focus of the movement was on achieving higher quality in manufacturing through reduction of the three evils. In the second phase (MMM II), the broad theme emphasized that by reducing the three evils Musashi could spring forward to become a factor in world industry. The objective of the third phase was more specific. The objective of the MMM 20 campaign was to increase efficiency in terms of output per worker by 20% in six months. After this specific objective had been met, another general objective was introduced. The MMM 80 campaign sought to challenge and defeat the top line brands of the world through reduction of the three evils. In 1981, a new theme was introduced with a specific objective. The MMM 200 UP program intends to double chip output in two years.

History of the MMM Movement at Musashi

	1975	1976	1977	1978	1979	1980	1981	1982
Theme	MMM	MMM II		MMM 20		MMM 80		MMM 200 UP

The MMM movement appears to have beeen an important instrument in introducing small group activity at the operating level. However, the MMM movement is only the very tip of the iceberg. Underlying this program was a complex and sophisticated organization built around the small group unit and concept.

Small Group Organization and Administration

The 2,700 workers at Musashi are organized into 360 groups. The typical group numbers 8 to 10 people. Group membership is determined largely by work station, although some self-selection is possible in certain work areas. Group members typically hold the same rank or position in the company, but groups often contain both sexes and different ages. Each group elects a leader from among its members. Small group systems are highly democratic at the group level.

Immediately above the level of the group leader, a hierarchy was developed to administer group activities. Each of the 20 departments within Musashi has its own department council, chaired by the department manager. At this level, the small group hierarchy closely parallels the formal structure of the Musashi organization. Each of the 20 departments also contains between 2 and 10 sections. A separate council was formed for each section. Participants in section councils come from almost the full range of the formal hierarchy. Section councils serve as the most important forum for exchange and communication between the top and bottom of the organization. Hitachi views these councils as a means of communicating policies and

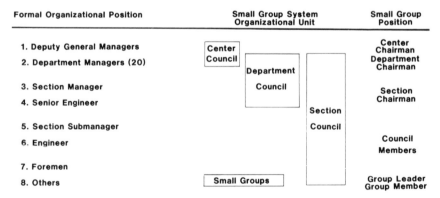

Formal Organizational Position	Small Group System Organizational Unit	Small Group Position
1. Deputy General Managers	Center Council	Center Chairman
2. Department Managers (20)	Department Council	Department Chairman
3. Section Manager		Section Chairman
4. Senior Engineer		
5. Section Submanager	Section Council	
6. Engineer		Council Members
7. Foremen		
8. Others	Small Groups	Group Leader Group Member

Figure 7-5. Relationship between formal structure and small group system.

objectives from management to the rest of the organization, particularly to the group level. Councils set specific objectives and themes for individual groups and review each group's performance on a monthly basis. However, it is very important to emphasize that communication between a council and a worker group is a two-way street. Worker groups are assigned objectives and themes by their section council, but they also choose a parallel theme for themselves. Groups have great latitude and self-direction in deciding the focus of their activities. Worker groups are given a great deal of discretion and autonomy in Hitachi's program. The sole constraint on group activities is that they be broadly consistent with the objectives of divisional management and Hitachi Corporation. Within the framework of the MMM movement at Musashi, worker groups are placed on an equal footing with management as a source of ideas to improve operations. The conceptual framework for the overall MMM movement is presented in Figure 7-6. In addition to communicating policies and objectives from management to workers, Hitachi describes the section councils as a means of achieving "technology transfer" from small groups to the management level. The vehicle for transferring technology, and indeed the focal point of the entire small group program, is something called the improvement proposal.

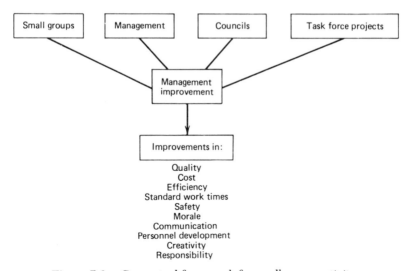

Figure 7-6.   Conceptual framework for small group activity.

Improvement Proposals

Improvement proposal generation, evaluation and implementation within a small group activity program is an extremely sophisticated process with far-reaching implications. The first improvement proposals were filed within Musashi Works in 1977, six years after the program began and three years after the first small groups were formed. An improvement proposal is submitted formally by a group to a section council. The proposal includes a statement of the problem, a proposed solution and in many cases a description of the actual results achieved under the new method. Proposals need not be approved before they are executed unless they involve major capital expenditures or adjustments at other work stations.

Groups were initially encouraged to identify areas within their work stations that could be improved to further the MMM movement. The first improvement proposals were voluntary. Later, council activity began to identify special areas and projects for specific attention. A committee structure was developed to provide a further layer of organization in the small group program. Project committees were composed primarily of junior managers and younger workers. An individual worker group could find itself working primarily with a project committee on a specific problem, depending on the priorities established in the senior councils. Where proposals required the involvement of more than one section or department, the groups involved would report to special project committees or coordinating councils.

By 1980, councils were asking groups to commit themselves to filing a certain number of improvement proposals each month. The level was negotiated individually with each group, but elements of competition and peer pressure clearly played a role in this process. Improvement proposals are typically handwritten. Typical proposals involve refinements in working procedures, work stations or production equipment.

Each group submits a monthly review of its activities in addition to individual proposals. These monthly reviews serve as the principal vehicle for control and feedback from management. Supervisors provide monthly feedback to individual groups praising their efforts or pointing out areas for improvement or emphasis.

Proposals play a key role in the small group system. The larger conceptual scheme in Figure 7-8 outlines the role of the improvement proposal in achieving the objectives of the MMM movement. Management support of the program, coupled with total employee participation, creativity and

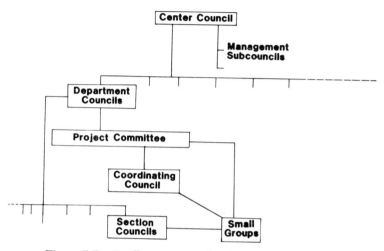

Figure 7-7. Small group council and committee structure.

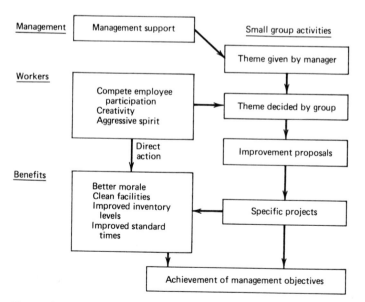

Figure 7-8. A conceptual scheme of a small group activity system.

299

aggressive spirit will lead to specific benefits in morale, quality and efficiency. Through the identification and implementation of specific improvement proposals, management objectives will be achieved. The improvement proposal submitted by individual groups is the key mechanism for achieving these objectives.

The first formal improvement proposals were filed at Musashi Works in 1978. By the end of the year, 26,543 specific proposals had been filed. Since that time, the number of proposals has grown dramatically. In the last six months of 1980, 112,022 proposals were submitted by the 360 workers groups within the Musashi factory. Of this total, 98,347 had been implemented by the end of the year. The average group completed about 45 improvements per month between July and the end of December in 1980.

Japanese small group activity systems are painstakingly and patiently nurtured into a highly sophisticated and powerful structure for achieving specific and general management objectives. Worker participation is encouraged by peer pressure, group affiliation benefits and the intergroup competition inherent in the system. The group structure is used to formalize specific objectives and commitments consistent with overall management strategy.

Managerial support and respect for the group system is critical in achieving success with such programs. Management reorientation is the first step in implementing a small group system. Management must be willing to permit the group system to exist outside the formal hierarchy if it is to be effective. Linkages between the group structure and the formal hierarchy are strong and sophisticated, however, to ensure monitoring and control of group activities. The Musashi example reveals the relative emphasis and sophistication of Japanese companies on the micro and informal dimension of organization design. Such approaches are becoming increasingly important in U.S. corporations. A recent survey estimated that more than 2,000 U.S. companies have adopted programs similar to small group or quality circle systems.[28]

KEY SUCCESS FACTORS

Another important principle in organization design is identification and emphasis of key success factors. Certain functions, such as coordination, communication, control and context management are essential for all organizations. For any given industry and company, however, certain other functions take on critical importance. Personnel development is essential for all organizations, but particularly for consulting companies. Labor relations are critical in other industries. Quality control is critical for pharmaceutical and processed food firms. Research and development assumes central importance for companies in high technology industries. In addition to the key success factors present in individual industries, specific functions become critical due to the nature of a firm's strategy.

Functional Requirements of Different Strategies

Strategic Emphasis	Key Functions
Global expansion	Resource transfer
	Government relations
Growth by acquisition	Legal and financial
	management
Cost reduction	Labor relations
	Engineering
Market development	Sales force development
	Marketing communications
Product differentiation	Design
	R&D
	Marketing communications
	Quality control

One of the key functions for firms pursuing a strategy of global expansion is resource transfer. The transmission of technology, capital, management, information, experience and strategies to foreign affilitates is the lifeblood of the global corporation. In selecting a structure, global corporations should seek to organize along lines that promote efficient, effective transfer of resources. Recent research suggests that different formal, macro structures exhibit very different capacities to transfer resources, principally technology, to foreign affiliates.

Structure and International Technology Transfer

It is widely held that international divisions create a barrier to the transfer of technology to foreign affiliates. The presence of an international division is thought to reduce direct communication between the domestic source of technology and the foreign market recipient.[29] In attempting to follow the principle of designing an organization around key functions, many global firms have been responsive to such logic. Concern for improved transfer of technology has been a factor in the general move away from international division formats toward global product and matrix structures.

In examining the record of organizational change for multinational corporations, one pattern dominates the overall trend. Many companies have made the transition to a global product structure. Among the 180 firms in the Harvard Multinational Enterprise Project study, 50 had adopted global product structures by 1980. In another recent survey of 105 U.S.-based multinationals, over one third of the respondents described themselves as organized primarily along global product lines. Only 22% of the respondents cited the existence of an international division.[30] There are several reasons for the trend toward global product structures. The need for cost efficiency in an increasingly competitive global environment has led firms to rationalize manufacturing. As cited earlier, the need for global strategic focus has increased. Portfolio planning systems and internal political pressures also contribute to this trend. However, concern for transfer of technology is also an important consideration. Global product structures permit direct, unified management of both technology sources and market recipients. This factor has supported the general move to global product structures.

An examination of the relative performance of different types of structure in transferring technologies reveals some surprising results. The results suggest that global product structures do not facilitate the transfer of technology. My study of 57 large U.S. multinationals found that new technologies introduced by firms organized along global product lines spread abroad more slowly and infrequently than new products of other companies.[31] More importantly, firms organized by global product lines were more likely to resort to the use of licensing rather than direct investment in developing foreign markets for their new products.

Table 7-3 classifies a sample of 954 significant new products according to the organizational structure of the parent firm and subsequent international transfer patterns. Note that less than 10% of all products introduced by global product firms are first transferred abroad within one year of U.S. introduction. Products introduced by firms in other structures spread abroad much more quickly. Fewer than two thirds of the products introduced by

TABLE 7-3. Structure and Technology Transfer Patterns

Parent's Organizational Structure	Number of New Products	% First Introduced Abroad in:					Total % Introduced Abroad as of 12/77	Average Annual Number of Transfers from Year of First Foreign Production to:	
		1 Year or Less	2–3 Years	4–5 Years	6–9 Years	10 or More Years		3 Years There-After	1977 Year-End
Domestic product divisions	128	13.8	17.8	8.5	7.8	21.2	69.5	.846	.261
Domestic functional divisions	84	19.1	10.8	12.0	11.9	20.3	73.8	.949	.277
Product with international division	403	19.6	12.7	13.2	17.4	20.8	81.6	.962	.296
Functional with international division	93	20.7	14.0	9.7	15.1	12.9	72.1	.979	.298
Global product divisions	140	8.1	11.4	10.7	15.7	17.1	64.3	.832	.266
Global matrix	106	23.6	20.7	13.2	13.2	8.5	55.9	1.189	.426
TOTAL	954	17.7	14.1	11.7	14.7	18.1	76.3	.952	.308

Source: W.H. Davidson, *Experience Effects in International Investment and Technology Transfer* (Ann Arbor: UMI Research Press, 1980).

global product firms had been transferred abroad at all by 1978, as compared to a rate in excess of 85% for global matrix firms. Even firms with no formal international structure exhibit greater transfer activity than global product firms.

One could argue that these findings do not necessarily reflect poor performance. They could be due to different industry classifications of these groups, but further examination revealed that firms organized along global product lines do not operate in industries significantly different from other firms. More importantly, examination of those firms organized along global product lines shows that they experienced a significant decline in transfer activity after the transition to global product status. These firms transferred technologies more often and more quickly before they adopted the global product structure. The observations in Table 7-4 are for only those firms organized by global product divisions. Since each of the 12 firms has remained in that structure, the two rows in the table are effectively before and after observations of transfer activity.

Still, the observation that global product firms are less active in transferring technology could reflect a change in corporate policy. As mentioned earlier, a primary benefit of the global product structure is manufacturing rationalization. Reduced technology transfer activity could be a result of a successful rationalization strategy as the number of locations manufacturing any given product is reduced. However, the greater use of licensing by global product firms suggests that another factor is at work (see Table 7-5). Over 30% of all international transfers of technology by global product firms are to independent foreign licencees. A similar rate is exhibited by firms with no formal international structure. Independent licencees are recipients of about 25% of all transfers by firms with an international division, and firms organized by global matrix use licensing in only 5% of all foreign transfers.

Global product companies view licensing more favorably than other companies. Why? The answer to that question may also explain the lower levels of technology transfer activity by such firms. The reasoning is that global product structures and the way they are introduced in U.S. multinationals tend to affect the valuation of foreign investment projects and market development proposals. This type of organizational structure affects the valuation of foreign projects in two ways. One is by its impact on the economics of foreign projects. Another is by its impact on the decision-making environment of the managers who make the commitment to pursue a project. On both counts, the global structure tends to discourage foreign initiatives.

TABLE 7-4. Technology Transfer Patterns for 12 Firms Before and After Transition to a Global Product Structure

Products Classified by Parent's Organizational Structure	Number of Products	% Introduced Abroad in:					Total % Introduced Abroad by 12/31/77	Average Annual Number of Transfers from year of First Foreign Production to:	
		1 Year or Less	2–3 Years	4–5 Years	6–9 Years	10 or More Years		3 Years There-after	1977 Year-end
Global product divisions	140	8.1	11.4	10.7	15.7	17.1	63.0	.832	.266
Other	101	13.9	13.9	11.9	14.9	29.8	84.4	.921	.296
TOTAL	241	10.5	12.4	11.2	15.4	22.5	72.0	.869	.278

Source: Compiled from W.H. Davidson, *Experience Effects in International Investment and Technology Transfer, op. cit.* (Ann Arbor: UMI Research Press, 1980).

TABLE 7-5. Licensing Rates for Firms in Different Organizational Structures

Organizational Structure of Parent at Time of Transfer	Number of Transfers	Percentage Via License
Domestic	798	30.2
International division	803	24.8
Global product	66	30.3
Global matrix	176	5.1
TOTAL	1,843	25.9

A Reduced Foreign Investment Experience Effect

Three factors play a major role in improving the economics of foreign projects. One is the company's ability to reduce costs through the sharing of resources. A second is the ability to reduce costs through the realization of learning benefits. A third is the ability to reduce risks involved in a project. All three factors, which we will jointly label "experience effects," are negatively affected by the transition from an international division to a global product structure. At the most basic level, the global product structure fragments the international resources of the company and in so doing raises the cost of executing foreign projects. Host country resources such as distribution facilities and sales personnel will become less than fully accessible to different product divisions. Duplication of overheads at the host country level can raise project costs significantly, as each division's project must pay for its own infrastructure and peripheral investments.

A similar effect occurs at headquarters. Global product structures can also fragment central resources such as administrative systems and corporate staff capabilities. Scale economies are foregone to the extent that each division or group develops its own support system. It also becomes very difficult to retain the foreign expertise embodied in the international division personnel once a firm starts to shift power from area units to product groups. In a global product company each division basically operates on its own learning curve with respect to international operations—even though the international activities of the various divisions may be concentrated in roughly the same countries. The fragmentation of information and know-how finally results not only in higher costs but also in much higher uncertainty levels about foreign projects. While the perceived risks of a project can be assessed precisely by experienced managers in an international division, risks will be perceived less accurately by a worldwide division manager making his first entry in a foreign market. A reduced ability to reap "experience benefits" vis-à-vis foreign investment results in higher costs and higher perceived risk for foreign projects. As a result, companies organized along global product lines can be expected a place a lower value on foreign investment projects and make greater use of licensing.

A Less Favorable Decision-Making Environment for Foreign Projects

The reduction in experience effects of course assumes investment decisions are made on financial return criteria. Foreign investmentt projects, like all others, are largely shaped by the perceptions and the career stakes of the managers who define, propose and support them. The nature of the decision-making process and the identity of the decision maker can change dramatically upon transition to a global product structure. More importantly, the behavioral characteristics of the decision environment in global product companies tend to discourage foreign activity.

It is widely observed that managers with little foreign experience will be highly risk averse with regard to foreign operations. It typically takes a number of years for firms embarking on international expansion to gradually overcome this risk aversion and adopt a policy of active international growth. This change in strategic orientation is generally embodied in the functions and personnel of the international division. The career stakes of the international division managers guarantee advocacy for foreign investment. Eliminating an international division and making product divisions responsible for worldwide investment decisions drastically changes the organization's perspective on foreign projects. Foreign investment projects typically become high-risk possibilities among a set of much less uncertain domestic investments involving cost reduction or market penetration. Chances are high that the worldwide business unit manager, often being less experienced and at ease in foreign matters and possessing low staff expertise, will be highly risk averse with regard to international operations.

In practice, the choice of worldwide business unit managers contributes to this phenomenon. In most U.S.-based multinational corporations, global product division managers are likely to be the former domestic division managers whose domestic business represented between 60 and 80% of worldwide product sales. Only a minority of such managers will have had a foreign assignment at any point in their career. These managers often retain a primary orientation toward domestic operations. Concerns for international considerations are likely to be strongly felt only when foreign competition threatens their domestic position.

In contrast, matrix structures exhibit sharply different patterns of technology transfer. The matrix format provides a different internal economic and decision-making environment. Area managers are responsible for ensuring the efficient use of local resources. Their incentive structures will encourage efficient allocation of local resources to investment projects. Product and functional managers will seek to maximize efficiency as well in allocating and applying resources to investment projects. The economics of investment projects will appear more favorable as a result. In addition, the decision environment in which investment projects are evaluated de-emphasizes the role of managers who have limited experience pertinent to any project. Besides maximizing the role of experienced managers in the decision-making process, the matrix stimulates sharing of resources, expertise and information. The matrix also balances and integrates technology and market forces in the project appraisal process.

This discussion shows how structure can affect key organizational functions. Choice of structure can have a significant effect on efficiency and ultimately competitive position. One of the most basic approaches to organizational design requires identification of functions or activities critical to the entity's success and selection of a structure that maximizes efficiency and effectiveness for those functions. Identification of critical functions is the first step in selecting a structure that promotes performance in these key areas.

A CONTINGENCY MODEL OF ORGANIZATION DESIGN

A wide range of internal and external variables must be considered in designing organizations. Environmental considerations have been widely discussed in relation to organization design. Burns and Stalker relate the level of change in the environment to structural needs.[32] Lawrence and

Lorsch summarize how a range of environmental factors relate to the effectiveness of different types of structures.[33] The environment also dictates certain critical success factors that must be addressed in selecting a structure.

Many of the structural imperatives drawn from assessment of the environment are first translated into strategic imperatives. If corporate strategy is responsive to environmental realities, structure can largely be designed to fit strategy rather than environment. The relationship between strategy and structure has been highly developed by Chandler.[34] Strategy dictates the structural requirements of the organization. Several elements of strategy are particularly important in that respect.

A firm's diversity of operations both in product and area dimensions represents a strategic choice with profound implications for structure. Diversity largely dictates the firm's ability to adopt a primary product, functional or area orientation in its operations. Vertical integration represents another strategic issue with important implications for structure. Vertically integrated firms require sophisticated coordination, communication and control mechanisms, often focused on functional activities. Arbitration and performance evaluation systems pose major challenges in such situations.

At the most basic level, the goals underlying the corporate strategy hold important implications for structure. Emphasis on rapid growth determines not only the nature of marketing, production and finance activities, but also how they should be integrated. Emphasis on profit maximization will require sophisticated management systems and profit center definition. Goals readily translate into key functions, such as cost minimization, global expansion, distribution, product development or personnel development, that can be emphasized in designing an organization.

Other elements of corporate strategy also have an important effect on organization design. Participation policy dictates the extent of integration of foreign affiliates with the rest of the organization. Sourcing strategy determines an important aspect of the choice between centralization, decentralization and integration of functions. The firm's technology and marketing policies also dictate the importance of these activities within the organization and determine the need for centralization or decentralization of management.

Consideration of all these factors will help in identifying the key functions around which to organize, in defining organizational subunits, in determining the choice between centralization or decentralization of different functions, in deciding which dimension—area, product or function—to emphasize, and how to link the various elements of the structure together through structural mechanisms and management systems. Implications for culture definition can also flow from this analysis. Although these factors play a large role in dictating structural choices, the availability of macro, micro, formal and informal design tools to meet structural needs permits a certain degree of flexibility. Once the needs of the organization are defined from analysis of its environment, its position and its strategy, the many possible structural configurations can be assessed to determine which options best meet the requirements and characteristics of the company in question.

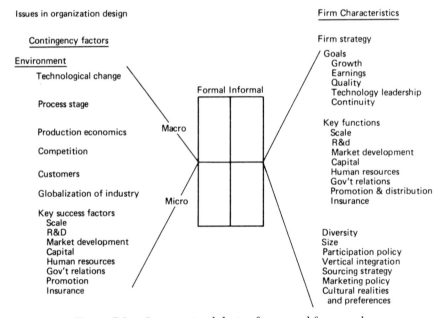

Figure 7-9.   Organizational design factors and framework.

NOTES

1.   Stopford, J. M. and L. T. Wells, Jr., *Managing the Multinational Enterprise* (New York: Basic Books, 1972); Fouraker, L. E. and J. M. Stopford, "Organizational Structure and the Multinational Strategy," *Administrative Science Quarterly,* June 1968, pp. 47–64.

2. Prahalad, C. K., "Strategic Choices in Diversified MNC's," *Harvard Business Review*, September—October 1976, p. 76; Dymsza, W. A., *Multinational Business Strategy* (New York: McGraw-Hill, 1972), Chapter 2; Doz, Y., "Strategic Management in Multinational Companies," *Sloan Management Review*, Winter 1980, p. 28.

3. Stopford, J. M. and L. T. Wells, Jr., op. cit., pp. 63—68.

4. Haspeslagh, P., "Portfolio Planning: Use and Usefulness," forthcoming, *Harvard Business Review*, 1982.

5. Jennegren, L. P., *Decentralization in Organizations* (Berlin: Institute of Management, 1974); Abell, P., The Task Determinants of Decentralization between HQ and UK Subsidiaries of International Corporations, unpublished paper, Department of Sociology, University of Birmingham, 1976.

6. This fundamental aspect of organizations is addressed in Chandler, A.D., *Strategy and Structure* (Cambridge: MIT Press, 1962).

7. Haspeslagh, P., op. cit.

8. Stopford, J. M., Growth and Organizational Change in the Multinational Firm, unpublished doctoral dissertation, Harvard Business School, 1968; Franko, L. G., "The Move Toward A Multidivisional Structure in European Organizations," *Administrative Science Quarterly*, Vol. 20, No. 4, 1976, pp. 493—506.

9. Doz, Y., *Government Control and Multinational Strategic Management* (New York: Praeger, 1979), Chapters 7—8; Brandt, W. K. and J. M. Hulbert, "Communication and Control in the Multinational Enterprise," in Keegan, W. J. and C. S. Mayer (eds.), *Multinational Product Management* (American Marketing Association Proceedings, 1974); Thompson, J. D., *Organizations in Action* (New York: McGraw-Hill, 1967).

10. The relationship between technology and organizational format is multidimensional. Woodward related process technology to structural requirements. Lawrence and Lorsch relate the rate of technological change to organizational needs. Woodword, J. *Industrial Organization* (London: Oxford University Press, 1965); Lawrence, P. R. and J. Lorsch, op. cit. Harvey, E., "Technology and the Structure of Organizations," *American Sociological Review*, No. 33, 1968, pp. 247—259. See also Jelinek, M., "Technology, Organizations and Contingency," *Academy of Management Review*, January 1977, pp. 17—26; Trist, E. L., G. W. Higgen, M. Murray and A. B. Pollock, *Organizational Choice* (London: Tavistock, 1963); Taylor, J.C., *Technology and Planned Organizational Change* (Ann Arbor: Brown-Bromfield, 1971). The need for centralized organization of research and production functions in high technology firms is cited in Vernon, R., "The Location of Economic Activity," op. cit.

11. This is essentially the nature of industries requiring centralized sourcing strategies as described in Chapter 5.

12. See the section "Choice of Technology" in chapter 5.

13. Lawrence, P. R., and J. Lorsch, *Organizations and Environment* (Cambridge: Harvard University Press, 1967).

14. Galbraith, J. R., *Organization Design*, (Reading: Addison-Wesley, 1977), Chapter 8; Farris, G. F., "Organizing your Informal Organization," *Innovation*, October 1971.

15. This phenomenon is described in Bartlett, C. A., Multinational Structural Evolution: The Changing Decision Environment International Divisions, unpublished doctoral dissertation, Harvard Business School, 1979.

16. From personal remarks to the author by Mr. Lyman Hamilton, former CEO of ITT. See also "ITT: Can Profits be Programmed?" *Dun's Review*, November 1965.

17. From comments made to the author by Mr. Robert Frederick, former head of General Electric's Planning Group and present head of GE's international sector.

18. Quinn, J. B., *Strategies for Change: Logical Incrementalism* (Homewood: Irwin, 1980).

19. Galbraith, J. R., *Organization Design* (Reading: Addison-Wesley, 1977).

20. Egelhoff, W. G., Strategy and Structure in Multinational Corporations: An Information Processing Approach, unpublished doctoral dissertation, New York University, 1980.

21. For case studies of this phenomenon, see The Galvor Company ICCH No. 9-313-035; Sigma (B) ICCH No. 4-377-086.

22. This broad subject has been addressed by a wide range of authors. See, for example, Emery, E.E. and E. L. Trist, "The Causal Texture of Organizational Environment," *Human Relations*, No. 18, 1965, pp. 21–31; Downey, H. K. and R. D. Ireland, "Quantitative vs. Qualitative Assessment in Organizational Studies," *Administrative Science Quarterly*, December 1979, pp. 630–37; Baker, E. L., "Managing Organizational Culture," *Management Review*, July 1980, pp. 8–13; Woodman, R. W. and D. C. King, "Organizational Climate: Science or Folklore?" *Academy of Management Review*, October 1978, pp. 816–26.

23. Athos, A. G. and R. T. Pascale, *The Art of Japanese Management* (New York: Simon and Schuster, 1981).

24. Ouchi, W. G. and A. M. Jaeger, "Type Z Organization," *Academy of Management Review*, Vol. 3, No. 2, 1978, pp. 305–14; Ouchi, W. G., *Theory Z* (Reading: Addison-Wesley, 1981).

25. Yoshino, M. Y., *Japan's Managerial System* (Cambridge: MIT Press, 1968).

26. Lifson, T. B., "An Emergent Administrative System: Interpersonal Networks in a Japanese General Trading Firm," working paper, Harvard Business School, 1979; Mattori, I., "Japanese Management Practices" in Ballon, R. J., *Doing Business in Japan* (Honolulu: University Press of Hawaii, 1976); Johnson, T., "Authority, Power and Decision-Making in the Japanese Business Organization," unpublished paper, Amos Tuck School, 1980; Ashwell, K. A., "Japanese Management Strengths and Weaknesses", Tokyo, Japan Productivity Center, September, 1981.

27. The author wishes to express his gratitude to the Worker's Council of Musashi Semiconductor Works for providing the materials presented here. This material is presented in detail in: Davidson, W.H. "Small Group Activity in Musashi Semiconductor Works" *Sloan Management Review*, Spring, 1982.

28. "Japanese Management Style Wins Converts," *Industry Week*, April 16, 1979, pp. 19–21; Cole, R.E., *Work, Mobility and Participation* (Berkeley: University of California Press, 1979).

29. This widely held opinion is reported by Davis, S. M., "Trends in the Organization of Multinational Corporations," *Columbia Journal of World Business*, Summer 1976, pp. 59–71.

30. Wicks, M. E., op. cit.

31. Davidson, W. H., *Experience Effects*, op. cit., Chapter 3.

32. Burns, T. and G. M. Stalker, *The Management of Innovation* (London: Tavistock, 1961).

33. Lawrence, P. R., and J. Lorsch, op. cit.

34. Chandler, A. D., op. cit.

EIGHT

Strategic Planning

Each of the preceding chapters described strategic issues and options important in developing and managing a global business. Strategic choices in each of these areas carry great weight in determining the ultimate performance of a global corporation. The means and processes for making these strategic choices are embodied in the firm's strategic planning function. Strategic planning can be performed in many different modes. Mintzberg describes three distinct modes of strategic management.[1] In the entrepreneurial mode, key strategic decisions often involve limited consultation, analysis or discussion. The strategic planning process is unstructured, personality-dependent and discontinuous in this mode. In the adaptive mode, administrative behavior is marked by incremental responses to strategic issues. In this form, strategic issues are addressed in a more structured manner, but formal planning processes are incomplete in scope and function. In the third planning mode, systematic, formal and interactive analysis of strategic issues and options is the rule.

It is common to assume that planning activities for individual organizations evolve along this spectrum, if at different rates. It is also widely held that the effectiveness of strategic decision making improves as planning processes evolve. Although planning practices within U.S. corporations vary widely, an increasing number of U.S. firms are adopting formal, participative strategic planning systems.[2] There is no guarantee that formalization of the strategic planning process will improve the quality of strategic decisions, however. Other modes and concepts of planning can achieve the overall objectives of strategic management. The planning practices of European and Japanese firms appear to differ sharply from those employed by many leading U.S. corporations.[3] Any process that systematically raises and

313

analyzes strategic issues provides a critical source of support to global managers. The design and use of an effective strategic planning system is of fundamental importance in global strategic management.

The roots of strategic planning are often traced to military origins.[4] Military concepts of strategic planning are widely used in the corporate world. Strategic planning, in an anthropological sense, can be traced to even more remote origins in the group hunting activities of prehistoric man. The basic framework of strategic planning predates its corporate applications by many thousands of years, yet it is often viewed as a novel approach to management. Much of this reaction is due principally to the formalization of the planning process. All organizations make strategic decisions, but many do not utilize a formal strategic planning system to analyze, structure and support such decisions. The steps in the strategic planning process, from definition of mission, selection of targets, formulation of strategy and specification of structure can be executed in many different modes.

There is no evidence that any one planning approach is superior to another. However, several important benefits can be derived from the formalization and systemization of strategic planning. Formalization can ensure a more thorough planning process. Formalization creates open forums for discussion of planning issues. Participation by a wider group of managers in these forums helps to build commitment to strategic decisions. Just as important, participation generates additional sources of information for use in the decision-making process. Formal planning systems can also be used to communicate objectives and responsibilities to line managers. Formal planning creates networks of information, forces operating managers to extend time horizons, influences attitudes and stimulates detailed analyses of pertinent issues. Systematic formal planning does not ensure the quality of decision making, but it can improve the quality of inputs in the decision-making process and the level of discussion involved in any decision. An effective strategic planning process:

Highlights assumptions

Raises strategic issues

Focuses managerial attention on key issues

Communicates objectives

Identifies options

Promotes strategic thinking

Provides forums for discussion

Fosters analysis

Reinforces decisions

Formalization of the planning process can assist in the realization of these benefits. However, extreme formalization of the planning process can restrict creativity, reduce diversity of thought and limit healthy ferment in strategic planning.

The benefits of formal planning are greater in some firms and industries than others. Lindsay and Rue find that formal planning is more likely to be adopted as the complexity and instability of the external environment increases.[5] Litschert relates the degree of formal planning to company size and technological variables.[6] Larger firms in more technologically dynamic environments exhibit higher degrees of formal planning.

Figure 8-1. Elements of strategic planning.

The ultimate goal of global strategic management is to locate and maintain a business in the best possible position and configuration in a dynamic environment. Strategic planning, whether done formally or informally, regularly or irregularly, frequently, infrequently or continuously, consciously or on a de facto basis, is the means by which this essential responsibility is managed. The health of the strategic planning function is a principal concern in diagnosing any business. For a global business, the principal concern involves the quality of the fit between the requirements of the business and the nature of its strategic planning philosophy and practice. Examination of different dimensions and elements of strategic planning can help in determining the appropriate planning approach for different types of global businesses. Strategic planning is a continuous, iterative, closed loop process. It does not follow specific sequences. A one-dimensional view of the different functions involved in strategic planning as presented here does not capture any of the full richness and complexity of the process underlying the formulation of strategy. However, it does provide some framework for discussion of different elements of the planning system. This chapter focuses on the ongoing process of formulating strategiees and structure for a single global business as presented in Figure 8-1.

DIMENSIONS OF STRATEGIC PLANNING

The basic objective in designing a planning system is the creation of a system that will fit the needs of the business. Different businesses exhibit different planning needs, in terms of the focus, frequency, formality, time frame and format of the planning function. Differences in business success factors and needs frequently frustrate attempts to initiate uniform planning procedures for diverse firms. Every business has different planning needs, just as every business has different organizational needs. The unique nature and needs of each business unit should be addressed in designing and executing the planning process.

The first step in the design of a planning system occurs in defining planning units. One of the most important issues in defining planning units is the familiar choice between centralization and decentralization of focus. This fundamental issue applies to planning as it does to every other function in global strategic management. The choice between a centralized planning focus of emphasis on individual markets is driven by what Vancil and

Lorange call the integrative and adaptive needs of the business.[7] Needs for integrated planning predominate in businesses characterized by rapid technological change, sourcing complexity, manufacturing capital intensity and global customers and competitors. Needs for differentiation or adaptive planning might predominate in businesses with limited economies of scale, stable technology, high market tailoring requirements and indigenous customers and competition. It is unlikely that any business will exhibit exclusively integrative or adaptive needs. However, analysis of characteristics such as those in Table 8-1 help in defining the planning needs of a given business. Such analysis is an important prerequisite in defining business planning units. The choice between centralized or decentralized planning focus can be based on analysis of such characteristics. For businesses that do not readily fit into one of these categories, a third approach can be used. Doz cites an approach based on "administrative coordination" for businesses that require dual focus on national and global planning dimensions.[8]

The choice between centralization and decentralization of planning focus for a given business rests primarily on such characteristics. Definition of

TABLE 8-1.   Business Characteristics and Planning Focus

Key Business Factors	Conditions Consistent with Integrative and Adaptive Planning Approaches	
	Integrative	Adaptive
Manufacturing		
Pace of technological change	Rapid	Stable
Complexity of sourcing	High	Medium/low
Manufacturing capital intensity	High	Low
Importance of scale economics	High	Low
Value added to weight	High	Medium/low
Marketing		
Stage of product life cycle	Developing/Mature	Maturing
Need for market tailoring	Medium/low	High
Nature of customers	Global	Local
Nature of competitors	Global	Local
Focus of competition	Price	Promotion
	R&D	Product tailoring distribution Government relations

planning units on a global basis is appropriate when the integrative needs of the business are significant. When adaptive needs are high, separate planning units for domestic and international markets for a given product will be justified. In such cases, the strategic thrust of management will differ sharply in different markets for the same product. A business that is mature or declining in the United States can be in very different stages of growth in foreign markets. Although domestic management will be oriented towards a cash cow or harvest strategy, foreign markets will require growth-oriented strategies and planning focus.[9] Planning units defined to reinforce these differences in strategic orientation will improve management responsiveness to the needs of the business. The definition of planning focus must also be sensitive to host country conditions. Conditions in an individual market may be so unique and so important to success that a market-based planning focus is required for all products in that market. These factors can dictate the definition of planning units along geographic lines. Such an approach is most appropriate for businesses with stable technology, significant marketing differentiation, low capital intensity, high gross margins, and significant government relations requirements. Other businesses will require a global, centralized planning emphasis. Businesses that will benefit most from a global planning focus generally exhibit low marketing complexity, low diversity of management requirements and objectives, low variance in operating conditions, global competitors, high sourcing complexity and integrated operations. Businesses with these characteristics require a centralized approach to planning and management. A shared or coordinated planning focus is warranted when responsiveness to both global and national imperatives is needed.

Each approach involves significant costs and benefits. A shared approach permits sensitivity to both global and national operating environments, but this approach involves significant conflict, ambiguity, administrative costs and management time. A global planning focus provides a worldwide perspective on opportunities and threats, but also results in insensitivity to local conditions. A global approach provides an excellent mechanism for strategic control of foreign affiliates, but restricts strategic flexibility and mobility in national markets. A national planning focus offers the same trade-off: this permits adaptation and flexibility, but at the cost of diminished integration and strategic control.

The focus of planning efforts on the market or product dimension is a fundamental issue in defining planning units. Other dimensions of the

TABLE 8-2. A Differential Approach to Global Planning

	Planning Approach		
	Global	Local	Shared
	Conditions Favoring		
Top management involvement	High	Medium/Low	High/Medium
Operating philosophy	Integrated	Adaptive	Coordinated
Marketing complexity	Low/Medium	High	Medium/High
Manufacturing complexity	High	Medium/Low	Variable
Diversity of management objectives	Low	High	High
Nature of competition	Global	Local	Unique
Variance in operating conditions	Low	High	Medium
Costs	Insensitivity to local needs; Inability to employ different strategies; Inflexibility	Lack of global perspective	High administrative commitment; High levels of ambiguity; Conflict; Slow decision making
Benefits	Global perspective and strategy; Vehicle for strategic control of subsidiary operations	Market adaptability	Concentration of effort; Combined global and local perspective
Key process characteristics			
Structure	Formal	Informal	Flexible
Predominant focus	Consistency Coordination	Adaptability	Both
Linkage of operations planning with strategic decisions	Tight	Loose	Tight

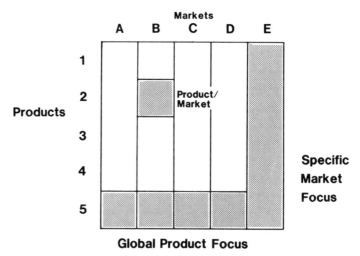

Figure 8-2. Planning unit definition.

planning system and process also require definition. The frequency of planning is an important variable. Many firms employ formal planning solely as a discrete diagnosis exercise to be completed once every 10 or more years. This examination can lead to fundamental reorientation of operations, objectives, strategic thrusts and even decision-making processes, but the formal planning process itself is not viewed as a continuing management activity. At the other end of the spectrum are firms that treat formal planning as a continuous process. The planning process in such companies is internalized into the firm's ongoing strategic management functions. A third group of firms lies between these two extremes. Such firms treat formal planning as an annual but discrete exercise. Planning activities are regularly scheduled, but often they are focused more on limited planning functions such as budgeting, operating plans and performance evaluation than on strategic decision making.

   In addition to focus and frequency, the format, time frame, and flexibility of the planning process also requires definition. Planning formats cover a wide range of options. The forms and procedures used in completing a planning cycle represent key dimensions of the planning system.[10] The design of planning forms, procedures, transmission media and input−output parameters requires extensive investment. Let us focus for the moment on planning procedures for unit and affiliate managers. These procedures can vary sharply. In some companies, completion of forms represents the culmination of planning activities for unit managers. More commonly, this step is followed by face-to-face dialogues about the assumptions, objectives, and resource requirements associated with the plan. The location, participants, duration, content, scope and intensity of these sessions can vary sharply. Most firms hold these planning sessions in regional or corporate headquarters. For the affiliate or unit manager, the culmination of the planning process is unlikely to be on his or her own territory. In some cases, each business unit manager must present and defend his or her plan before the corporation's board of directors. In others, regional, divisional or functional management provide the critique and endorsement of unit plans. Other unit managers are active in this process in many companies. Planning staff can also fill this role.

Planning procedures, location and participation are largely dictated by the content and scope of the plan itself. Of prime concern is the emphasis on operating versus strategic planning. Operations planning can be regarded as encompassing principally the budget process. The main purpose of such planning is the determination of unit operating budgets and standards. Such issues can also be addressed in planning systems oriented more toward broader strategic planning. The degree of integration of operations and strategic planning is a key issue in the design of a planning system. Many firms segregate the two types of planning completely; others address both simultaneously through the same channels. The level of strategic planning content in the planning system depends on the relative emphasis on the following variables:

Unit mission
Unit objectives
Environment analysis
Competitive analysis
Internal and external constraints
Long-range forecasts and scenarios
Strategies
Programs
Resource requirements
Contingency plans

These issues need not be addressed at the unit level, but their presence and emphasis in the planning process determines the level of strategic, as opposed to operations, planning content and scope.

The planning process, from initial preparation of business unit plans to acceptance, can take three to six months for unit managers. Of course, the amount of time spent on planning activities increases for managers placed higher in the organization. The amount of time involved in completing a planning cycle is an important variable. The time horizon of the planning process also affects the focus of planning activity. At one extreme, planning can be oriented essentially toward short-term operating considerations. In this mode, planning is designed principally to communicate objectives and ensure consistency between the organization's strategic thrust and its operating subsystems. The planning system serves important communication and integration purposes in this mode, but it does not support the process of strategic decision making. At the other end of the spectrum, the planning process focuses on long-term, strategic issues. In this mode, the planning process permits more participation in fundamental strategic decisions by operating management.

The overall strategic direction of a company is presented to operating managers in the planning system with varying degrees of clarity and fixity. Many managers view the annual budget and planning cycle as anything but an exercise in strategic decision making, or even communication of strategy. The key variable in this regard is the degree to which the strategic thrust of the company is treated as fixed or flexible in the planning process. If the general strategic direction of the company is considered fixed in the planning process, planning must essentially be viewed as a management system designed to integrate operating plan subsystems with the overall strategic direction of the company.

The planning process can be distinguished in terms of three distinct levels of focus: corporate or macro strategic planning, business unit or program planning, and function or operations planning. Each has a distinct focus, time frame and purpose. Corporate or macro strategic planning focuses on long-run positioning issues. The time horizon for this process is 3 to 10 years, and the process is continuous. Business portfolio planning is commonly the core framework for planning activity at this level. Outputs from this level include sector priorities, broad strategic guidelines and objectives, resource allocation criteria and constraints, coordination of business unit plans, and structural changes.

Business unit planning focuses on a specific strategic business unit. Resource allocation issues tend to be dominated by geographic choices, whereas resource allocation at the corporate level focuses on industry sector choices. The time horizon for business unit planning is a medium-term orientation, and the process is semicontinuous. Strategic and operating issues both appear in the business unit planning process. Operations planning by contrast is short-term, operational and discrete.

These distinct levels in the planning process can overlap to varying extents. The broad strategic direction of the company can be determined and dictated to the rest of the organization by an elite, private council, or it can be tested in a flexible, open, continuous forum. If macro strategy is treated as fixed, unit and operating plans will follow directly from this base. There will be relatively little discussion of macro strategic choices at the program planning level and little discussion of program planning options at the operating plan level. The flow of the planning process is essentially one-way and hierarchical in such a system.

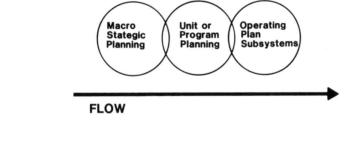

FLOW

Issues	Issues	Issues
Target sectors	Market selection	Production planning and
Positioning	Participation policy	scheduling
Resource allocation	Product planning	Inventory and purchasing
Structure (macro and micro)	(product line)	Personnel
Objectives	Marketing mix strategy	Cash management
Strategic orientation		Funding
		Exposure management
	Capital budgeting	Sales force planning
	Sourcing	Promotion planning
	Capital intensity	Facilities planning
	Repatriation	Capital expenditures
	R&D	

Figure 8-3.   A fixed planning hierarchy

TABLE 8-3. Organizational Dimensions Within the Planning Hierarchy

Organizational Dimensions	Corporate/Macro	Business Unit/Program	Operating Functions
Focus of effort	Strategic Long-run effectiveness Organization is variable Qualitative	Strategic/Operational Medium-term effectiveness Organization is adaptive within limits Mixed	Operational Short-term operational efficiency Organization is fixed Quantitative
Information focus	Broad trends and key business and market indicators	Specific industry trends and key market indicators	Specific business trends and key performance measures
Time horizon	3–10 years	2–5 years	1–3 years
Time cycle	Continuous	Semi-continuous	Discrete
Outputs and objectives	Alignment of corporate position with the key trends in the environment Development of corporate performance variables and targets by *business and market* Definition of business acquisition and resource allocation criteria Coordination of unit/program activities	Identification of key success factors and development of business strategy by *market* Clarification of industry niche and refinement of resource allocation patterns and performance expectations	Developmnt of key planning programs across functions, consistent with the overall business/market strategy Optimization of efficiency given available resources and proposed sequence of resource allocations

In a flexible planning system, the hierarchy and flow of the process become diffused. The degree of interaction between each of the three levels of planning increases, and the flow of the process becomes more iterative. In such an approach, all macro strategic parameters are not fixed when operating managers engage in the planning cycle. Operating decisions must then be discussed within a framework that openly evaluates broader strategic options. This approach can be extremely expensive in terms of management time consumed, but it also offers the benefits of management participation and commitment to ultimate strategic choices.

The degree of flexibility in the planning system can be designed into the system, but it is largely a matter of the planning culture.[12] Planning culture is an excellent example of an informal aspect of organization design, as discussed in Chapter 7. The creation and management of the desired planning culture is as important as design of the formal planning system. Many of the same issues and options arise in molding a planning culture as appear in managing an overall corporate culture. A planning culture can be quite distinct from the prevailing culture within an organization, however. In some cases, such contrasts can promote planning effectiveness. In some otherwise tight-lipped organizations, planning can play the role of the confessional to raise doubts, concerns, problems and conflicts. In organizations with a high degree of strategic autonomy, planning can provide strategic auditing and control as well as integration benefits. Design of planning culture requires sensitivity to the existing corporate culture and its shortcomings. However, attempts to use planning as an audit, control and integration mechanism can provoke powerful resistance in organizations permitting extensive autonomy.[13]

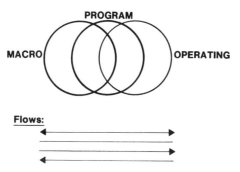

Figure 8-4. A flexible planning approach.

Organizational Linkage

The relationship between planning and broader corporate cultures represents one important dimension of linkage between the planning system and the rest of the organization. Formal linkages are also important.[14] At the most basic level is the relationship between business planning units and operating units. In some cases, the definition of a planning unit is different from that of a formal organizational operating unit. Haspeslagh found that in 20% of the Fortune 250 firms using a portfolio planning system, all planning and operating units did not coincide.[15] However, most of this variance is due to the aggregation or segmentation of operating units. Only in 7% of all cases did planning units actually cut across organizational lines. Pressures for parallel unit definition can result in compromises at both the planning level and the formal organizational level. The adoption of planning systems can provide a powerful stimulus for organizational change. When planning structure differs from formal structure, the principal causes are the desire to integrate or coordinate activities of different units or subunits and the desire to further differentiate activities within an individual organizational unit. Such cases are examples of the use of planning to meet a formal structure's secondary integration and differentation needs.

Another important organizational linkage involves the position of the planning manager in the firm's reporting and responsibility framework. Reporting and responsibility linkages have a great impact on the nature and perception of planning objectives, purposes and procedures. Planning units responsible to the corporate controller can be effective as audit mechanisms, and in integrating operating plans with budgets and performance evaluation. Such planning units are likely to be less effective if the planning process is intended to promote strategic discussion and decision making. Planning units responsible to the chief financial officer can also be effective in tying the planning process to capital budgeting and performance evaluation, but the strategic impact of such planning systems may also be low.

Planning units that operate within the general staff of the chief executive officer can be more effective in ensuring strategic content in the planning process. At the same time, such planning systems run the risk of being perceived as an intangible exercise. Divorced from the budgeting and evaluation processes, planning can be viewed as an academic exercise with little impact on operations. The degree to which this occurs depends greatly on the culture of the organization and ultimately, on the CEO's emphasis on planning. When the CEO uses strategic planning as the principal basis for resource allocation decisions and development of objectives and strategic orientation for business units, such an approach can be highly effective.

As current generations of MBA's work their way towards the top of their corporate organizations, an increased emphasis on the use of formal strategic planning can be expected. These managers generally are trained to use formal planning at the chief executive officer level. Their emergence at the senior management level often leads to an attendant change in planning culture. An example of this process can be seen within the American Standard Company. One of the first steps taken by its new chief executive officer in 1971 was to disengage the strategic planning unit from the rest of the general staff and establish more direct and powerful ties to his own office. [16] Increased emphasis on strategic planning as the principal decision support system for senior management can be expected to occur in other companies over time. Linkages between the planning unit and the CEO's office strengthen the strategic content and impact of the planning process.

Implementing the Planning Process

Elevation of the planning function into a focal point for strategic decision making does not occur instantaneously. Planning outputs represent only one of many inputs into strategy and policy decisions. It is not easy to displace other contributors to and participants in these decisions. A principal challenge in implementing a planning system is the need to convince management to channel their strategic inputs through the planning process. The transition from an informal strategic decision-making system to a formal process involves significant modification of behavior, attitudes and activities.

Informal inputs and processes dominate strategic decision making in many organizations. The participants, analysis patterns, discussion formats, time frame and ratification requirements for strategic decisions in such organizations can vary significantly from decision to decision. Guidelines for analysis, discussion and confirmation, if they exist, will tend to be implicit and imprecise. Such organizations can exhibit strict adherence to implicit norms of conduct in matters of strategic choice. However, decision making processes tend to be "organic"—flexible and adaptive but with the potential for inconsistency and incompleteness. Organizations with informal decision-making processes also face the problem of potential loss of strategic control. Unless consistency of goals, objectives and policies is enforced in all strategic decisions, the organization can easily drift away from its charted course. Formalization of the strategic decision-making process is an important means of ensuring strategic control although perhaps at the cost of some creativity and entrepreneurship.

The displacement and rechanneling of informal strategic inputs and processes typically occurs over an extended time period.[17] In the first stage of implementing a formal strategic planning system, activity often focuses on operating and financial information systems and planning. The development of annual, quarterly and monthly budgets for existing operating units often represents the first step in implementing a planning system. The process of negotiating and establishing budgets creates a foundation for further strategic communications between top and line management. The financial and operating information generated by this system provides important inputs in decisions regarding unit and system strategies.

In the second stage of expansion, the short-term operating plans can be enhanced by extension of the budgeting time frame and emphasis on scenario development. Long-term resource and functional planning can be accomplished against a backdrop that begins to recognize key trends, variables and alternative paths of development in the external environment. Exercises of this sort can highlight potential problems, deficiencies, needs and opportunities. Specific program responses to identified areas of concern provide further vehicles for expansion of strategic analysis and communication within the formal planning system.

Discrete program planning offers a valuable vehicle for implementing a planning system because of the concrete and immediate nature of such efforts and outputs. Program planning provides a base for the transition to broad-gauged, macro strategic planning. However, a quantum leap in the level, scope and nature of planning activity is needed to effect this transition. Strategic planning is not an extension of financial and operating plans. The two overlap significantly, but they can be regarded as distinct exercises and processes. Consequently, the transition from operations planning to strategic planning is not straightforward. The outputs of the strategic planning process will be less immediate and tangible than those of the budgeting or operations planning process. Unit managers may not see the immediate value or need of strategic planning. Linkages to resources allocation and other strategic choices must be established to stimulate serious involvement in the planning process.

Increased emphasis on environmental analysis occurs during the early

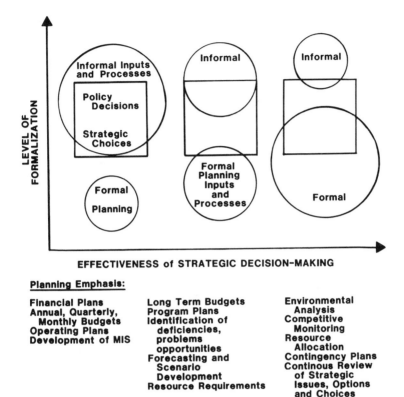

Figure 8-5. Formalization of planning and strategic decision making.

stages of strategic planning implementation. Formal competitor, market, industry, political and socioeconomic analyses will be generated for each business unit. Although the immediate value of these exercises will be questioned in many cases, they form the basis for evaluating present strategies and exploring alternatives. Several means can be used to involve unit and affiliate management in the environmental analysis exercise. They can be asked to submit reports prepared by their own staff for one or more of the dimensions of the exercise. In many cases, especially in the initial stages of implementation, this may not be feasible. Whenever possible, however, assignment of such responsibility does ensure some commitment and participation by line managers. A less demanding format emphasizes the completion of forms in which key variables and trends are specified. Management responses to the forms can be used to test assumptions and confidence levels, to assign data collection and monitoring priorities and to generate alternative environmental scenarios. An iterative process can be used to refine initial assessments and move toward a more fluid and integrated assessment of the environment. This assessent will provide an important part of the framework for evaluating unit strategies.

Once environmental assessment capabilities have been established and linkages between the planning process and strategic choices are confirmed, the strategic planning process can serve as a channel for communication and analysis of strategic inputs, options and issues. As the planning process becomes increasingly formalized and effective, strategic assumptions will be explicit and consistent, issues and options will be commonly recognized, analysis and discussion will become continuous and planning outputs will increasingly determine strategic choices.

Affiliate Resistance

For global corporations, implementation rarely occurs as smoothly as this scenario suggests. Foreign affiliates generally resist the implementation of information and planning systems. Within many global firms, foreign affiliate managers possess an unparalleled level of autonomy. Such autonomy stems from more than the physical and environmental distances between parent and affiliate. In most global firms, international markets represent principal areas of growth. Strict financial and operating controls typically are not applied to fast-growing business units. The managers of such units tend to be entrepreneurial in nature; their personalities, by nature or force of habit, resent and resist the imposition of operating and strategic controls. The level of resistance tends to be greatest in joint ventures, acquisitions and older affiliates.

The implementation of a planning system in a joint venture raises the immediate issue of strategic control. Institution of a formal planning process can be seen as a means of injecting one parent's goals, objectives, and decision-making processes into the power structure of the joint venture. Many partners will resist the implantation of a formal planning process. In acquired and older affiliates, long histories of independence, established norms and procedures and entrenched management lead to resistance. In such cases, it is imperative that the initial steps of implementation focus on areas where the parent can contribute to the affiliate's immediate performance. In some cases, the application of data processing systems to basic payroll, cash management and accounting functions can provide such a vehicle. If data processing systems precede management information systems, some opposition can be neutralized. Widespread and significant resistance to the development of planning systems can be expected at the affiliate level. Much of the resistance typically is focused on the implementation of operations planning and budgeting systems. Confrontations in these areas can create a culture that is not conducive to effective strategic communication and planning between parent and affiliate. Additional resistance can be met in attempting to upgrade an operating/budgeting system into a management system with broad strategic planning and control applications. A gradual, phased approach to implementation of information, planning and control systems can aid in overcoming opposition. The design and development of information systems provides an excellent starting point in this process.

Management Information Systems

Management information systems serve as the foundation for strategic planning and control functions. Design and implementation of these systems is central to an effective global management. The starting point for design of an MIS system is determination of information priorities. At the most basic level, a set of subsystems dealing with specific aspects of operations typically receive initial priority.[18] These subsystems generate information that permits the review and control of individual aspects of operations.

Another level of information systems can be created around analysis and planning activities for specific functional areas. Extensive analysis of marketing activities can be generated through the accumulation of computer-based information. Such analyses can model the effects of promotions, advertising, pricing and other marketing initiatives on product sales and margins, for example.[9] Product line analysis by host country can provide significant insights useful in plannning of product introductions and other aspects of marketing strategy. Similar planning subsystems can be used to improve production scheduling, capacity management and facilities planning at the affiliate level. Financial and personnel management can also be facilitated through the development of the following information and planning subsystems. The transfer of management procedures and software packages for these subsystems provide important linkages between a parent firm and its affiliates.

Management Information and Planning Subsystems

Operating Data	*Functional Analysis and Planning*
Customer order entry	Marketing research
Invoicing	Market forecasting
Inventory	Product line analysis
Purchasing	Mix analysis
Routings	Sales force planning
Expenditures	Production planning and scheduling
Payroll	Capacity planning
General ledger	Maintenance planning
Accounts receivble	Inventory control
Accounts payable	Shipping scheduling
Depreciation	Financial planning
Financial statements	Budgeting
Tax statements	Funding
	Capital cost analysis
	Personnel planning

The development of functional information bases often results in immediate identification of affiliate problem areas. Problems in forecasting, inventory control, working capital management, productivity, customer service, production scheduling and other functional areas can be identified and isolated. Individual units can then engage in program planning to address the specific problems identified by the information system.

One of the first issues in designing an information and planning system is assigning priorities to the different areas of information gathering and analysis. Establishment of information and planning subsystems according to the resulting priority schedule is the first step in implementing an information and planning system. These subsystems can be developed individually, but a master plan is essential to link and integrate these subsystems into a cohesive general system.

The creation of functional planning subsystems often occurs without extensive central management direction or knowledge. Affiliate and functional managers often develop independent information bases and planning models for their own use. The availability of distributed data processing systems further promotes this possibility. Although such independent creativity provides significant improvements in efficiency and effectiveness, it can lead to problems of inconsistency, integration and control. If functional planning formats and frameworks vary from unit to unit, global planning effectiveness for such functions will be compromised. The ability to integrate discrete functional plans into multifunctional plans will also be restricted if information bases, analytical frameworks and planning formats are inconsistent. The ability to evolve from operating to functional, program and business unit planning and ultimately to broad strategic planning will be inhibited by the proliferation of independent planning models and systems. Integration of the basic information and planning subsystems is essential to effective evolution of a strategic planning system. Independent information-gathering, analysis and planning activities can reduce or retard integration of the overall system. The result is a loss of cohesiveness and control in strategic analysis, planning and decision making.

Centralized direction and coordination is needed to ensure consistency in the design of information and planning subsystems. In addition to system consistency, the central architect also must be sensitive to the information processing and transmission requirements of the system. Integration of the various subsystems requires the design of effective transmission, analysis and consolidation mechanisms. These architectural elements can only be designed by central managers. Questions regarding the extent, format and frequency of information flows can be resolved within the context of a system such as that presented in Figure 8-6. Additional architectural elements such as amplifiers, hot lines, one-way versus two-way transmission lines and traffic control mechanisms can be applied within this framework as well.

The design of an integrated information system requires sensitivity to the information needs of all members of an organization. At the most basic level, it is imperative that information be transmitted back to affiliate management. Flows of information from affiliates to senior management can be overemphasized. Many otherwise very sophisticated information systems lack the capability to process and transmit information back to the field units. One means of ensuring effective and efficient transfer of information within the organization is the specification of an information grid. Such grids specify all pertinent types of information and the transmission patterns for each type. Construction of such a grid can help identify the information needs of the organization and ensure timely transmission to appropriate areas within the organization.

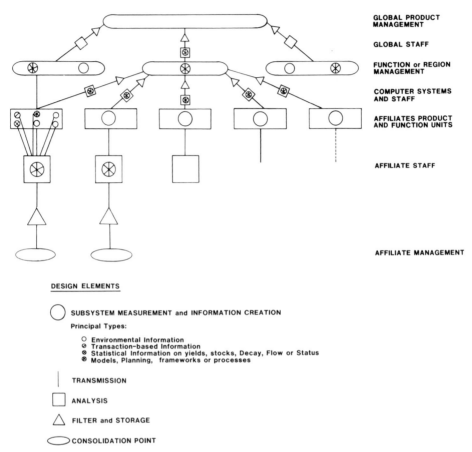

Figure 8-6.   Information system architecture.

The grid presented in Figure 8-7 drastically oversimplifies the dimensions of the information-processing matrix. Each of the information types can be broken down into subcategories with unique transmission patterns. The number of managers and organizational units requiring information also will be much greater and more complex. In addition, while a general transmission category can be applied to each cell in the grid, different categories will apply to different types of information flowing through each cell. Finally, the grid can vary by individual product line and by affiliate. The complexity of

Organizational Location	Monthly summary of operations	Cost accounting	Product line analysis	Market forecasting	Capacity	Sales force	Accounts receivable	Competitive data	Government relations	Inventory	Order status	Customer data
101 Corporate CEO	2											2
102 Marketing staff											2	
103 Manufacturing staff	3									2		
104 Procurement staff		2		2	2							
105 Personnel staff												
106 Financial staff	3	2	3	3			3			3		
107 Legal staff								1	1			
Division:												
201 Corporate CEO												
202 Marketing staff		2		2	2		2	3		3	2	2
203 Manufacturing staff	2	2	2	2			2			2		
204 Procurement staff		2								2		

Figure 8-7. Global information grid for a product line within a foreign affiliate. Information transmission categories: 1 = real-time transmission; 2 = scheduled transmission; 3 = access available.

Continued

335

Special Categories

Information Type

Information Type	205 Personnel staff	206 Financial staff	207 Legal staff	Region: 301 Corporate CEO	302 Marketing staff	303 Manufacturing staff	304 Procurement staff	305 Personnel staff	306 Financial staff	307 Legal staff	Sister Affiliates: 401 Corporate CEO	402 Marketing staff
Monthly summary of operations			3									
Cost accounting												
Product line analysis		2										
Market forecasting												
Capacity		3										
Sales force												
Accounts receivble												
Competitive data			1									
Government relations			1									
Inventory		2										
Order status		3										
Customer data												

Organizational Location

403 Manufacturing staff

404 Procurement staff

405 Personnel staff

406 Financial staff

501 Corporate CEO

502 Marketing staff

503 Manufacturing staff

504 Procurement staff

505 Personnel staff

506 Financial staff

· · ·

n01 · · ·

n07

Figure 8-7. (*Continued*)

337

defining and designing an effective information system poses a major challenge to global managers. Furthermore, this framework describes only the gathering, transmission and processing of information. The decision and implementation aspects of the planning system occur, to a large extent, outside this framework. The information system serves principally as a foundation and support for planning, strategic decision-making and control processes.

The implementation of information and planning systems at the operating, functional and program levels results in immediate and tangible outputs and activities at these levels. At the broader strategic planning level, the immediate result of activities is often seen in resource allocation patterns. The use of planning outputs and processes in resource allocation decisions is an important vehicle for establishing the legitimacy and scope of strategic planning activities.

Resource Allocation

The formalization of capital budgeting procedures provides an important opportunity to apply the planning function. In most firms, the capital budgeting process revolves around pro forma financial statements for individual projects. Envionmental analysis and strategic assessments also carry varying degrees of weight in the project review process. The planning unit often plays a key role in analyzing environmental issues related to individual projects. Planners also frequently aid in the assessment of a project's fit with the firm's strategic posture and direction. As a result of these activities, the planning unit can have a significant impact on resource allocation decisions. It is also important to note that the planning unit can play a major role in the development of project financial estimates.

In most firms, financial estimates are prepared largely by affiliate management. Country managers and staff play the key role in identifying, defining and estimating project opportunities. As the need for global integrated management increases, however, it is likely that a central product management perspective will develop within the firm. These central managers will also identify and define opportunities and estimate project returns. The result can be a conflict in resource allocation priorities. In Figure 8-8, country and product managers have each calculated potential returns from

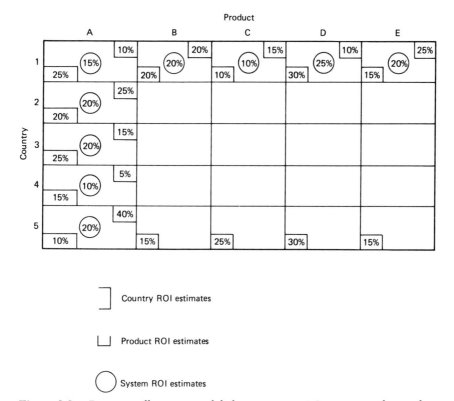

Country ROI estimates

Product ROI estimates

System ROI estimates

Figure 8-8. Resource allocation in global corporation: ROI estimates by product and country management.

incremental investments in each sector. Although product managers for Product A place high priority on Country 5, country management will not wish to pursue a project in that sector, preferring investments in other product areas. Similarly, management in Country 1 will place high priority on investment in Product A, while managers for that product will prefer to invest elsewhere.

Differentials in project return estimates result from several factors. Host country resources and facilities will exhibit varying degrees of transferability to individual products. Returns for a similar project in several countries depend greatly on whether the host country has already invested in complementary products or component lines, for example. Country management returns will reflect the extent to which such economies can be realized. Central product managers' estimates will be more sensitive to the degree to which a standardized product and strategy can be used in a given host country. Markets that require significant modifications in product design and unique production and marketing activities will be less attractive to central management. In addition to such differences of perspective and focus, project return estimation will vary because of different information, assumptions, preferences, uncertainties and project analysis procedures.

Resource allocation under such conditions can prove to be an extremely difficult process. Country management priorities will differ sharply from product management priorities. Resolution of product and country management priorities into a system resource allocation schedule will involve extensive debate and conflict. The planning function can play an important role in resolving the potential ambiguities, inconsistencies and conflicts inherent in the capital budgeting process under such conditions. At one extreme, the planning unit can be given responsibility for estimating the overall system ROI for each cell of the product−market matrix. Once such estimates have been generated, the resource allocation process can be reduced to a relatively smple exercise. It is unlikely, however, that the planning unit will be capable of generating realistic project estimates without the aid of product and country managers.

The planning process can be used to bring together the perspectives and information of both sides to yield an overall system return estimate for individual projects. The planning function also can be used to raise assumptions, address uncertainties and unify project analysis procedures. The result will be more effective allocation of corporate resources.

Formalization of capital budgetng procedures within the framework of the planning function also encourages improved environmental analyses and strategic assessments. Planning staff can initiate formal analyses of broad environmental conditions and trends in different host countries and industries. These studies will highlight key issues that affect resource allocation decisions. They can also be used to address other strategic choices. Resource allocation discussions provide an excellent forum for addressing other strategic choices. Strategies can be discussed and defined prior to the commitment of resources. Through activities focused on resource allocation decisions, the planning process can extend its impact to other areas of strategic choice.

INTEGRATED GLOBAL PLANNING

Strategic decision making in firms with highly evolved planning systems exhibits several key characteristics.[20] Three characteristics in particular distinguish the strategic decision making process in such firms from other modes of strategic management. First, planners and analysts play a major role in strategic decisions. Second, the decision process emphasizes systematic analysis of competing strategic options. Third, the context in which decisions are made emphasizes the integration of strategic issues. In addition to stimulating greater activity in these dimensions of the decision process, planning reduces other types of activity. The evolution of the planning process creates a decision environment that limits:

Opportunistic behavior
Disjointed decisions
Withholding or camouflaging information
Reactive behavior
Dictated decisions
Failure to address uncertainties
Emotional decisions

These changes in the decision environment have a significant effect on individual managers. Argyris cites several effects of formal planning that can lead to negative responses from management.[2] First, the flexibility, discretion and autonomy of unit managers will be reduced as a result of integrated planning activities. As decisions are made on an increasingly systematic basis, managers may exhibit a classic response. The automation of an essential part of their work can result in the same type of response and sabotage that occurs on the factory floor. As the system assumes responsibility for decisions, managers may resent and resist the loss of control and function. Individual managers become increasingly dispensable as the system assumes greater importance in the strategic management process. In addition, the integration and coordination of activities reduces unit identity, which can drain morale and reduce drive. All these factors, when combined with the restructuring of strategic processes, control and power, contribute to the universal tension between formal planning and other modes of strategic management.[22]

The tension between formal planning and more discrete, decentralized and informal modes of strategic management is perhaps greater in global corporations than in any other type of organization. The need for coordination in global firms is significant, complex and increasing. At the same time, the costs and problems involved in designing and implementing global information and planning systems greatly exceed those for national organizations. Arguments for affiliate autonomy carry great legitimacy in many sectors and countries. However, the long-term success of a global corporation depends fundamentally on its ability to coordinate and control its diverse operations. Global firms exist because a network of related affiliates is superior to a set of independent, unaffiliated entities as a form of economic and strategic organization. Only by maximizing the benefits of system affiliation can the global corporation ensure its continued advantage over rival global firms and over other forms of economic organization. The foundation of a global firm's existence is built on a global strategy, integrated

Figure 8-9.   Figure 8-9.   A continuous planning process.

operations, a worldwide information system, coordinated planning and effective strategic control. Information, planning and control systems provide the mechanisms for developing and maintaining a responsive global strategic posture. The design and development of these systems is the ultimate challenge of global strategic management. These systems provide the means of managing the strategic decision making process for global businesses.

The performance of a global enterprise rests inevitably on the quality of its strategic choices. The responsibility of positioning and maintaining the enterprise in an optimal configuration within a dynamic environment requires constant, continuous management attention. Formal strategic planning systems can provide excellent support in pursuit of this objective. In the end, management's ability to formulate and execute an integrated global strategy requires effective information, planning and control systems.

NOTES

1. Mintzberg, H., "Strategy Making in Three Modes," *California Management* Review, Winter 1973.
2. Haspeslagh, P., "Portfolio Planning," *Harvard Business Review*, January–February 1982.
3. Comparative planning practices have been evaluated by Horowitz, J.H., "Strategic Control in Three European Countries," in *Top Management Control in Europe* (London: MacMillan Press, 1981); Capon, N., J.U. Farley and J. Hulbert, "International Diffusion of Corporate and Strategic Planning Practices," *Columbia Journal of World Business*, Fall 1980, pp. 5–13; Hayashi, K., "Corporate Planning Practices in Japanese Multinationals," *Academy of Management Journal*, Vol. 21, No. 2, 1978, pp. 211–226.
4. Several of the classic works in this area are: Von Clausewitz, Karl, *(On War* New York: Modern Library, 1943); Sun Tzu, *The Art of War* (Harrisburg: Military Service Publishing Company, 1949).
5. Lindsay, W.M. and L.W. Rue, "Impact of the Organization Environment on the Long-Range Planning Process: A Contingency View," *Academy of Management Journal*, Vol. 23, No. 3, 1980, pp. 385–404.
6. Litschert, R.J., "Some Characteristics of Long-Range Planning: An Industry Study," *Academy of Management*, September 1968.
7. Vancil, R.F. and P. Lorange, "Strategic Planning in Diversified Companies," *Harvard Business Review*, January–February 1975, pp. 81–90.
8. Doz, Y.L., "Strategic Management in Multinational Companies," *Sloan Management Review*, Winter 1980, pp. 27–46.
9. This issue is addressed in Abell, D. and J. Hammond, *Strategic Market Planning* (Englewood Cliffs: Prentice-Hall, 1979). An excellent example of the problem is found in the Petro-Tex (A and B) Harvard Business School case.
10. For useful examples of MIS formats, see Corning Glass Work Information Systems

Planning, ICCH No. 1-181-024; Note on the Use of Market Attractiveness/Business Position Matrices for Strategic Market Analyses and Planning, ICCH No. 1-581-028.

11. The distinction between strategic and operating plans is widely used. It was first developed in Anthony, R.N., *Planning and Control Systems* (Boston: Division of Research, Harvard Business School, 1965).

12. The issue of planning culture is addressed in Hussey, D.E. and J. Langham, *Corporate Planning: The Human Factor* (Oxford: Pergamon Press, 1979); King, W.R. and D.I. Cleland, *Strategic Planning and Policy* (New York: Van Nostrand Reinhold, 1978), Chapter 12. For a discussion of the broader issue of strategic control in multinational corporations as it relates to culture, see Prahalad, C.K. and Y.L. Doz, "An Approach to Strategic Control in MNC's," *Sloan Management Review*, Summer 1981.

13. V.T. Dock, V.P. Luchsinger and W.R. Cornette (eds.), *MIS: A Managerial Perspective* (Chicago: Science Research Associates, 1977), Section 10; Ross, J.E. and F. Schuster, "Selling the System," *Journal of Systems Management*, October 1972.

14. Shank, J., et al., "Balance Creativity and Practicality in Formal Planning," *Harvard Business Review*, January–February 1973, pp. 87–95.

15. Haspeslagh, P., op. cit.

16. From personal discussions with American Standard management.

17. Ansoff, H.I., "The State of Practice in Planning Systems," *Sloan Management Review*, Winter 1977. Gluck, F.W., S.P. Kaufman, and A.S. Walleck, "The Evolution of Strategic Management," McKinsey Staff Papers, October 1978.

18. An excellent example of this process can be seen in: MECCA International Suits Corporation: Business Systems Planning Report (White Plains: IBM, 1980). In this company, subsystems were implemented in the following order of priority: buying, inventory control, shipping and receiving, order control, vendor data, receipts data, and then marketing/production and planning systems.

19. See, for example, Montgomery, D.B. and G.L. Urban, "Marketing Decision-Information Systems: An Emerging View," *Journal of Marketing Research*, May 1970.

20. The characteristics of different stages of planning are discussed in Mintzberg, H., op. cit.; Mintzberg, H., et al. "The Structure of Unstructured Decision Processes," *Administrative Science Quarterly*, June 1976, pp. 246–75.

21. Argyris, C., "M.I.S.—The Challenge to Rationality and Emotionality," *Management Science*, February 1971.

22. The relative roles of formal and informal planning processes are described in Quinn, J.B., "Formulating Strategy One Step at a Time," *Journal of Business Strategy*, Winter 1980.

Index

345